KITCHEN GARDENS OF AUSTRALIA

Kate Herd is a passionate kitchen gardener, writer, artist and designer. Her interest in food production comes from her 'free-range' out-of-doors childhood spent up trees, in vegie gardens and hanging around paddocks and animals. Kate's love of good food is equaled by the pleasure she gets from growing produce, and she has developed a fascination with heritage food plants as well as with the stories that accompany them. Garden history, Australian plants and bush revegetation are all interests that inform her writing and her garden design practice. Kate creates gardens to be beautiful, functional and sustainable, whether for residential or commercial projects. She has contributed articles to *The Age* and other publications. This is her first book.

KITCHEN GARDENS OF AUSTRALIA

Productive gardens for inspiration and practical advice

KATE HERD

Photography by Simon Griffiths

LANTERN
an imprint of
PENGUIN BOOKS

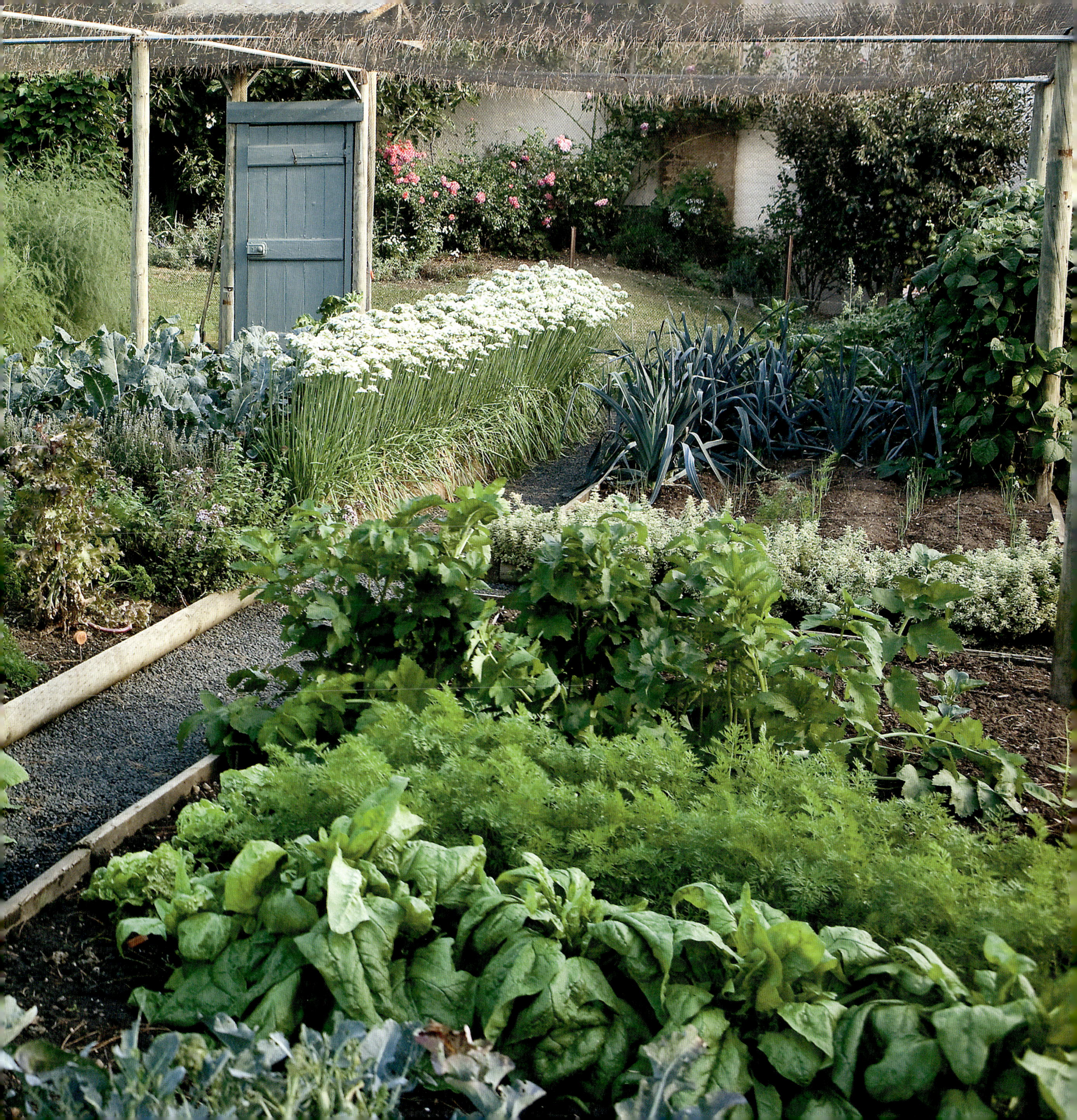

SECATEURS

GARDEN RAKE

DIGGING FORK

Malabar Nightshade (White)

DIGGING SPADE

For the gardeners who have inspired me: Neil, Prue and Philip

CONTENTS

Introduction		1
The Benefits of a Kitchen Garden		5
1	Ampelon: A Kitchen Garden in Sunraysia	12
2	Markos Dymiotis' Mediterranean-style Backyard	22
3	The Kitchen Gardens at Heide: Art, Love and Gardening	32
4	Karen Sutherland's Urban Eden	46
5	Bellis: Jeremy Coleby Williams' Sustainable Garden	56
6	Vaucluse House: A Colonial Kitchen Garden Lost and Recreated	66
7	Marangy: A Walled Kitchen Garden in Rural Victoria	78
8	Locavores in the Red Centre: The Brock Family's Backyard	90
9	Conmel Cottage: A Productive Garden in the Tamar Valley	102
10	La Huerta: Gay Bilson's Country Kitchen Garden	114
11	Edible Gardening in Suburban Perth	124
12	Villa Lettisier's Walled Kitchen Garden	136
13	Leonie Norrington's Tropical Food Garden	146
14	Josh Byrne's Sustainable Backyard	158
15	Kitchen Gardening in Capricornia	168
16	Panshanger: Self-sufficient Gardening on an Historic Tasmanian Farm	178
17	Paradise in South Australia: Armando and Maria's Garden	190
18	A Garden of Plenty on the Sapphire Coast	200
Footnotes		210
Plant List for the Kitchen Garden		213
Resources		216
Bibliography		218
Photographic Credits		219
Acknowledgements		220
Index		221

INTRODUCTION

At a young age I learnt that productive gardens come in many forms. My green-thumbed neighbours had a circular garden of vegetables, roses, perennials and herbs within their transpiration bed; my farming relatives boasted a neat fruit and vegetable garden encased entirely within a wire netting cage. Another neighbour had a small market garden, and yet another a sprawling edible landscape that made him almost self-sufficient. My memories of these gardens are unashamedly nostalgic: picking posies of flowers for the table, eating apple cucumbers while standing among the vines, hiding in a corn field taller than my head munching on ripe corn, pulling up carrots . . . For a free-range child like me, picking things by myself for myself to eat was deeply satisfying. And of course, the more illicit the act of picking and eating, the more delicious it tasted!

Whether we call it a decorative vegetable garden, an ornamental vegetable garden, a *potager*, a vegie patch, an edible garden or a plot in an allotment, community or school garden, all are kitchen gardens. What distinguishes the kitchen garden is the combination of the useful, edible and attractive that elevates it above the simply utilitarian. A kitchen garden is one in which you grow the things you bring into the kitchen – herbs, vegetables, fruit and flowers. I like to define the kitchen garden as a domestic-sized garden in which a combination of these four elements is grown.

Twenty years ago my stepfather was horrified when my mother planted corn in our 'nice' and 'respectable' front garden in the Melbourne suburb of Kew. For him it was embarrassing; it smacked of urban peasantry: 'What will the neighbours think?' Thankfully, vegie gardens are again a more accepted part of the urban landscape. Groovy inner-city cafés boast their own *potagers* and there are monthly neighbourhood vegetable 'swap-meets' where fresh unused or excess backyard produce is swapped for the different surplus of others. The busy city family doesn't even need to get its hands dirty to benefit from its own garden any more – you can pay companies to install and maintain your vegetable garden for you. On the other hand there are gardening makeovers based on reciprocal volunteerism like those instigated by the organisation Permablitz, where volunteers will come over and transform your garden into a productive space in a single weekend.

Digging up the front lawn for a productive garden might still constitute an anti-social act of radical gardening in some suburbs – and should by all means be encouraged! For those without land or an appropriate space of their own, a plot in a community garden or a land-sharing arrangement of some kind can be the answer. I love that a contemporary kitchen garden might be created on some unused urban land appropriated by a guerrilla gardener somewhere in a street near me; a 'vegieplante' who risks a council notice or two to make a low-tech and affordable edible garden out of recycled materials like pallets or car tyres. The country or rural kitchen garden is a different matter; regional gardens being marked by their access to open space and to large quantities of resources like manure and straw and, often, by their isolation. These days, however, country and city produce gardens can be equally challenged by lack of water.

Nineteenth- and twentieth-century produce-gardening discourse often equated busy hands and thrifty self-sufficiency with moral and physical health. Written at the end of the nineteenth century, Frank Finedon's language is representative of such value-laden ideas about the benefits of kitchen gardening for the mind, body and household/society: 'A well laid out and carefully kept kitchen garden is pleasant to the eye; the labour expended upon it is healthy and interesting, and a very profitable investment, commercially and otherwise.'[1] Garden writers today are just as likely to wax lyrical about the joys of self-sufficiency, 'getting one's hands in the dirt', experiencing the 'rhythms of natural processes' – and these are valid and worthy incentives. Contemporary texts as much as those of previous centuries invoke the Garden of Eden (that original pre-agrarian garden), Paradise, arcadia, the garden of earthly delights or nature's pantry, and use words such as cornucopia, profusion, abundance, bounty, plenty and harvest to supply a fertile imagery. They idealise kitchen gardens as spaces where humans are at their most natural, productive and contented.

For me, a kitchen garden is the ultimate *locus amoenus* (Latin for 'pleasant place', and a literary term that generally refers to an idealised area of safety or comfort). What other type of garden engages four senses – taste, smell, sight and touch – simultaneously? I wonder whether my passion for productive gardens is because they replicate the archetypal 'clearing in the primordial forest' and epitomise domestication, safety and prospect. Perhaps my almost Pavlovian response to a vegie patch in full production, to the stimuli of verdant vegetation and brightly coloured fruits, is a particular manifestation of 'biophilia' (the term used by biologist Edward O. Wilson to describe the instinctive human desire to connect with nature, particularly those landscapes featuring vegetation and water). Our brains are conceivably hardwired to favour the patterns of a garden divided up into regular shapes and the patterns of crops. Whether a garden is planted in straight lines of a miniature farm, or an intricate symmetrical vegetable *parterre*, an informal permaculture mandala or a meadow-like profusion – they all boast an edible tapestry of foliage of various shapes, sizes and colours; of flowers, seed heads and fruits that have universal appeal.

Writing back in 1897, Frank Finedon was quite right – kitchen gardens are a profitable investment, although Frank didn't consider them within a framework of their 'sustainability' – by which I mean management practices that conserve and sustain the resources of the soil, water, forests and habitat. Nor would he have considered backyard food production, as modern gardeners increasingly do, in the specific context of water and climate change – two defining issues of the early twenty-first century. I have found that produce gardeners tend to be especially conscious of the need to both reconsider our food system – the price, quality, security, resilience and the environmental impact of the food we eat – and to take into account a warming, drying and increasingly unpredictable climate. Healthy foods, people, farming systems and the environment are intrinsically interconnected. Consuming food that is produced organically is beneficial both for our own health and that of our environment and growing your own food can be a wonderful way of minimising your own individual 'ecological debt'. Produce gardening contributes to more than just a sense of personal virtue; growing food really can lessen your helplessness and your dependence on the mainstream food system and teach you to provide for yourself without detriment to the environment. It's by no means 'rocket science', yet it takes care, skill and practice to achieve a succession of fruits, vegetables and herbs for the table.

In writing this book I wanted to visit productive gardens and tell the food-growing stories of the people who tend them. Visiting the eighteen gardens that are featured in this book and meeting the garden makers has been an immense pleasure. All the gardeners are practical, imaginative and passionate about growing beautiful and tasty food plants, often despite a shortage of water and difficult conditions. The gardens are various – large and small, historic and new, urban and rural, coastal and inland, formal and informal and in-between – and all are inspirational. It's been a privilege to talk with these gardeners, who have so generously shared not only their knowledge with me but cups of tea, meals, produce and favourite recipes. The connection between the garden and the kitchen, is, I hope, just one of the many things this book celebrates.

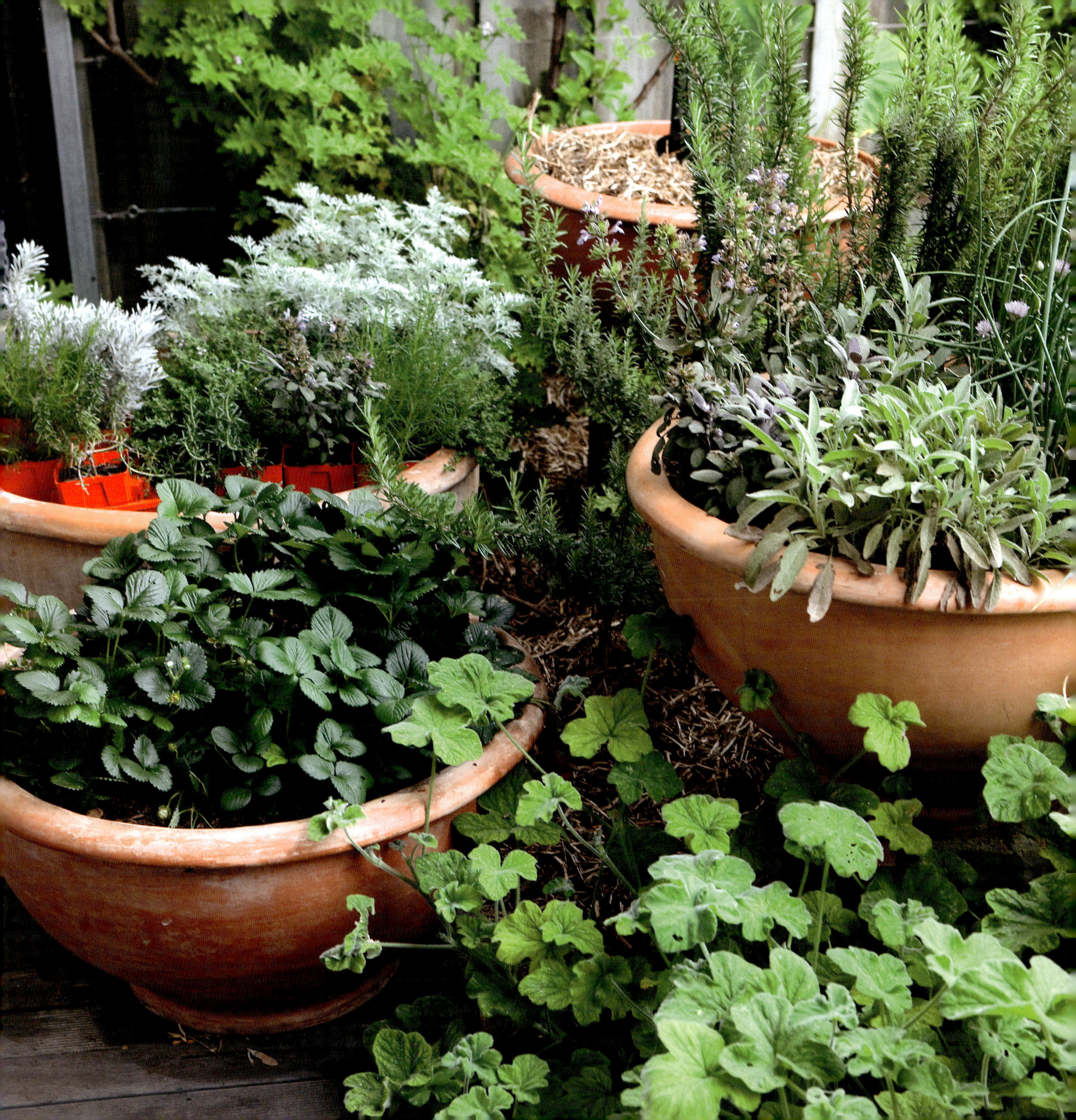

THE BENEFITS OF A KITCHEN GARDEN

There is much to be said for a garden in which one can grow plants to eat as well as to smell, pick, admire, climb and sit under. There are multiple benefits of growing your own food – not only will we 'walk more lightly' on the planet and reduce our national and individual 'ecological footprint' but we can secure a real quality of life for ourselves and our kids in the process. A garden culture that celebrates home-grown 'real' food is not only achieved via a back-to-the-land brand of survivalist gardening, it can be accomplished through changing the way we inhabit our cities in which the majority of us live and how we use our backyards and community spaces. Living well is as much about the food we eat – its nutritional value, freshness, diversity and affordability – as it is about access to clean water and air, or education and housing. Obesity, diabetes and other health problems associated with the Western diet, climate change, chemical use on our food, environmental degradation associated with conventional agriculture, decreasing plant biodiversity, genetically modified foods, preserving our cultural and horticultural inheritances, and rising food prices: all are reasons why people are rediscovering produce gardening. What others have known for years is that nothing tastes as good as a home-grown strawberry, peach or tomato, or beats the satisfaction and pleasure gained from creating a meal from fresh herbs and vegies from your own garden.

Grow your own food and reduce your carbon footprint

Calories are not the only form of energy embodied in our food: every single component of what we eat uses resources such as fuel and electricity. Each item of food we consume generates environmental impacts through the way it is grown, fertilised, irrigated, harvested, dried, processed or manufactured, packaged, transported, stored or refrigerated, displayed and sold and even purchased by us, the consumer. Australia has a history of cheap, abundant and high-quality food, but this is changing. Food prices are already rising owing to increasing fuel costs and prolonged drought, and many scientists and economists predict that climate change and 'Peak Oil' will ultimately trigger all manner of crises in regard to food.

Our food system is responsible for nearly 23 per cent of Australia's greenhouse pollution, with agriculture accounting for around 16 per cent of the national total.[1] While the production of fruits and vegetables is responsible for around 1.5 kg of GHG emissions per kg of food, meat production emits a whopping 25.2 kg.[2] The easiest way of reducing your carbon footprint, therefore, is to eat less meat. In addition to this, avoid buying bottled water, and purchase local and less-processed food. Growing your own fruits, herbs and vegetables is also one of the most rewarding ways to achieve a diet that is low-carbon and low-environmental impact.

A seasonal diet based around the organically managed and compost-centred home garden results in almost zero pollution. There are certainly no 'food-miles' involved in eating from your home garden as there is no transport required in the journey from backyard patch to plate. But of greater significance in cutting food-related carbon pollution is reducing the 'embodied' energy entailed in food processing, refrigeration and packaging. In the home garden there is no packaging that is not either edible or biodegradable and little food-related processing is required, as fruit and vegetables are almost never better than when eaten fresh. (Preserving the harvest for the longer term through age-old methods like drying, pickling and bottling is an alternative to refrigeration and freezing.) The beauty of growing your own plant foods is that your consumption and meals change in direct response to the seasons, enhanced by what home-made preserves you may have stored in the cupboard.

Use alternatives to biocides

Biocides are substances designed to kill living organisms designated as 'pests' – whether vegetable or animal – and they include herbicides, insecticides, bactericides and fungicides. Such substances vary in toxicity but all have potentially negative environmental impacts. Given that the health of our soil and water is fundamental to all horticultural pursuits, not to mention human life itself, the use of biocides is of concern.

We know too well the disastrous story of agricultural insecticides like the now-banned organochloride DDT, and other persistent organic pollutants (POPs) that endanger the food web, but even those products marked 'environmentally friendly' can still have a serious ecological impact. For example, the plant-derived and relatively non-toxic insecticide pyrethrum is non-selective – meaning it will take out the beneficial insects along with the target pest insect.

In the home garden we have the opportunity to create a resilient multi-species ecosystem teeming with life above and below the soil, and which, being complex and biodiverse, is not nearly so susceptible to pest attack as a simplified garden or monoculture. For pest and disease control in the home garden, start by building healthy compost-enriched soils, practice crop rotation, use green manure crops,[3] encourage biological controls like predatory insects and birds by planting beneficial insect-attracting and bird-attracting plants, or conduct physical management (such as squashing pests!). Other alternatives include using traps for fruit fly, codling moth and even mice and rats; fruit bags to exclude fruit fly; releasing the bacteria *Bacillus thuringiensis* to control caterpillars; ladybird larvae to predate aphids; and using ducks or resident blue-tongue lizards to eat snails.

Alternatives to using herbicides like glyphosate to kill weeds in the kitchen garden include hand-weeding and hoeing existing garden beds to remove annual weeds. Follow weeding by mulching with soft organic mulches like pea, barley and lucerne straw, sugarcane bagasse or aged sheep manure mixed with compost to suppress weeds and conserve moisture. Pine oil is a non-systemic herbicide that is totally biodegradable and non-toxic to garden critters. In preparing a new vegetable garden area, you could use plastic to solarise the weeds over the summer months – if it gets hot enough, much of the dormant seed bank in the upper soil can also be killed. Other weed-killing alternatives include using steam-weeders, boiling water, and for stubborn broadleaf weeds, a treatment of iron sulfate and sulphate of ammonia can be effective. (The downside of all of these methods is that they also kill off soil life.) A schedule of rotary hoeing, green manure and slashing followed by thick mulching can be used to thoroughly prepare a new area. Sandwich mulching involves feeding and watering your weeds to promote active growth, then covering them (they may need to be slashed first) with multiple sheets of well-overlapping newspaper, then at least 10 cm of mulch such as pea straw. Add some blood and bone to aid decomposition and leave for 4–6 months. Another option is to create no-dig beds – the depth of the combined layers of manure, straw, leaves, clippings and compost will kill most weeds growing beneath. (Persistent weed species like couch grass, kikuyu or blackberries will require a serious and sustained eradication campaign, however.) By gardening without biocides, you can help reduce the overall presence of these substances in our environment and food chain.

Make compost rather than synthetic fertilisers the centre of your gardening practice

Synthetic or inorganic fertilisers are the junk food of the plant world and their use in agriculture has been shown to cause long-term environmental harm. Synthetic fertilisers are manufactured from non-renewable resources via energy-intensive chemical processes that emit greenhouse-gases like methane, CO_2 and nitrous oxide. These processes themselves require vast quantities of electricity (produced from fossil fuels) and natural gas. The misapplication and overuse of synthetic fertilisers – nitrogen and phosphate fertilisers in particular – have caused tremendous damage to our farming land and ecosystems. Excess nitrogen fertilisation results in volatile losses in the form of nitrous oxide (N_2O) – a major greenhouse-gas that is some 300 times more potent than carbon dioxide. Being highly soluble, nitrogen fertilisers leach nitrates into groundwater as well as our surface water systems – where they can cause algal blooms that kill native fish and fauna. Nitrogen fertilisation can also destroy soil biota, affect the decomposition of organic matter and the take-up of nutrients by plants. It also increases the soil's susceptibility to erosion and can cause soil acidification.

The most desirable way of maintaining soil fertility is to increase soil organic matter. Home gardeners can most easily achieve this by way of inputs such as organic fertilisers, green manure crops and compost. Compost has been called the vital foundation of gardening and farming, and as my favourite super-gardener Peter Cundall says, 'Compost is so bloomin' beautiful, you could eat it'. Compost is the magic component of any productive garden. The natural process of decomposition is what the clever gardener uses to turn waste into beautiful plant food. By composting kitchen scraps, green waste, dead plant material from the garden, lawn clippings and even the kids' dead budgie, you also reduce the amount of organic matter going to landfill. Sending compostable waste to the tip is an opportunity missed and places further strain on already pressured (and methane-emitting) landfill sites. Why send this marvellous resource away, only to drive to the nursery and buy it back again in plastic bags? By incorporating crumbly, dark-chocolate-coloured, sweet-smelling compost into your soil you increase its organic content and the population of beneficial bacteria. You simultaneously improve the soil's fertility, air porosity, structure and water-retaining ability, thus creating optimal growing conditions for your plants which will feed you leaves, fruits and nuts in return. Not only does making compost sequester carbon, using well-made compost as a garden fertiliser won't pollute groundwater and streams. Vermiculture, or worm farming, is another excellent way of converting household waste into plant food. Worms enjoy most organic matter (except citrus and onions) which they gradually consume, leaving behind their castings – 'black gold' – for the garden. 'Worm juice' is one of the best plant tonics/foliage fertilisers/soil conditioners around. Dilute 1 part liquid from the worm farm to 9 parts water and apply with a watering can, and your soil and plants will thank you.

Green manures also add organic matter to the soil, improving soil structure and water penetration. By using leguminous green manure crops that are planted and dug under a month or so later, you harness the biological nitrogen cycle. (Decaying legumes make nitrogen available to other plants, thanks to nitrogen-fixing bacteria in their root nodules.) Using these methods in combination with the occasional targeted application of minerals, rock dust or trace elements if necessary, and use of blood and bone, seaweed concentrate, compost tea or worm liquid to stimulate plant growth, constitute environmentally friendly alternatives for managing produce gardens. While growing your own fruit and vegetables at home will not ameliorate the damage caused by unsustainable agriculture, it will benefit your local ecosystem and decrease your consumption footprint.

Create an edible garden and increase your food choices

Our commercially produced food supply is generally based on intensive industrial agriculture that focuses on producing vast monocultures of a very limited number of crop species. Both traditional plant breeding as well as the modification of plant genes has been used to achieve the genetic uniformity of crops such as wheat, corn, rice and soybeans, but also of common vegetables. Thousands of varieties of plant foods have been lost to cultivation as a handful of genetically similar cultivars have come to dominate agriculture. This loss of agricultural and genetic diversity not only makes crops (and the world's food supply) more vulnerable to pests and disease, it has also harmed many traditional farming societies. Only a fraction of all the global varieties of plant foods are available at the local green grocer or supermarket – thus growing your own is a fabulous way to expand your choice of fruits and vegetables, and it is also an answer for those who want to avoid consuming genetically engineered plant material.

For many Australians, growing your own fruit and vegetables may be a way of affording organic produce. It can prove cheaper to grow annual and many perennial food crops from seed than it is to buy punnets of seedlings (one packet containing 200 broccoli seeds is the same price as a punnet of twelve broccoli seedlings). The choice of plants in seed form is also a thousand times of that available as seedlings in nurseries. Many old varieties of fruit and vegetables have been handed down over generations because they have been selected for flavour and hardiness or satisfied specific uses like storing, drying, pickling or bottling. These are commonly known as heirloom seeds, which are open-pollinated (non-hybrid) seeds that grow 'true-to-type' – meaning they can be saved to reproduce the same variety year after year (provided you prevent cross-pollination).

Modern hybrids have been primarily bred for yield and uniformity and while there are many well-performing and tasty hybrid varieties, you cannot save hybrid seed as it does not grow true-to-type. F1 (first filial cross) hybrids are one-shot wonders – which suits commercial seed companies just fine. Saving your own seed is a wonderful way of preserving our seed heritage and maintaining genetic diversity of food plant varieties. The easiest types to save are the self-pollinating ones like most varieties of tomatoes, lettuce, peas and beans, and a good general rule is to select the best (for seed saving) and to eat the rest. Growing from seed is satisfying, meditative and hands control back to the home-producer, with the opportunity to garden organically from seed to plate.

Make good and efficient use of the water available to you

Using water to feed yourself is the most valid of human activities, but one that is increasingly regulated in terms of how and when it is carried out. Australia is the driest habitable continent on the planet. It has high evaporation rates that significantly exceed rainfall in all but the wettest areas, one of the highest water footprints,[4] and nearly every one of our capital cities is on water restrictions of some kind. In this context, even a simple thing like watering high water-use plants like annual vegetables raises some real issues!

Fresh, unprocessed fruits and vegetables have the lowest water-for-food ratio or 'water intensity' of all foods, with a high yield per water application. Through home food gardening, however, we save 'embodied water' – the water used to produce, process and transport all the food we purchase. In growing your own food, the water price tag is visible and can be monitored. There is some evidence that home-grown vegetables use as little as 20 per cent of the amount of water per dollar-value of produce that commercially grown ones use, but whether or not this is the case, there is no doubt whatsoever that clever and sustainable design of edible gardens can minimise their water use.

Temperature, wind, evaporation, humidity, sunshine hours, the time of year and soil type and organic matter content all affect how much water is required for plant growth and fruit production. If planning a vegetable garden, one way of estimating how much water it will require is to multiply the 'crop factor' by the daily evaporation rate to get the daily number of litres needed per square metre of garden. Crop factor is the rate at which plants transpire water in relation to the daily evaporation rate. For the purposes of home production, annual vegetables can be said to have a crop factor of 0.85. If the daily summer evaporation rate in your region is 10 mm, the calculation is 10 × 0.85 to give 8.5 litres of water per square metre per day during the warmer months; if it is 5 mm, then you will need only 4.25 litres. This is particularly useful for estimating your potential water needs over summer when there may be three or more months without much rain.

Conserving precious water from aquifers, dams, rivers, tanks and reservoirs is crucial for our drinking supplies, household needs and the ecological health of our catchments as well as for food production. Water restrictions make it extremely difficult to keep vegetable gardens alive (let alone thriving) if you are using only mains water. Ideally, mains water should be a last resort for watering productive home gardens, because of the fact that drinking water is more expensive than non-potable water. Unlike private water from dams, bores or rivers, or rainwater harvested in tanks, potable water requires vast infrastructure to purify and distribute it to households, and therefore costs both urban consumers and the environment more than non-treated water costs other users.[5] Storing rainwater in tanks for garden use makes you less dependent on mains supply and helps reduce the demand on reservoirs, rivers, creeks and dams or aquifers. Even the smallest garden can probably fit a slim-line water tank or even store water underground. The secret is to obtain as much water harvest out of your 'roof catchment' as possible.

Clockwise, from top: **No wallabies or bowerbirds will break into this space-age fruit cage; cherry tomatoes; glorious produce; baby carrots.**

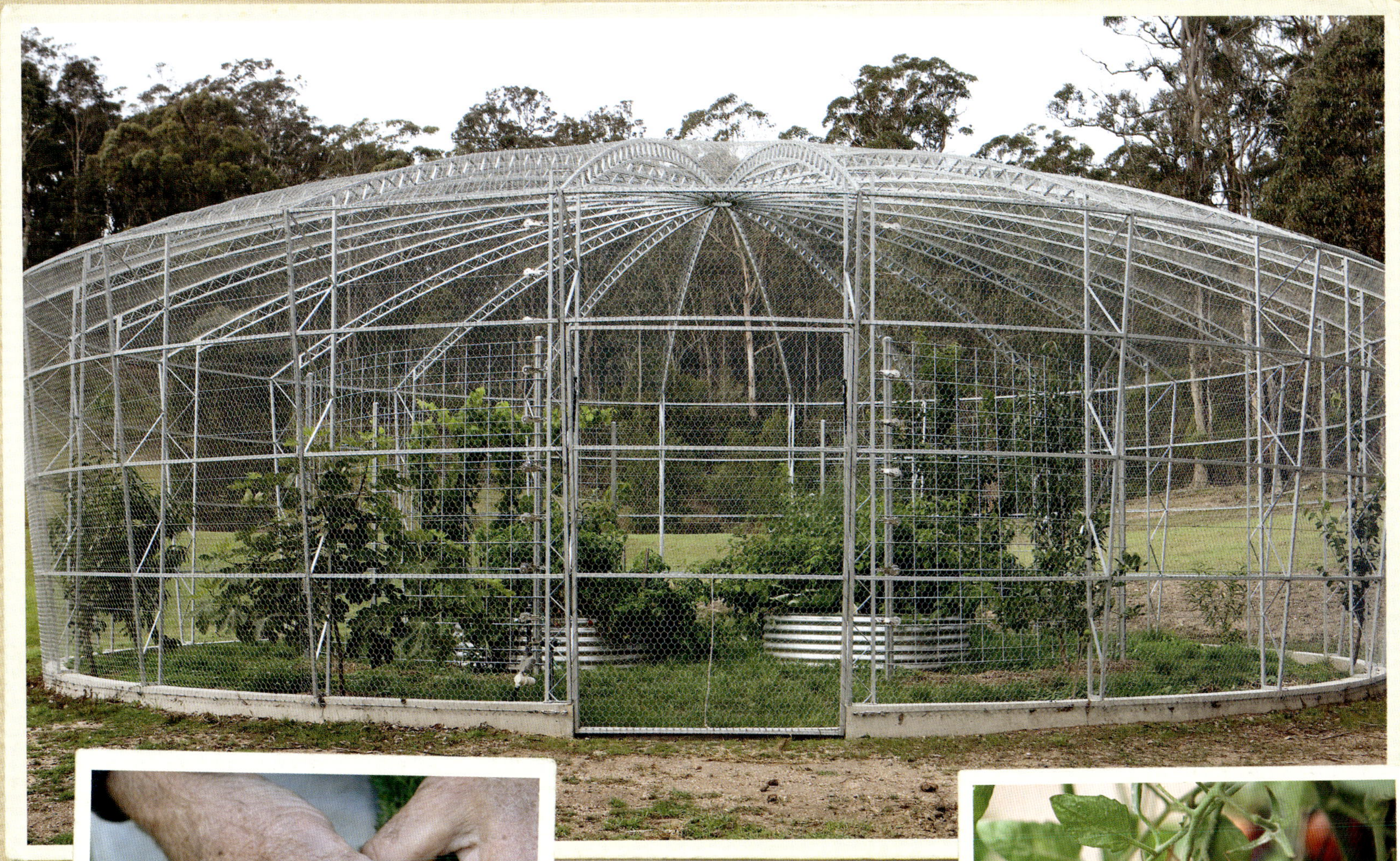
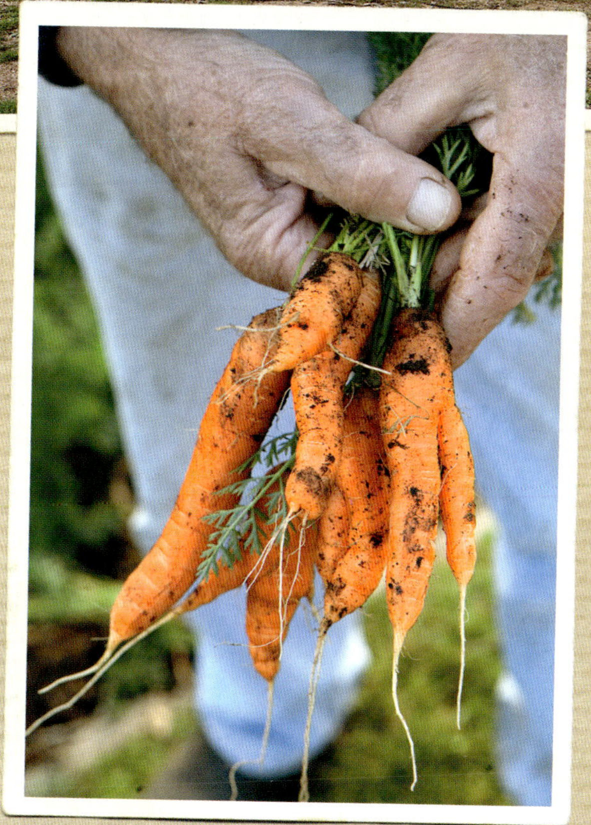
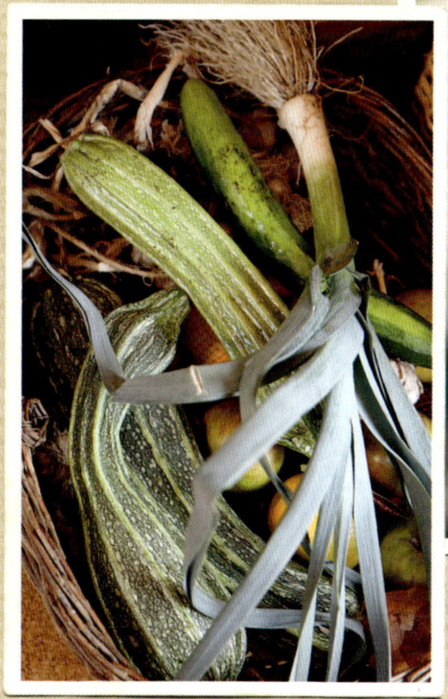
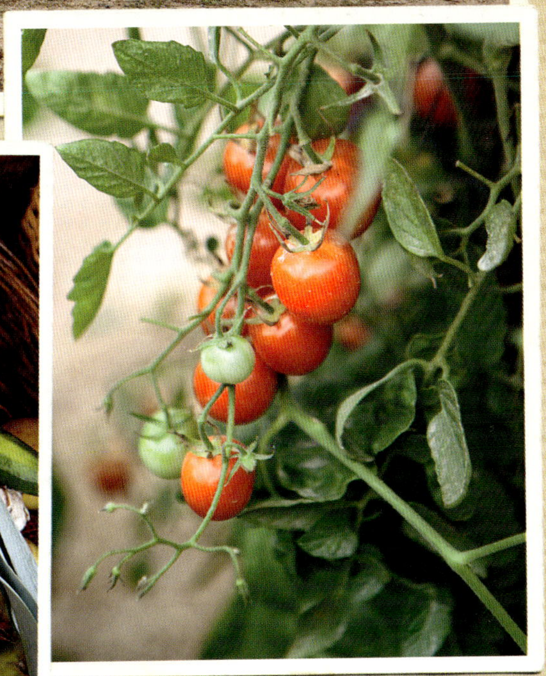

Greywater (non-toilet wastewater) is not always an option for the kitchen garden: the EPA recommends not irrigating food crops like leafy green vegies or root crops with untreated grey water as this would pose a health risk (check with the EPA and your local council and water authority). Fruit trees, however, can be safely irrigated beneath soil level or via drip irrigation under mulch with high-quality untreated greywater (non-kitchen water that is low in potassium, sodium, phosphorus and nitrogen). Some experts now recommend only shower and bath water and not water from the washing machine be used on the garden. There are now a variety of systems that treat domestic greywater to a Class A grade approved by the EPA and local councils. Class A water is suitable for use on vegetable gardens.

Recycled blackwater (waste water and sewage) treatment systems that produce Class A water are an increasingly affordable, if still expensive, option for those who want to close the loop entirely. An efficient irrigation system like dripper irrigation can reduce water usage and is less wasteful than sprinklers or micro-sprays. With weeping hose, drip emitter or integrated drip-line systems, water is directed to plant roots and is not lost through wind, evaporation or overspray. Growing plants appropriate for your climate and during the right season is essential. The other important means of saving water in the vegie patch are to have compost-enriched soil and to use mulch to reduce both evaporation and decrease soil temperatures during summer. Constructing 'wicking beds' or other growing systems that water plants from below the root zone, and shade structures to minimise evapotranspiration, can also help cut your water use.

Your kids will eat vegetables

There are countless studies that demonstrate how garden-based food education positively impacts kids' fruit and vegetable intake and increases their preferences for plant foods. But all we really need to see is their delight when they pull carrots from the soil (rude bifurcated ones are the best!), 'bandicoot' potatoes (dig up potatoes without removing the whole plant) engrave their names in zucchinis, or pick peas and beans to eat raw on the spot. Magic! Such first-hand experiences often translate into a willingness to try new and unusual fruits and vegetables. The vegetable garden should be a place for children to discover a diverse, beautiful and delicious assortment of plant foods. Caring for food plants and making a real and practical connection with nature is something that many kids never get to experience. Many primary schools are seeking to remedy this, however, by establishing school kitchen gardens to provide garden-based learning about fruit, vegetables and herbs. Such programs intend children to benefit from eating fresh produce as well as learning about cooking and nutrition. Not only will they know how to stuff an artichoke, it is hoped that such early experiences will a have long-lasting positive impact on their adult health.

Grow 'real' food and eat more fruit and veg

Home gardening can contribute significantly to household consumption. According to 1992 Australian Bureau of Statistics data,[6] home gardens produced 6 per cent of Australia's total vegetable production and 4 per cent of its fruit production. This manifested in an average of around 50 kg of fruit and 70 kg of vegetables per productive backyard annually! Going by more recent data we consume more than we grow: during 2001–3 Australians consumed 100 kg of vegetables and 99 kg of fruit per person annually.[7] These quantities might sound large, but we are in fact a nation of low consumers (we don't eat the recommended five serves of vegies a day[8]) and big wasters of fresh fruit and veg.[9] It is especially worrying that fruit and vegetables are so undervalued, because a plant-based diet is an important factor in preventing chronic diseases like cancer and cardiovascular disease, while conversely, low fruit and vegetable consumption is a risk factor for obesity. A garden-based seasonal diet high in vegetables and fruit can circumvent those negative aspects of the Western diet – specifically food that is high in calories, fats, salts and sugars yet nutrient-poor, which has resulted in the phenomenon of people being overfed at the same time they are undernourished. Backyard vegetable gardens can therefore be considered as being in the front line of preventative health care!

Kitchen gardens can play a role in rethinking our relationship with food. Growing our own produce encourages us to get reacquainted with 'real' or whole food as opposed to industrially processed super-refined edible substances. Writer Michael Pollan makes a great argument for eating from the garden; it is hard to eat badly from your garden, he claims. Not only does growing your food enlist your body in participating in 'the intricate and endlessly interesting processes of providing for our sustenance', it is the 'surest way to escape the culture of fast food'.[10] The produce you harvest from your kitchen garden will be perfectly imperfect – more than likely, it will have a slug or dirt on it – and it does not come individually wrapped in plastic! Fresh fruit and vegetables taste better, but studies show they are also higher in nutrients and antioxidants than ones that have been transported and refrigerated – perhaps for weeks before they get to you. Growing an edible garden makes you a primary producer in your own backyard, all-knowing about the provenance of your food.

Planting a productive garden is fun!

The cultivation of food plants not only sustains us but, like the growing of ornamental plants, it is also immensely enjoyable and potentially addictive! Pottering in the vegie garden is one of life's simple pleasures. Deciding what you'd like to eat and thus what you'll grow is a form of creative expression in itself. Gardening is outdoor work in the changing seasons, enjoyable physical exertion far from the maddening gym, and is immensely therapeutic. Kitchen gardens are places for playing and experimenting with plants; vegetables, herbs and fruit come in all the colours of the rainbow and somehow a mixture of orange marigolds, red nasturtiums and purple basil never looks garish in the kitchen garden. Meet the neighbours by gardening in the front yard, meet other growers by attending a monthly 'vegie swap' or join a local seed-savers network. Sharing or swapping surplus produce with friends, and comparing notes and competing for the first-tomato-of-the-season award in your street can all be highly enjoyable and encourage a sense of community. While all kitchen gardens require regular attention, how much work they need depends on their design, size and the type of food plants. Some necessitate a daily visit, others get by with attention at weekends, but generally kitchen gardens with their rituals of sowing, planting, tending and harvesting are a wonderfully mindful and tangible endeavour.

AMPELON'S KITCHEN GARDEN

Size	22 × 22 m (484 m²)
Climate	Grassland – warm (persistently dry)
Soil	Loam with a high iron content
Average annual rainfall	250 mm
Frost	Yes
Water source	Murray River
Irrigation method	Spray and drip irrigation and hand-watering
Compost and fertiliser	Composted food scraps and plant material, sheep manure, pelletised chicken manure
Mulch	Mushroom compost, leaves, lawn clippings, grape marc
Biggest challenges	Water, heat and frost
Favourite herb	Parsley
Favourite food plant	Tomato

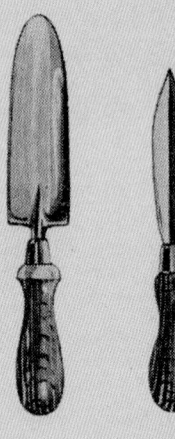

CHAPTER 1

AMPELON

A Kitchen Garden in Sunraysia

Why, you might ask, would anyone living in the area regarded as Australia's food bowl bother growing their own fruit and vegetables? The Sunraysia region of the Murray River Basin (from Swan Hill in Victoria to the South Australian border) produces nearly 5 per cent of the nation's total fruit and vegetables, not-to-mention about 20 per cent of our citrus and 30 per cent of our table grapes. Yet, despite the local bounty, Margot and Dennis Mills, who grow wine grapes and citrus at Gol Gol, New South Wales, choose to grow their own. But then, the Mills are not your average Sunraysia 'blockies' (local speak for fruit growers). Although they are locals born and bred, they have also travelled widely and are keen and knowledgeable foodies.

Here, on the northern side of the River Murray, ten minutes from Mildura, they have created an extensive and romantic garden over a period of forty years. Today, their property Ampelon is a cool and green-treed haven rising up from the surrounding grid of citrus trees and grape vines. (In Greek mythology Ampelon was supposedly the garden of Zeus and it is also the Greek word for vineyard.) Over the last five years Margot has rendered their place even more fruitful by transforming an old horse paddock into a kitchen garden that supplies herself and Dennis as well as their adult children and their families with an abundance of organic vegetables, fruit and herbs. Growing their own fulfils the Mills' desire for a diverse variety of beautiful fresh foods, for a garden-based diet based on the seasons, and for the daily beneficial interaction with the earth that goes with it.

Food growing in this region has a long history, one that is inseparable from the story of Murray River irrigation itself. In the 1830s the search for the mythical inland sea resulted instead in the naming of the Darling and Murray rivers by Charles Sturt. Settlers took up land for sheep grazing from the 1840s and in the late 1880s, the enterprising Canadian Chaffey brothers, at the invitation of prime minister Alfred Deakin, travelled from California to set up an irrigation colony at Mildura following the establishment of one at Renmark, South Australia. They saw irrigation as the saviour of the dry inhospitable continent, as transforming the desert into an oasis – a food bowl that would feed and build a nation. The region's first horticultural industry was dried fruits (raisins and sultanas) followed by citrus after World War II. The post-war settlement, particularly of the Mildura area, saw an influx of both Anglo–Australians – mostly returned soldiers under settlement schemes, and migrants from Mediterranean and European countries. It became commonplace for blockies to grow fruit and veg for their own consumption in addition to the food plants they grew to make a living. Today, the Sunraysia district has people who have come from more than twenty-five different countries and boasts diverse national and regional migrant cuisines.

To reach the kitchen garden at Ampelon you must first walk through the garden itself, beneath shady trees planted by Margot and Dennis as newlyweds four decades ago – homestead tree-planting being a rite of passage for any farming family. Like many farmers, the Mills understand that trees can do more for us than air-conditioners can – creating shade and reducing wind that makes life more bearable in this dry inland, where summer temperatures regularly reach the high forties. The kitchen garden is at the southern end of the homestead garden within the floodplain of the Gol Gol creek, a tributary of the Murray. The garden is perfectly situated to receive full sun all day long and is protected by the mature trees of the main garden to the north and a patch of remnant indigenous saltbush and black box (*Eucalyptus largiflorens*) to the south. A young hedge of cypress 'Leighton's Green' defines the east side and one of olive trees, the west.

Measuring 22 × 22 m, the symmetry of Ampelon's kitchen garden is a formal delight. A central circular bed features a sundial amid marigolds, various herbs, red and green lettuces and beetroot, and the whole bed is edged with box. The quadripartite paths intersect with perpendicular ones to create three progressively larger right-angled garden beds in each quadrant of the garden. Margot does love symmetry, she says, particularly the formal and classical designs of nineteenth-century European gardens. With help from local landscaper

The kitchen garden at Ampelon
is a formally laid-out delight

AMPELON'S KITCHEN GARDEN

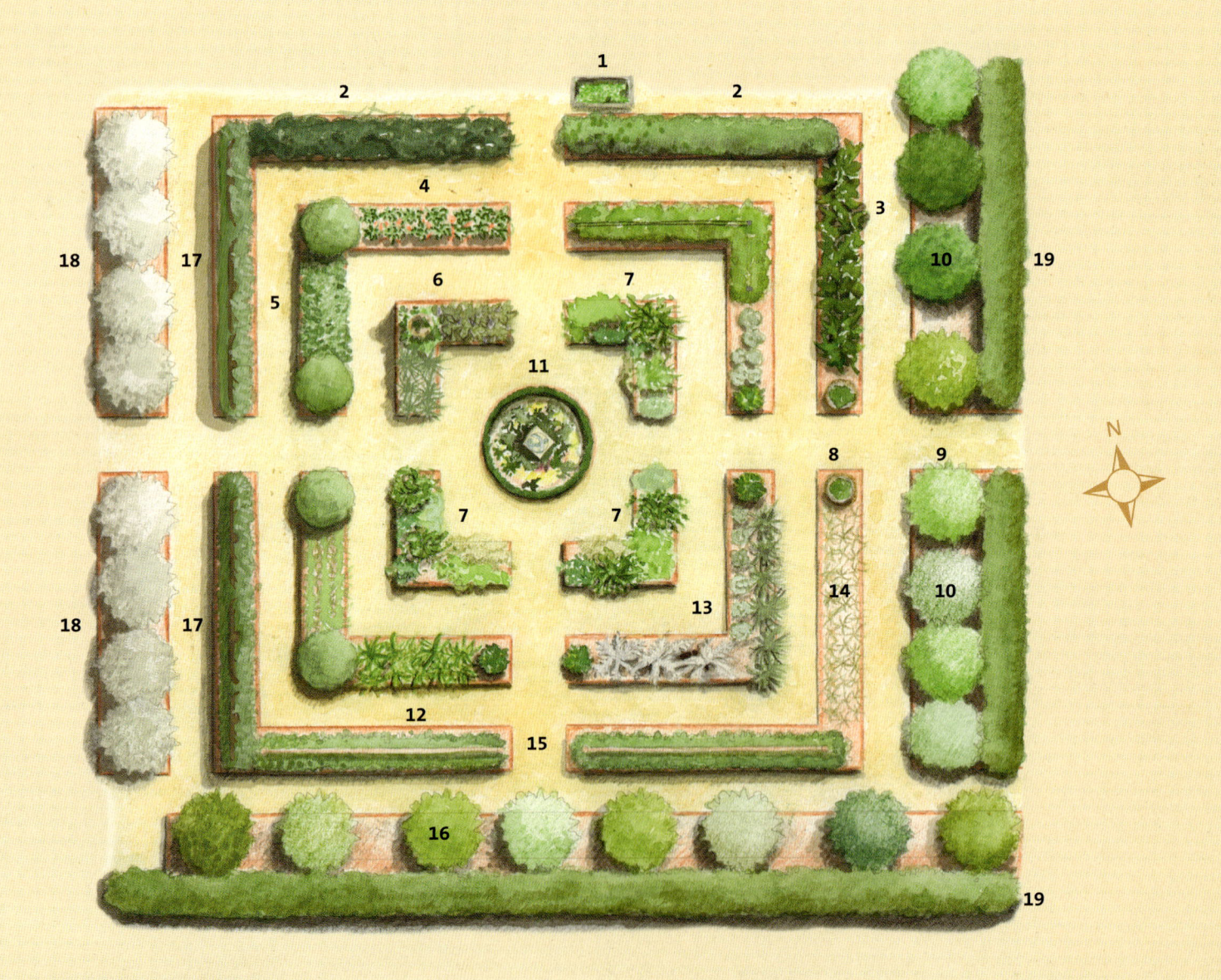

1	Mint in trough	11	Beetroot, lettuce, African marigolds
2	Passionfruit	12	Ballerina apples, chives and sweet corn
3	Tomatoes	13	Spring onions, globe artichokes and garlic
4	Capsicum, chillies and basil	14	Onions
5	Potatoes	15	Table grapes on trellis
6	Eggplants, climbing beans and spring onions	16	Assorted fruit trees – fig, peach, nectarine, plum, apricot
7	Herbs	17	Espaliered apples and pears underplanted with strawberries
8	Chives and cabbage	18	Olive tree hedge
9	Zucchini	19	Cypress hedge
10	Fruit trees: figs, persimmon, cherry, almond and apricot with sweetpotato and pumpkins underneath		

Chris Dawe, they have constructed her garden from Margot's carefully drawn plan. They used old local bricks laid on edge to define the beds and then a local 'crusher dust' (a quartz-gravel) as a surface for the generous paths. Pairs of standard roses and potted miniature stone fruit function as living statuary at the end of the beds. The effect is immensely pleasing – it's neat and bountiful, and at the same time the garden is accessible and easy to work.

Margot has improved the soil in the kitchen garden beds with its calcerous clay subsoil by using red loam and mushroom compost from the nearby Merbein Mushroom Farm. Cow manure, blood and bone and pelletised chook manure have also been used as soil conditioners. The recipe is obviously an excellent one, for the plants are all mouth-wateringly healthy – the foliage of the figs, grapes and raspberries is deep dark-green against the ochre soil. It is an amazing thing, this soil, its colour quite astonishing – made red by particles of iron oxide. It is the stuff of myth and legend: the fragile interior, with the addition of water from the life-giving and once-mighty Murray, rendered so productive. The hot and dry climate is ideal for fruit, nut and vegetable growing, and fungal diseases are minimal thanks to the low humidity. On the other hand, being inland, there is little cloud cover in winter, so frost can be a big problem for fruit growers. One winter the Mills lost all their lemon trees to an exceptionally severe week of −5°C temperatures.

Margot's tomatoes would make a southerner weep with envy, and not only are they incredibly healthy, they normally start fruiting in early December. She has devised a most clever and practical method of staking her plants: they are simply hedged within double strands of fencing wire strung between star-stakes and tensioned with the old Walker fence strainers. As the plants grow she just has to add another row of wire to keep them controlled and never fusses about pinching out the laterals. She likes to try many different varieties for salads and for cooking, particularly the heirloom tomatoes that she sources from the Digger's Club in Victoria – flavour being most important.

The humble tomato (*Solanum lycopersicum*) would have to be Australia's favourite food plant, being the subject of more garden magazine column space, over-the-back-fence conversations and garden-radio-show talkback questions than even the lemon tree. (According to ABS statistics, tomatoes account for 18 per cent of Australian home garden vegetable production, ahead of pumpkin, cabbage and Brussels sprouts, lettuce and potatoes, in that order.[1]) Tomatoes were eaten in Britain by the late-1700s, most often in the form of sauces, but in Australia, according to food researcher Barbara Santich, the history of the tomato is one of rather slow utilisation post-white settlement. Tomatoes were available in the colony of New South Wales from at least 1827,[2] when they were listed in the 'List of esculent vegetables and pott herbs cultivated in the Botanic Gardens, Sydney' compiled in December of that year. This document, like early nursery catalogues, named tomatoes as the 'love-apple' or *pomme d'amour*, whereas from the 1840s, named cultivar and generic currant, pear, globe and plum types of 'tomato' are specified. Santich charts the tomato's journey from unfamiliarity and obscurity where cooks were unsure what to do with them, to increasing popularity and consumption in the 1880s and 90s with varieties such as 'Large Red', 'Mammoth', 'Trophy', 'Acme' as well as cherry, currant and pear types being in favour.[3]

> 'It is an amazing thing, this soil, its colour quite astonishing – made red by particles of iron oxide.'

The tomato is now classified as a fruit – a berry, in fact – but is still commonly regarded in culinary terms as a vegetable. (In an 1893 court case in the US, a John Nix sought to avoid a 10 per cent tax on imported fruit by claiming that the tomato was a vegetable – with the Supreme Court ruling in his favour that in the common language of the people, tomatoes were a vegetable.) Thankfully Australia's love-affair with the tomato has moved on from white bread, tomato and iceberg-lettuce sandwiches to embrace the full culinary potential of this amazing berry.

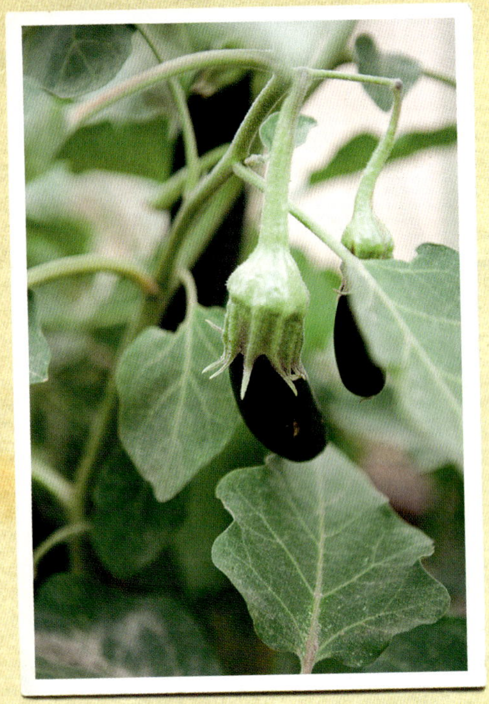
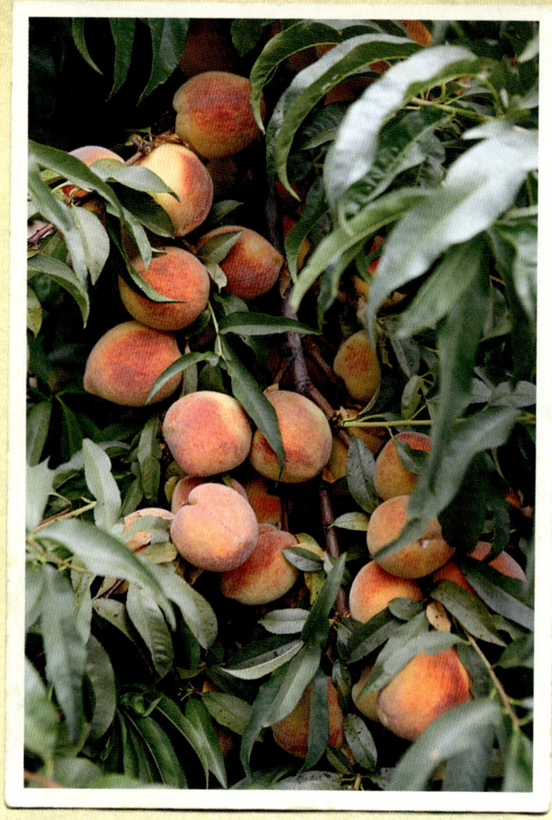
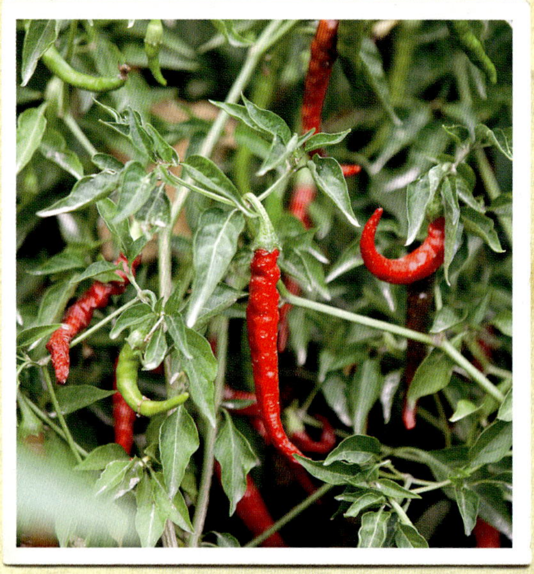
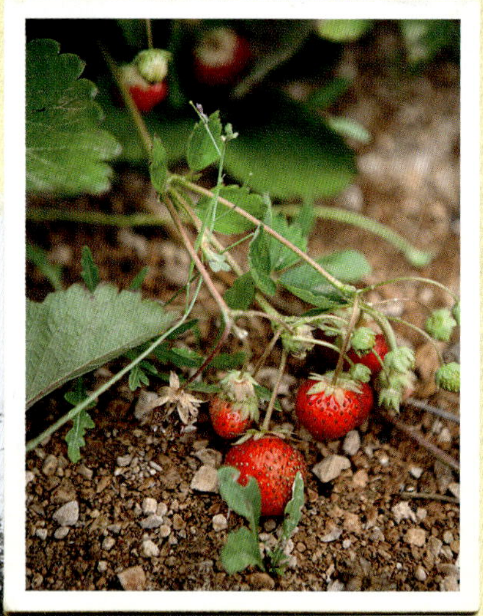
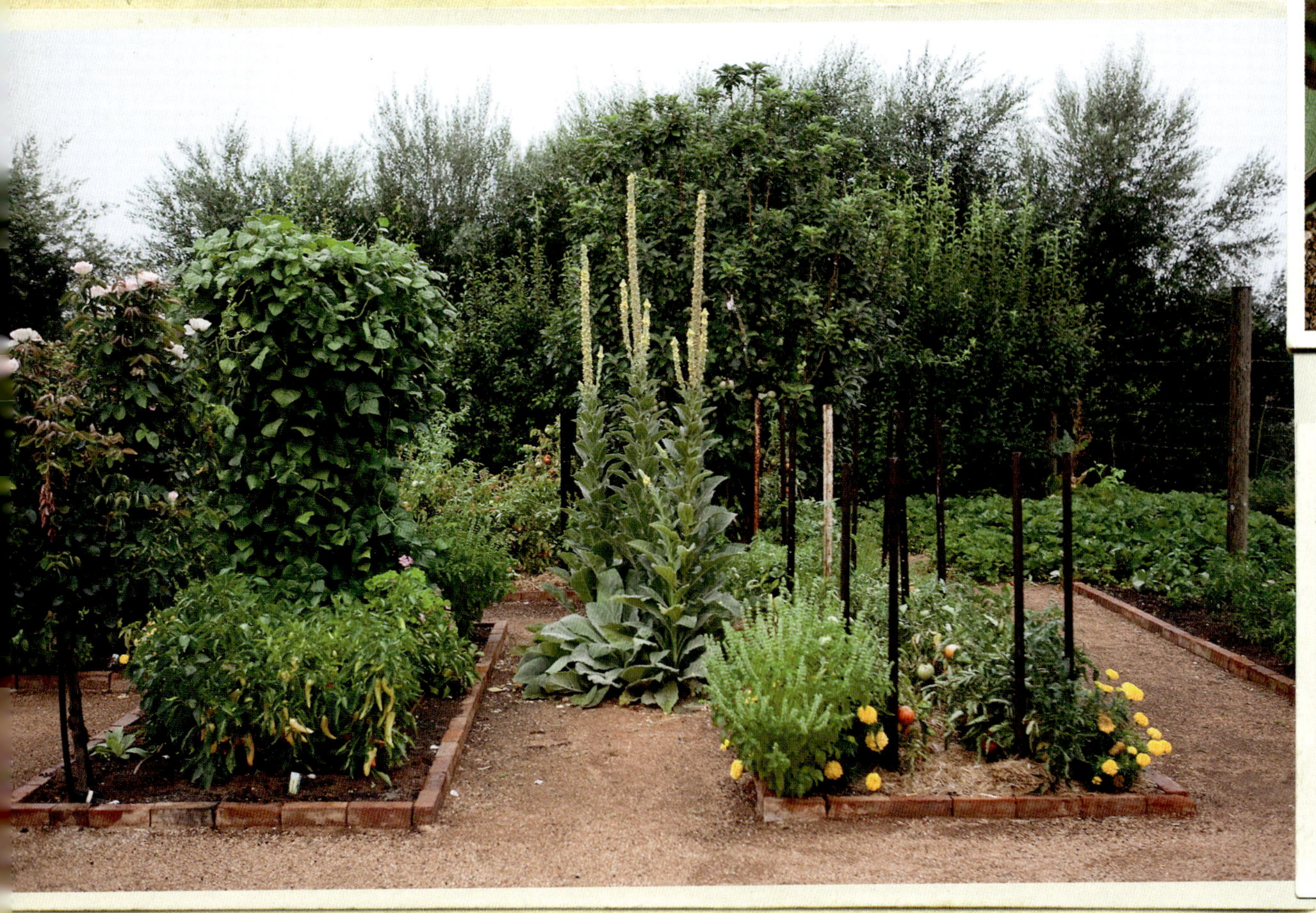
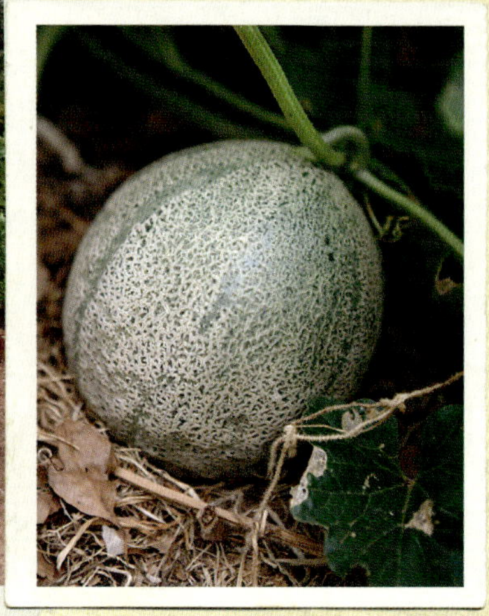

Other members of the solanum family also thrive in Margot's garden: capsicums and chillies develop in dark-green rows, eggplants in grey-green-foliaged ones. Herbs flourish throughout the beds: garlic chives, fennel, rosemary, oregano and thyme – both the common and variegated forms, and common and Vietnamese mint are planted in one of those old concrete laundry troughs once common in every Australian home. There is a good-sized patch of asparagus, a bed of shallots, one of potatoes, and climbing beans and corn are summer staples. The main food crops are rotated so as to prevent a build-up of diseases. Some of the globe artichoke plants are left to flower as Margot loves their electric mauve-blue stamens. There is salad burnet and wild rocket (arugula – *Eruca sativa*), which is an enthusiastic self-seeder. In winter Margot's crops include broad beans, onions, broccoli and peas.

> **'Food is best when it doesn't have to travel far before it reaches the table.'**

Margot is in complete agreement with local cook and restaurateur Stefano de Pieri about the value of the local Sunraysia produce: 'Food is best when it doesn't have to travel far before it reaches the table . . . The citrus, dried fruit, the river: they are all part of the Murray food experience,'[4] he says. But you'd think living in the citrus and grape capital, Margot wouldn't bother growing either of these fruits in her garden, but she has planted a number of table grapes on a trellis along one side of her kitchen garden. The varieties of red grapes include 'Cardinal', 'Ruby seedless', 'Crimson Seedless', 'Flame seedless' and the white grapes 'Menindee Seedless', 'Doro', 'Sultana' and 'Gordo'. The staggered fruiting times keep the house supplied with grapes for months. (The Mills are also 'bacchanalian blockies' and celebrate a true Dionysian vision at Ampelon in making and drinking their own wine.) The ubiquitous citrus, however, is to be found out on the blocks, where nearly all the fruit of the oranges, tangelos and lemons are destined for export to the United States.

There is plenty for eating, juicing and marmalade for the house too. 'Lane's Navel' and 'Barnfield Navels' are late-fruiting orange varieties, 'Washington Navels' are early- to mid-fruiting, and Dennis also grows a small number of the famously bitter Sevilles, which, of course, make the best marmalade of all. Dennis recommends the lemon variety 'Fino' as a prolific fruiter. 'Fino' is probably an old Spanish variety known as *Mesero* or *Primofiori* and was imported into Australia from Spain in the 1990s. It's a winter producing lemon, with production of one main crop in winter and early spring in southern Australia. In mild climates, however, 'Fino' produces fruit throughout the year, similar to the 'Eureka' lemon.

Margot has planted an assortment of fruit trees within and around Ampelon's kitchen garden: cherries, almonds, plums, apricots, a persimmon, figs 'Brown Turkey' and 'Black Genoa', 'Beurre Bosc' and 'Williams' pears and 'Granny Smith', 'Pink Lady' and 'Jonathan' apples. She has made an impressive job of her espaliers, teaching herself from books how to prune and train the apple and pear trees in fan shapes against wires. Underneath grow strawberries, which are a great favourite with Margot's grandchildren. 'Ballerina' apples have outgrown their promised small stature and columnar shape in these ideal conditions to become tall and upright feature trees in two of the long beds. Outside the kitchen garden grow avocado trees: 'Feurte', 'Hass' and 'Bacon' are varieties that do well in the district. The fruit trees are netted as required but the local birds have yet to cause havoc despite their very healthy numbers.

More than a third of Australia's farms are located within the Murray–Darling basin and over one hundred years after irrigation began, the entire region is a landscape changed beyond all recognition. The Murray–Darling basin system is fed by a total of twenty rivers (of which all except the Paroo

Clockwise from top left: **Lebanese eggplant; mouth-watering 'Elberta' peaches; long, thin Cayenne chillies; strawberries; cantaloupe; a verbascum has escaped the confines of the neat garden beds.**

River are dammed or regulated by weirs) across Queensland, New South Wales and Victoria, and the Murray River itself flows for 2530 km through New South Wales, Victoria and South Australia. Water is *the* political issue here – not only is there insufficient water to go around, the sharing and management of the water of the Murray–Darling is so complicated and fraught that even billions of government spending appears unable to bring about a solution.

Irrigators are subject to increasing state and federal government regulation and intervention as water licences are bought back and allocations are reduced. The push is also for growers to improve their water efficiency and change to more sustainable practices if there is to be any future for the industry. Managing and mitigating the environmental consequences from irrigating from the Murray – including the degradation of the river's ecology, the loss of red-gum forests, salinity and rising water tables – are all fundamental to our water and food security. And because we are all irrigators by proxy (any Australian who buys Australian-grown foodstuffs, be it orange juice, wine, rice, a muesli bar with dried fruit, lamb, pork, beef, dairy products, or fresh fruit and veg, eats or drinks products grown with water from the Murray–Darling system) these are problems for us all.

Unlike the produce grown out on Ampelon's blocks, the bounty from Margot's kitchen garden is not measured in terms of a yield basis as in kg/ha, $/ha or $/ML. Her own measure is the immense satisfaction and pleasure of creating beautiful, delicious and healthy meals from the fruit and veg she grows at Ampelon without chemicals and synthetic fertilisers. Of climate change, Margot says that certainly 'The weather is different now'; Gol Gol has not received its average rainfall of 250 mm since 1996. The 100 mm that fell in 2008 is far from adequate to grow food, let alone maintain mature trees, gardens and lawns. Gol Gol, on the New South Wales side of the Murray, is part of the Buronga irrigation system, and is piped, pressurised and privately owned. Margot is subsequently able to water her kitchen garden via a combination of micro-sprays and drippers, and mulching is imperative given the extreme temperatures of the region. Limiting evaporation is one of the gardener's first priorities.

Mulching the garden proper at Ampelon has been by means of sheet-mulching the beds – layering pelletised chook manure, newspaper, lawn clippings and grape marc (the leftover grape skins and seeds from the winemaking process) on top of the soil and weeds. Margot says she finds that if she spreads the marc on thickly, grape seedlings don't tend to germinate everywhere as I've noticed in gardens elsewhere. On the kitchen garden beds she's tried sugarcane straw with good results. It is most impressive that Margot maintains the entire garden of 1.6 ha (3.9 acres) by herself, with her trusty ride-on mower and trailer. She keeps the grounds immaculate for the many weddings and music events that take place in the garden beside the small waterlily-festooned lake under a weeping willow – picturesque surroundings indeed.

Margot's favourite time in the garden is January, despite the heat, because all of her favourite vegetables are in full production. Eggplant, tomatoes and zucchini make a fabulous trio and are natural companions for basil – all constitute the ingredients of her much-loved recipe for eggplant parmigiana. At this time of year, Margot will visit the garden daily to harvest vegetables, and reckons she probably uses parsley just about every day. Her enviable pantry is stocked with beautiful jars of jewel-coloured marmalades, jams, relishes, chutneys and preserved olives – such 'kitchen literacy' is something that is celebrated in the district. Margot and Dennis work hard and live well; no doubt they give daily thanks for the soil, water and sunshine as their kitchen garden continues to provide for the delights of the table.

Clockwise from left: **Margot hand-watering the central bed; Gol Gol has the perfect climate for growing tomatoes; luscious 'Brown Turkey' figs; repeated elements in the form of trees, standard roses and pots emphasise the formal design of Margot's** *potager.*

vait des plaintes au perfide.
e toucher il prit un air timi
mes pieds, en pleurant, il tomba.

MARKOS' KITCHEN GARDEN

Size	House block 16 × 45 m (720 m^2)
Climate	Temperate coastal
Soil	Sand
Average annual rainfall	Around 576 mm was the average per year during 1999–2009
Frost	No
Water source	Tank water
Irrigation method	Hand-watering
Compost and fertiliser	Composted food scraps and plant material, sheep poo
Mulch	Compost
Biggest challenges	Drought
Favourite herb	Oregano
Favourite food plant	Fig

CHAPTER 2
MARKOS DYMIOTIS' MEDITERRANEAN-STYLE BACKYARD

According to one of his fellow gardeners, productive gardening is more than Markos Dymiotis' passion, it is his life. Like the next urban food grower, Markos loves the 'pleasure and beauty' of harvesting his own fruit and vegetables. It is, however, just as important to him to pass on his food-growing knowledge to others as it is to share his produce. This seems natural, given that he is a cook, writer and teacher as well as a gardener. Markos is also a proud conservator of his Cyprian heritage and culture — most particularly with regard to all aspects of food — its growing, preparation and preservation. Breadmaking, preserving olives, oven building, growing vegetables, winemaking, composting and soil improvement are among his many skills; skills he has passed on to countless people in his role as a teacher at Melbourne's CAE (Council for Adult Education) for twenty years. Markos' Hampton home and garden is but a tomato's throw from the trendy and affluent beachside suburb of Brighton, but no box hedging and fashionable water feature for him! Instead, his less-than-a-quarter-acre-block boasts a Mediterranean-style productive garden that combines vegetables, herbs, vines and fruit trees, with nary a centimetre left uncultivated.

Markos was born in Agros (meaning 'the field'), a village of the Troodos mountain range in central Cyprus, and famous for growing *Rosa* × *damascena* for making rosewater. Steep terrain and impoverished soils characterise the region — serious mountain goat country, the hills dotted with small vineyards and olive groves. While Markos had no garden adjoining his house while growing up, his family cultivated a number of plots nearby to provide them with fresh produce: 'In every village, everybody's a gardener,' he jokes. Rather than return to his partitioned homeland after the crisis of 1974, Markos came to Australia from Germany where he was undertaking postgraduate study in civil engineering. In Melbourne he found a strong Greek–Cypriot community and like them, he 'put down roots' here in making a home and garden.

On this block measuring 16 × 45 m Markos packs in an amazing quantity of food plants that he cultivates organically, without synthetic fertilisers or pesticides. The north-facing rear garden receives ample sunshine and, situated only 2 km from the beach, it is not affected by frost. The front garden is ornamental as well as productive. Here the Salvia Study Group of Victoria maintains a collection of salvias that provide a colourful display for ten months of the year. Among the salvias grow three varieties of cherry, two pomegranates and grapes, trained on a trellis of posts and wire. On the northern side of the house is a shady undercover 'cave' that features two impressive brick ovens built by Markos over twenty years ago. The small oven is for roasts while the larger one — for baking bread — squats like a fat open-mouthed deity who demands offerings of wood, and olive and vine prunings. To the south and west, more grapevines cover pergolas and supply both grapes for eating and winemaking. Markos also uses the vine leaves, which he preserves by freezing the young leaves, for making the traditional *koupepia* — the Greek *dolmades*, a dish of which he is especially fond.

At the rear of the backyard a network of narrow concrete paths weave between vegetable beds. This entire area was raised to overcome the issue of soil contamination caused by an incinerator previously used on the property. Here the serious crop growing takes place in eight main beds — carrots, potatoes, broad beans, leeks and onions — plants that benefit from yearly rotation. At ground level, ornamental plants soften the spaces in between fruit trees — roses, jasmine, honeysuckle, and annuals like nasturtiums, borage, marigolds, zinnias and sunflowers are valued for their cheerful flowers, for attracting bees and as companion plants. The orchard comprises apricots, lemon, mandarin, numerous figs, olives, four varieties of plums, pears, a persimmon and loquat trees. Many of these are grafted fruit trees with two or more varieties on the one rootstock, which results in even more plant diversity per square metre — on the three olive trees, for instance, grow seven varieties of olive!

Beneath the fruit trees grow self-sown greens like silverbeet, dandelion and amaranth. These greens feature daily in Markos' cooking — the frequent use of leafy vegetables being typical of the Mediterranean-style diet, a diet also characterised by its use

Narrow concrete paths enable Markos to access all of his vegetable beds

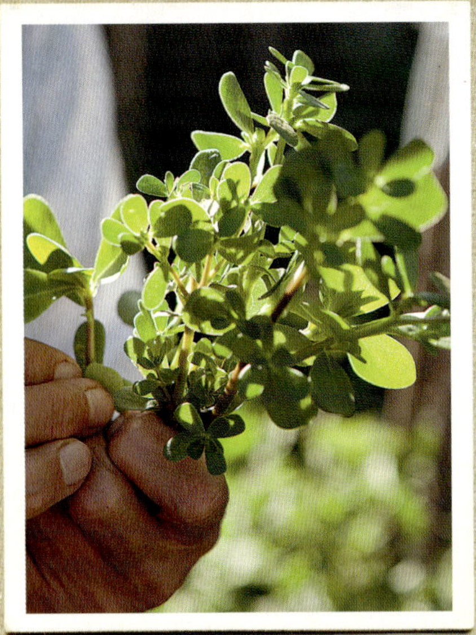
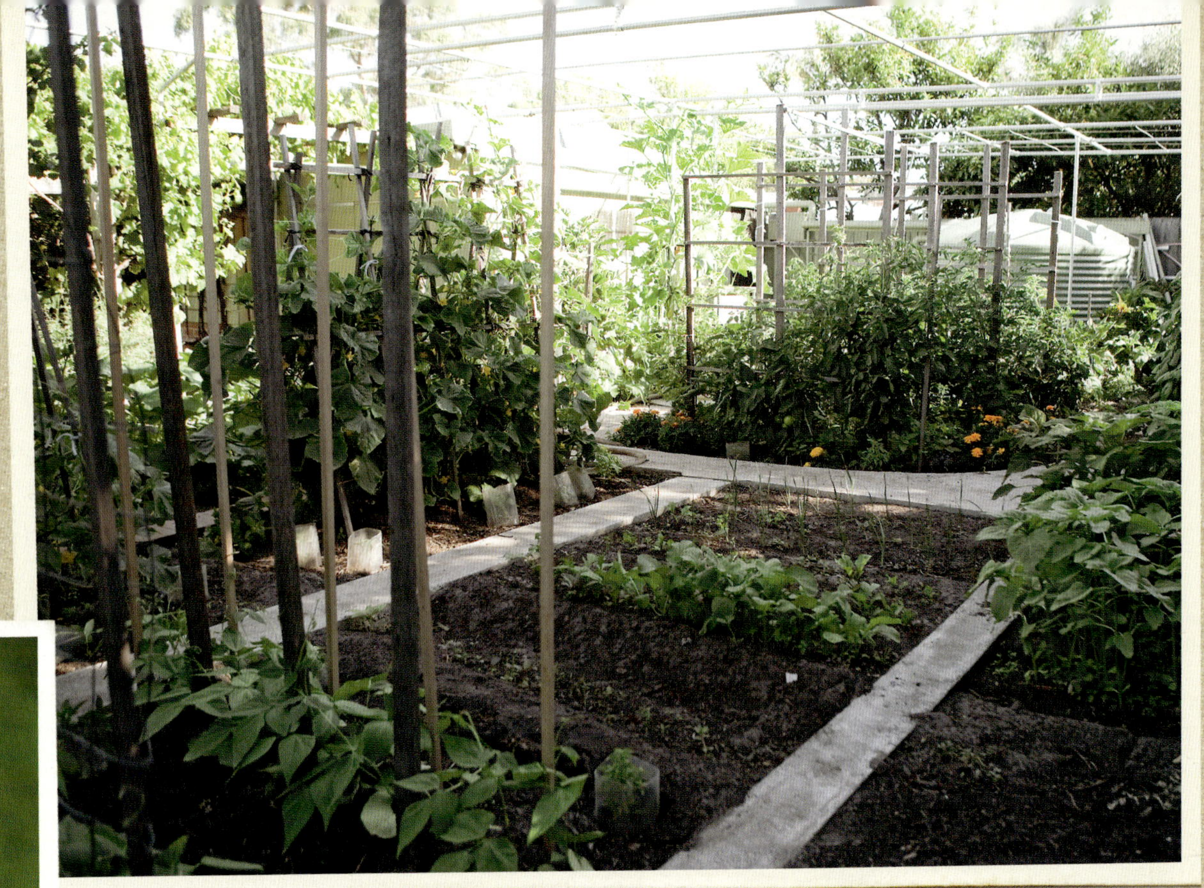
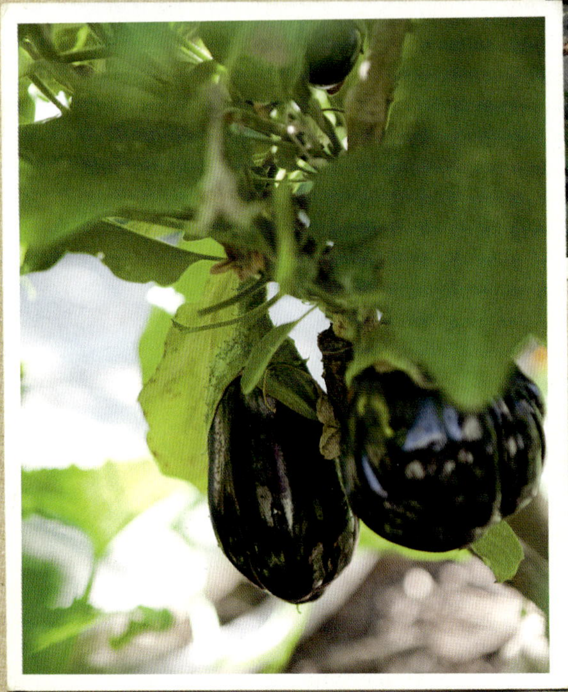
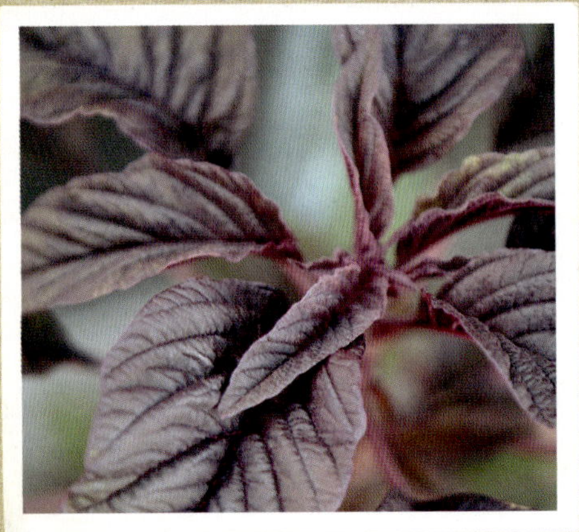
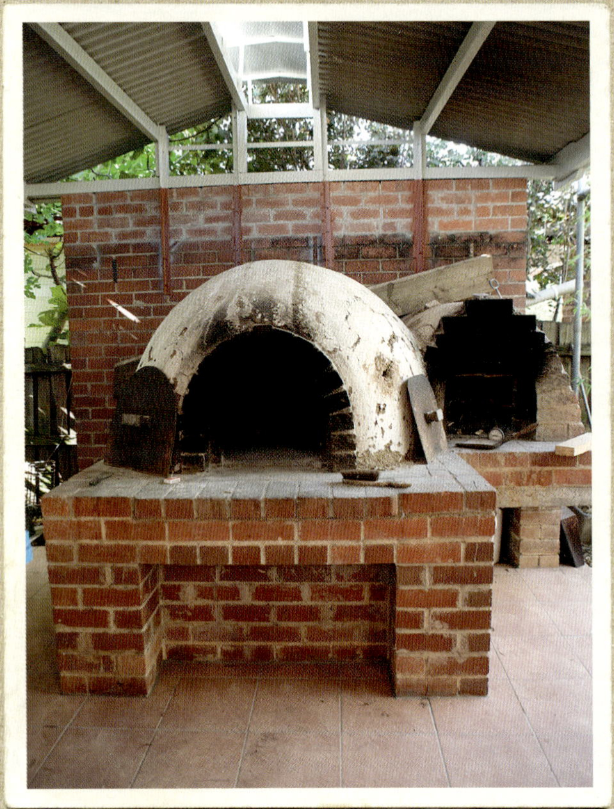
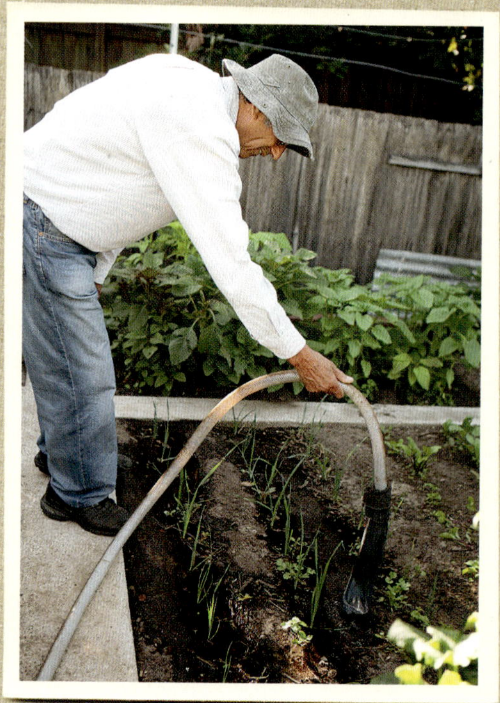

of olive oil, high consumption of legumes, unrefined cereals, fruits, vegetables, moderate consumption of dairy products (mostly in the form of cheese and yoghurt), moderate to high consumption of fish, low consumption of meat and meat products, and moderate wine consumption. Herbs are also important to many of the dishes Markos creates – particularly basil, parsley, oregano and mint, but he also grows rosemary, thyme, Greek sage (*Salvia fruticosa*) and lemon verbena.

Eating seasonally is the only way to live in Markos' book. Spring brings globe artichokes, broad beans, spring onions and celery. In summer, if he has the water, he grows chillies, capsicum, corn, beans, tomatoes (he gets his seedlings from an Italian gardener in Oakleigh), zucchini and cucumber. Markos plants garlic in March and usually harvests the bulbs around December. He has a saying about planting the cloves: 'Plant the best and eat the rest', which ensures good-quality crops year after year. I am particularly envious of his eggplant 'tree', an eggplant grafted onto a rootstock of *Solanum capsicoides* that extends the eggplant's lifespan into that of a true perennial and increases yield. The big problem in growing the heat-loving eggplant or aubergine (*Solanum melongena* – the main solanum species eaten by humans) from seed or seedlings in Melbourne is that they take most of the first summer to set their first crop, by which time it's too cold to get successive crops, and in frosty areas they won't survive winter at all. *Solanum capsicoides*, also called cockroach berry and devil's apple, is an extremely prickly shrub in the Solanaceae family native to eastern Brazil and the Gulf of Mexico. Markos allows the rootstock to leaf over winter, but will cut the foliage off near the graft once spring arrives. He has grafted the eggplant 'Bonica' and the long Lebanese variety on to a rootstock which is now eight years old. Despite the hardier rootstock and the lack of frost, the plant still requires its own plastic igloo in order for the grafts to survive the winter.

Early autumn is a time for feasting upon figs – Markos grows a number of varieties including the queen of all figs, *Ficus smyrna*, which needs to be pollinated by a variety called the 'Capri' fig and by the tiny fig wasp which lays its eggs in this variety. Figs are at optimal ripeness when the skins just begin to crack and the insides become like the most divine red jam – it is sacrilegious to cook figs, Markos asserts: they are best eaten straight from the tree. Later in the season there are hairy brown Chinese gooseberries (kiwifruit) hanging from the female vines. May or June is olive harvest, followed by the pruning of his trees. In winter, he picks mandarins from the dual-graft mandarin tree and there is broccoli, cauliflower, cabbage, bulb fennel, rocket and coriander (which he plants only as a winter herb) in the vegetable beds. With salads being so essential to his diet, Markos plans to have greens growing all year-round.

This abundance is remarkable, given the drought. Melbourne, like many parts of southern Australia, has endured twelve years of below-average rainfall – a historically unprecedented record in the last 150 years. May 2006–07 was Melbourne's driest twelve months on record, with a paltry 316.4 mm – less than half its average yearly rainfall of 648 mm. The opinion is that this may be the new climatic normal. The suburban vegetable garden has arguably become politicised: Stage 1 water restrictions were introduced in 2002 and Stage 3A in April 2007, under which plants can only be watered two mornings a week. In Markos' view these restrictions 'punish backyard fruit and vegetable growers who produce a basic food which has important health, environment and social benefits with higher water charges'. He argues that the short periods of watering permitted under restrictions 'does not allow enough time for effective watering of the deep- and medium-rooted plants (e.g. tomatoes, pumpkins, beans, capsicums)'. He writes that it leads to superficial watering, depriving these plants 'of the ability to develop deep roots – vital for good production and for good plant development to cope with harsh conditions.'

'Watering is an integral part of gardening, which is daylight

Clockwise from top left: **Purslane (*Portulaca oleracea*) is a highly nutritious edible weed; all is functional and productive in the backyard; Markos demonstrating his preferred method of watering; Markos' two brick ovens; amaranth features regularly in Markos' cooking; eggplants growing on *Solanum capsicoides* rootstock.**

MARKOS DYMIOTIS' MEDITERRANEAN-STYLE BACKYARD

1. Compost bay
2. Olive trees
3. Dual-graft mandarin
4. Lemon tree underplanted with herbs and flowers
5. Fig
6. Grapevine
7. Triple-grafted pear
8. Apricot
9. Plum
10. Pomegranate
11. Persimmon
12. Cherry
13. Sink for washing produce
14. Marrows
15. Grafted eggplants, fennel, silverbeet and amaranth
16. Tomatoes and capsicums
17. Gourds, amaranth and silverbeet
18. Black-eyed peas and climbing beans
19. Amaranth and sunflowers
20. Beans – climbing and bush, leeks, fennel and beetroot
21. Cucumbers and corn

work,' says Markos. He uses a large diameter hose to water via furrows in the garden beds and it disappears quickly into his compost-rich soil. By using three water tanks totalling 21 000 L (complete with an ingenious homemade filtration system), Markos aims to capture every drop off his assortment of roofs. Household water helps the garden survive too. In preparation for a long dry summer he radically reduces his planned crops. Pumpkins and marrows will be planted to scramble all over plots that would normally contain a diversity of food plants; Markos figures they will at least provide some yield and cover and protect the soil at the same time.

It is only to be expected that in the course of being independent from the supermarket one will exert some physical labour. Growing his own food is daily work for Markos, and his work and gardening ethic is coupled to his dedicated environmentalism, a desire to improve the planet and reduce his own ecological footprint in the course of his daily connection to the backyard. The embedded environmental costs of conventional food production and its final packaged form in the supermarket concern him greatly; as does the huge consumption of water, greenhouse-gas emissions, pollution, land clearing for agriculture and the amount of waste and packaging going to landfill. (Markos puts his rubbish bin out only once every few weeks and his recycling bin out only every few months – and most of its content is junk mail.) Markos' emphasis on recycling and frugality is a result of the nexus between utility and self-sufficiency in the Mediterranean everyday diet. The functional is at the heart of Markos' garden; things don't have to look pretty – they just have to work! Fruit-juice containers make great seedling protectors and a stainless-steel sink for washing vegetables is positioned outside in the garden itself, so that the water can run straight back into the vegetable garden.

All of Markos' ideologies come together in his compost making. In pride of place, at the 'centre of his universe', is the compost-making space. Made from recycled hardwood it comprises a single three-sided bay with a grapevine growing overhead. It is arguably the most lovingly attended pile in Melbourne; Markos' religion must surely be compost – he is the demigod of decomposition! The pile of garden and vegetable waste and lawn clippings is turned every second day with a garden fork for two weeks, and by then is usually miraculously decomposed and ready for use. Kitchen scraps are composted in a separate plastic compost bin in order to prevent flies and rodents. This is the closed loop of nutrient cycling at work, composted dead plants feed new plants, which in turn feed Markos. The velvety brown compost is both dug into his soil – which is naturally sandy, due to the bayside location – and used on top of his vegetable beds. Markos attributes the absence of problem pests in his garden to the fertility of his soil as well as practising good garden hygiene.

> 'In pride of place, at the "centre of his universe", is the compost-making space … It is arguably the most lovingly attended pile in Melbourne.'

In an assortment of backyard sheds Markos carries out various alchemies of the culinary kind. In one room he makes wine from his own grapes, including 'Shiraz' grapes, as well as from fruit harvested from other sites. Because he uses low pH grapes – generally cool climate varieties – he says that his wine requires no added preservatives. He also makes *petimezi* (*vino cotto* in Italian), a sticky sweet reduced grape syrup used as a sweetener and glaze. *Petimezi* is made from fresh cloudy grape juice that Markos simmers for over ten hours until reduced to a fraction of the original liquid. Grape juice can also be made into a typical Cypriot sweet called *mustalevria* by simmering it with flour to set the juice to a firm jelly-like consistency. The addition of chopped almonds or walnuts make for a nice dessert. When it comes to olives, Markos has a couple of methods of preserving them – green or firm black olives can be pickled in a 10 per cent brine solution, whereas the other method sees ripe black olives layered in pure salt to make the traditional 'shrivelled olives', which gives fairly speedy results and intense-flavoured wrinkly olives. He freezes his tomato harvest to save time instead of the more labour-intensive process of bottling them. Requiring a bit more time and love is his bread-making, that most basic human ritual that he has taught for twenty years at the CAE, along with how to build the ovens in which to bake the loaves.

The importance of gardening to migrants is increasingly being recognised. For Markos, a first-generation migrant, the influence of culture and memory on the way he initially began to garden and cook was very strong. 'When I came to Australia I felt a desire to go back to my roots and have natural foods, but always the flavour. That is a big thing of mine.'[1] Olive oil, herbs and greens are simply everyday foods – Markos believes there is no need for additional processed foods and artificial flavourings when you use good home-grown ingredients. He is a teacher who also likes to learn from others – he says he 'must go out with the Greeks' on weed-gathering expeditions so he can increase his knowledge of edible greens. There are edible weeds growing on abandoned land, in parks, beside railway lines and under bridges all over the city, which are, of course, free (yet ruinous for our bushland). Such wild foods are regarded as especially desirable, being something that the domestic safety of the cultivated kitchen garden cannot supply.

The wild food knowledge networks in Melbourne are well established; you can bet that old lone olive tree in a nearby park or golf course or that patch of brassica greens, often referred to collectively as *horta*, has its regular harvester and beware those that tread on another's patch and pinch their harvest! Markos, however, has many of these wild foods growing in his garden already: fennel, purslane (*glistrida* or *andrakles*), stinging nettles (*tsouknithes*), chicory, rape, sow thistle (*tsochos*), dandelion, and cat's ear – *Hypochoeris radicata*. They do quite well without any interference from him, particularly leaf amaranth (*vlita*) – that most weedy yet nutritious of food plants, and arugula – the 'wild rocket' now readily found in the greengrocer, a species that has been cultivated since ancient Roman times. Many of these greens are quite bitter – the plants' inbuilt protection system is their sap and cells – and their bitterness gives them the edge over their sweet fleshy domesticated cousins. Scientists studying the properties of such wild and weedy greens believe these plants may be an important factor in the Mediterranean diet. Bitter greens have been found to stimulate liver function and bitterness is a trait associated with high levels of phyto-nutrients containing powerful antioxidants, that can help fight cardiovascular disease and cancer.

To the dismay of many, particularly the older first-generation migrant population, the tendency has been for gardens of intensive production like Markos' to virtually disappear within a generation of migration.[2] The appeal of leisure and accoutrements of 'lifestyle' in the backyard – lawns, swimming pools, trampolines and 'entertaining spaces' – eventually seem to win out over labour-intensive food growing. 'They are missing out on the wonderful and fresh flavours of natural foods!' laments Markos. On trips to Cyprus and Greece Markos likes to research national dishes and food rituals. He has also interviewed many of his gardening 'elders' – older and mostly Greek and Italian people – about their food practices at home in the suburbs of Melbourne. His thinking is in line with psychologist Paul Rozin, who believes that some of a 'culture's accumulated wisdom about food' is embodied in its cuisine.[3] Through gardening and teaching others his methods, Markos is ensuring the continuity of his accumulated wisdom about food in a society increasingly lacking in 'food literacy'. As the sign to his garden reads: 'Welcome to simple living. Environment's only serious hope.'

Clockwise from left: **Markos' tomato trellis system with both horizontal and vertical hardwood stakes to 1.8 m high; Markos is a great ambassador for garden-based living; beautiful cucumbers; ripening figs.**

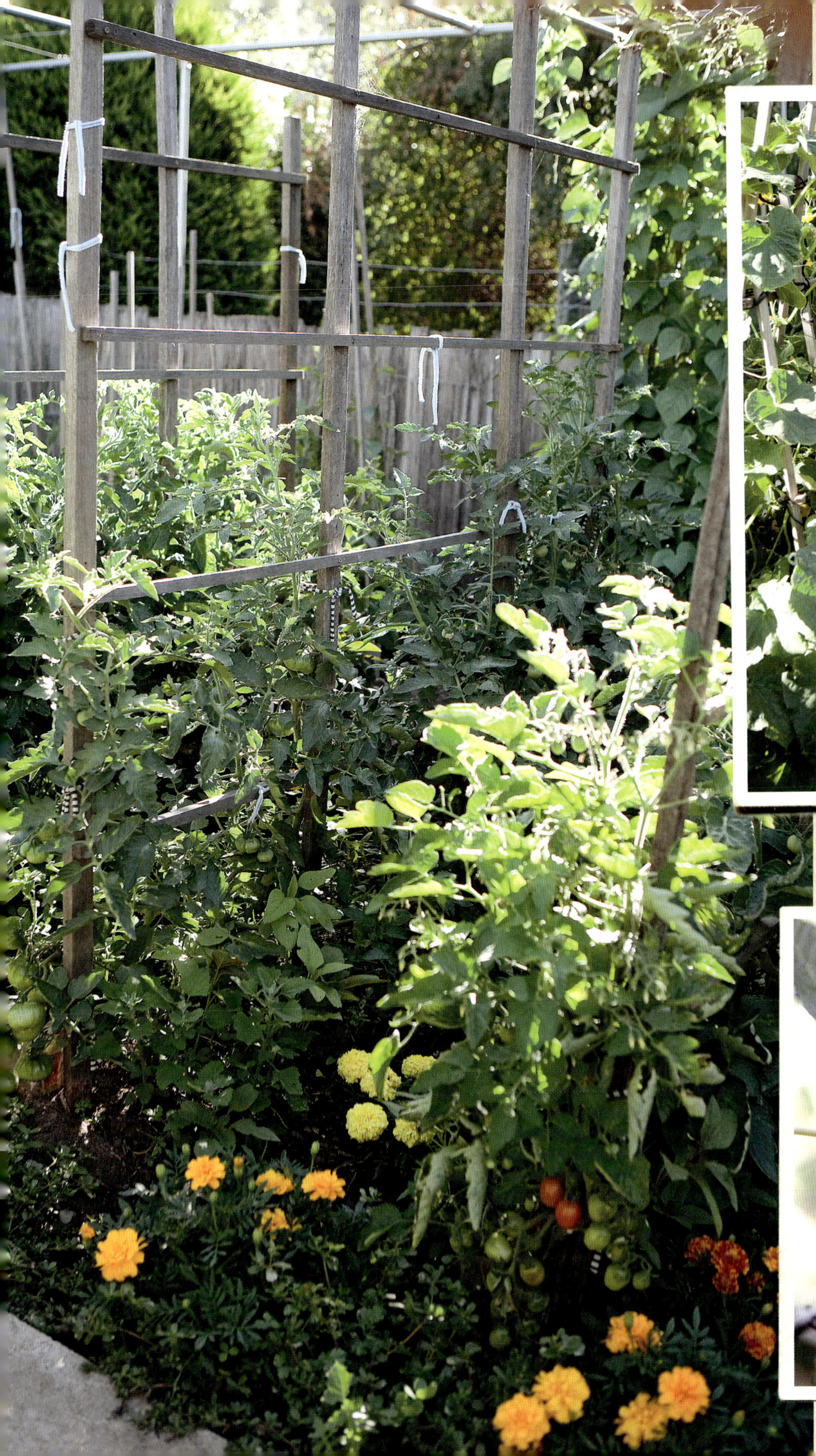

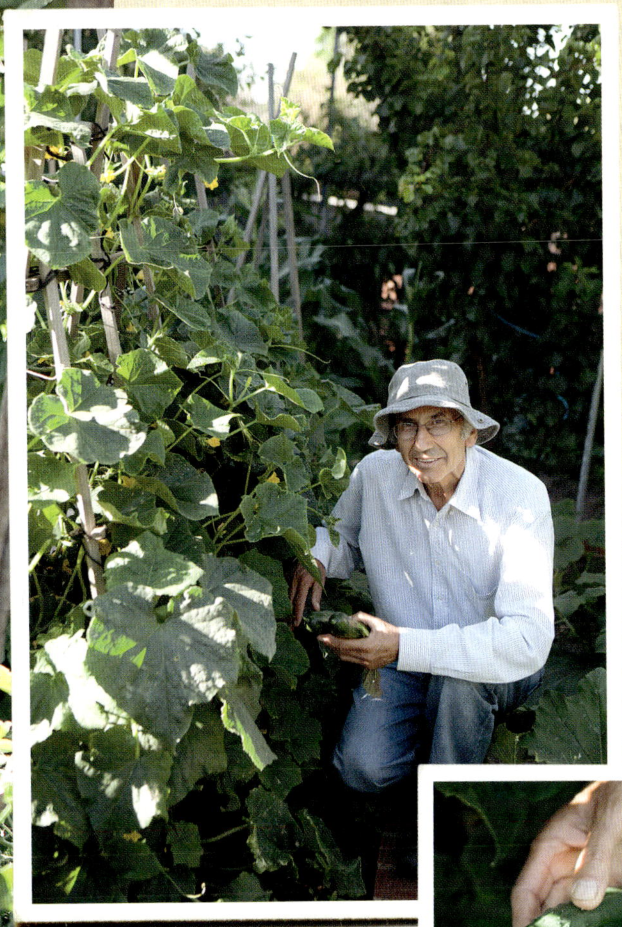

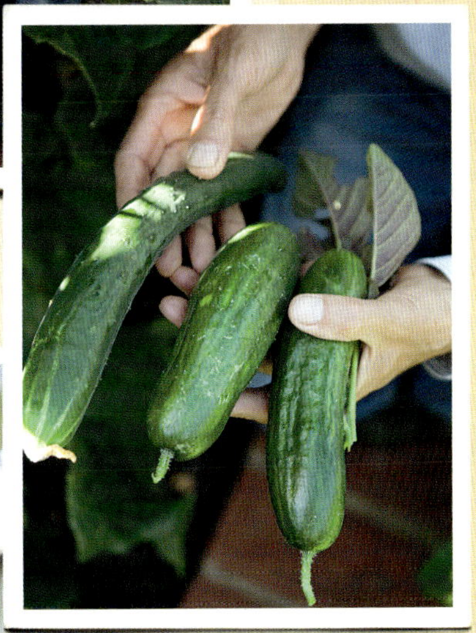

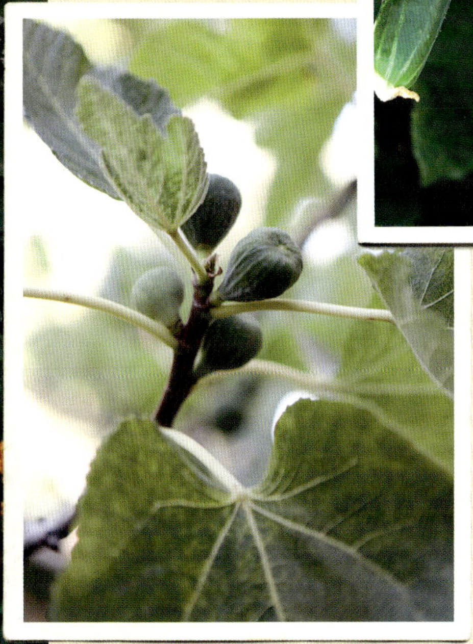

THE HEIDE KITCHEN GARDEN

Size	340 m²
Climate	Temperate (warm summer)
Soil	Clay
Average annual rainfall	500 mm
Frost	Occasional
Water source	Yarra River, rainwater, water captured from the gallery's climate-control system
Irrigation method	Hand-watering
Compost and fertiliser	Compost
Mulch	Pea straw
Biggest challenges	Watering and soil improvement
Favourite herb (Dugald's)	Sage
Favourite food plant (Dugald's)	Sweet corn

CHAPTER 3
THE KITCHEN GARDENS AT HEIDE
Art, Love and Gardening

'It is a pity one cannot have an aussie kitchen garden . . .'[1] Sunday Reed once lamented to her friend, botanical artist Jean Langley. By 'aussie kitchen garden' Sunday may have meant a kitchen garden composed entirely of Australian native bushfood plants – it was the 1970s, after all. On the other hand, she may have intended that her own 'working garden' on an old farm on the suburban outskirts of Melbourne was but a poor cousin to the kitchen gardens or *potagers* she had been so entranced with on her travels through France. If so, such 'garden cringe' proved short-sighted and pessimistic: at her home Heide in Melbourne, Sunday created a romantic garden of roses and flowers, vegetables and herbs that has been much loved and admired. While it might have been *Provençal* in inspiration, this garden was essentially home-grown in its adaptation to local conditions – a true-blue kitchen garden surrounded by gum trees and complete with tiger snakes and blue-tongue lizards.

In 1934 Sunday and John Reed purchased the 6.5-ha (16 acre) property on the Yarra River in Bulleen that their friends named Heide. Here, the Reeds established not so much an artists' colony as a household with their non-artist selves as patron/friends to live-in artists such as Sidney Nolan, Albert Tucker and Joy Hester. Consequently they wrote themselves into the story of Australian modernist art. Comparisons have been drawn with England's Bloomsbury set, and the Heide circle was similarly intellectual, artistic and engaged in formulating 'a new visual language'. Life at the semi-rural idyll of Heide – from kitchen to library, bedroom to garden – was often intense for its rather self-consciously bohemian and liberal participants. Albert Tucker described the atmosphere as a 'hot-house': an appropriate garden analogy for the affairs and 'goings-on' that no doubt shocked the Reeds' neighbours and conservative Toorak relatives. Notwithstanding all the tumult of the Heide circle, Sunday and John shared a love of art as well as an interest in plants and a passion for gardening. Both art and gardening were, for them, acts of cultivation that were ideally nurturing and transformative and both facets of their creative defiance of the Establishment. The transformation of the Heide landscape would be a shared project for the couple over the five decades they lived there, and they created not one but two kitchen gardens in that time.

The first kitchen garden was begun in 1935, on the site of the vegetable garden belonging to the original 1860s weatherboard house. It faced north and was exposed to the hot northerly summer wind. The soil was awful – clay over rock, very hard to work and improve – but nonetheless the two vegetable gardening amateurs created their garden here, in close proximity to their kitchen. Sunday's travels through France with her first husband in the 1920s almost certainly inspired her vision for the Heide garden. In France she had fallen in love with the sun-drenched hills of the south – the gardens were fabulous and the summer-dry, winter-rainfall climate of the Riviera seemed relevant to that of her hometown. In Nice, Cannes and Marseille as well as near Paris, she would have seen the kitchen garden at its peak; integral to daily life, producing fresh, good and delicious food. The French kitchen gardens – the formality of the classic quadripartite paths, the box hedging, the fruit trees either espaliered or hedged in cordons – would have appealed to Sunday as works of art in their own right. Her impulse was to recreate that aesthetic at home – to continue her love affair with the French lifestyle – aspiring to all she felt that small-town Melbourne in the 1930s, and in the middle of the Depression, was not.

The Heide kitchen garden evolved upon fairly orthodox lines – Sunday liked a classical layout and things to be 'neat' – so there were hedges of southernwood (*Artemesia abrotanum*), lavender and box, and rectangular beds with gravel paths. By January 1936 the garden contained beans, onions, lettuces, strawberries, tomatoes, marrows, parsley and raspberries. The couple had bought *French Market Gardening* (1909), which proved to be a useful handbook for their gardening ventures.

Clockwise, from left: **the romantic mix of flowers, herbs and roses that characterise the Heide garden; the entry to the second Heide kitchen garden; one of Sunday's beloved old-fashioned roses; gravelled paths and timber edging define the geometry of the beds.**

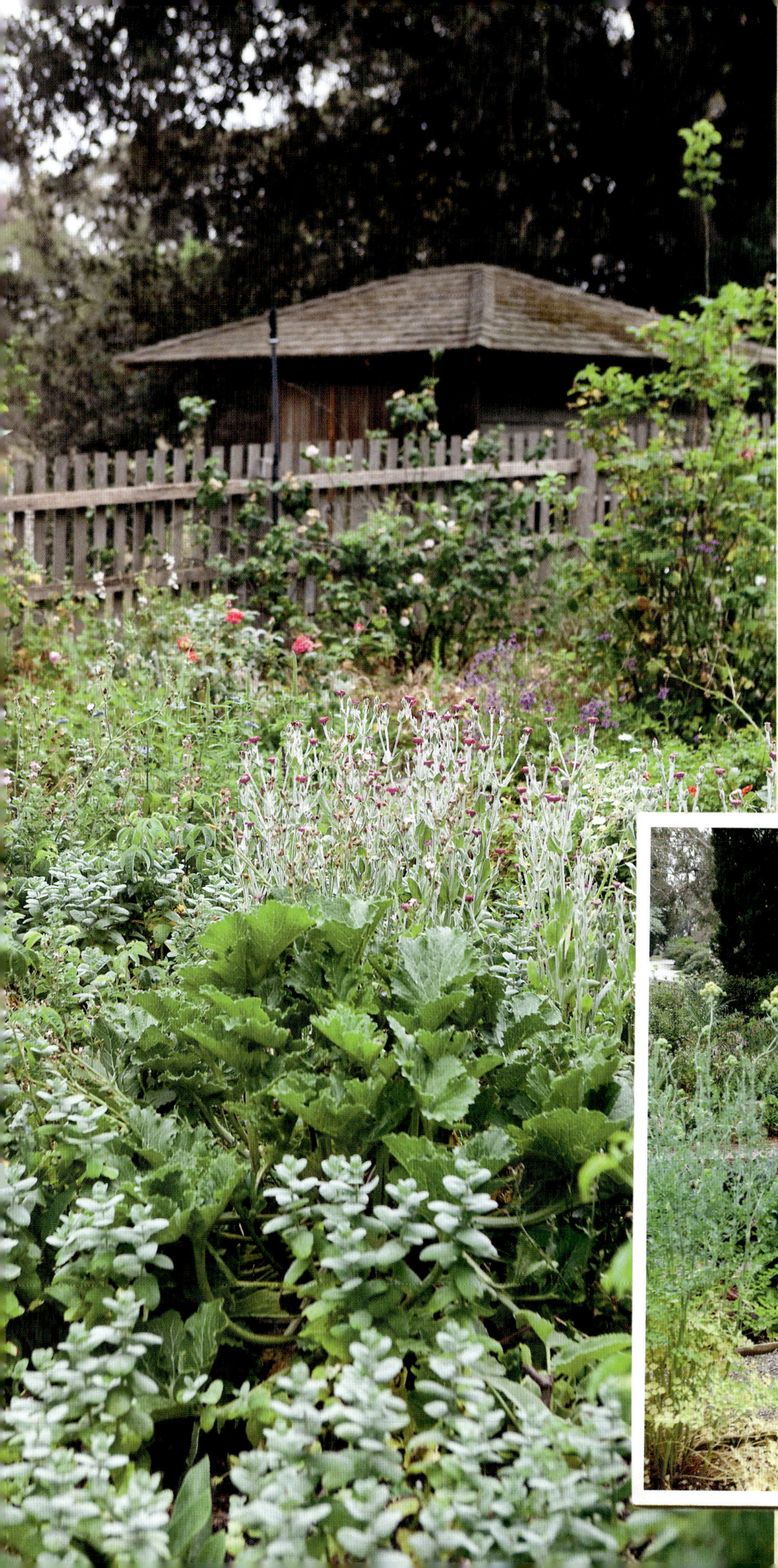

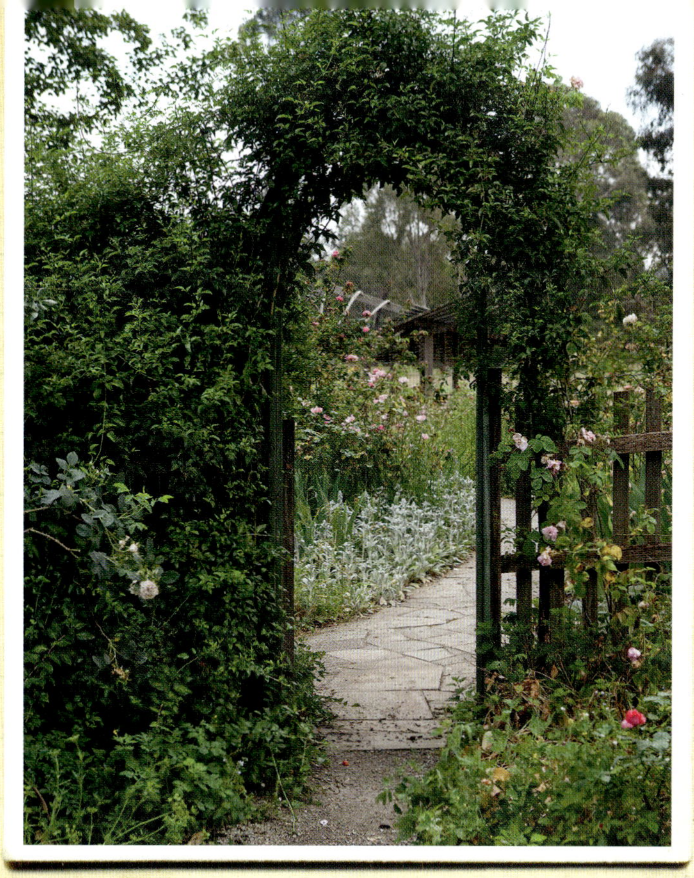

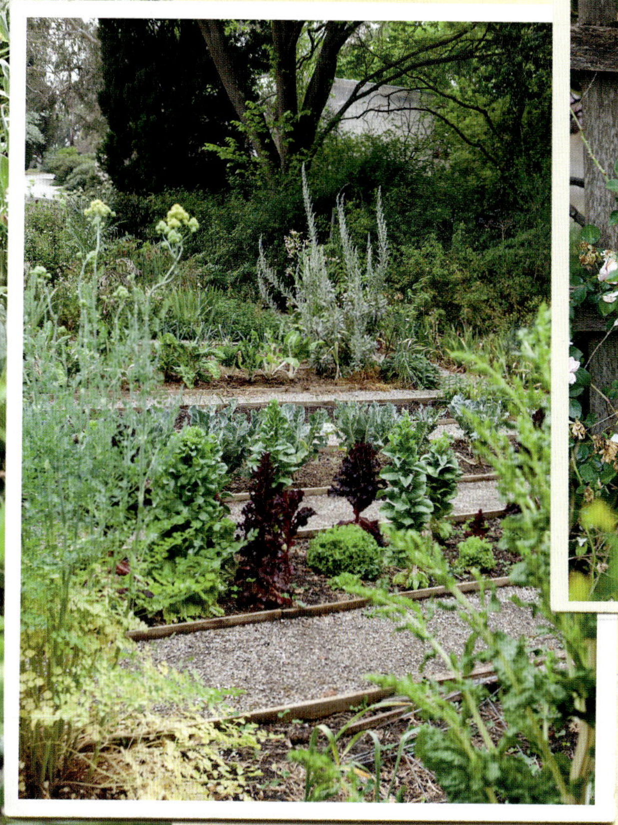

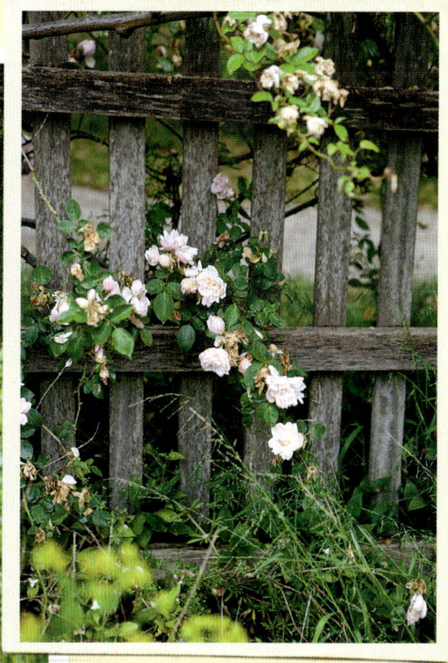

KITCHEN GARDEN I AT HEIDE

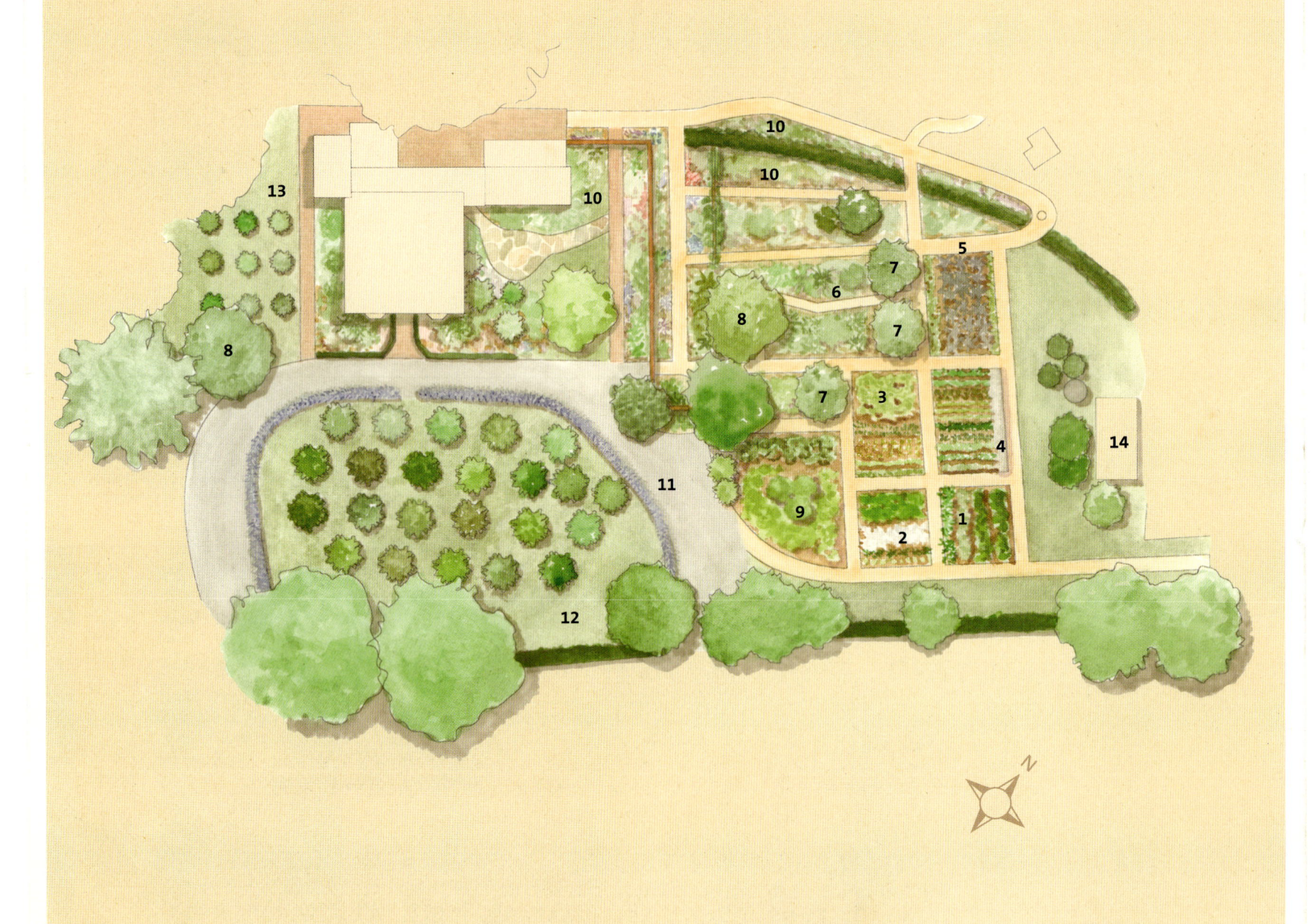

1. Tomatoes, eggplants, chillies and capsicums
2. Florence fennel, sorrel, globe artichokes and potatoes
3. Cucumber, radish, lettuce and oregano
4. Parsley, endive, carrots, onion, turnip, parsnip, beetroot, swede and angelica
5. Black kale and lettuce
6. Remnants of the native garden planted by Barrett Reid
7. Eucalypt
8. Mulberry tree
9. Pumpkins, zucchini and apricot trees
10. Roses and perennials
11. English lavender hedge
12. Orchard
13. Pome fruit orchard
14. Shed with compost area

Most useful of all was the Reeds' friend and gardener, Neil Douglas, whose advice, energy and encouragement was inestimable to the Reeds in creating the garden. He assisted with sourcing plants, propagation, much hard yakka, and provided lively conversation and company when living on site at Heide three days a week. His working relationship with John and Sun, as he called her, continued for a decade from 1936, and his friendship and love of the Heide garden until the Reeds' deaths in 1981.

As well as having green fingers, from all accounts, Sunday was a good and innovative cook. She created a food culture to which fresh vegetables were central. They also kept chooks, ducks and a house cow for milk, butter and cream. Although never totally self-sufficient, they liked to be as independent of the shops as possible; the garden, and the fact that they were independently wealthy, meant they were in many ways cocooned from the privations of wartime. Melbourne in the 1930s and 40s was a meat-and-three-veg town without a coffee machine. Olive oil could only be purchased at a local chemist. Petrol, butter and tea were rationed until as late as 1950. But Melbournians were an enterprising lot, and domestic vegetable production peaked in Melbourne during the 1940s – in the vicinity of Heide almost 80 per cent of residents produced some of their own food.[2] The Reeds were old hands by 1943, when the government introduced the national 'Grow your Own' campaign to encourage Australians to play a part in the war effort. Sunday and John, however, gardened because they wanted to, not because they needed or were encouraged to.

Throughout the 1940s and 50s the kitchen garden continued to be an essential resource for Sunday's largesse – manifested in the moveable feast and gifts of produce for their struggling artist friends. John and Sunday gardened at Heide together for nearly thirty years and, like many Australians, underwent a 'conversion' in the 1960s and started planting Australian native and indigenous plants. This was synonymous with a decline in working their original kitchen garden, yet not with gardening with exotic plants entirely – their purchasing of roses and herbs continued unabated. In 1967 the Reeds built a new house further down the hill designed by architect David McGlashan and named it Heide II. Here, on the north slope below their new contemporary home, Sunday began another kitchen garden. Being Yarra floodplain, the soil was rich with silt deposits and organic matter and the garden-making proved much easier than at Heide I. In this project Sunday had assistance from John and many friends, particularly Susie Brunton and Peter Hobb, but it was always Sunday's garden, created with buckets of her own sweat, designed by her, made with love and much laughter.

> '**Throughout the 1940s and 50s the kitchen garden continued to be an essential resource for Sunday's largesse – manifested in the moveable feast and gifts of produce for their struggling artist friends.**'

The new kitchen garden measured 23 × 46 m and was initially fenced with posts and wire, and later, to mitigate the effects of flooding, with a 1.2 m-high unpainted picket fence. The layout of beds was geometric, with rectangular beds sloping across the hill north-west to south-east and separated by earth paths. This was the canvas on which Sunday could arrange all her favourite plants: roses, herbs, flowers and vegetables. As Jean Langley wrote of her friend, 'Sunday was an artist, an artist who did not paint . . . but someone whose every touch was a touch of magic.'[3] That the garden should be beautiful as well as productive, that art should direct nature, was a given.

According to an inventory of the herbs in the kitchen garden made in 1981 there were all the common varieties: chamomile, comfrey, rosemary, feverfew, mint, angelica, rue, sage, elderflower and Sunday's beloved lavender. Rarer herbs included poison hemlock (*Conium maculatum*), coltsfoot (*Tussilago farfara*) and elecampane (*Inula helenium*) – Sunday

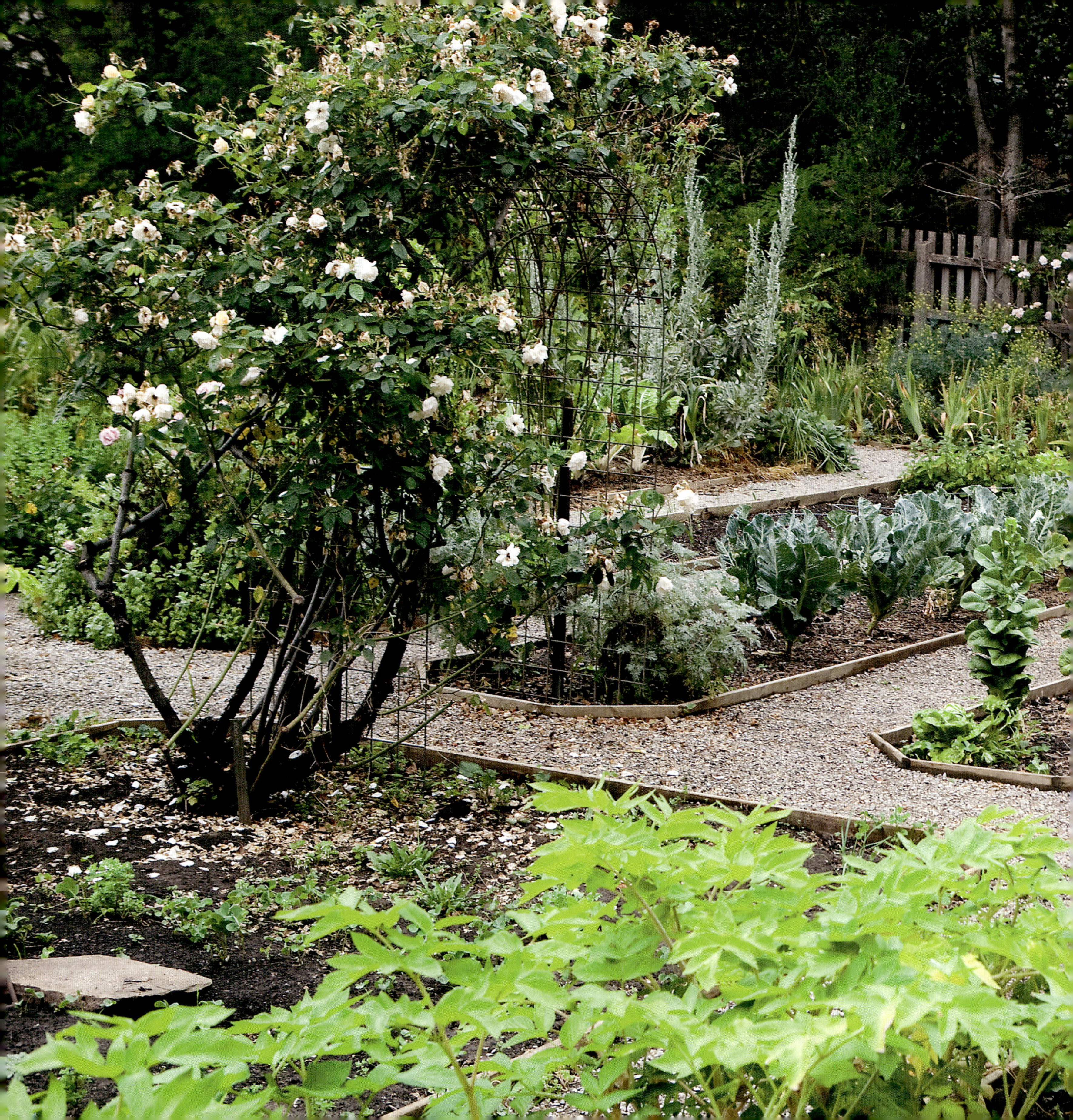

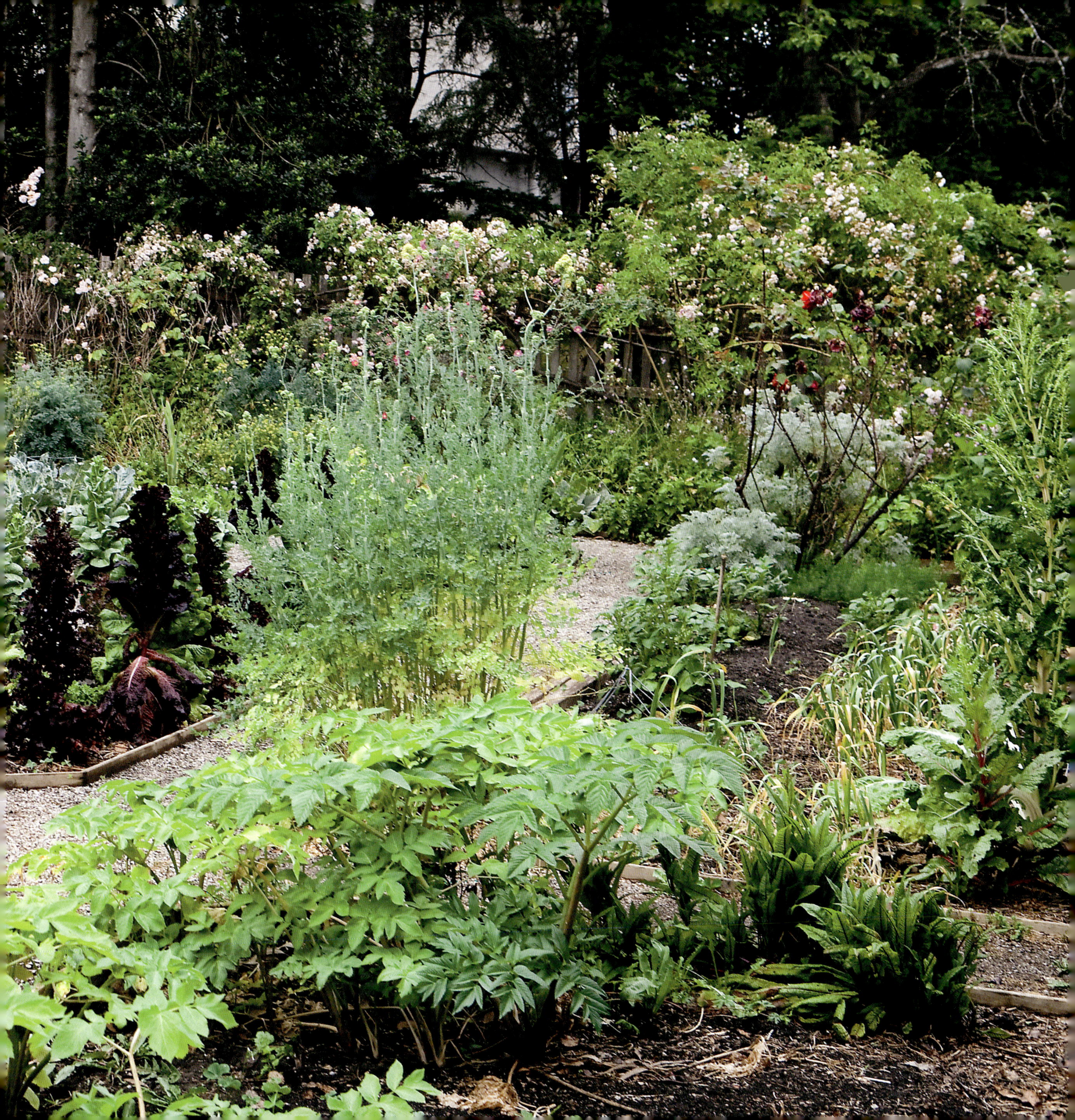

Heide
Museum of
Modern Art
Heide
→ Kitchen Garden
BEWARE
SNAKES

had inadvertently become quite a collector. If Sunday was in fact a 'witch', as one acquaintance suggested, then her kitchen garden would have amply supplied her simples and potions! In corresponding with Guy Smith of the Herb Society (who consulted on and worked in the kitchen garden after Heide II was sold), she wrote: 'I would like the garden to be remembered just as a kitchen garden I made and not as a "herb" garden.'[4] There is a total of 104 different genera on this list (not including the roses) and at least forty-five of these have herbal or edible uses. Sunday's botanical knowledge was extensive by this time – she knew the tricks to getting difficult seeds to germinate; she even smuggled chervil seeds from France so she could grow the aniseed-flavoured leaves for her salads.

Roses reigned supreme in the kitchen garden: over a hundred species were planted here. Sun's favourites included *Rosa* 'Fantin-Latour', *R.* 'Cecile Brunner', *R.* 'Souvenir de la Malmaison', damask roses, rugosas and species roses like *R. bracteata* and *R. spinosissima*. Roses terminated each end of the vegetable beds as well as being densely planted around the perimeter. A central rose arbour with seats supported the striped Bourbon rose 'Variegata di Bologna'. Everywhere were the fluffy flowerheads of red and white valerian, purple yarrow, drifts of the yellow flowered tansy and evening primrose – though the soft colours of pink, mauve, blue, purple and white predominated as Sunday was not a fan of loud oranges and yellows. Other ornamental plants were rose campion (*Lychnis coronaria*), soapwort (*Saponaria officinalis*), scented-leaf pelargoniums and marguerite daisies. Blue was her favourite colour, and thus there was a profusion of love-in-the-mist, bearded iris, cornflowers, delphiniums, borage and forget-me-nots.

The soft and romantic Heide II garden was both the antithesis of both Sunday's ultra-modern new home and the manicured gardens of Toorak and Sorrento of her childhood

Pages 38-39: **Roses, herbs and perennials are planted around and among the vegetables in the kitchen garden and Heide II.**
Clockwise, from top left: **Evening primrose; seedhead of salsify; Heide is ideal tiger snake habitat; Rosa 'Constance Spry'; love-in-the-mist; edible flowers of globe artichoke.**

and adolescence. Her gardening style had evolved from her more formal approach of the 1930s and 40s to a cottage garden style *sans* box hedging. The tendency has been for writers to see Sunday's gardens as an extension of her identity: one part vanity, one part creativity, one part practicality, one part sanctuary – a refuge from the dramas of her social world, her love affairs and disappointments. In her book *The Heart Garden* historian Janine Burke posits Sunday as an Earth Mother personified: 'The Heide garden was a potent symbol of Sunday's creativity. It was meant to enchant and animate . . .'[5] This bountiful cultivated garden has also been read as a particularly poignant space given Sunday's own infertility, and we shouldn't underestimate how much its care was a daily ritual necessary for her psychic wellbeing.

In 1980, after years of negotiation, Heide II and the surrounding six hectares was finally sold to the Victorian government by the Reeds. The institution Heide Park and Art Gallery (later Museum of Modern Art at Heide) was inaugurated and John and Sunday subsequently moved back to their original home at Heide I that same year. On her return to her old home, Sunday supposedly never visited her kitchen garden again – she must have felt great grief and loss for her creation. She was anxious about how it would be cared for and maintained by the new owner, but obviously felt the break had to be final. (After the Reeds' deaths in December 1981, their friend Barrett Reid lived at Heide I and cared for the place as best he could until his death in 1995.) Under museum director Maudie Palmer the kitchen garden at Heide II was restored – David Kirkpatrick and Simon Dickeson being the gardeners there at that time – but it wasn't until 2003 that the renovations of Heide I's kitchen garden began. Landscape architect Elizabeth Peck and Heide's gardeners have now reconstructed the layout from old photos and the memories of people who knew the garden.

Today, visitors can wander into the Heide II kitchen garden after seeing an exhibition at the galleries at Heide II or III. Entry to the kitchen garden is via a banksia rose-covered archway in the timber paling fence as in the Reeds' day. The large 'Beware Snakes' sign is a reminder that all is not entirely idyllic in this Garden of Eden: tiger snakes and flooding have both affected the garden regularly over the years. The kitchen garden is only 1000m² but it is a feature of the whole property. It is one of the most intensely cultivated part of the Heide garden – which is 'what gives it the strength and sense of place you get when you're in there: it's a concentrated little rectangle and once you pass out of it through the gates, you are back into open parklands'.[6] In this respect it is a *hortus conclusus*, a feeling enhanced by the mature surrounding trees.

The gardeners here are committed to improving the garden and simultaneously respect the history of the place without believing in the garden's museification. They never garden with the feeling of Sunday's ghost watching over their shoulder. It is important to the gardeners not to alter the feel of the kitchen garden; that they don't 'change the overall sense of bounty and produce' but that they instead 'attempt to maintain that sense of dynamics: change of season, massive height in all the plants, changing colours throughout the season so that you really know that you are in a kitchen garden'.[7] Kitchen gardens are not static spaces, after all; they manifest more than any other type of garden the cycle of decay and renewal.

In summer, height within the plantings is provided by the roses, Jerusalem artichokes, tree dahlia (*Dahlia imperialis*), *Salvia guaranitica*, lemon verbena and golden rod. Low-growing herbs intertwine with strawberries and ornamental bulbs planted by Sunday like pineapple and belladonna lillies and Solomon's seal. The ongoing management of this space involves caring for the ageing roses and eradicating some environmental weeds that have found their way in – the noxious horsetail (*Equisetum hyemale*), for example. Vegetable crops were grown in the beds at the western end of the garden by Sunday. In the future, however, only perennial vegetables like asparagus will be grown in the Heide II kitchen garden as the food production has been shifted from the lower garden back up to the original kitchen garden at Heide I. Head Gardener Dugald Noyes has overseen the redevelopment and extension of the old kitchen garden where food plants are now being cultivated to supply the gallery's café–restaurant.

Dugald has a great love of kitchen gardens, fostered when he started working for the National Trust at the historic Melbourne homes Como House and Ripponlea and on the kitchen gardens at those properties. The Heide I kitchen garden is designed as a workhorse, with a focus on high turnover, on growing 'baby vegetables', edibles that were grown by Sunday and French heirloom varieties. Two of Dugald's favourite heirlooms are the 'Jersey Royal' potato – a beautiful kidney-shaped potato developed on the island of Jersey in 1878 – and pumpkin *Rouge Vif D'Etampes*. The latter, with its squat and deeply ribbed red-orange form, is the classic 'Cinderella' pumpkin and is an heirloom that dates from the early 1800s.

> **'Even as suburbia has steadily encroached, the park-like feel remains at Heide.'**

The garden is managed according to organic and sustainable methods, with compost (made on site) comprising the essential 'engine' by which the clay soil is replenished, and enabling such intensive and constant vegetable production. Come December and the garden boasts sorrel, parsnips, swedes, carrots, globe artichokes, zucchini, cucumber and masses of salad greens, mint and parsley, all destined to supply the café's kitchen. In order to fulfil the Heide chef's wishlist and maintain a continuity of supply, Dugald says he needs to practice 'strategic' kitchen gardening: 'It's all about the real estate,' he says, meaning making careful decisions on which vegies are a priority, where they can be fitted in and following what crop rotation. There are also plans for a bushfood garden to be planted in the remnants of the native garden established by Barrett Reid upon the Reeds' original kitchen garden. This recently proposed garden 'layer' could be a lovely *dénouement* in light of Sunday's idea of an 'aussie kitchen garden'.

Dugald prefers to water the kitchen garden by hand, which adds considerably to his daily summer work, but he likes to

Head gardener Dugald Noyes amongst cauliflowers and lettuces in the Heide II kitchen garden

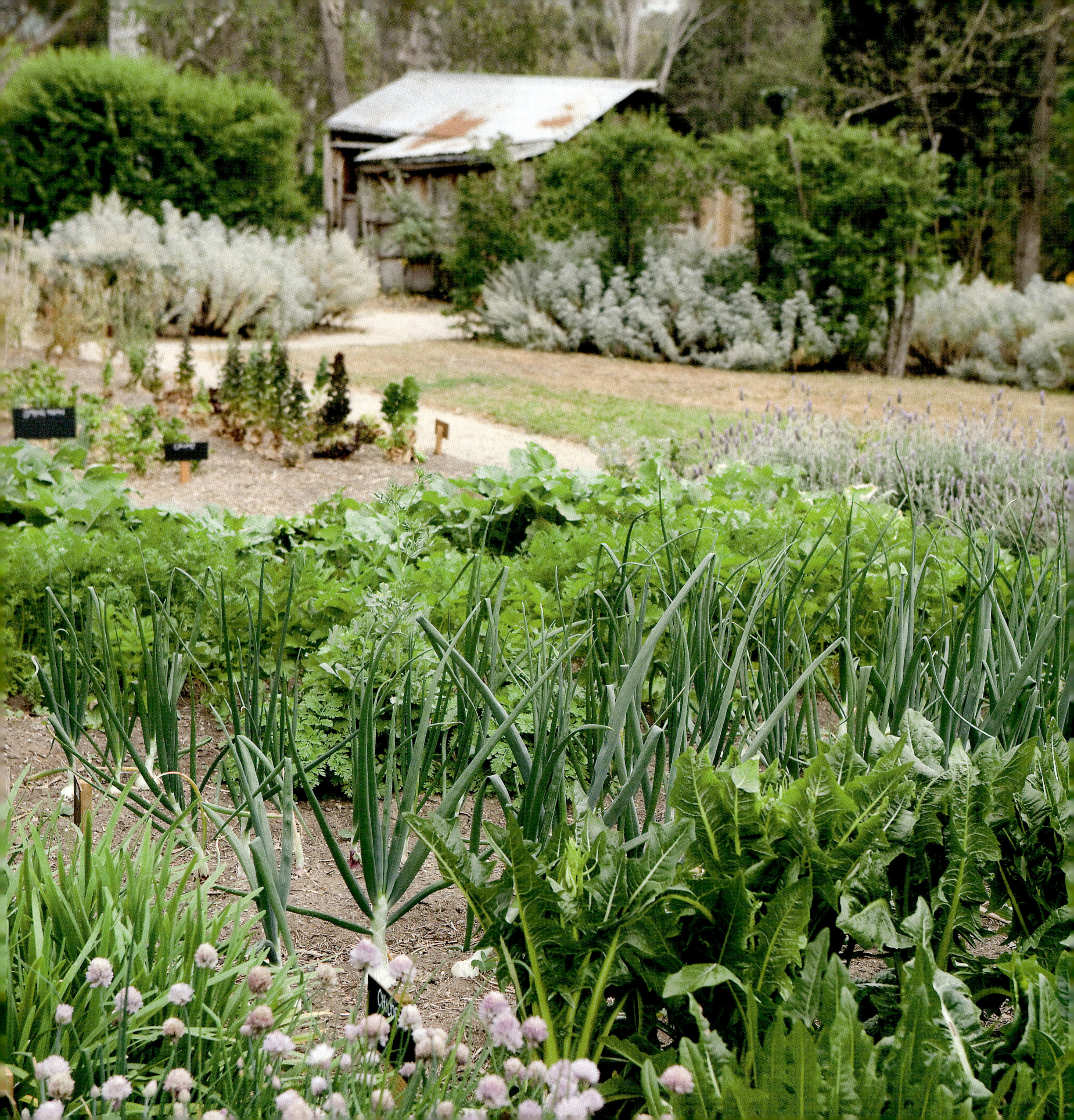

see the water 'going on' to the soil and uses this task as a time to inspect the plants. Over the course of Melbourne's more than decade-long drought, water has been available for the Heide gardeners (owing to a licence from Melbourne Water) to pump a limited annual quota from the Yarra River. However, watering with mains and river water is still limited to two days a week, so huge tanks have been installed to catch rain from the roof of the Heide III gallery as well as the condensation resulting from the operation of the gallery's climate-control system.

Even as suburbia has steadily encroached, the park-like feel remains at Heide. Wombats have their burrows down by the river and the remnant riparian vegetation – river red gums, tree violet (*Melicytus dentatus*), poas and lomandra – suggests what must have been. The challenges of maintaining a heritage garden and a public one too are varied. In particular, the issue of senescent trees – many planted (and over-planted) by the Reeds and their friends – demonstrates the trade-off between heritage considerations, arboreal health and public safety. There is the odd theft of vegetables and fruit (either opportunistic pilfering or organised gleaning), but by and large visitors are respectful.

Sunday Reed could not have foreseen the many gardeners who have gardened in her footsteps, each responsive in their own way to her legacy; each, like her, a plant-lover: 'I love my kitchen garden so much. It is a pity one cannot have an aussie kitchen garden yet it is true that all these flowers and herbs are my closest friends.'[8] Yet it proved possible, after all, and we appreciate that this intense and creative woman had the vision to ensure that we all might visit her home and her garden: a gift, with love, from Sun.

Left: **Chives, chicory and onions with the building known as the 'Doll's House' in the background.**
Above from top: **The heirloom potato 'Jersey Royal'; cabbage 'Red Drumhead'.**

KAREN SUTHERLAND'S KITCHEN GARDEN

Size	13.5 × 38 m (513 m²)
Climate	Temperate
Soil	Heavy clay
Latitude	37° 44' S
Average annual rainfall	650 mm (less than 500 mm annually from 1996–2009)
Frost	No
Water source	Tanks, mains and greywater
Irrigation method	Drip irrigation and hand-watering
Compost and fertiliser	Homemade and purchased compost, pelletised organic fertiliser and liquid seaweed plant conditioner
Mulch	Compost, partially composted pine bark, straw in vegie patch
Biggest challenges	The changing climate (more heat, less water, more insects)
Favourite herb	Lemon . . . verbena/myrtle/grass
Favourite food plant	Flat-leaf parsley/globe artichoke

CHAPTER 4
KAREN SUTHERLAND'S URBAN EDEN

It is a rare individual who can say that after a hard day at work they'll come home and happily do more of the same thing, and then do it again on the weekend too. Karen Sutherland is one such person. A professional gardener as well as a designer and teacher, Karen is passionate about creating gardens that are edible. Her own garden in suburban Melbourne fits the typical nicest-garden-in-the-street scenario: a lovely combination of flowers, trees and shrubs with attractive slate paving and granitic sand surrounding her Californian bungalow home. Who would guess that most of the plants are edible? Silver-foliaged globe artichokes are grown with Mexican sage and lamb's ears, rosemary 'Blue Lagoon' is planted among purple pennisetum (a sterile form, *P. advena* 'Rubrum'), and citrus and Warrigal greens are combined with purple statice. Karen's garden proves that vegetables need not be confined to a backyard vegie plot, herbs to a herb garden or fruit trees to an orchard! Produce gardens can be as ornamental as gardens designed for aesthetics alone. Karen has a particular interest in herbs, perennial vegetables, and unusual fruits. She started her first vegie garden at the age of eight and is now a serious plant collector (her garden contains over 150 different edible and useful plants). She qualifies as a true *maven* in the Hebrew/Yiddish sense of the word of one who is experienced or knowledgeable and who seeks to pass knowledge on to others. Focused on the warming and drying climate, she is designing gardens (both her own and for others) according to sustainable and organic principles.

Edible landscaping is about using productive plants in an ornamental way – combining fruit and nut trees, berries, vegetables, herbs and edible flowers with ornamental plants. Edible landscaping became popular in the US in the 1980s thanks to pioneers such as garden designer and writer Rosalind Creasy, whose 1982 book *The Complete Book of Edible Landscaping* came out at a time when 'there seemed to be an unwritten law against vegetables in a suburban front yard'.[1] It coincided nicely with the development of the heirlooms movement and middle-America went mad for rainbow-coloured vegies in the home garden – everything old was new again.

In her own design business Edible Eden Design, Karen encourages clients to think creatively about making spaces that are beautiful and productive. In designing a garden Karen might suggest using purple beans and climbing plants on decorative trellises, edging beds with gorgeous pale-pink-flowered strawberries, or with chives and curly leaf parsley. Structure is important too – hedges can be created using rosemary, bay trees or guavas, she says. 'Screening plants can be shrubs yielding fruit, flowers and leaves for herbal teas', and shrubs and trees can be 'espaliered on fences to bring colour and texture into the garden and to attract bees for fruit and vegetable pollination'.[2] Repeated plantings of the same species can give a sense of design rhythm to the garden whereas feature plants draw the eye – Karen suggests a standard bay tree in the centre of a garden bed to create visual impact. There is a serious philosophy behind these beautiful edible gardens, however. Apart from the sheer pleasure of it, Karen believes there are a number of benefits of growing your own fruit and vegies. The freshness of the food means it has better nutritional value; there's no travel time from garden to plate and thus no food miles or greenhouse-gas emissions; and you know that no chemicals have been used in its production. 'Lower impact on the environment and seasonal foods equal healthier cooking,' says Karen – growing your own is 'a recipe for better health of body and mind'.

In her home garden Karen has built up the heavy northern Melbourne clay soil (gluggy and unworkable in winter, impenetrable and cracked in summer) over twenty years. After removing extensive concrete with a crowbar and sledgehammer, she dug the soil by hand, she says, adding gypsum and homemade compost. Today, the soil in mounded garden beds is about 15 cm high, is well drained and full of life. Fruit trees are thriving in the west-facing aspect – this is what she calls her 'Mediterranean garden'. There's a carob tree (*Ceratonia siliqua*), olive, bay tree and pomegranate 'Ben Hur', the orange varieties 'Lane's Navel', 'Valencia' and a blood orange as well as the dwarf lemon 'Lots-a-lemons'. Bordering one side of the driveway are feijoas that Karen has cleverly espaliered in a strip of garden bed only 20 cm wide. The 1.5-m-high espalier shows

Karen hand-watering in the backyard vegetable patch

off the feijoa's many-stamened red blooms and the knobbly grey-green oval fruits. Underneath she's planted the strappy-leaved society garlic *Tulbaghia violacea* which, despite being tough, evergreen, and having pretty lilac flowers, is not often planted. Perhaps the garlicky fragrance of the foliage deters some gardeners as well as pests.

There are native plant foods planted in the front garden too: Warrigal greens scramble over a garden bed, midyim berries (*Austromyrtus dulcis*) promise to do well in the semi-shade of an ornamental pear, while some coastal dune-loving muntries (*Kunzea pomifera*) are an 'experiment' in full sun. Karen is excited about the culinary and garden potential of native Australian myrtles. She grows the lemon-scented (*Backhousia citriodora*), the aniseed (*Anetholea anisata*) and the cinnamon myrtle (*B. myrtifolia*) in pots as she's found they require filtered light and protection from hot winds. Individually and combined together, the leaves (fresh or dried) make a lovely tea. In another pot is the pink-fleshed form of the native finger lime *Citrus australasica*, a thorny tree of the rainforest understorey of northern New South Wales and southern Queensland. Pots enable Karen to grow yet more food plants upon her outdoor surfaces, to move them around and to give tender plants extra love or shelter. Take the saffron crocus – its tiny bulbs would get forgotten in the garden proper, so Karen has them in pots on the front steps and hopes one day to again pick the tiny golden stamens worth more by weight than gold.

Karen is a 'herb fanatic' so there are herbs galore – elderberry, lemon verbena, and many different species of thyme and savory. One of her sources is Island Herbs and Perennials in Tasmania. From Island Herbs she has obtained such unusual edibles as chives that grow throughout winter and vanilla grass (*Hierochloe odorata*), a perennial poa to 40 cm high that has soft leaves that taste of vanilla. The leaves can be dried and burned as incense to give off the sweet vanilla fragrance or, as they do in Poland, added to a bottle of vodka to steep and infuse. It has creeping roots that can quickly spread so it is best planted in a pot. From a blue glazed pot tumble the beautiful silver felted leaves of Cretan dittany, a low-growing herb and member of the oregano family. *Origanum dictamnus* is endemic to the mountainous hillsides of Crete and has traditionally been used by locals as both a medicinal 'cure all' and a culinary herb. The flowers are covered by lovely nodding pink bracts like the ornamental varieties of oregano. This unassuming and pretty perennial has a history filled with passion: it was reputed to be an aphrodisiac and Cretan men risked life and limb to collect the flowers from cliffs and dangerous rocky terrain as love tokens and proof of their huge machismos. Such foolish men were known as *Erondades* (love seekers). Karen, on the other hand, although herself an experienced rock-climber, had only to stroll down the street for her cutting from a Cretan neighbour.

Pascoe Vale is a multicultural neighbourhood with many first-generation Greek and Italian migrants. Lots of these residents are gardeners and Karen has enjoyed their immense plant knowledge and generous advice over the two decades she's lived here. Gardening in the front yard can be a communal experience! While her front yard and nature strip have a Mediterranean flavour (in keeping with the cultural demographic) the backyard has a tropical one. As Karen explains, this is a great example of different microclimates at work and how to plant with aspect, slope, prevailing wind direction, heat traps or shady spots in mind. Buildings and pavement in full sun will act as thermal mass creating a 'heat island effect' whereas slopes can be sinks for cold air or frost and bodies of water can work as natural air-conditioning. In this part of urban Melbourne frost is not an issue; Karen's rear garden is sheltered from the wind and the trees, foliage and the lawn increase the humidity.

Karen plants trees for multiple purposes in the garden: for shade, to filter city air, cool the house in summer, for structure in the garden, their leaf colour and spring blossoms,

Clockwise, from top left: **Karen's aquaponic set-up; the front garden with potted edibles; aquaponic lettuces growing in scoria; the backyard patch and fruit trees; thornless blackberries.**

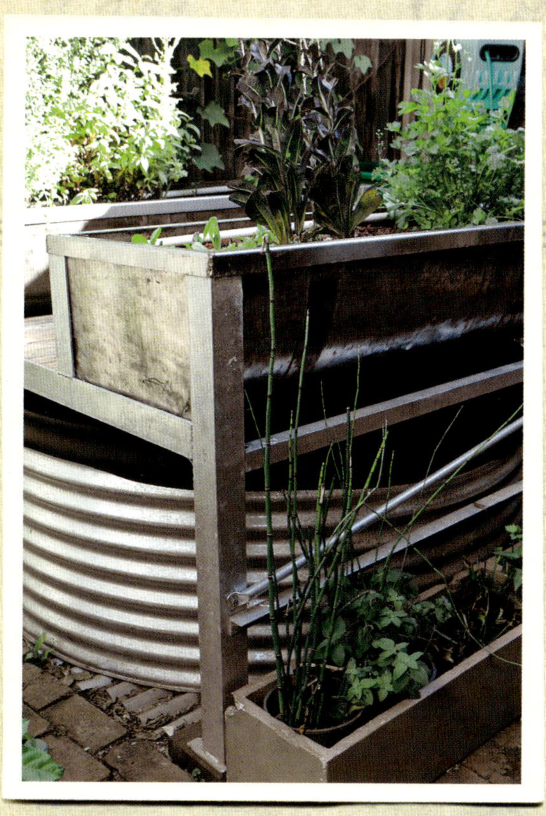
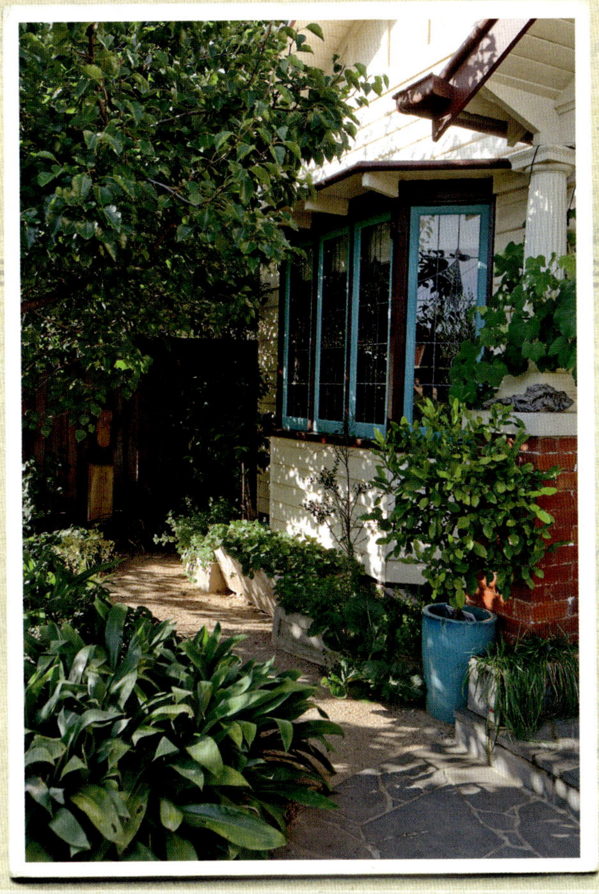
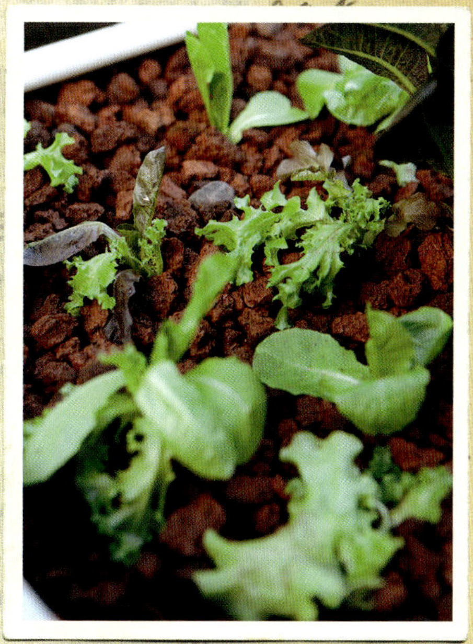
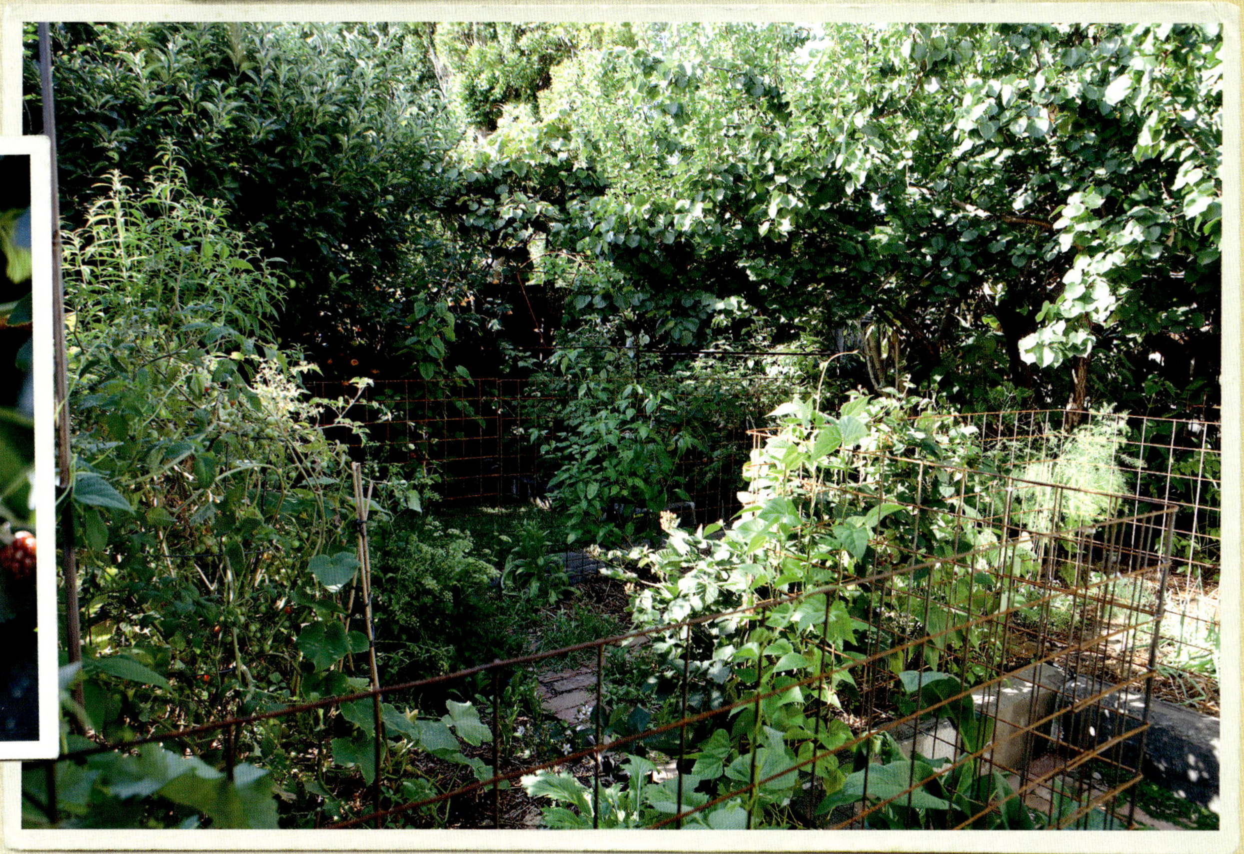
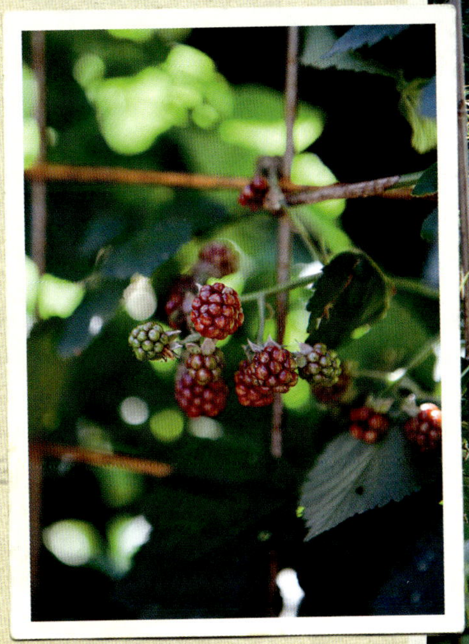

KAREN SUTHERLAND'S URBAN EDEN

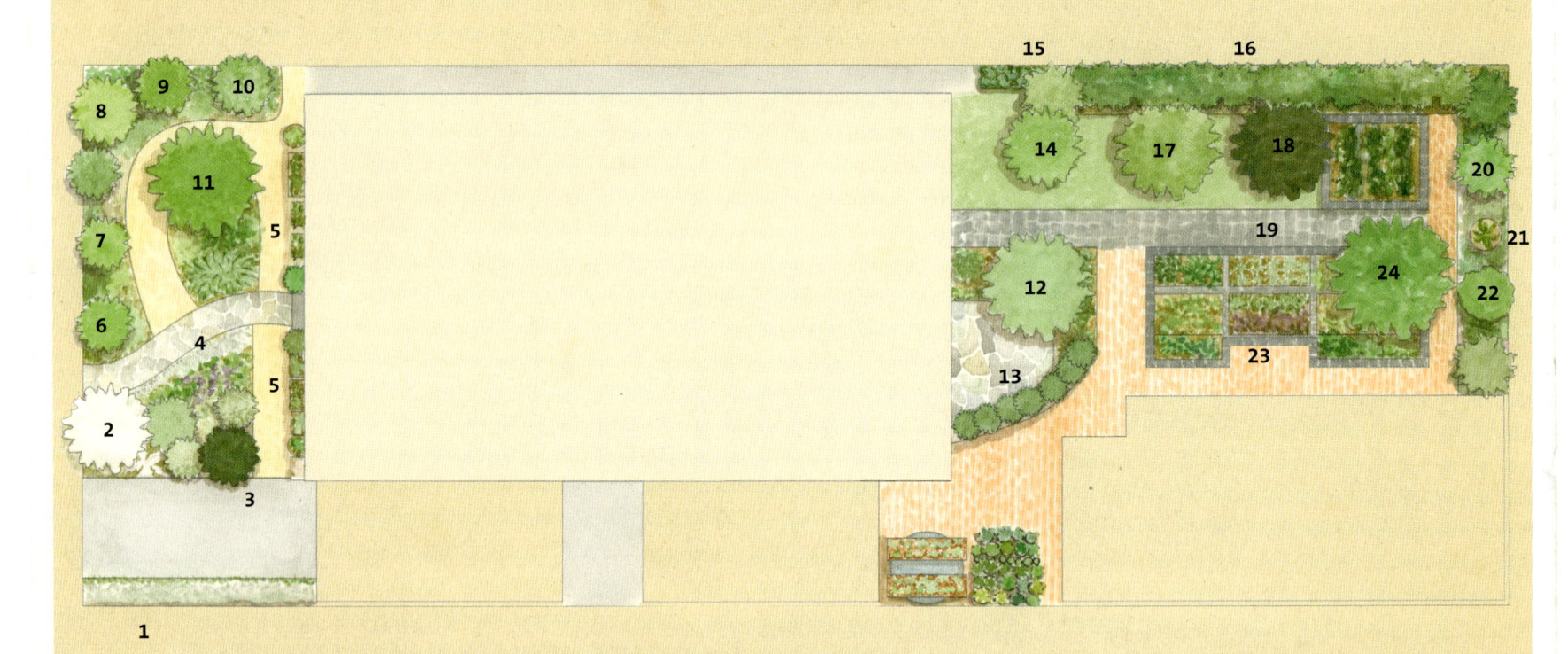

1. Espaliered feijoas
2. Olive tree
3. Carob tree
4. Rosemary 'Blue Lagoon', 'Lots-a-lemons', lamb's ears
5. Pots of herbs and native food
6. 'Lane's Navel' orange, thyme and Natal plum
7. Valencia orange and muntries
8. Pomegranate 'Ben Hur'
9. Blood orange
10. Persimmon
11. Ornamental pear with midyim berries
12. 'Weeping Wandin Pride' apple with assorted citrus, and yacón, pepinos and lemongrass
13. Strawberry guava hedge
14. Almond
15. Monstera and macadamia
16. Kiwifruit, dragon fruit, naranjilla
17. Apple
18. Mulberry
19. Raspberries
20. Babaco and white sapote
21. Banana in pot
22. Mango, avocado 'Bacon' and *Actinidia arguta* growing on the fence
23. Vegetable garden
24. Apricot

as well as for their fruit and nuts. Hers is a food forest that includes apples, a mulberry, an apricot, lots of citrus, tropical fruits and nut trees. Nut trees appeal to Karen for their beauty and delicious bounty and she has an almond and a grafted macadamia in the rear garden and has planted pistachios in the nature strip. She intends to add a Chilean hazelnut (*Gevuina avellana*) to the pistachios, a nut tree related to the macadamia, but with soft-shelled nuts that turn red when ripe. Originating from Southern Chile, the Chilean hazelnut grows well in a cool temperate climate and looks to be the most ornamental shrub or small tree with cream grevillea-like flowers – not surprising, as it is a Gondwanan relative of our own Proteaceae family.

Karen likes 'low input' edible plants as well as multipurpose ones. Low input vegie gardening can mean planting annuals that grow easily from seed sown (or self-sown) direct in the garden like lettuce, rocket, flat-leaf parsley and giant purple mustard, and also growing perennial vegetables and fruits that give you leaves or fruits over a number of years. This means using different methods than those in annual crop rotation – you have to sow seeds, transplant self-seeded plants, pull weeds and add compost around the more permanent framework. 'My favourite year-round vegetables are perpetual spinach, perennial leeks and silverbeet,' says Karen, and of course there is always rhubarb. In addition, she grows spring onions, French sorrel, thornless blackberries, galangal, lemongrass, pepino and a chilli which is proving perennial in the sheltered garden. (Wild foods are also allowed to grow and are harvested: dandelion, cleavers and nettles.) These edibles emerge from among borage and violas in raised beds constructed from old blocks of bluestone. Karen's winter plantings might include snow peas (a beautiful semi-dwarf heritage variety called 'Delta Louise', with pink and purple flowers), lettuce and lots of Chinese greens. Her spring plantings are likely to be more lettuce, cherry tomatoes, basil, beans (including an heirloom variety of bush bean called 'Preston', originating from a nearby suburb) and pumpkin. New seedlings are fertilised with compost, and Seasol® or cow and chicken manure is applied during the growing season. A lot of food is produced from this plot of 3 × 7 m – Karen estimates that she grows about half of the vegetables consumed by her household of two people, with some to share with friends, neighbours and relatives. The vegetable garden is watered from the tanks, and the fruit trees and ornamental plants receive greywater from the washing machine and shower. To buffer the effects of using greywater, once a year Karen applies Earthcraft compost, a slow-release organic fertiliser and gypsum.

> '**The fruits of South America hold a fascination for Karen ... perhaps it was her gardening apprenticeship at the Melbourne Zoo that awakened her interest in exotic botanical wonders.**'

The fruits of South America hold a fascination for Karen – she likes tropical and subtropical fruits almost more than she does herbs. Perhaps it was her gardening apprenticeship at the Melbourne Zoo that awakened her interest in exotic botanical wonders, or perhaps the sheer diversity of fruits arising from the one continent. Latin America has many rare and mysterious fruits but it has also been the source of foods we now take for granted like the potato, tomato and passionfruit. One of the most unusual South American fruits Karen grows is the Lúcuma (*Luke*-Mah) tree, *Pouteria lucuma*, a relative of the sapote, with fruit said to taste like 'maple syrup flavoured ice-cream'! Guavas are another favourite – for their evergreen form and their amazing fruit flavours – although they can be frost-tender and are somewhat slow to establish. They come from an assortment of genera: there's the Chilean guava (*Ugni molinae*), which grow to less than a metre; the tropical guava (*Psidium guajava*); the strawberry guava (*Psidium littorale* var. *longipes*); and of course the pineapple guava or feijoa (*Acca sellowiana*), which fruits so well in cool climates.

Karen has also planted white sapote, babaco, cherimoya and tamarillo trees. There is a hedge of strawberry guava as a screen around the outdoor sitting area, an avocado 'Bacon' (said to perform well in cool climates), a fruit salad plant (*Monstera deliciosa*), pepinos, yacóns and a naranjilla – delicious Latinos each and every one. Naranjilla (*Solanum quitoense*) or 'The Golden Fruit of the Andes' originates from Ecuador. It is a prickly and highly ornamental shrub with orange fruit that have kiwifruit-like flesh that is used to make a popular Andean drink known as 'Nectar of the Gods'. The pepino is an amazingly tough small shrub to around 1 m high with attractive dark green leaves. The flesh of its oval melon-like fruit tastes rather like a bland rockmelon but is very nice dressed with passionfruit or mint sugar or added to a fruit salad. With the yacón or the Peruvian ground apple, it is the tuber that is eaten. The long storage tubers have a crunchy texture and a flavour somewhat like an apple and the plant is closely related to the Jerusalem artichoke.

In designing her edible garden Karen has not neglected the vertical growing spaces that walls and fences afford. On a specially built steel structure (welded by Karen's father) along her long northern boundary grow monstrous male and female kiwifruit vines. Hanging baskets fixed to the fence underneath contain young plants of dragon fruit. Climbing the rear fence is the kiwi's little cousin *Actinidia arguta* that bears grape-sized hairless fruits and a choko vine scrambles along the southern fence. Grapevines are also trained against the fascias of the house and the studio. The variety of climbing plants add texture and atmosphere to the tropical plantings in the garden. Past the raspberry bed, a banana in a pot makes a focal point at the end of the cobblestone path. The banana and a mango tree are Karen's 'future plants' for the warming climate – the way things are looking for southern Australia, Pascoe Vale might soon inherit the macroclimate of the dry subtropics!

Top to bottom: **Karen has made use of every inch of her garden for growing food plants; kiwifruit; tools and seedheads.**

In her home town of Shepparton, Karen's grandparents were accomplished vegetable gardeners and 'everyone preserved fruit', says Karen. No locally-grown SPC (Shepparton Processing Company) tinned fruit for the Sutherlands – they bottled their own stone fruits and made sauces and jams. Karen carries on the tradition by bottling, drying and making jam from her harvest. Using an electric fruit dehydrator she makes fruit leather and dries apple, apricot, grapes and even feijoa – which makes an intense and piquant dried fruit. What a joy it is to be able to use your own fruit in the kitchen, but preserving is a skill that has largely been lost in the suburbs and is thus something that Karen enjoys teaching in her weekend classes. Karen and partner John have constructed an air-cooled pantry to keep their vegetable seeds, homemade produce and bought dry goods cool and help them keep longer. This is achieved by drawing cool air from under the house up through the back of the pantry as the warm air is drawn up and out via a whirlybird ventilator on the roof.

Aquaponics has presented Karen with a new challenge. Her homemade combination aquaculture-hydroponic system comprises a 2-m-diameter tank containing the six original 'starter' goldfish and some fifty tiny silver perch, below two stainless steel 'grow beds' made by the 'two Johns' – her partner and her father. The nutrient-rich water of the fish tank is pumped through the garden beds fourteen times per day. The plants sit directly in the growing medium – in this case, large aggregate scoria – and feed upon the nutrient-rich fish water which then drains back into the tank, having been cleansed by the plants. Bacteria living on the scoria also feed upon the nutrients ultimately converting ammonia into nitrates – the perfect plant food. There are many advantages to this nutrient-cycling system of food production – apart from having fish to go with your home-grown chips and salad (eventually, Karen would like to be able to eat one fish a week from her pond). Karen believes it is a sustainable way of producing protein, especially considering the dire state of our rivers and oceans – where wild-harvesting has devastated fish stocks globally and aquaculture can have all manner of negative environmental impacts. The grow beds are raised and being soil-less there is no digging or compost required. However, there are many variables when you bring creatures into the mix and keeping the fish happy has been a case of trial and error for this inventive designer.

> **'Edible landscaping is not only a great way to grow your own food, it is a beautiful approach to living within one's own means as well as the planet's.'**

Karen's plant knowledge and gardening wisdom, passion and practicality are evident in every (mostly edible) square metre of her Pascoe Vale garden. It shows in the number and diversity of the fruit trees, herbs and vegetables, in the care and attention given their cultivation and their resulting produce. Edible landscaping is not only a great way to grow your own food, it is a beautiful approach to living within one's own means as well as the planet's. As Karen writes: 'It's time for a new kind of suburban garden, one that feeds us, body and soul, and is sustainable in these times of climate change, irregular rain and temperature.'[3]

THE BELLIS KITCHEN GARDEN

Size	20 × 20 m (400 m²)
Climate	Subtropical
Soil	Silty clay
Average annual rainfall	1100–1200 mm
Frost	Rare
Water source	Recycled household wastewater
Irrigation method	Hand-watering and natural rainfall
Compost and fertiliser	Composted food scraps and plant material, mineral rock dust, poultry manure, liquid seaweed plant conditioner
Mulch	Sugarcane straw, home-grown mulches
Biggest challenges	Drought, killer winds, growing food for three on 350 L of water a day, capricious rainfall: often the site receives heavy rain in the Dry and insufficient rain during the Wet, plus regularly it can receive one to two months' average rainfall in one or two hours
Favourite herb	Coriander
Favourite food plant	Sweet chestnut

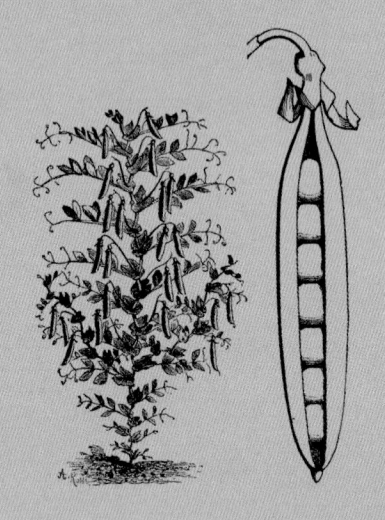

CHAPTER 5
BELLIS
Jeremy Coleby Williams' Sustainable Garden

Even from the glance of the casual passer-by, the home of Jeremy Coleby-Williams and Jeff Poole is not your average Brisbane residence. To the initiated, the nature strip is a dead give-away that brazen practitioners of guerrilla gardening live on the other side of the footpath – guerrilla gardeners who think appropriating neighbourhood land for growing food is a perfectly logical urban intervention. Their weapons of beautification: Golden foliaged sweet potato (*Ipomoea batatas* 'Marguerite'), which covers their verge, *Aloe vera*, which thrives in front of their fence, and the dragon fruit which they've snuck in beneath the street trees across the bitumen. Inside their own front fence the bounty continues – a veritable cornucopia of fruit, vegetables and herbs (about 150 cultivars), many of them rare and interesting, flourishes despite five years of drought here in Brisbane.

These 'two mad Poms' have created a sustainable backyard here in the land of the big pineapple – and not only do they grow most of their own food in their backyard garden, they've also renovated their home to become a sustainable dwelling. Named Bellis, the entire property has been designed, says Jerry, 'to reduce my ecological footprint, slash my household bills and grow organic food'.[1] They harvest rainwater, treat and recycle wastewater onsite and create their own power, and in the process of all this retrofitting, have confounded council, local residents and plumbers alike.

Jerry, a horticulturalist and curator, is the first to admit that his garden might not quite be the one he'd maintain purely for himself. Thanks to his role as a presenter on ABC1 Television's *Gardening Australia*, the garden is regularly filmed, which means it is worked intensively and on a daily basis. Add to this, numerous visitors to Bellis for open-garden scheme, community and sustainable-house events, including sustainability students, conservationists, architects, town planners, overseas television and radio crews. It's easy to see how what began as a sustainable home and garden of their own is now listed as an official Queensland government experiment and has become an educational facility complete with its own website! Nonetheless, the garden gives both Jerry and Jeff great pleasure, is highly productive, and is a place in which Jerry can 'play with conventions' and subvert the Aussie gardening orthodoxy, as he is wont to do.

Born in south-east London, Jerry is a fourth-generation gardener, who trained at Kew and the Royal Horticultural Society (RHS) and fell in love with the flora of Western Australia as an honours student. His grandfather Connor was one of his horticultural mentors: 'We used to compete with each other comparing the amount of crops we could raise from our gardens and he gave me advice on traditional organic gardening techniques.' Jerry began gardening at four and helped run his family household at ten – according to Jerry, his mother told him 'she didn't want him to be a liability like his father'! The ensuing sense of independence has evidently been advantageous for his travelling and own home-making in the far-flung antipodes.

Jeff and Jerry share a long-held belief that the West's dependence on fossil fuels and other non-renewable resources is both unsustainable and unethical. Having lived through the 'Oil Shocks' of the 1970s in England, peak oil is a reality they readily accept. Australia is already experiencing the effects of anthropogenic climate change and the couple believe we are living way beyond our means. Michael Pollan writes that 'we can, if we bother to try, find ways to provide for ourselves without diminishing the world'.[2] And we find in Jerry and Jeff, a couple who *do* bother, who practice what they preach, who walk the talk. They have pushed their 800m^2 site to the limits – their expectations of what was possible on a residential block were high. Not only did they require their property to produce much of their food (both are vegetarians), Jeff says they wanted to 'mimic a natural system' working toward a state of equilibrium where system inputs are balanced by system outputs.

They set about making a garden here systematically – starting with the soil, for as Jerry says, 'Getting the soil right can eliminate half the common gardening problems.' The backyard had no earthworms and 'soil like cement that broke a rotary hoe', says Jerry. So, over six months, they undertook a strenuous program of soil rehabilitation. First, a green manure

Jerry's eight vegetable beds are surrounded by bales of sugarcane straw to protect the plants within from drying winds.

of millet was sown, which was rotary hoed, followed by a second planting of sunflowers that was slashed and mulched with barley straw, bark and bush mulch, grass clippings and mushroom compost. It was conditioned with minerals, lime and organic fertiliser and left to the fungi and microbes to do their work. A final green manure of peas, barley and sunflowers was sown and dug in. As the site was potentially contaminated (a previous owner had scrap metal and car bodies on the property) follow-up testing was carried out to make sure toxic heavy metals weren't present. Jerry then designed the garden around a simple geometry of eight rectangular productive beds with perimeter beds, a small lawn, a nursery area and spaces for sitting and enjoying the garden. The maturing kitchen garden offers edible delights at every step, and enough variety to make any herbivore happy.

It is the lack of 'quality and variety' of bought food that makes home-grown such an appealing and satisfying option for the Bellis household. Jeff and Jerry are just about fully fledged locavores, growing about two-thirds of their food, which is one way of giving unsustainable agribusiness the finger! And aren't they lucky in Brisbane with the sheer diversity of plants they can grow? (To southern gardeners, not only is it bizarre to be able to grow coconuts and hydrangeas side by side, but it verges on the improper.) A medley of tropical plant species including pineapples, bananas, pawpaws and various spices thrive in the almost frost-free site. Jerry's edible plantings show just how ornamental the pineapple plant can be – the strappy leaves of this South American bromeliad are gorgeous in their own right and provide perennial form among the fruit trees in the perimeter garden bed. Not only are pineapples beautiful, you get to eat them (or make a *piña colada*). So why not plant pineapples instead of cordyline, astelia, yucca or phormium? Jerry grows five varieties in the garden including *Ananas comosus* 'Mareeba Sweet' – probably the most commonly grown pineapple in Queensland – 'Queensland Rough Pineapple', 'Smooth Cayenne', 'Spanish Red' and the species *A. bracteatus* 'Variegatus', which has beautiful variegated leaves. As the sections of the fruit develop from the intriguing flowers they reveal a Fibonacci spiral with its two characteristic interlocking spirals, eight spirals in one direction and thirteen in the other.

Bananas also feature in the Bellis backyard – they provide rapid-growing height in the young garden and beautiful huge green leaves. Domestic production of bananas is, interestingly, regulated by the Department of Primary Industry in Queensland as protection (or protectionism) for the banana industry. Residential growers may only plant a maximum of ten plants made up from seven varieties, and only after obtaining written approval from a DPI inspector! The permitted varieties are 'Blue Java', 'Ducasse', 'Kluai Namwa Khom' (Dwarf Ducasse), 'Bluggoe' (plantain or cooking banana), 'Goldfinger', 'Ladyfinger', and 'Pisang Ceylan' (meaning 'Ceylon banana') and Jerry grows all seven varieties here at Bellis.

> **' Every year Jerry will have a "passionate affair" with a particular variety of food plant – this last season it has been the "Green Zebra" tomato.'**

Jerry hasn't abandoned the food plants of his English childhood, though – take for instance mangolds or mangel-wurzels, a root crop associated in Australia with the Depression, drought and livestock food. The humble mangel-wurzel (*Beta vulgaris*) is a root vegetable of the saltbush or Chenopodiaceae family, and a close relative of silverbeet and beetroot that Jerry plants as a winter crop. Both the roots and leaves are highly nutritious – the leaves can be lightly steamed or boiled as with English spinach – while Jerry uses the huge turnip-like roots in curries. Another favourite is the humble pea, which is a particularly nostalgic food plant for Jerry: 'I get such a happy feeling observing our growing peas. The seeds feel lovely to the touch; they unfurl and push through the soil so eagerly as they germinate; their leaves are very soft and often delicately patterned. But most of all they remind me of my childhood,

THE BELLIS GARDEN

1. Screw pine (*Pandanus silvestris*), spindle palm and dwarf palmetto
2. Chilean wine palm (*Jubaea chilensis*)
3. Hedge of *Hibiscus insularis*
4. Sweet potato (*Ipomoea batatas* 'Marguerite')
5. Nursery tables and compost bin
6. Alongside fence: coffee 'First Fleet', *Citrus australasica*, *Cinnamomum zeylanicum*, *Citrus australis* and Davidson's plum
7. Arrowroot
8. Along back fence: false cardamon, lemon 'Lots-a-lemons', lemon 'Meyer', Oldham's bamboo, Tahitian limes, pawpaw and 'Monastery' bamboo (*Thyrostachys siamensis*)
9. Concrete water tank
10. Pandanus surrounded by bananas: 'Ducasse', 'Bluggoe', plaintain, 'Ladyfinger' and 'Pisang Ceylan'
11. Kale 'Red Russian', kohlrabi 'Purple Vienna' and borlotti beans
12. Snow peas 'Delta Matilda' and 'Oregan Sugar Pod' and potatoes 'Pink Fir Apple' and 'King Edward'
13. Bean 'Purple King', silverbeet, lettuce 'First Fleet', huauzontle and radishes
14. Snow pea 'Dwarf Skinless', parsley, Chinese celery and mustard 'Osaka Purple'
15. Daikon, radishes 'White Icicle', 'Long Red' and 'French Breakfast' and peas on bamboo frames
16. Cabbages 'Couve Tronchuda' and 'Women Meet and Gossip', zucchini 'Gold Rush' and tomatoes on frames
17. Mangel-wurzel, tomato 'Tommy Toe' on wigwam, peas on frames and black mustard
18. Potato 'Kipfler'
19. 'Dwarf Ducasse' banana, pawpaws, 'Blue Java' banana, 'Goldfinger' banana and pineapples
20. Compost bins
21. Cocoyams and plantain bananas
22. Herb and spice bed
23. Wastewater treatment system

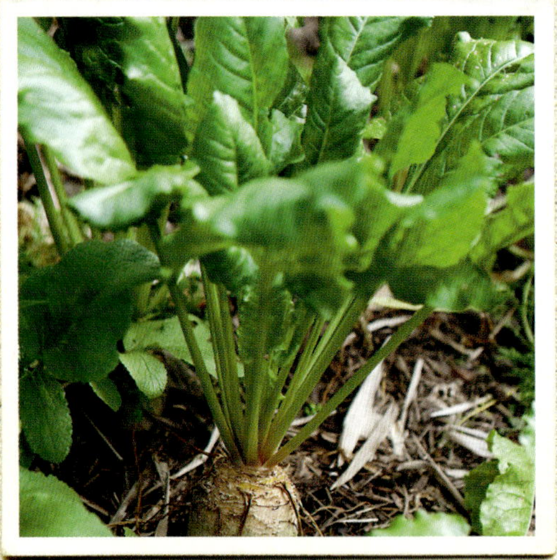
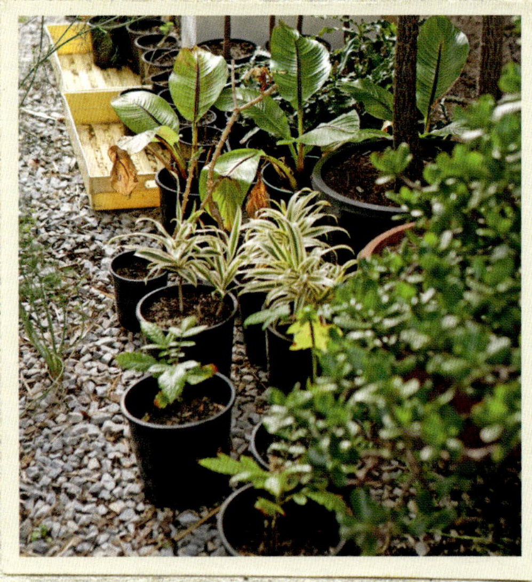
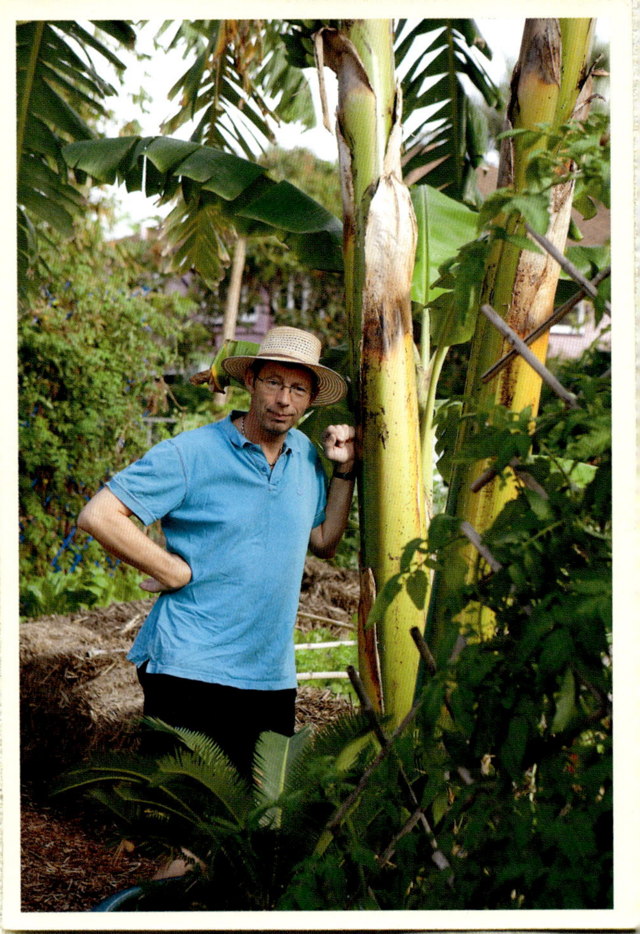
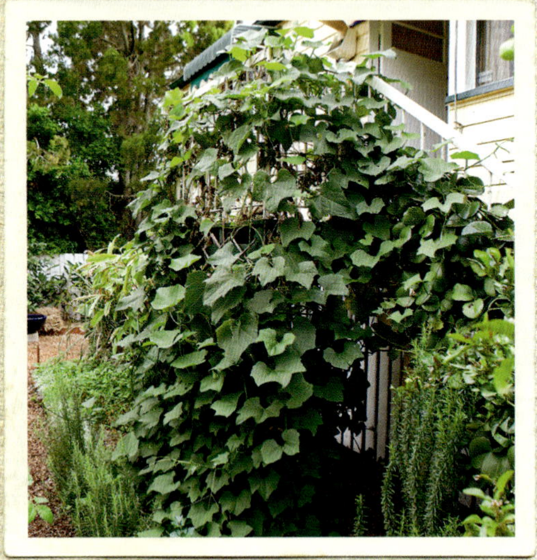
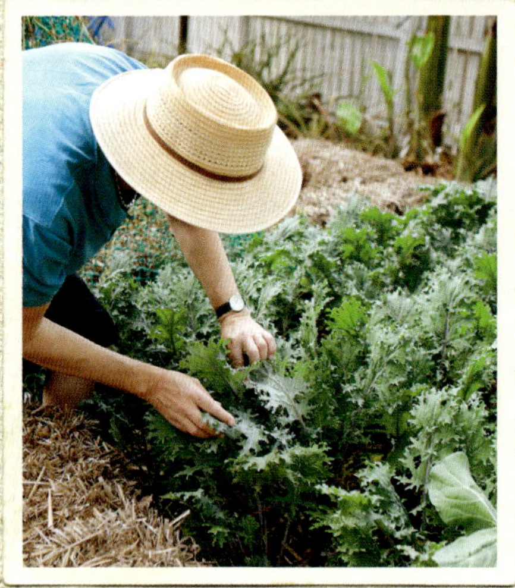
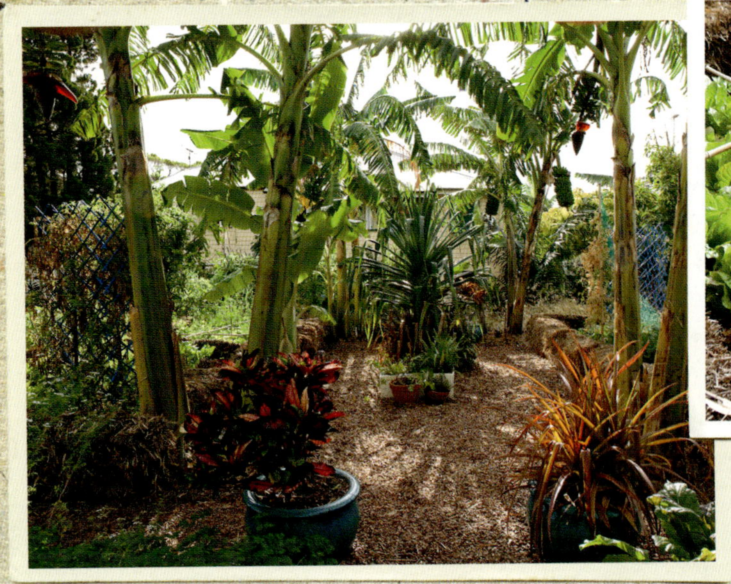
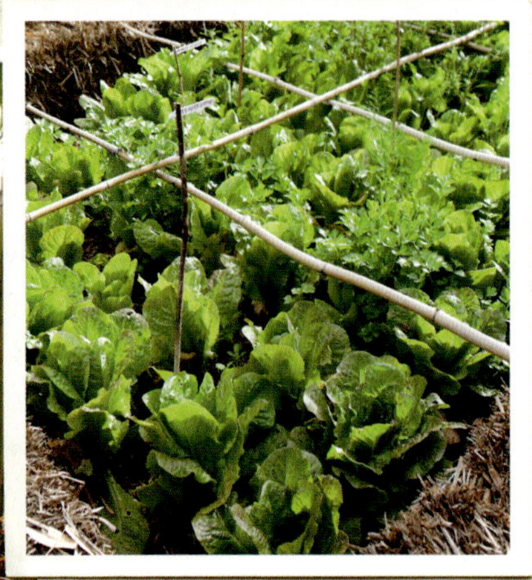
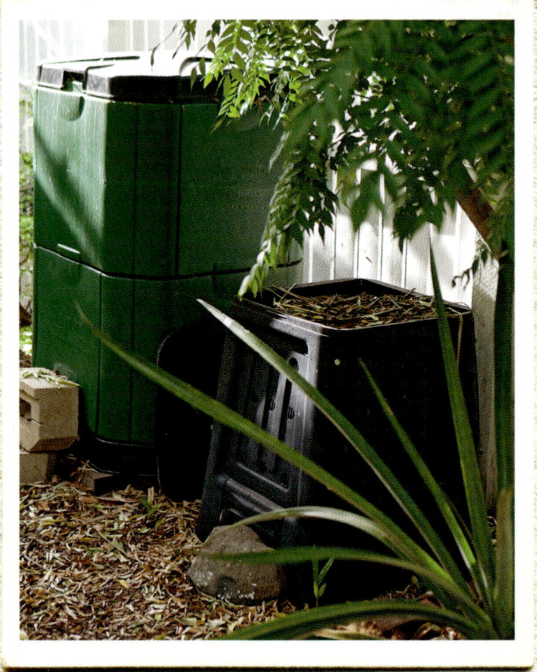

when my family used to go on weekend drives to country farms in Kent.' Here, peas grow on bamboo lattices painted a brilliant cerulean blue and make edible screens between the beds.

Every year Jerry will have a 'passionate affair' with a particular variety of food plant – this last season it has been the 'Green Zebra' tomato. The trick with tomatoes in this subtropical climate, says Jerry, is to simply only grow tomatoes in the Dry season rather than have to deal with all the pests that plague them in the Wet, as is demonstrated by a tee-pee of self-sown 'Sweet Bite' cherry tomatoes towering 3.1 m into the blue winter sky! Jerry adores kale 'Russian Red' for its ornamental value as much as its culinary use, as well as the leaves of 'Purple Osaka' mustard, beetroot and kohlrabi. Jerry has obtained both lettuce and coffee seeds grown from seeds brought to Australia on the First Fleet. The lettuce was originally grown at Sydney's settlement at Farm Cove and Jerry says he really appreciates 'having a little bit of heritage side salad'. In fact, he is 'currently growing a seed crop to send some to the Queen's new vegetable garden in Buckingham Palace'. This strikes him as a wonderful subversion of tradition: 'Republican gardener sends monarch convict lettuce!'

One of the most delightfully named plants in the garden here is the cabbage 'Women meet and gossip', a loose-leaf form of cabbage from Ethiopia. It towers over its squat European-bred hearting cousins and the large green leaves can be picked individually from the stem. Growing such fabulous old varieties, it's no surprise that Jerry is the director of the Seed Savers' Network in Australia, a not-for-profit community organisation that aims to preserve open-pollinated and heirloom seeds and the genetic diversity of plant varieties.

Bellis is a timber Queenslander built in 1914 and a classic example of the Australian tropical vernacular. The house, enthuses Jerry, 'is the place where century-old single-storey houses on stilts prove that climatically appropriate design can be elegant and simple'. Michael Mobbs, a sustainability coach, has project-managed retrofitting the house, which now boasts an aerated wastewater recycler and photovoltaic solar panels. The in-ground concrete rainwater tank has a capacity of 21 000 L. The entire site is designed to capture water, to prevent any of the precious 'cloud juice' getting away. Unlike most suburban gardens, stormwater is treated as a resource. Today, 95–8 per cent of the water that falls on the property is captured on the site and directed to soak into the soil. (Even during five years of ongoing drought, Bellis has been 98 per cent self-sufficient in water.) A lawn of Durban grass is never watered but doubles as a catchment area. The paths through the productive garden are constructed from water-permeable bark mulch, and other areas are covered with gravel.

It has taken five years to get the soil just as he wants it, says Jerry. The garden is managed organically, but not on permaculture principles as some might think. Compost is integral (there is conventional compost as well as a bin for making leaf-mold), as is crop rotation and non-chemical pest management. Mulch is fundamental: both the foliage of arrowroot (*Canna edulis*), lemongrass and sugarcane straw are used to conserve moisture, encourage earthworm activity and improve the soil. Sugarcane straw in bales is cheap and local and Jerry puts it to an innovative use: by laying entire straw bales onto the soil inside the edges of the garden beds (made of recycled timber sleepers) he makes 'gardens within gardens' – protective microclimates which slow evaporation, shelter plants from the 'killer winds' of early spring, and generates the most fabulous compost *in situ* as the bales decompose over a year.

July to September is the Dry season in Brisbane and a great time in the vegetable garden. October and November is the build-up to the subtropical Wet season – a time of year characterised by extreme UV, heat and humidity but no rain; a period Jerry calls 'crematoria'. The intensity builds until storms bring welcome relief, but potentially damaging downpours,

Clockwise, from top left: **Mangel-wurzel; the nursery area; Jerry; compost bins; the lettuces thrive in the protected garden bed; a grove of bananas in the middle of the vegie garden; a choko vine covering the stairs.**
Centre: **Jerry checking out his crop of kale.**

hail or cyclones. Brisbane's average rainfall is around 1200 mm (1182 mm is the fifty-year average), but over the last five years, drought has taken a toll. With global warming, scientists predict hotter and drier conditions in much of Australia. Writes Jerry: 'Global Warming is having the same effect as putting Brisbane on a trailer and slowly dragging it to Rockhampton. We'll arrive in that climate around 2030.' (Rockhampton marks the southern line of the Tropic of Capricorn, and thus the start of the tropical zone.) There will be more frequent extreme weather events: an increase in severe tropical cyclones on the east coast, in flooding in northern Australia and drought in southern and eastern Australia, and in the number of summer days of high fire danger.

The implications of higher average temperatures for agriculture and food production are numerous: first and foremost, winter frosts will cease in some areas and the range of some food plant species will expand and others will contract accordingly, as will the range of pest species. This will potentially manifest in reduced productivity and species diversity of food crops and increased food prices generally.

So, Jerry asks the question: Given limited water and higher temperatures, how are we to grow our own food? During the worst of the drought the Bellis household undertook a self-imposed challenge to grow food for three people on 350 L of recycled water per day rather than use precious rainwater directly on the garden. 'If we hadn't had a sewage system, we wouldn't have a garden,'[3] says Jerry, referring to their wastewater treatment system. The combined household black and grey water is processed via two tanks, then a sand and gravel filter with water passing through a UV filter for sterilisation before use in the toilet for flushing or gardening. The clean, disinfected water has been tested regularly and classified as suitable for use on vegetables. The produce garden is watered by hand using this recycled water – as Jerry says, it's 'the most efficient way to distribute our modest volume of water, and it's also the most effective way of ensuring gardener and plants regularly interact'.

Jerry has been contemplating the potential for wild and ancient species of food plants to adapt to a warmer and drier climate better than their domesticated relatives. His interest in what he terms 'famine foods' – undomesticated plants not normally considered as crops but which are eaten in times of

> **'Weeds are also great contenders as alternative food crops – including common garden seeds such as purslane and swine-cress.'**

famine or war – is linked to his concern about climate change and food security. This category includes plants like huauzontle (pronounced 'wah-zont-lay' – *Chenopodium berlandieri,* syn. *C. nuttalliae*) and the native Australian spinach: Warrigal greens, which are more heat tolerant than traditional leaf crops like English spinach. Jerry describes huauzontle as an ancient Andean 'pseudo-grain' that makes a good substitute for spinach, and is excellent in curries. The 'Palestinian radish', a black-skinned, mild-tasting radish, is a 'climate-change ready radish' says Jerry, thanks to its Middle Eastern provenance. Weeds are also great contenders as alternative food crops – including common garden weeds such as purslane and swine-cress (*Lepidium didymum*) – a member of the Brassica family, which Jerry's great aunt used to grow as a water-saving substitute for watercress during World War I.[4]

Other tough food plants growing at Bellis with limited irrigation include pawpaw, bamboo, false cardamom, sweetpotato, arrowroot, curry leaf, Natal plum (*Carissa macrocarpa*), choko and cassava. While cocoyam (*Xanthosoma sagittifolium*) and celery stem taro (*Colocasia esculenta*) might look like thirsty specimens given their huge fleshy green leaves like elephants' ears, they are, in fact, also fairly drought-resistant food plants. The cocoyam (or 'white taro' as it is known in Queenland), a subtropical member of the Arum family, is a starch staple whose roots are eaten cooked like potatoes – both the root or corm and smaller offset cormels.

Their taste has been described as earthy and nutty and they are commonly used in soups and stews. They may also be eaten grilled, fried, or mashed. Celery stem taro is also an aroid and the stems and leaves need to be boiled for ten minutes before they are eaten in order to leach the oxalates that can be potentially harmful consumed in large amounts. Jerry waters both these species only once every few weeks.

The bounty doesn't end there: Jerry also grows malabar spinach, Chinese celery, okra, yam, air potato vine (*Dioscorea bulbifera*), winged yam (*Dioscorea alata*), eggplant, Jerusalem artichoke, snake bean, Oldham's bamboo (*Bambusa oldhamii*), hibiscus spinach (*Abelmoschus manihot*) and silverbeet. Herbs include basil, lemon grass, parsley, Moroccan mint, Kaffir lime, golden oregano, culinary pandanus, ginger, garlic chives and a cinnamon tree. The true curry leaf (*Murraya koenigii*) makes a lovely small tree and is a relative of the ornamental murraya (both are now rather weedy in Brisbane so it's best to prune off flowers before their seed ripen). Lemons, Tahitian and Kaffir limes, mandarin and red and yellow forms of Panama passionfruit give abundant fruit, as do the native Australian fruits Davidson's plum and midyim berry. Other native bushfood includes the common succulent pigface with its edible leaves and fleshy red fruits, and the native plum, *Planchonella australis*.

The life of a gardener who grows their own food is very much about making daily decisions, observing the weather, the health of their plants, the progress of compost and monitoring water use. Is there enough water in the tank? Is there rain forecast? Should I sacrifice one of the thirsty crops? Observing and managing are integral to the cycle of productive gardening. While many of the big global problems seem insurmountable, Jerry and Jeff show that they can be tackled in meaningful ways through the manner in which you live, work and garden. They are certainly providing for themselves without diminishing the world and having a good time in the process.

Top: **Jerry also makes room for ornamental plants at Bellis.**
Below: **A bunch of green bananas.**

VAUCLUSE HOUSE KITCHEN GARDEN

Size	1200 m²
Climate	Temperate coastal
Soil	Sand
Average annual rainfall	1242 mm
Frost	No
Water source	Mains and tank water
Irrigation method	Hand-held hoses/watering cans
Compost and fertiliser	Composted food scraps and plant material, animal manures
Mulch	Stable straw
Biggest challenges	Summer heat and sandy base soil
Favourite herb	Basil
Favourite food plant	White bush scallop squash (White pattypan squash)

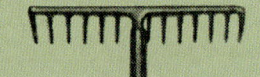

CHAPTER 6
VAUCLUSE HOUSE
A Colonial Kitchen Garden Lost and Recreated

At its peak in the mid-1800s, the property Vaucluse House near Sydney had an estate inventory that read like a settler's wishlist: 208 ha (515 acres) on a spectacular site on Port Jackson, fine house, servants, grand stables, dairy, furnishings imported from Germany, a boat and boathouse, not to mention a beautiful and much-admired garden – a seemingly splendid remedy for any case of colonial status anxiety. The garden was a veritable cornucopia complete with kitchen garden, vineyard, orangery, small banana plantation and orchard. 'In this garden there grows the most delicious fruit in the colony' declared *The Australian* in January 1830.[1] The garden produced prize-winning fruit and vegetables, including the famous '9-inch peach' of 1830, and a variety of subtropical crops and herbs from the colonies, Americas and far reaches of the globe as well as the more familiar fruits and flora of 'mother England' and the Continent. The drought and crop failures of the 1790s that brought the colony to the brink of starvation had given way to a dependable food supply by the late 1830s, yet even so, such productivity must have appeared truly wondrous.

Two fascinating sets of owners occupied Vaucluse House in the nineteenth century: in 1803 unconventional Irish convict Sir Henry Browne Hayes purchased the land, began clearing it and established a stone cottage with fenced cultivated garden and several thousand fruit trees. In 1827 William Charles Wentworth bought the property and carried out extensive modifications to both the house and garden until his death in 1872. With wife Sarah Cox, who was also Australian-born, he further developed the botanical capital begun by Hayes. The grounds of Vaucluse House tell the national story writ small; they speak of clearing the bush with convict labour and, of course, Aboriginal dispossession. The Cadigal clan were the traditional owners of the area and the Vaucluse property itself was a site of great ritual importance to them. The arrival of the First Fleet was tragic for the Cadigal – not only was their land stolen but their people were decimated by the smallpox brought by the European invaders – by as early as 1790 the fifty-strong clan had been reduced to just a few members.

Vaucluse House is now one of Sydney's best preserved and authentic nineteenth-century remnant harbour-side estates comprising 10 ha (25 acres) of park that is open to the public. An eccentric amalgam of Gothic Revival and earlier colonial Georgian architecture, the home operates as a house–museum, a time capsule for life in the 1800s. The immaculately maintained grounds are dotted with arboreal wonders such as Bunya, Hoop and Norfolk Island pines, *Brachychitons* and palm trees. There is a lovely pleasure garden, and to the north, across Wentworth Road, a beach paddock that adjoins Vaucluse Bay. One part of the garden that did not survive into the twentieth century, however, was a kitchen garden, and thus the story of the garden that is now in existence is one of recreation and interpretation with all the challenges that these endeavours entail.

In the 1990s the Historic Houses Trust of New South Wales (HHT) felt there was an opportunity to recreate the southern portion of the Vaucluse House kitchen garden and recapture the essence of the nineteenth-century original. The garden would be as authentic to the period as possible and provide an educational resource in terms of schools' programs and public events that explore themes of food and gastronomy from the early nineteenth century to the present. The HHT curators, with head gardener David Gray, went about this in a variety of ways: firstly, in determining the original location of the garden, then working out its layout and construction, and lastly, by planting varieties of fruit and vegetables that were available in Sydney prior to 1900. Thankfully, there are numerous letters and records that detail the lives of the owners and managers and the evidence reveals that the land on the western side of the creek was an intensively worked site with orchards, vineyards, vegetable plots and a kitchen garden.

Two images were integral in recreating the kitchen garden: Conrad Martens' pencil sketch *Vaucluse from the Road* (1840) and a 1930s aerial photograph of Vaucluse House. Surveyors' field notes from an 1884 Sydney Survey book plan also guided the reconstruction. The sketch shows the view to the north-west of the house and linear patterns of vines and orchards, although a distinct, fenced space not far from the kitchen yard

Clockwise, from top: **Looking across the kitchen garden to Vaucluse House, behind the old laundry; Vaucluse House today;** *Vaucluse,* **1851, oil painting by George Edwards Peacock.**

is not shown. In the aerial photo there is a clear geometry of crop marks suggesting fences and a road. It is frustrating that with all the wealth of historic material depicting Vaucluse House – there are many paintings and sketches, and numerous photographs of the house and the pleasure gardens – not a single image shows the kitchen garden! An archaeological dig carried out in 1999, however, exposed physical evidence of trenching, the site of an old wooden shed (that may have been the greenhouse), the position of fence posts and a regular layout of pits where fruit trees were likely to have grown.[2]

The story of the Wentworths, their ten children and their social aspirations in the colony is fascinating for both the drama of William's political objectives and the personal narrative. Sarah Cox was a 'currency lass', the child of convict parents, William the son of the infamous D'Arcy Wentworth – a well-born doctor acquitted for highway robbery. A wealthy barrister and pastoralist, William was one of the trio who crossed the Blue Mountains in 1813, our first native-born politician, and a difficult and domineering man. Both Sarah and William were ostracised by Sydney's bigoted social elite, partly for their birth and convict connections, partly for having had two children out of wedlock, and also for William's radical politics. Although literate, Sarah Wentworth had a limited education. She proved an excellent manager of her household, overseeing a workforce of servants and convicts. Although they were a most peripatetic family they continued to manage Vaucluse House and the garden from Europe during their numerous stints abroad.

From the family's letters they evidently gained much pleasure from their garden and its produce, and both William and Sarah were involved in transforming the Vaucluse landscape. Sarah was fond of gardening, and had a gardener to carry out the heavy manual work. She wrote that she was 'particularly happy gardening' – an enjoyment that was perhaps nuanced, given her exclusion from the colony's social scene.[3] William's 1820 text *A statistical, historical, and political description of the colony of New South Wales, and its dependent settlements in Van Diemen's Land* includes an appendix called 'The Colonial Garden' containing cultural notes and local anecdotes on common fruits and vegetables and their cultivation in the colony. His numerous entries of fruit and vegetables in agricultural shows in the mid-1800s also attest to his interest in food production – but were perhaps as much about cultivating status as they were about plants.

> **'The story of the Wentworths, their ten children and their social aspirations in the colony is fascinating for both the drama of William's political objectives and the personal narrative.'**

The lost kitchen garden at Vaucluse House is a place in which English landscaping traditions would have been both continued and discarded. Rather than being facsimiles of the English kitchen garden, the Australian versions were transformed by isolation, climate and the materials that were locally available. Contemporary gardening books from both Australia and England were used to help recreate the layout of the garden at Vaucluse. The ideal kitchen garden was square or rectangular form with rectilinear beds[4] or 'a parallelogram, lying east and west'[5] as espoused in the mid-1800s by the likes of English gardening writer J C Loudon, and locally, in the lectures and writings of Thomas Shepherd and George McEwin. At Vaucluse, the traditional English distinction between 'front: lawn' and 'rear: productive zone' was preserved. Following advice to maintain uninterrupted views of the pleasure grounds so as to preserve a park-like pastoral landscape, the service areas, stables and animals were kept to the rear of the house. This had the added benefit of preventing the household and guests having to encounter the 'undesirable traffic' of servants across the lawn!

The recreated kitchen garden at Vaucluse House is a working garden with earth paths and mounded beds that cover an area of about one 1.4 ha (⅓ acre). It is an unpretentious garden; not elaborate nor overly 'prettified'. The gradient is

VAUCLUSE HOUSE KITCHEN GARDEN

1. Water tanks
2. Asparagus
3. Pineapples
4. Cape gooseberry, 'Lacinato' kale, marrowfat pea and purple-podded Dutch pea on trellises and cut flowers
5. Onions
6. Chicory, salsify, carrots and silverbeet
7. Endive, scorzonera, salading and the currant tomato
8. Jam melon
9. Rhubarb 'Victoria', beetroot, broad beans 'Aquadulce' and 'Early Long Pod' and nasturtium
10. Indian fig hedge
11. Rough lemon hedge
12. Fruit trees
13. 'Thousand Headed' kale, green manure of white mustard, rosella, sugar peas
14. Cardoon, tomatoes, capsicum 'Bell Lantern', alpine strawberry, radish 'China Rose' and 'White Icicle', kale 'Red Russian'
15. Artichoke, strawberry spinach, parsnip 'The Student', rhubarb, Warrigal greens
16. Green manure
17. Compost and mulch piles

Clockwise, from top left: Radishes; bean teepees made of bamboo; gardener Naomi Jeffs at work in her favourite part of the Vaucluse House garden; Warrigal greens (*Tetragonia tetragonioides*); black kale.

quite steep and the sloping dirt paths are maintained to cope with stormwater and minimise damage to the beds. The rectangular space is enclosed with a fence of wire netting and timber posts as was common, and two five-barred timber gates designate an old road that bisects the garden. Three sides of the garden feature an attractive hedge of 'rough lemon' (*Citrus jambhiri*) or bush lemon, valued in colonial gardens for its thorny stems and dark evergreen leaves. On the garden's north-western fenceline grows an incredibly healthy hedge of what looks like the common prickly pear, the noxious weed *Opuntia vulgaris*, but is in fact *Opuntia ficus-indica*, the edible Indian fig – considered an exotic and choice plant in the 1800s.

Naomi Jeffs has taken over from David Gray as the gardener responsible for the Vaucluse House kitchen garden, a project originally overseen by David. Over the last eight years David and Naomi have trialled many plants, with over thirty varieties initially being experimented with in the garden in 2000. The trials continue today, but a core inventory has eggplant 'Early Long Purple'; tomato 'Red Pear' and 'Yellow Pear', the tiny currant tomato and the German variety 'Riesentraube'. There is the potato 'Pink Fir Apple'; capsicum 'Bell Lantern'; 'Purple Cape' cauliflower; 'Early Purple Sprouting' broccoli, borecale or kale, and cabbage 'Red Drumhead'. Root vegetables include carrot 'Early Horn' and 'Long Red Surrey'; radish varieties 'French Breakfast' and 'Black Spanish Round'. The bean 'Windsor Long Poz' and the runner bean 'Painted Lady' with scarlet and white flowers are grown upon rustic bush-pole tee-pees.

Of the leafy 'salading' plants: lettuce 'Royal Oak Leaf', 'Green Cos' and 'All Year Round'; purslane, chicory and endive are grown. The latter two, Naomi believes, are too bitter for the modern palate, raised as it is on sugar, but were very popular greens in the nineteenth century. 'Warrigal greens' was also cultivated in the mid-1800s colonial garden. We think it's a trendy bush-tucker plant but 'New Zealand Spinach', as it was first named, was collected in New Zealand by Joseph Banks and Daniel Solander on Captain Cook's 1770 voyage. As its name suggests, it was boiled and eaten like spinach. Banks took seeds back to Kew Gardens in 1771 and it subsequently became popular in England later that decade and in Australia by the 1830s.[6] What distinguishes it from any other plant grown in the Vaucluse kitchen garden or any garden in Australia today is that it was the only plant indigenous to Australia to be collected prior to British settlement and cultivated as a vegetable internationally.[7]

It is interesting to consider just how much rested upon the DNA of the seeds of these vegetables and fruit – a whole pioneering potential was contained within their germplasm, the survival and success of the settlers, and also a link with their culture and the familiar. The subsistence value of kitchen gardens in nineteenth-century Australia shouldn't be underestimated. Planting a garden, like an orchard, to paraphrase Michael Pollan, was one of the earliest ceremonies of frontier settlement.[8] In the new colony of New South Wales not only did kitchen gardens provide sustenance, but they also contributed to the settlers' sense of independence, status and permanence. The gardeners and curators researched catalogues of Sydney nurseries of the era, the records of the Botanic Gardens, the list of seeds brought on the First Fleet ships and the Vaucluse House property records to ascertain what food plants were grown in Sydney between 1800 and 1900. They also sought help from the Henry Doubleday Association in Britain (a heritage seed library), and more recently, the Digger's Club, Eden Seeds and the Lost Seed Company, which have stocked the appropriate historically-documented cultivars.

Perennial food plants grown in the Vaucluse kitchen garden include cape gooseberry (*Physalis peruviana*), artichoke, cardoon, a green-stemmed variety of rhubarb known as 'Victoria', pineapple and asparagus 'Mary Washington'. Of the varieties of pumpkin, the most remarkable-looking cucurbit grown would have been 'Turk's Turban', with its stripes of orange, cream and green. It was first seen in the UK in the 1840s and was more popular as an ornamental than an edible. Pumpkin was 'A thing little used in England, but of great use in hot countries'[9] as William Cobbett wrote in his 1833 book on kitchen gardens and, he suggests, best used in pies or as cattle food. 'Turk's Turban' has a pleasant nutty flavour and is extremely long keeping. The books and catalogues of the early 1800s list many esculent plants or esculents (meaning edible) that are rarely cultivated for eating today: samphire, sea kale, skirret, cardoon and purslane, for example. Another forgotten esculent is the jam melon (*Citrullus lanatus* var. *citroides*) – also known as the citron. It resembles a watermelon in shape, size and colour but its flesh is pale, denser and much less sweet. While jam melon is rather bland, the addition of sugar and flavourings make it good in jams and pickles, cakes and puddings. Jam melon, like pumpkin, was a great pioneer food in that it was easily grown, prolific, and was a good source of calories that could be stored for a long period.

In Victorian England, of all the fruits grown in the kitchen garden, perhaps none were more prized than pineapple and melons, and among the vegetables, the cucumber. As Naomi confirms, pineapples were a Victorian symbol of status and hospitality – they were expensive and hard to grow and thus an impressive item to offer guests. No wonder new migrants were incredulous – at home vast wealth was required to force these tropical plants into fruition in an adverse climate. Pineapples were grown in heated pine-pits, melons in a melon-ground and cucumbers in hot houses where their tendency to bend was curtailed with long glass cylinders hung over the immature fruit. The expense and effort of such pits let alone the full extravaganza of heated-brick-walled kitchen gardens or 'flued' walls with multiple fireplaces was considerable. In Sydney there wasn't even the need for simple hotbeds of manure; such tender plants bore fruit out in the open ground in this warm temperate climate. Melons – including rockmelons, cantaloupes and watermelons – were no rarity to the Australian-born Wentworths, the melon crops of the antipodes being 'such as to encourage their cultivation not simply as articles of luxury but of food'.[10] Sarah brought several melon varieties with her on returning to Australia in April 1861 and by December she wrote to her daughter Thomasine of growing 'a great many vines of different melons in hope of a good feast for Papa [William] enjoys a good mellon'.[11]

William was also especially fond of peaches, waxing lyrical in his 1820 book about New South Wales: 'Of all the fruits . . . the peach is the most abundant and the most useful . . . This fruit grows spontaneously in every situation, on the richest soils, as on the most barren; and its growth is so rapid that if you plant a stone, it will in three years afterwards bear an abundant crop of fruit. Peaches are, in consequence, so plentiful throughout the colony, that they are everywhere given as food to hogs . . .'[12] Fruit trees grown in the kitchen garden at Vaucluse today include apple 'Gravenstein' and 'King of the Pippins', the 'Moorpark' apricot, pomelo, loquat, strawberry guava, greengage plum, medlar, fig, quince, custard apple and olive.

> **'In Victorian England, of all the fruits grown in the kitchen garden, perhaps none were more prized than pineapple and melons, and among the vegetables, the cucumber.'**

The efforts made to recreate an authentic colonial garden here at Vaucluse House are admirable – while the gardeners use modern tools, not even mechanically-baled straw is deemed appropriate as mulch; instead, loose stable straw is used from the nearby Equestrian Centre at Centennial Park. The sandy soils leach nutrients and need regular improvement so compost is made on site and utilises the manure of the property's goats and chooks. In recreating the kitchen garden, more than 100 tonnes of compost were initially incorporated into the soil! Sydney's coastal suburbs are, naturally, surrounded by the harbour, and consequently temperature conditions are buffered. There are first settlement records, though, that note the occurrence of frost, and Naomi wonders whether climate change is responsible for the fact that in the mid-1800s the garden grew wonderful stone fruit (like the peach with the 9-inch (23 cm) circumference) but that in 2010 not even the apricots set fruit readily. Perhaps it's the heat-bowl effect, or is it the grim reality of global warming?

In autumn the pumpkins and pie melons are harvested and

The gate to the kitchen garden intersects a hedge of Indian fig
(Opuntina ficus-indica) growing along the north-east perimeter

Clockwise, from top left: Jam melons; a basket of oyster plant roots (Salsify – *Tragopogon porrifolius*); parsnip 'The Student'; many types of salad crops can be used as 'cut-and-come-again' seedlings; a flowerhead of the purple-leaf form of amaranth; a pea trellis is constructed from stakes, sticks and bamboo.

piled on the long workbench in the shed. 'The first thing I do every morning is to check the kitchen garden,' says Naomi – she goes straight there even before collecting her tools to see how the vegetables are doing. In her tours of the garden Naomi demonstrates her considerable knowledge of garden history – she's not only a gardener but effectively a curator too. She loves the book *A History of Kitchen Gardening* by Susan Campbell for its detailed depiction of the bygone era of kitchen gardening of the most labour-intensive kind, and the gorgeous illustrations of old tools and plants.

The property at Vaucluse remained in the Wentworth family until 1910 when the New South Wales government resumed it to provide parkland on the Sydney Harbour foreshores and the HHT has endeavoured to restore it as the Wentworths would have known it. If you stand in the garden shed looking across the garden towards the slate roof of the house and its eccentric castellated façade, you may well think you have stepped through a portal to Sydney's past. At the same time as this heritage is being preserved, it is good to know the property is not simply a colonial theme-park but actually has some relevance to twenty-first-century living and gardening. In 2006 a new kitchen garden shed was built to provide storage space and an accessible area for working with produce. Two corrugated-iron tanks to harvest rainwater for irrigating the garden have also been installed. Sydney receives an average of 1242 mm of rain annually, but few years are average years these days. The suburb of Vaucluse might be one of the highest water-using localities in New South Wales but at Vaucluse House the garden's water use has been stable over the last few years – maintained at a surprisingly low level for such a large garden (an efficiency of which the gardeners are justifiably proud). The kitchen garden has a small but regular group of volunteers, and a number of Year 12 food technology students from the local high school have been making use of the garden for their studies. All around is the expensive and exclusive suburb of Vaucluse, where giant SUVs choke the narrow streets, but down below the sandstone escarpment with its remnant bush, angophoras and gymea lilies, in the little valley at Vaucluse House, all is peaceful and productive.

THE MARANGY KITCHEN GARDEN

Size	180 m² (kitchen garden 15 m in diameter)
Climate	Temperate (hot summer)
Soil	Free-draining loam (lots of organic matter)
Average annual rainfall	780 mm (580 mm average from 1996–2009)
Frost	Yes
Water source	Dam, tank and town water
Irrigation method	Spray irrigation
Compost and fertiliser	Pelletised organic fertiliser
Mulch	Composted pig manure
Biggest challenges	Wildlife, frosts, summer heat
Favourite herb	Rosemary
Favourite food plant	Asparagus

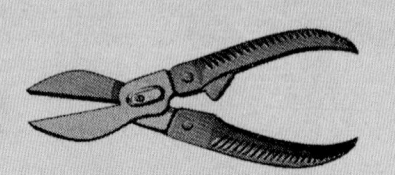

CHAPTER 7
MARANGY
A Walled Kitchen Garden in Rural Victoria

There are very few walled kitchen gardens in rural Victoria, let alone contemporary ones that feature sensuously curved semi-circular walls. But then, Sally Gamble likes to do things differently and loves design that, as well as being beautiful, enhances her life in functional ways. At their property 'Marangy' just outside of Benalla, she and husband Gerard Brownstein have created a charming garden since they moved here from Melbourne in 1991. Around the few existing exotic trees, they have established a gravel garden filled with tough perennials and evergreens that survive the harsh conditions – the summer heat and the winter frosts. Echiums, perovskia, sedums, yuccas, bearded iris and ornamental grasses are planted in great informal sweeps – Chatto-esque islands of foliage and texture in a sea of gravel punctuated by statuesque and spiky specimens of *Agave americana*.

The garden is the ongoing project of a couple who enjoy tackling the dilemma of country gardening – how to maintain a shady oasis, stop the wind and grow lovely plants, yet also minimise the amount of precious water needed to maintain such as oasis. Benalla hasn't received good or even 'normal' rainfall since 1996, yet despite this Sally and Gerard enjoy the fresh local food characteristic of the country life of yesteryear by growing their own vegetables, citrus and herbs as well as olives for olive oil. For this family, it is apparent that gardening is a little bit science, a little bit art, some hard physical work and a whole lot of common sense.

Walled gardens were designed to be impressive status symbols as well as productive mini-farms: in their hey-day in Victorian England the diversity of food plants, the detailing of the architecture and the formal layout manifested an elegant blend of the aesthetic and the practical. They were not a British gardening tradition that was maintained in Australia, however. Here they are few and far between because the Australian climate was too warm to necessitate such a massive microclimate creation – old walled gardens are most often found in the Southern Tablelands of New South Wales and the colder inland areas of Tasmania. Tasmania's cool temperate climate meant that the storage of heat and protection from frost was an important factor in extending the growing season at either end and ripening fruits properly. In our 'upside down' continent the heat-storing walls so important in growing tender food plants in the northern hemisphere (of course reversed to face north) were rather redundant. Take the walled garden that landscape designer Edna Walling (English-born) designed for Keith and Elisabeth Murdoch at Cruden Farm – the garden proved too hot for the espaliered fruit trees and the space was quickly converted to an enclosed flower garden. As Dame Elisabeth recounts: 'The espaliers that Edna Walling planted on the west-facing wall were impossible – the fruit stewed as it hung on the branches!'[1]

While Sally's garden is not a true walled garden in the sense of being fully enclosed by walls on four sides (the wall of the weatherboard house forms the opposite boundary, while the two ends are open to the rest of the garden), the single wall separates the space from paddocks and the bush beyond. Built from recycled red bricks, the wall measures 1.8 m high – tall enough to protect the plants within from the southerly winds if not from all of the severe frosts the area receives each year. Being eye-level it allows views through to the gum trees and olive grove. The garden occupies a space 15 m in diameter with four raised curvilinear beds and a single large bed at the base of the curved wall. Gravel paths flow between the beds and around a central glazed pot of deep cobalt blue emerging amidst the red and yellow flowers of gaillardia and the delicate seed heads of switch grass – *Panicum virgatum*. The garden recalls courtyard gardens of Spain in that it is strongly symmetrical and unashamedly colourful. The formal design gives the garden year-round structure, as Sally says: 'The garden can be dormant, you can cut everything back, but it still looks fantastic.' And as the centre of the garden lines up with the kitchen window, there is always something edible to contemplate while doing the dishes.

The garden was constructed in 1999 under the guidance of local landscaper and friend Ken Bourke. His input was to suggest the curved wall and productive garden to replace a group of senescent desert ash trees on the south-east side of the house. The result is a far more sympathetic treatment of the site than a predictable layout of straight lines and 90-degree

A blue glazed pot and the colourful flowers of gaillardia make a decorative central feature in this Benalla kitchen garden

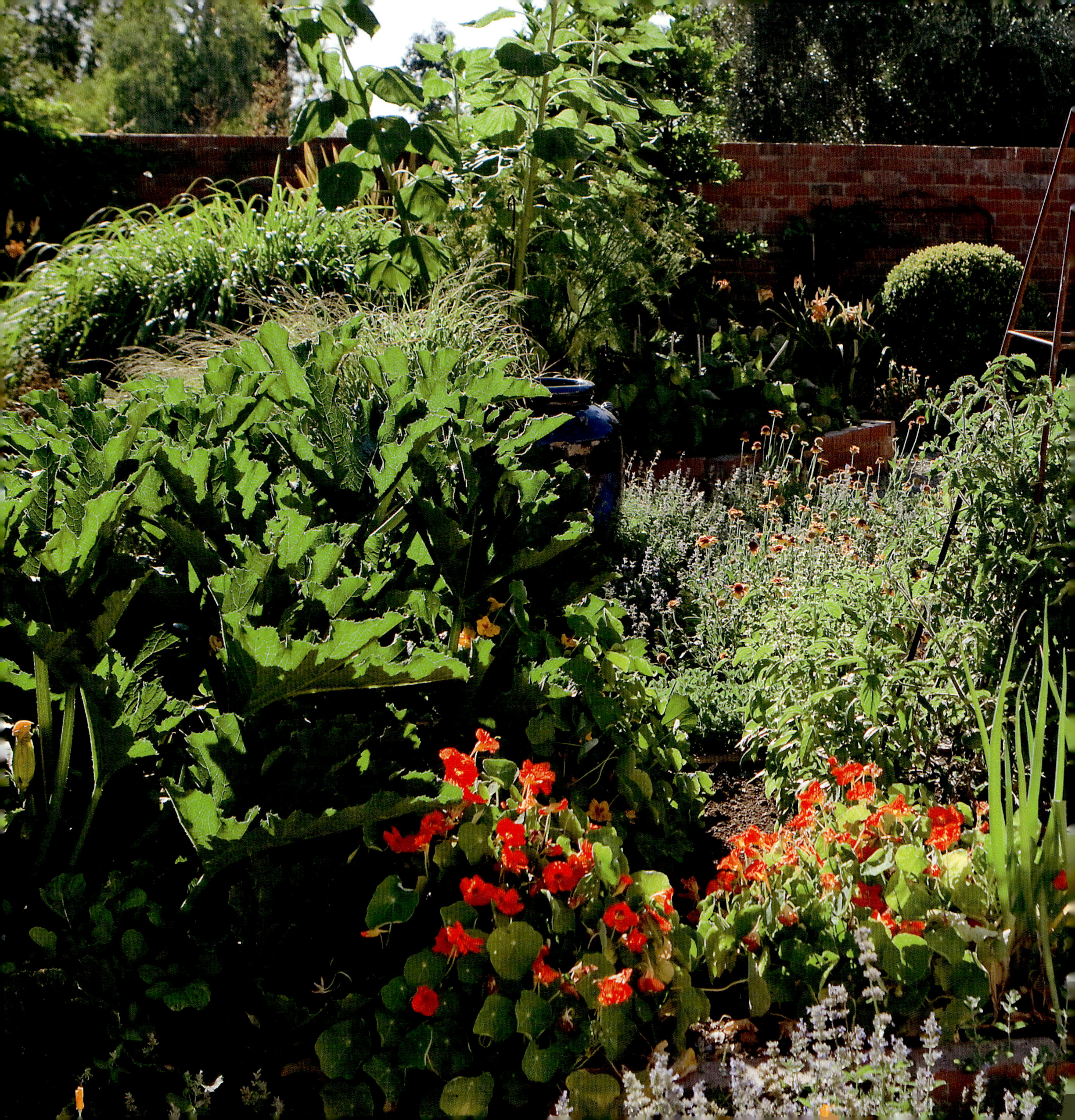

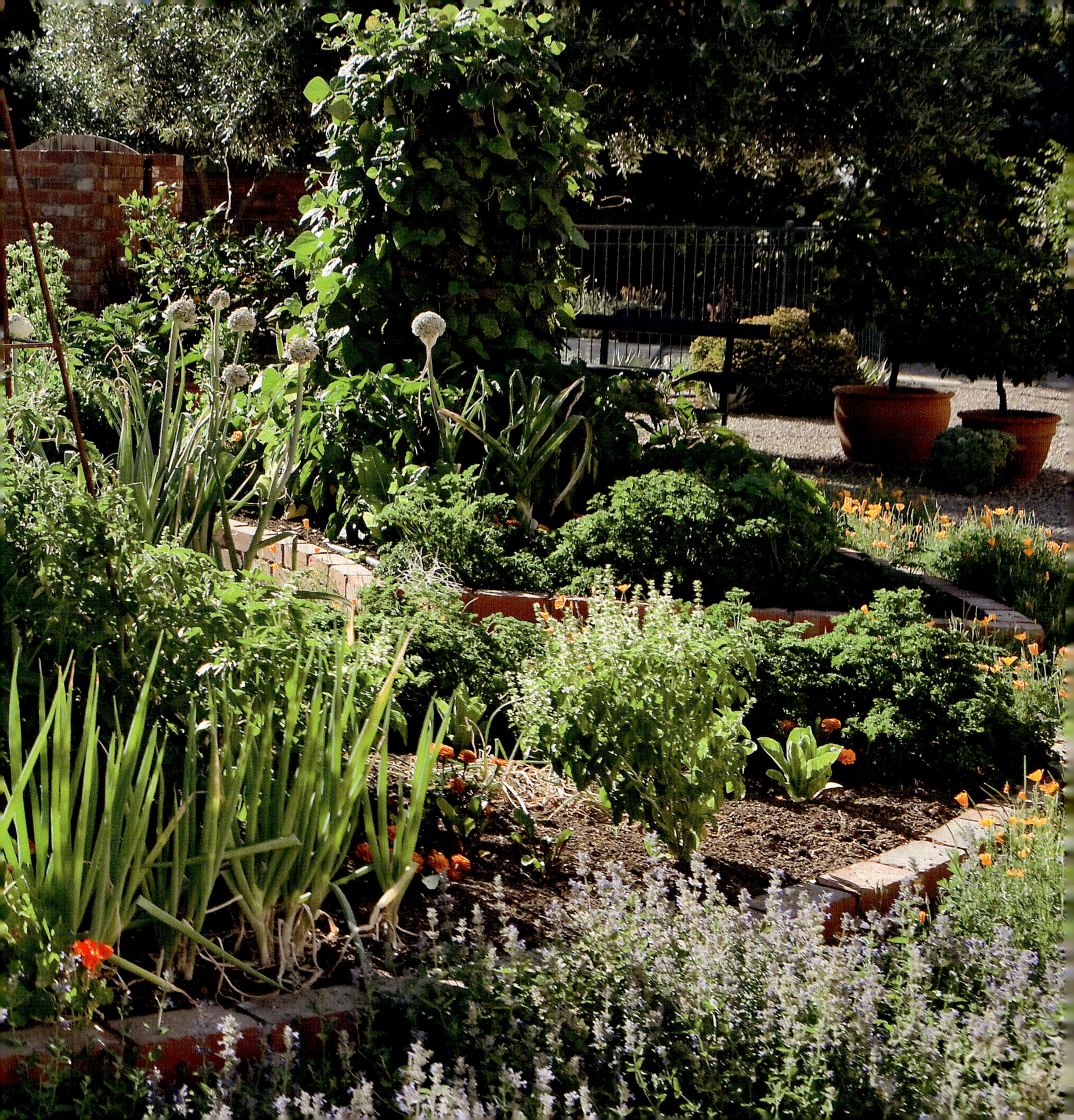

angles would have proven. Setting the garden beds 4 m away from the house means they are out of the shade cast by the building while the raised beds aid drainage and emphasise the design. One of the four smaller beds is devoted entirely to asparagus, which gives the family an almost continuous crop of green spears through the spring. Another features the best patch of lemongrass in country Victoria. Sally plants her annual food crops very much in anticipation of the weather and seasons. In summer, zucchinis are a staple vegetable, planted in combination in one of the curved beds with 'Black Russian' tomatoes, basil, parsley, lettuce, shallots, beetroot and red bunching onions. (Seeds and seedlings are sourced from either the Digger's Club or the local nursery.) In the neighbouring bed Sally has planted parsley, capsicums, eggplants, leeks, heirloom climbing beans, garlic, borage and celery. Brassicas star during winter, as do salads, herbs and spring onions.

Sally's parents live on the neighbouring property and her father is a retired agricultural scientist so it is no surprise that he has an impressive vegetable garden of his own. Sally therefore tries to avoid doubling up on what her dad is growing next door — especially blackberries, stone fruit and pumpkins — as there is no winning those particular competitions. Each season features its different food plants but the rituals associated with the kitchen garden remain fairly constant — planting, mulching, tending, harvesting and making compost. Then there are the annual jobs like pruning the fruit and olive trees and adding composted pig manure to the kitchen garden beds. This year Sally will also remove non-edible plants that have taken over the kitchen garden; for example, purple-foliaged canna lilies will be replaced with the edible *and* ornamental purple-headed globe artichokes.

Against the curved wall grow a Tahitian lime tree, table grapes and a pomegranate tree. The trio of citrus, grapes and pomegranate conjures up images of walled paradises of ancient times — Iranian gardens full of scent, fruit and flowers. Who can resist a ripe pomegranate with its tough skin bursting to reveal the ruby juice and seeds within? There are few more evocative symbols of fertility, abundance and renewal in the plant world. The Bible contains multiple references to pomegranates and some scholars regard the pomegranate as the original forbidden fruit rather than the infamous apple. In Jewish tradition the seeds in a pomegranate fruit are said to number 613 — one for each of the Bible's 613 commandments. And in the Koran, the representation of Paradise is of an afterlife in which the gardens contain date palms, grapes, olives and pomegranates. Pomegranates are not only long-lived and beautiful deciduous trees to 6 m tall, they are incredibly tough, have golden autumn foliage, bright orange flowers and the fruit is delicious and high in antioxidants — what's not to love?

Sally's pomegranate is the dwarf form *Punica granatum* 'Nana', which has none-the-less grown to 2 m. There are hundreds of named pomegranate varieties in the world, and the number available in Australia is finally increasing. Named varieties include: 'Gulosha Rosavaya', 'Gulosha Azerbaijani', 'Nabha', 'Chawla', 'Achik Dani', 'Isseka', 'Big Red', 'Ben Hur', 'Wonderful', 'Griffiths', 'Shepherds Red', 'Jennings' and 'Elche'. Some of the best varieties for the size of their fruit and juicy red flesh are 'Gulosha Rosavaya', 'Gulosha Azerbaijani' and 'Wonderful'. The 'Wonderful' variety was a chance seedling discovered in Florida that has become the dominant commercial cultivar in California. Many of the plants sold in Australia as 'Wonderful', however, are not in fact the true cultivar — which can prove most disappointing after years of waiting for your trees to bear fruit!

Citrus also do well in the climate here — orange, lemon and mandarins thrive and are the only fruit trees to escape the notice of the birds. The local bird life is a blessing rather than a curse, but as the garden is not enclosed Sally and Gerard realise

Previous page: **The combination of colourful flowers and the verdant foliage of summer vegetables in Sally's garden is quite enchanting.**
Clockwise, from top left: **Dahlia 'Bishop of Llandaff'; climbing bean 'Rattlesnake'; potted tomatoes; bright blooms of gaillardia; Lebanese eggplants; Sally in the kitchen garden; Gerard's stacked-stone sculpture; a steel obelisk made by Gerard.**
Centre: **Bean 'Puple King' with zucchini flowers.**

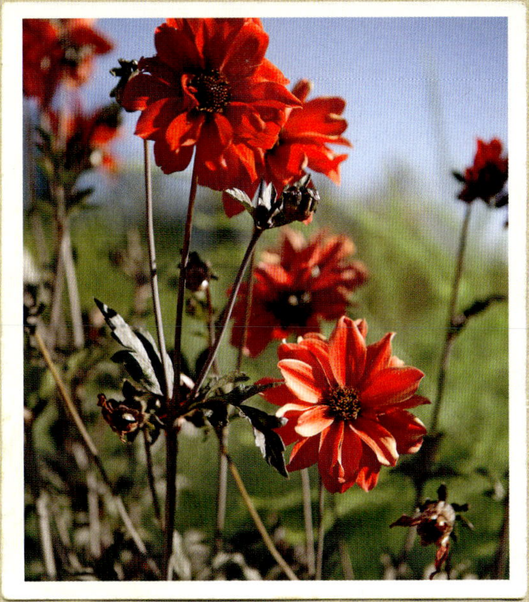
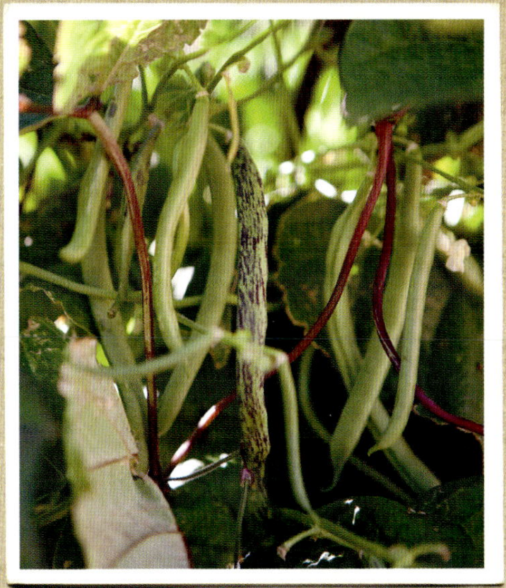
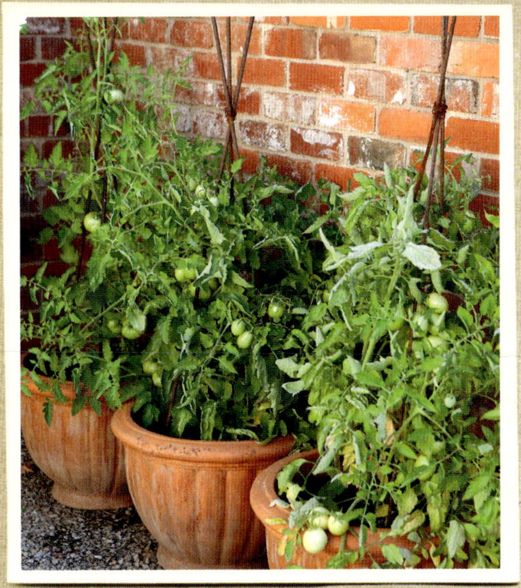
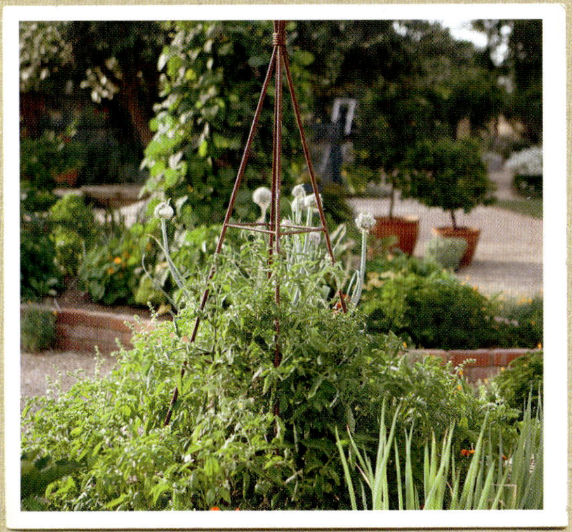
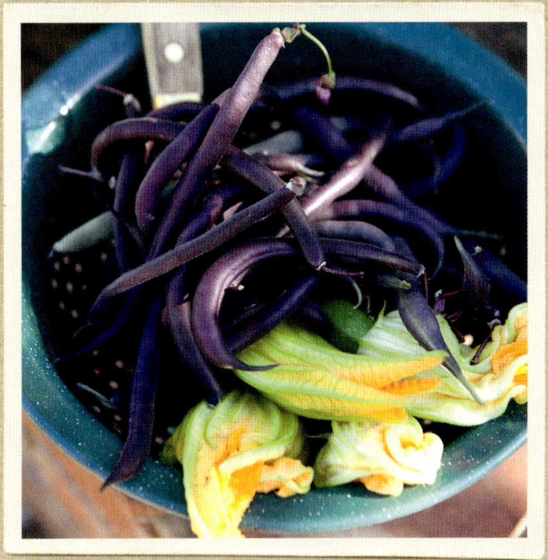
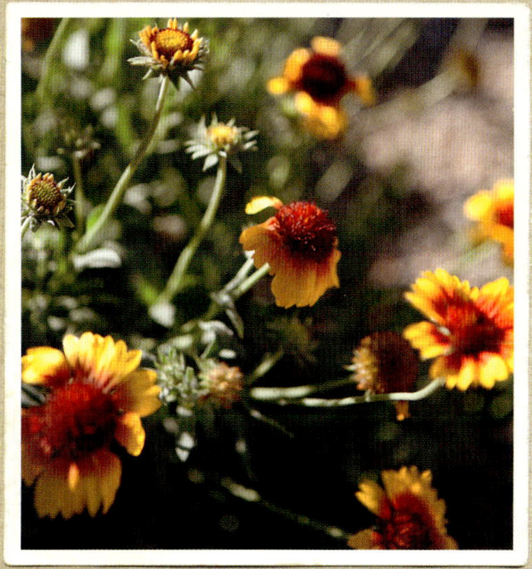
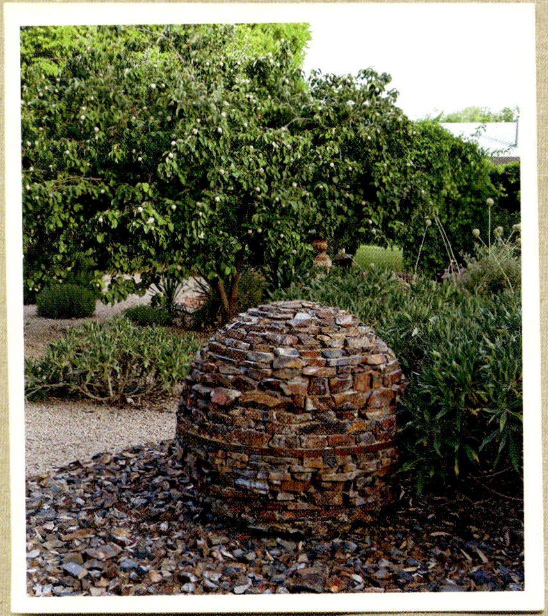
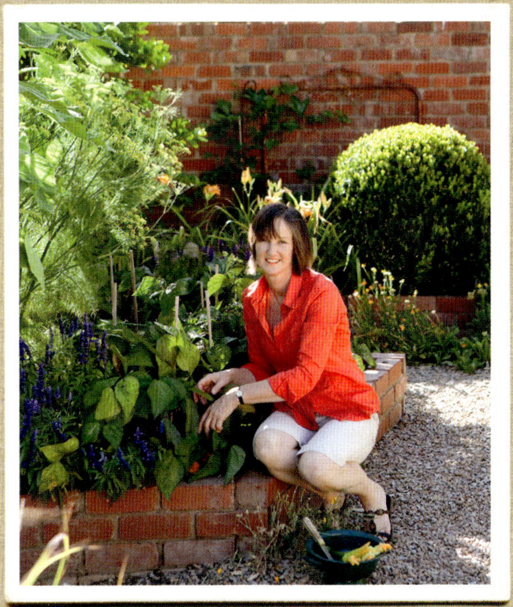
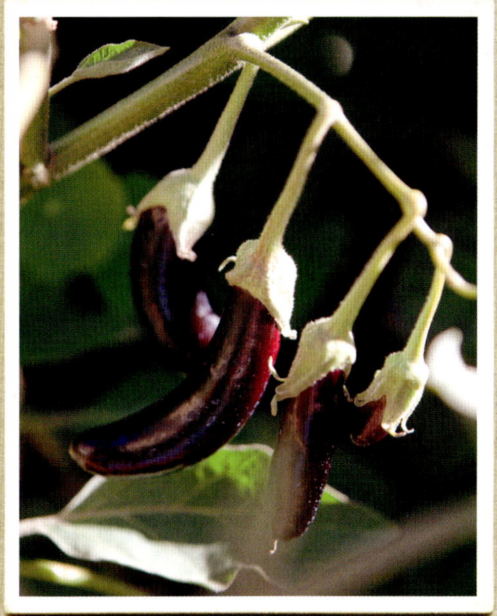

THE MARANGY GARDEN

1. Kalamata olive tree and potted citrus
2. Tahitian lime
3. Pomegranate tree
4. Globe artichokes
5. Grapevines and tomatoes in pots
6. Asparagus
7. Lemongrass, zucchini and silverbeet
8. Spring onions, peas
9. Eggplants, herbs and lettuce
10. Ceramic pot

they have little choice but to share their bounty with the avian residents. King parrots and crimson rosellas loved the stone-fruit trees that Sally and Gerard initially planted – but they were nothing compared to the naughty cockatoos that played destructive teamwork and broke off entire branches with their

> ' The family is totally committed to Benalla – its challenges and delights alike – and understands that it is we humans who have to adapt our practices to the bush environment.

beaks. The King parrots devour the pomegranate fruit but their jewel-like colours are too beautiful for Sally to mind. Hawks ate some of their chooks, the foxes finished off the remaining ones and rabbits and hares are a pain in the neck – but these are not the complaints of disaffected 'tree-changers'. The family is totally committed to Benalla – its challenges and delights alike – and understands that it is we humans who have to adapt our practices to the bush environment.

Blue wrens and honeyeaters are the gentler face of local biodiversity in the garden. They and their kind will all benefit from the nearby Regent Honeyeater habitat restoration project with which Sally is involved – making and improving wildlife corridors from the hills to the river and creeks. Living in the country, Sally is well aware of how its bushland has been degraded and fragmented by land clearing and conventional farming practices, and thinks it is imperative to restore the bush and local ecosystems. For farmers and gardeners, this has the added advantage of creating habitat for beneficial predators (insect, spider, bird, marsupial and reptile) of garden pests. Increasing local and regional biodiversity is a great principle of both sustainable horticulture and agriculture – but such 'farmscaping' has other benefits: it assists in regulating both surface and ground water, with riparian stabilisation, it can double as windbreaks, it helps prevents erosion and sequesters carbon.

The family is very much an advocate of the stewardship model of land management on their small farm and sees conservation plantings as a necessity rather than a nuisance. Behind the kitchen garden wall lies a new garden bed of native plants – many of them local species such as *Dodonaea viscosa* and *Acacia flexifolia,* and threatened ones like *Goodia medicaginea*: the small shrub called Western Golden Tip with its beautiful foliage and yellow pea flowers. With the iconic forms of *Xanthorrhoea*, river red gums and corrugated-iron tanks how could you be anywhere else but Australia?

A riot of colour explodes from the kitchen garden – there is the pretty (but still useful) bronze fennel, happy-faced sunflowers and orange-flowered calendulas among the red blooms of purple-foliaged dahlias and grey-blue cabbages. The irrepressible Californian poppies are at home in the gravel paths. Just as Sally likes to mix ornamentals in the kitchen garden, *vice-versa* there are edible plants elsewhere in the garden at Marangy. Sally will happily 'incorporate herbs and edible plants into the ornamental garden' – and thus there is parsley planted among the perennials and thyme under the trees. Even the spiky giant agaves (*Agave americana*) in Sally and Gerard's gravel garden are useful, being edible (well, drinkable) and a source of fibre for weaving and rope in its land of origin. This species of Mexican agave (also known as century plant or *maguey*) is the source of the distilled liquor *mescal* (it is *Agave tequilana* which produces the more famous tequila). Mescal is made by cutting the thick agave flower stem before it flowers thereby making it exude a sweet liquid called *agua miel* or 'honey water'. This liquid is then fermented to produce the drink called *pulque*, which when distilled becomes mescal – the ancient drink of pre-Columbian Mexico.

In 2004 English garden designer and author John Brookes conducted a garden masterclass at Marangy as part of the biennial Benalla Botanica conference. Brookes' own garden Denmans in England is well known for its use of gravel and plant foliage form, textures and colour. Sally was impressed by his design philosophy and has endeavoured to focus upon creating vistas in the garden and forming naturalistic and generous plantings of a few chosen drought-tolerant species. Gerard has a similarly creative approach to the landscape – he might be a GP but he has the soul of an artist, and a number of his sculptures are placed around the garden. In the kitchen garden stand a pair of steel obelisks – the product of a local metal-working workshop, which make an impressive support for snow peas, sugar snap peas and climbing beans. In the gravel garden he has constructed a beautiful sphere from local stone. The red and blue-grey rock is cleverly stacked to form a textured lithic globe of a sculpture, emerging from among plants and gravel.

Water is a big issue in the Goulburn–Broken Catchment – local communities feel beleaguered by the city of Melbourne's thirst for water from the Goulburn River system. As elsewhere in rural Australia the great local river on which the surrounding region depends is in crisis, and a total solution to the dilemma of limited water is seemingly unattainable. The house here is on town water, and the household's wastewater is recycled through a water treatment plant onto some of the ornamental garden. Rainfall has averaged 580 mm annually since 2000 and Marangy's two dams have not filled naturally since 1996, and thus supplies for the garden have been supplemented with limited pumping from Hollands Creek. (The property name *Marangy* is the Aboriginal name for the islands and many small waterways that dot the Broken River near its confluence with Hollands Creek.) Luckily the vegie garden has three large rain tanks to draw its water from.

On a gentle rise to the north-east of the house is an olive grove planted a decade ago. Sally and Gerard were not concerned to establish a grove of one single variety, planting instead 200 trees of a number of different ones including: 'Kalamata', 'Corregiola', 'Frantoio', 'Spanish Mission' and 'Verdale'. Both this grove and another that lies to the south beyond the magnificent old river red gum act as windbreaks for the house zone and the silver-foliaged olive trees look at home in their bush setting. The trees are not watered and because of the different varieties there tends to be a crop every year – overcoming the tendency of some types to bear biennially. Sally and Gerard like their multi-variety grove as it means their oil tastes different from year to year depending on which variety has the best crop. Oils are as varietal as wine, after all. Some years the oil might be fruity and spicy, in other years, green or herbaceous in flavour. It is encouraging to see a small-scale hands-on family enterprise that (unlike the large-scale production behemoths in northern Victoria) is cultivated without the use of copper sprays (for fungal leaf spot), without pesticides or 'chemical fruit loosening agents'.

Olive harvest is a happy ritual that involves family and friends. Picking starts early, with a break for morning tea and again for an enormous lunch – it's a little bit of the Mediterranean lifestyle in Benalla. Cold fingers pick the fruit on a freezing weekend morning in May or June and the olives are driven to Milawa in the nearby King Valley where they are processed into liquid gold. Bottled, the beautiful extra virgin oil is part of Sally's daily table as well as being sold locally. Part of the proceeds of the sales is donated to Benalla's Tomorrow: Today Foundation, a foundation that Sally has helped set up to assist in funding community and environmental projects in the area. It is a wonderful reversal of the general trend that the Gamble–Brownstein family has moved to, rather than away from, rural Victoria. They have been busy getting their hands dirty ever since and are obviously glad to eat well and look after the land at the same time.

A little bit of the Mediterranean in rural Victoria

THE BROCKS' KITCHEN GARDEN

Size	20 × 24 m (480 m^2)
Climate	Arid
Soil	Fine textured sandy silt
Average annual rainfall	280 mm
Frost	Yes
Water source	Alice Springs aquifer
Irrigation method	Drip irrigation
Compost and fertiliser	Composted food scraps and plant material, composted chook manure, cow manure
Mulch	Buffel grass, anything they can find
Biggest challenges	Nematodes
Favourite herb	Thyme
Favourite food plant	Fennel

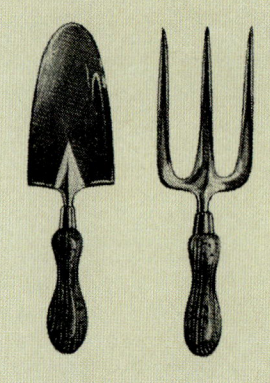

CHAPTER 8
LOCAVORES IN THE RED CENTRE
The Brock Family's Backyard

Alice Springs is a town of contradictions. It is an urban village in the pastoral heart of Australia, its suburbs rapidly expanding into the ancient rocky landscape. Homes and bitumen streets are flanked by the ochre and purple MacDonnell Ranges, by ghost gums and spinifex. Known as *Mparntwe* by its traditional Arrernte owners, Alice Springs is one of the driest places on the driest habitable continent on the planet. It has an annual rainfall of just 280 mm and a big river – the Todd – in which water rarely flows.

Consider the following: water comes from an aquifer south of the town and there are no residential water restrictions; in summer they have nearly three months of temperatures in the high thirties, and in winter experience cold nights to minus zero with occasional frosts (it has even snowed!). However, fruit and vegetables *can* thrive in this semi-arid climate. Then add to this a local commercial horticultural industry that is in its infancy and the fact that most of the food for the population of 30 000 is transported 1500 km from either Adelaide or Darwin . . .

Such factors are some of the reasons why Chris and Helen Brock choose to grow their own food at home in the Alice Springs suburbs. They love living in this unique environment but the climate does prove challenging for gardening. Still, because they believe it is better for the environment's health and for their own, and because fresh food is pretty expensive in the supermarket up here, they figure the effort required to grow their own is worth it. Chris and Helen and their kids Lily (four) and Giles (three), epitomise the kind of kitchen-literate and environmentally conscious family who would take up a locavore challenge. This means that they try to buy, grow or source food grown close to where they live, aware that food production (its growing, harvesting, processing, transport, refrigeration, etc) accounts for nearly 50 per cent of Australia's total eco-footprint.[1] The idea is eating perishable food that is local and seasonal, in addition to organically produced (if and when it is available), which is more energy, carbon and water efficient than purchasing conventionally produced food which has been refrigerated and transported over long distances. (The huge dependence on road transport in the Northern Territory would probably account for the state having an eco-footprint that is 4 per cent higher than the national average of 6.4 ha (16 acres).[2]) Obviously Alice Springs is rather short on dairy farms, but Chris and Helen grow most of their own vegetables and eat locally raised protein in the form of their own eggs and rabbits as well as buying meat that's been grown and processed nearby (a quarter of a camel to stock their freezer, for instance). The Brocks' Araluen backyard, measuring 24 × 25 m, accommodates the vegetable garden, citrus and mulberry trees, the chooks, the rabbit hutches, indigenous plants and trees, a poly-house and sandpit as well as the ubiquitous Aussie trinity of the lawn, hills hoist and shed.

When Chris and Helen bought the property much of the backyard was covered in carpet (an unusual outdoor room perhaps!) but it was beneficial as it had eradicated couch grass from the soil – weed enemy number one of both gardens and the bush throughout the Centre. They constructed their kitchen garden at the rear out of recycled timber posts and chook netting and added an old hand-forged iron gate they'd found on their honeymoon through outback South Australia and the Northern Territory. On the inside they built six beds of varying shapes with timber edging that today boast a charming tangle of vegetables, flowers and herbs. Next, they created runs for the chooks and rabbits and planted some of the beautiful grevilleas, eremophilas and grasses to be found growing in the region. Two olives and a pomegranate tree were added to the existing plantings of mulberry trees (both the white- and pink-fruited forms). The mulberries fruit in September and excess berries are dried and eaten as snacks like you would sultanas. There were also mature existing citrus trees including numerous oranges – 'Valencias', 'Lane's Navel' and 'Washington Navel' – and a grapefruit, and their size and abundance has to be seen to be believed.

Clockwise, from top: **The backyard patch with broccoli and the Ethiopian cabbage 'Women Meet and Gossip'; the vegie patch is enclosed by the 'honeymoon gate' and a fence of chook netting; Chris, Helen, Giles and Lily.**

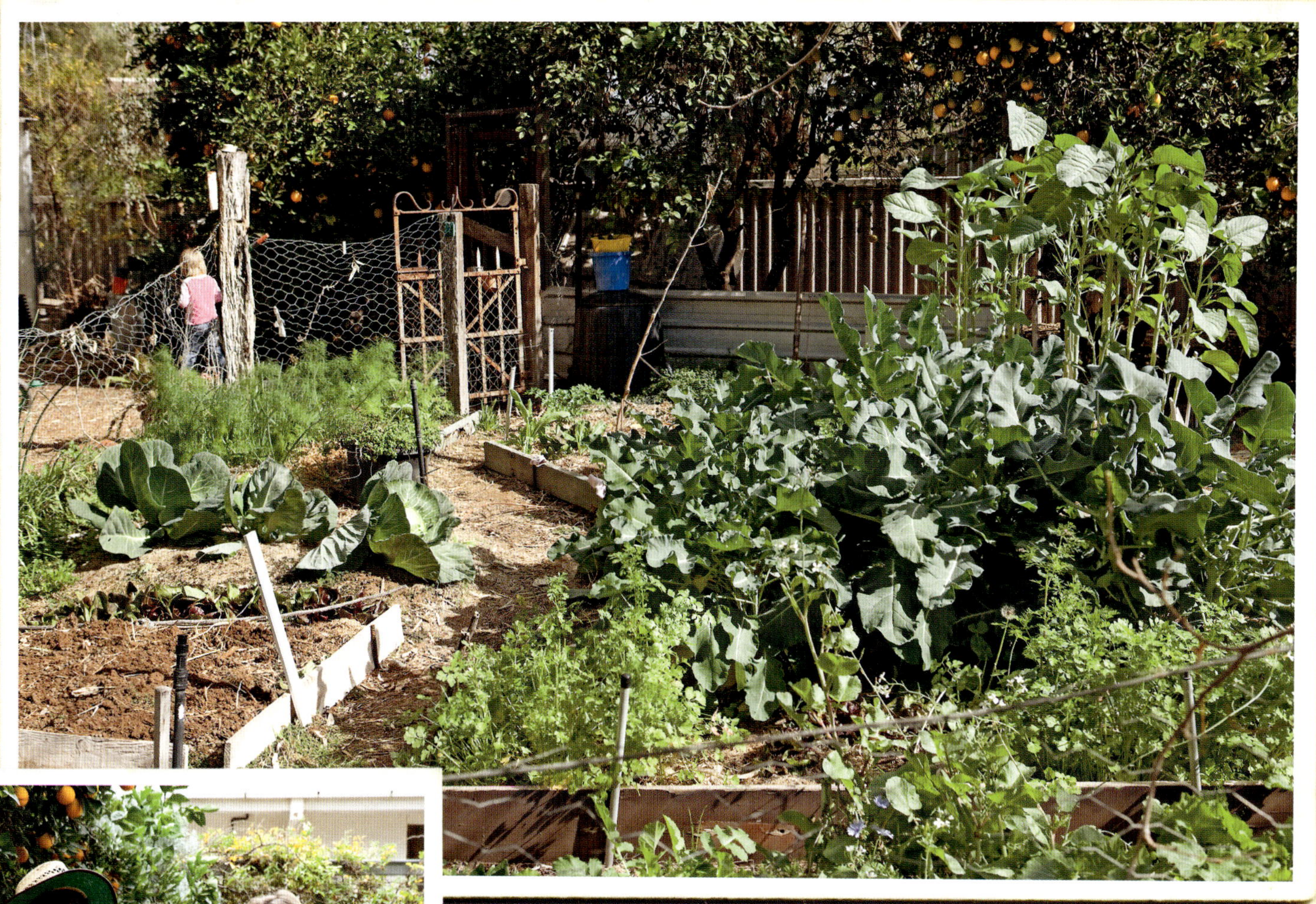

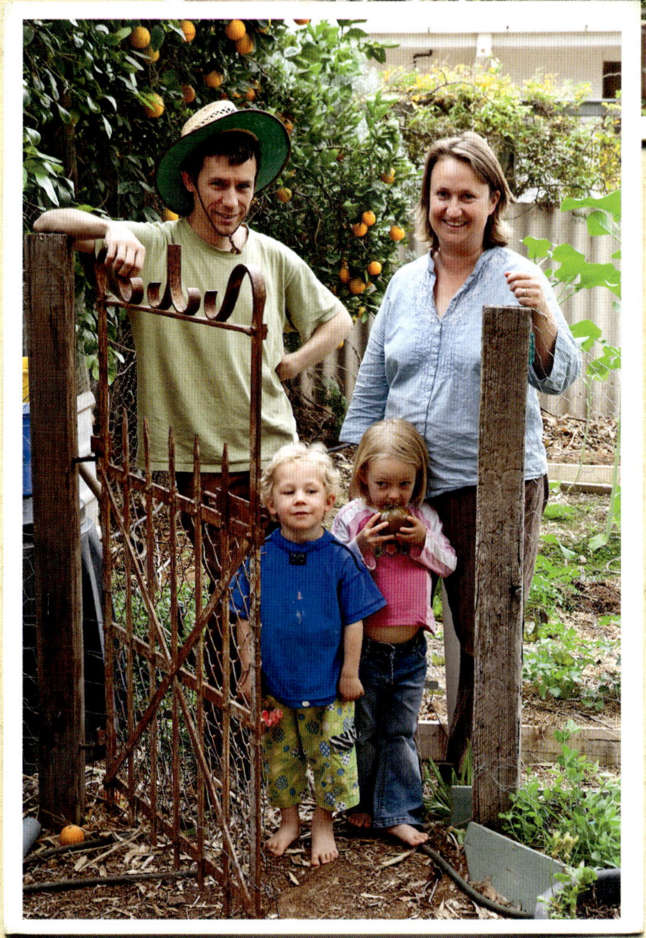

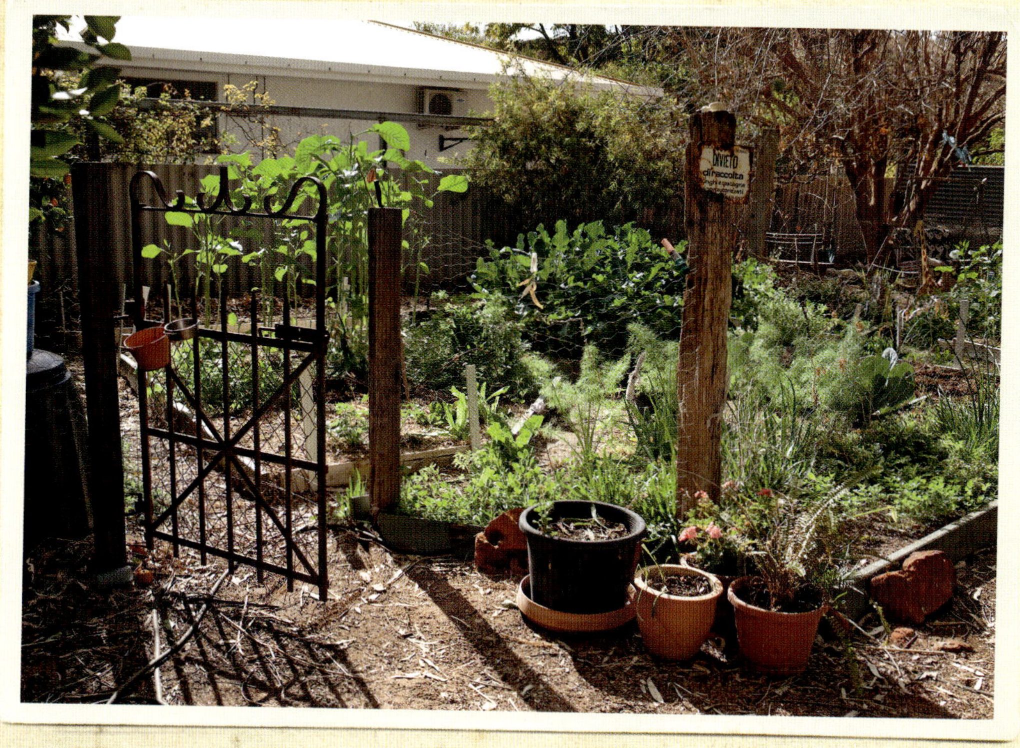

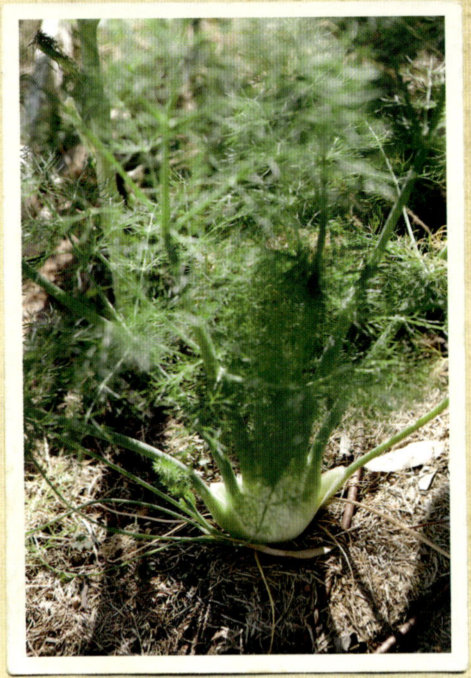
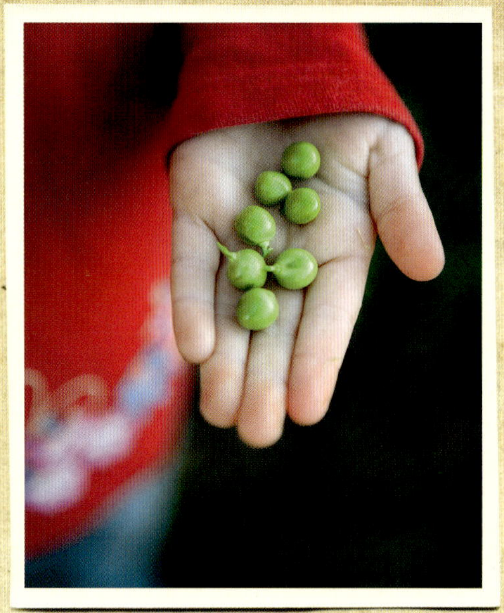
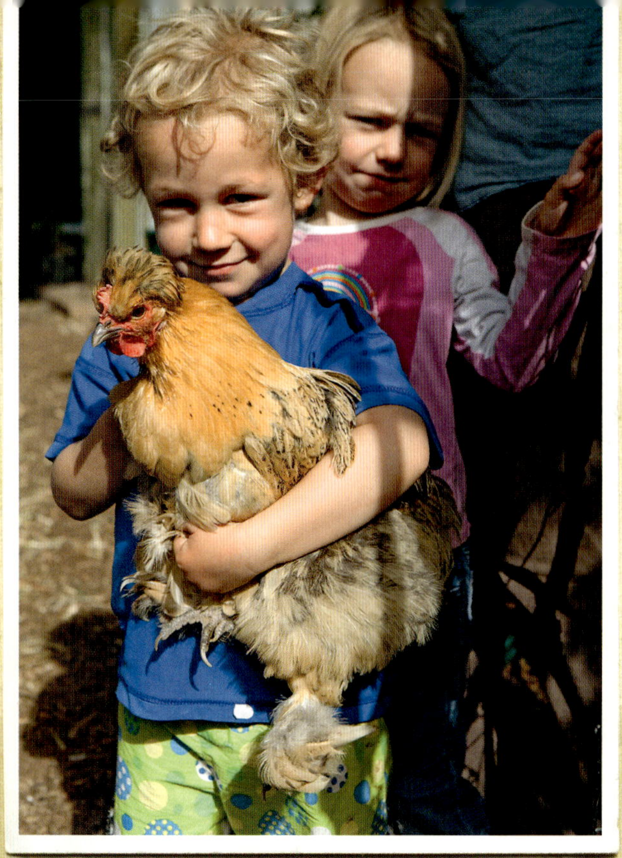
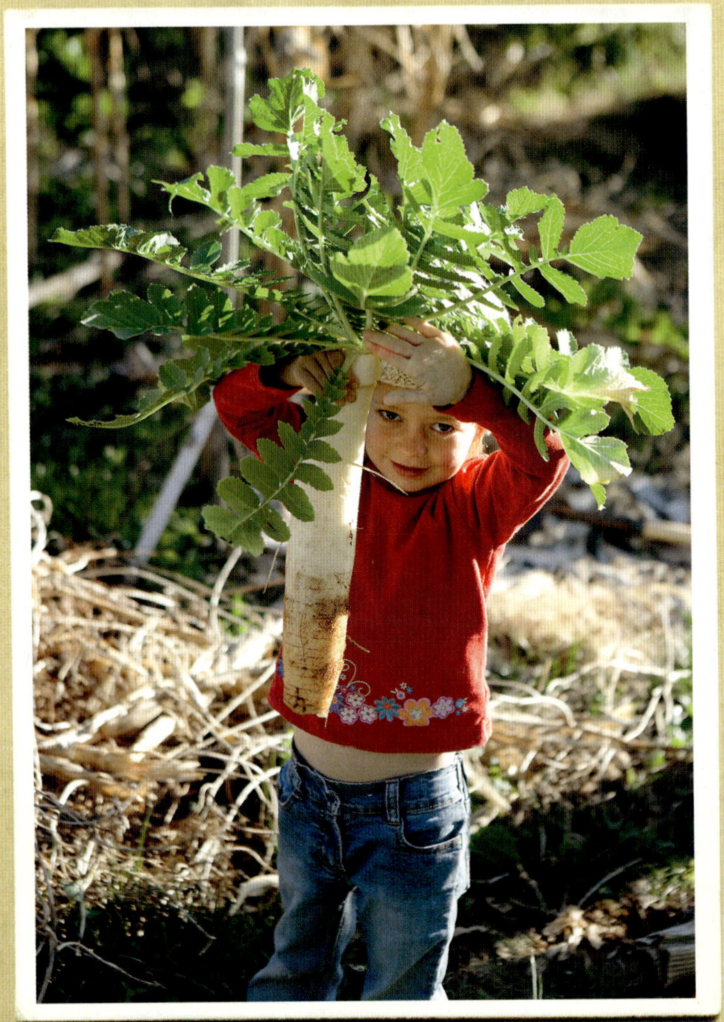
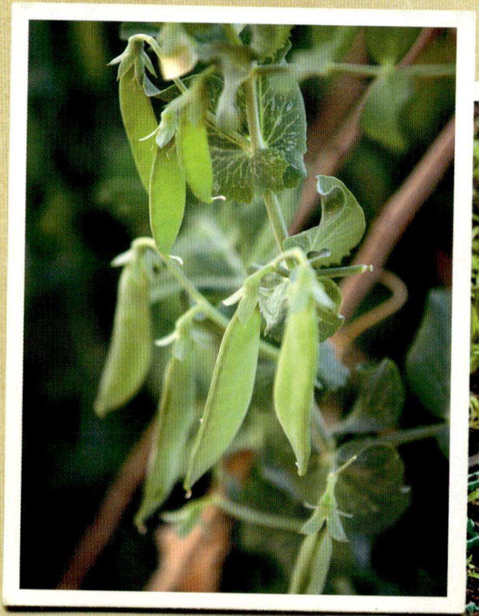
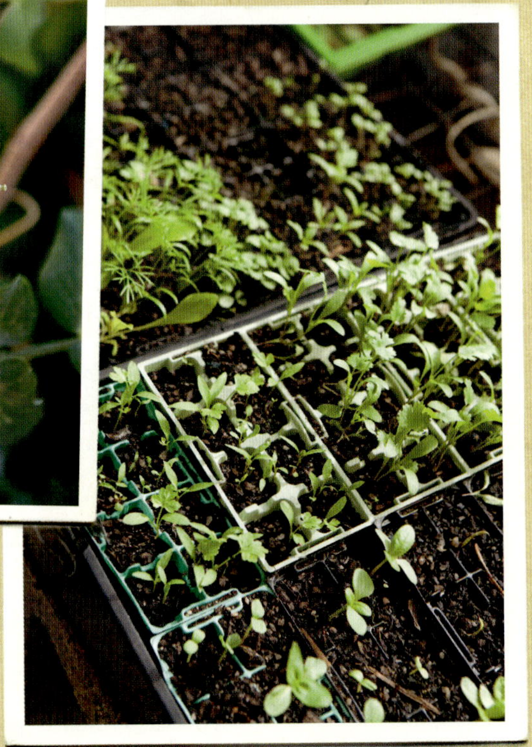

Given the low rainfall across the year (summer storms are periodic and unreliable), vegetables are irrigated year-round in this arid climate, if less frequently during winter. The duration of the summer heat, the high soil temperatures and evaporation rates seem so prohibitive for growing cool-climate food plants but techniques such as choosing appropriate plant varieties, and using compost, mulch and drip irrigation are very effective. In contrast to the easy-going open-endedness of 'Territory Time', growing food in Alice is all about accurate timing. There are only short windows – with April and August being the optimal months – for getting seedlings of annual plants, particularly cool climate vegies, into the ground in summer. Too late . . . and they've 'bolted'! The Brocks grow all the heat-loving annual food plants including tomatoes, eggplant, snake beans and basil. Gardeners can even get two summer crops if they plant, say, one lot of zucchini seedlings in September, and another in January.

Desert soils are unique soils, the result of the weathering of rock formations over millennia and here, within the Todd River System, alluvial deposits over thousands of years more. Given water and compost, the fertility of the red earth is truly astonishing. (It is possible to eat fruit from a passionfruit vine in ten months from planting!) During summer, daily watering of seedlings and tender greens is essential as is mulching the garden beds to conserve soil moisture. Chris uses a mulch of buffel grass (*Cenchrus ciliaris*) – an introduced grass that has invaded central Australia and is thus readily available. Sunburn and wind burn can occur during spring and summer, so some gardeners like to use a 30 per cent shade cloth to give their plants some protection.

Lackadaisical gardeners will miss the food train if they fail to schedule their planting calendar. As soon as the nights get cold in March or April, it's time to plant coriander. Late February is time to plant cauliflower, potatoes and broad beans, while tomatoes can be planted from July (if frosts have passed) to early September. In winter Chris and Helen grow many of their family's favourites: broccoli, peas, carrots, cabbage, spring onions, pak choy, tatsoi, wombok (Chinese cabbage), coriander, rocket, celery, fennel and daikon (a long white Japanese radish). They also grow asparagus in two huge beds (the salt-tolerant perennial is surprisingly happy growing in gardens all over Alice Springs) and the non-hearting Ethiopian cabbage 'Women Meet and Gossip', which grows to 1.5 m tall and has tasty tips and leaves.

The Brocks also have a vegetable plot west of town that Chris shares with friends. This is where they grow some of the vegies that take up a bit more space. There are great long rows of peas and tomatoes, as well as potatoes, eggplants, watermelons, pumpkins and more brassicas. Okra, snake beans and rosella all thrive here, but some of the more exotic food plants include the Turkish leopard melon, the Armenian striped cucumber and the African horned cucumber. The latter, also known as *Kiwano*, is a crazy-looking cucurbit of southern and central Africa that is covered with short spikes or 'horns'. It is eaten either young when green or ripe when yellow/orange and the somewhat tangy flavour is said to be like a cross between a cucumber and a zucchini. Chris has access to such treasures through his role as coordinator of the Alice Springs Seed Savers Network. The group might only number in the dozens of members, but it is a fantastic resource in growing and sharing seeds that are heirlooms or not commercially available. The gardening culture in Alice Springs is very cooperative – sharing makes it fun and easier – not to mention social too.

The family's chooks are a mix of Isa Browns and Australorps – excepting the tame hen 'Buttercup' who is a Buff Orpington/Silkie cross. Buttercup has the run of the whole garden and patiently submits to cuddles from the kids. She is quite spoilt by the abundance of 'clucker tucker' growing in the garden. With the productive garden, the compost bins, the chooks and rabbits (they breed the variety 'British Giant') and their manures, Chris and Helen have established an effective backyard system of nutrient cycling.

Clockwise, from top left: **Fennel; peas!; the kids and Buttercup the chook; Chris raises most of his vegetables from seed; snow peas; a huge daikon.**

THE BROCKS' GARDEN

1. Asparagus
2. Cabbage 'Women meet and gossip', coriander, daikon and parsley
3. Cabbage, broccoli, coriander
4. Daikon and herbs
5. Cabbage 'Women meet and gossip' and fennel
6. Cabbage, radicchio, spring onions
7. Herbs
8. Herbs, rocket, celery
9. Olive tree
10. Mulberry tree
11. Orange
12. Grapefruit
13. Compost bins
14. Chook run
15. Rabbit cages
16. Potting bench
17. Polyhouse
18. Sandpit

Chris's interest in meat rabbits stems from his South Australian childhood: 'They are in my blood, I suppose. I grew up trapping, shooting and eating rabbits and my granddad would also process them for sale in pubs. We were eating rabbit all the time – especially when we went to granddads,' he says. Growing rabbits for meat represents one simple solution to the 'omnivore's dilemma' and in Chris and Helen's book it constitutes ethical eating. In addition, this micro-farm takes up little room, has a quick turnaround (after all, they breed like rabbits) and stocks the freezer with excellent lean meat. Great care has to be taken in harvesting greens from elsewhere for their rabbits so that the feed isn't picked from places wild rabbits have been, as there is a risk of transferring calicivirus. Favourite ways of cooking rabbit include what Helen calls 'grandma recipes' and casseroles using fennel and olives, which they like to serve scattered with a *gremolata* of preserved lemon and coriander.

It is important to both Chris and Helen that their kids grow up understanding where their food comes from. Giles and Lily are free-range kids that will eat every plant food offered to them and happily munch on vegies straight from the ground. Growing your own is about being familiar with traditional foods rather than enduring a situation where 'your whole diet can be manipulated by outside forces', says Chris. Travelling in Italy in 2008 they were excited by the regionalism of Italian cuisine, by the harvesting of mushrooms, chestnuts and beautiful wild greens, and by the intensive nature of the food production. Better to live like the Italian villager and work for your food than to be a passive consumer of industrial agriculture! As a botanist and a bird-observer, Chris is very conscious of the impact of farming and human activity upon fragile ecosystems. Helen is a wildlife biologist and they share a love of camping and wild places. Both like to cook and also to preserve fruit and veg in the form of jams and chutneys (Chris also makes a mean sauerkraut!) The whole family has great fun entering these preserves in the Alice Springs Annual Show.

With Lily attending the Alice Springs Steiner School kindergarten, Helen has become involved with the school's garden. The school has a sustainably designed 'no dig' vegetable garden that was established in 2005. The raised beds are lined with plastic to help combat couch grass and to conserve water and were built by parents, staff and students. The garden is integrated into the school's curriculum, and excess produce is often gifted to parents. The school has also developed a market garden as a fundraiser and a more impressive produce garden would be hard to find anywhere in Australia. Lush, thickly planted strips of coriander, black kale, carrots and broccoli and virescent rows of tatsoi, lettuce, rocket and silverbeet, would have thrilled the great Rudolph Steiner himself (if he wasn't humus). The produce is picked on Saturday mornings and sold through 'Afghan Traders', an organic food shop established by and affiliated with the school, the profits going back into the garden enterprise and school.

> 'Growing your own is about being familiar with traditional foods rather than enduring a situation where "your whole diet can be manipulated by outside forces", says Chris.'

That water equals life is more palpable in the arid inland. A permanent groundwater supply was an understandable preoccupation for the European settlers choosing the site of Alice Springs in 1871. Nineteenth-century ideas of the 'fertile desert' sought to render the 'wilderness' tame-able and surviveable, but a 'just-add-water' mentality and ignorance of the environment saw repeated failures to secure a food supply. Conflict with the Arrernte, floods and fire all took their toll. Today, old date palms form remnant markers of the longed-for oases in this contested landscape. The settlers in the first instance failed to acknowledge just how bio-diverse this semi-arid region in fact was, nor that it was the land of the Arrernte, who had managed the land for thousands of years and held

This page, clockwise from top:
The student vegetable garden at the Alice Springs Steiner School; their experimental crops watched over by an obliging scarecrow; harvesting early on a Saturday morning.
Right: **Volunteers picking vegies in the Steiner School's market garden to send to the local organic store.**

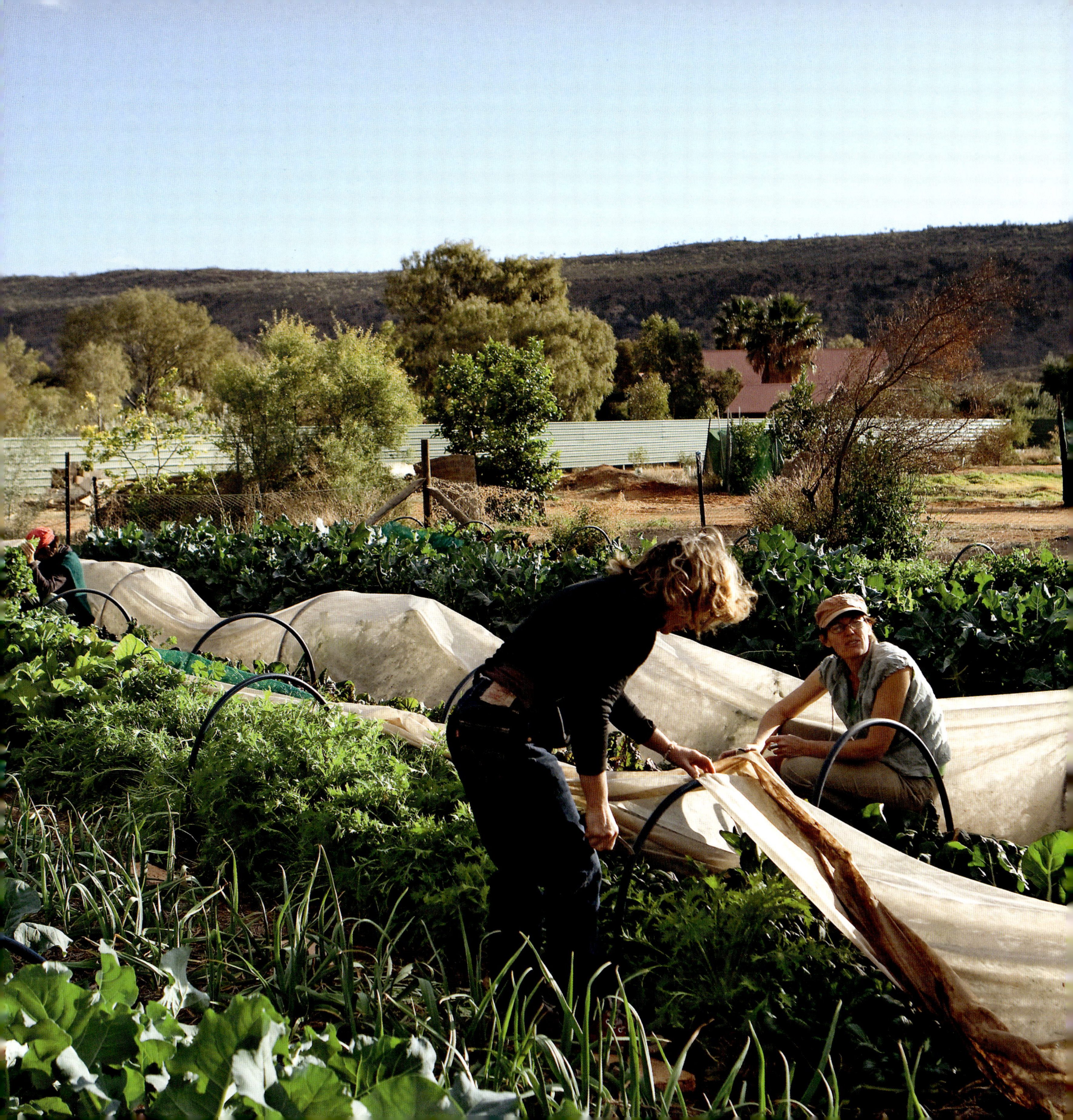

immense knowledge of its plants and animals.

Gardening sustainably in Alice involves using drip irrigation to minimise water loss though evaporation. Over-watering lawns and gardens has had a damaging impact – in some places raising the level of the water table and causing salinisation of the upper soil profile. In addition, pH is an issue: the bore water is slightly alkaline and it is necessary for gardeners to monitor the alkalinity of their soil – Chris has had soil pH rise to 14! Sulphur is required to bring the pH down to a more optimal range for plant growth (6.5–7.5) in which nutrients and minerals are available to plants. Water extraction from the Roe Creek borefield is also taking its toll (Alice Springs has the highest per capita household water use in Australia, at about 1500 L per household per day!) and the ultimate life of this precious resource is hard to put at only a hundred-years plus.

Vegetable gardeners are ever-aware that it is a biotic jungle down below the soil's surface. In Alice Springs another of the gardening challenges is nematodes, also known as eelworms, which are microscopic worms that feed on algae, bacteria, fungi, and plants and animals both alive and dead. Some species are beneficial and innocuous but the nasty 'entomopathogenic nematodes' parasitise the roots of vegetable crops causing the plants to weaken and die. In gardens they prefer warm, moist conditions and sandy soil that Alice vegie gardens supply perfectly. They infest plants and anything that comes in contact with the soil, including equipment, animals and stormwater. Total elimination is not possible but they can be controlled through measures like crop rotation, resting the soil, soil solarisation, and by adding organic matter to increase the biological activity of the soil. The latter encourages beneficial micro-organisms, including predatory nematodes, which can help suppress nematodes and pathogens.

Chris has found that green manure is his best weapon against nematodes. In winter he sows mustard and barley seed, and in summer, sorghum, all of which he grows for 4–6 weeks before digging back into the soil. Growing these crops with their resilient root systems has proven very effective. Mustard also has biofumigant properties – something that farmers and gardeners have been exploiting in their crop rotations to suppress pathogens. Chris has observed that earthworm activity among the dug-in green manure, even after only a few weeks, is enormous – far greater than when compost alone is incorporated into the beds. He has also installed a root barrier around his large mulberry tree – a favoured host of nematodes – to prevent them re-invading the vegetable garden. Caterpillars, slaters, millipedes, aphids, slugs and snails can be more periodic pests: 'The balance of nature is not so balanced in desert regions where plant and animal populations experience boom and bust cycles,'[3] says Chris.

> 'Bushfood is currently in the process of transforming from a niche market into a sustainable industry – hopefully one that supports and is owned and run by Aboriginal communities.'

Take grasshoppers, for example: they can descend suddenly (akin to a biblical locust plague) and in such numbers that all you can do is cover your veg up with netting cages.

The Todd River floodplain on which Alice Springs has developed is a unique ecosystem dominated by river red gums (*Eucalyptus camaldulensis* var. *obtusa*) and Coolabah trees (*Eucalyptus coolabah* subsp. *arida*). Underneath, and within the surrounding vegetation communities, grow a multitude of edible plants: mulga (*Acacia aneura*) and witchetty bush (*A. kempeana*), native lemongrass (*Cymbopogon ambiguus*), ruby saltbush (*Enchylaena tomentosa*) with tiny red fruits and konkleberry (*Carissa lanceolata*). There's bush tomato (*Solanum centrale*) known by the Arrernte people as *katyerre* and quandong (*Santalum acuminatum*) – known as *merne pmerlpe*. Quandong is a shrub to small tree common to inland Australia. The fruit can be eaten fresh or turned into jellies and jams, as well as dried and reconstituted. It is high in vitamin C and the oily kernal inside the hard textured seed is also edible and can even be roasted and turned into quandong flour.

The trees of Alice Springs bear over a period of a month in spring, and it's a race for quandong lovers – Aboriginal and whitefella alike – to get their fill of the beautiful red fruits. Quandong is one of the few native plants to be seriously explored for commercial production. Although it is tough and adapts to a wide range of conditions, its domestication has proven rather difficult. Firstly, it's hard to germinate, and secondly, it is partially parasitic and requires a host plant to sustain it. Bushfood is currently in the process of transforming from a niche market into a sustainable industry – hopefully one that supports and is owned and run by Aboriginal communities. There is also a developing Aboriginal horticulture industry in Alice Springs driven by local and state-level Aboriginal organisations and Central Australian communities themselves. They are seeking to establish commercial crops like table grapes, citrus, mangoes, asparagus and dates on Aboriginal land, providing communities with income and jobs.

Trial and error are obviously integral to gardening success in Alice Springs, as is dedication, and despite the numerous challenges, the Brock family is succeeding where many might think it's all too hard. They've adapted their gardening methods to the climate and put their philosophy into action. Working toward a level of self-sufficiency is a pleasure rather than a millstone around this modern family's neck. Chris and Helen ignore the tyranny of distance to grow beautiful, delicious produce, and are quiet practitioners of a deep conviction that we owe it to ourselves and to our kids to put good food on the table.

Top: **Lily with a rabbit kitten.**
Below: **Citrus thrive in Alice Springs.**

THE CONMEL COTTAGE KITCHEN GARDEN

Size	36.5 × 15.5 m (565.75 m^2)
Climate	Temperate (mild summer)
Soil	Heavy loam over clay
Average annual rainfall	600 mm
Frost	Occasional
Water source	Mains water
Irrigation method	Spray and drip irrigation and hand-watering
Compost and fertiliser	Composted food scraps and plant material, sheep and cow manure, pelletised chicken manure, blood and bone
Mulch	Pea straw
Biggest challenges	Sparrows and blackbirds
Favourite herb	Basil
Favourite food plant	Broccoli 'Romanesco'

CHAPTER 9
CONMEL COTTAGE
A Productive Garden in the Tamar Valley

Not many vegetable gardens have as beautiful a view as the one from the kitchen garden of Geraldine and Bret Flood. Below Conmel Cottage – Bret and Geraldine's home of over thirty years – meanders the Tamar River, wide and shining in the fertile Tamar Valley. Here lies the riverside village of Rosevears – originally established as a ship-building port and the point from which John Batman departed aboard the *Rebecca* in 1835 to cross Bass Strait and ultimately settle Melbourne. The Floods' 2.4-ha (6-acre) property is surrounded in all other directions by vineyards (the famous Ninth Island is just up the road); it is one very productive neighbourhood a mere twenty minutes from Launceston. The kitchen garden that the Floods have created here is the product of a wonderful partnership of thirty-six years, and now they are both retired, Bret and Geraldine are able to devote even more time to gardening, cooking and the general art of living well.

'They can be quite picturesque,' says Bret of vegetable gardens in general, sounding somewhat surprised that something so functional can be also pretty, and yet his own vegie patch is no exception. As Joy Larkcom, the undisputed guru of creative vegetable gardening says: 'Why choose between food or frivolity when the answer could be to have both?'[1] The Floods agree that the productive garden is Bret's domain; the ornamental garden the providence of Geraldine, a rose enthusiast. But it was Geraldine who, after a trip to England over a decade ago, during which she visited beautiful kitchen gardens such as the restored Victorian walled garden at West Dean in Sussex, was 'bitten by the bug'. She returned home eager to extend and improve their own vegetable garden. Their horse paddock fence was subsequently pushed outwards up the hill on three separate occasions.

Entering the hillside kitchen garden through a timber gate is to arrive in a world of order and fertility. A 32-m-long gravelled path bisects the space, and a central rose arbour divides the garden in the opposite direction. Within a perimeter hedge of privet, fifteen rectangular garden beds provide ample room for a mosaic of vegetables. In each of two beds to the rear of the main garden the Floods have espaliered a fruit tree: a 'Beurre Bosc' pear and a 'Bramley's Seedling' apple – regarded as the world's best cooking apple. Trained in the classic *formes fruitières* or espalier pattern of four horizontal tiered cordons, the trees' thick cordons or lateral branches are festooned with fruit in late summer like a couple of multi-armed tree goddesses. Aromatics and vegies intermingle between internal hedges of Japanese box and French lavender; an exuberant riot of flower and foliage colours and textures spill from within the formal edges.

Roses have asserted their presence even in the vegie garden – it is a pleasure garden too, after all, and we shouldn't forget how important fragrance is. A hedge of *Rosa* 'Paul Ricault' is a sight to behold in November, covered entirely with scented, fat blowsy cerise blooms. Over the central arbour grows 'Pinkie', 'Cloth of Gold', and individual arches support 'Apricot Nectar', 'Mary Rose', 'Alchemist' and the thorny evergreen 'Laevigata' or 'Cherokee' rose. Not only do roses do well here, the entire *Rosaceae* family thrives in Tasmania: the weedy genera – blackberries and hawthorn – flourish, as do the domesticated ones of strawberries and cherries, but most climate-suited to Tasmania of all the family is the apple. It is no surprise that most of the deciduous fruits commercially grown in the world today are from the *Rosaceae* family – humanity has such a collective sweet tooth. Tasmania was once known as the 'Apple Isle' by virtue of being the world's biggest apple producer during the early half of the twentieth century. The apple, as Michael Pollan describes so beautifully in *The Botany of Desire*, was a pioneer plant of colonial domestication, which represented the familiar, a reminder of the British Isles, as well as bearing fruit that could be stored or made into alcohol. The Tasmanian climate was perfect – it had the crucial long winter chill factor allowing for over a thousand hours below a temperature of 7°C – in Van Diemen's Land the settlers had found a new Eden for apples.[2]

In its peak in the 1930s, Tasmania was producing about six million bushels of apples a year and apple orchards covered 11,000 hectares (27 170 acres). Despite the decline of the apple industry from the 1960s, the landscape remains marked by

The Tamar River glitters behind the vegetables and herbs in Conmel Cottage's kitchen garden during high summer

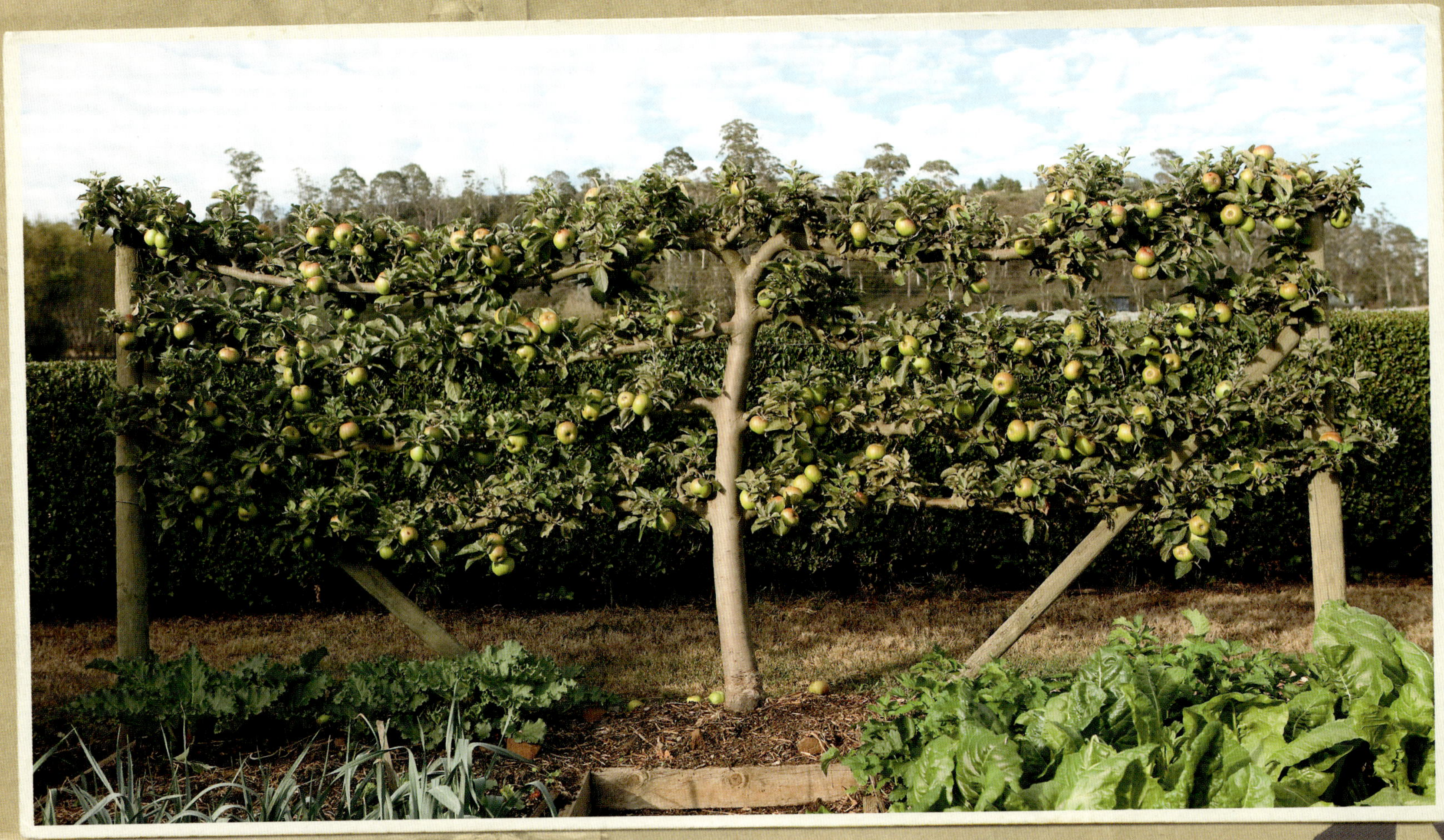

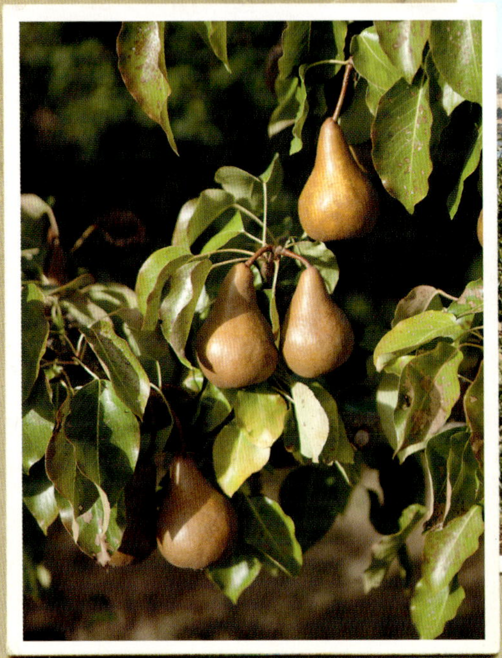

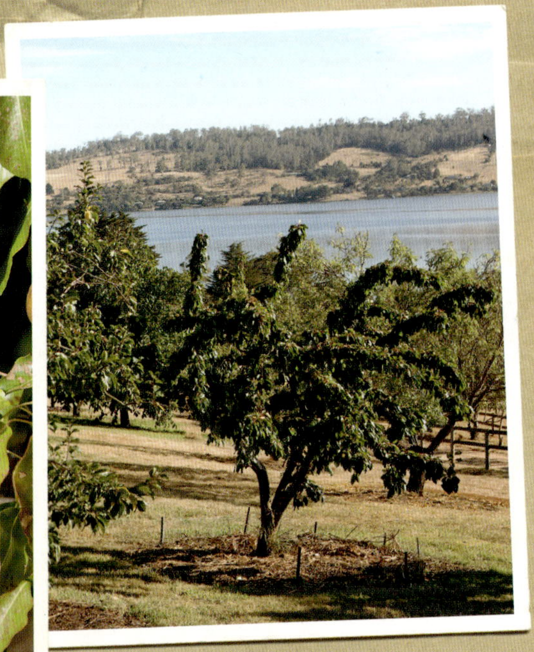

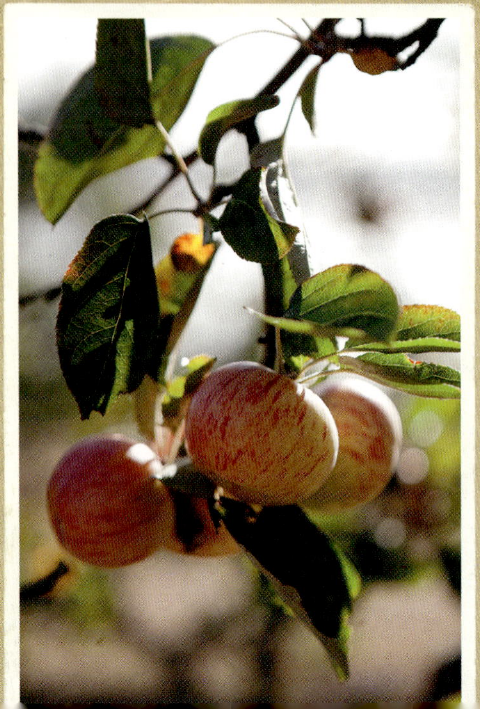

it – the ubiquitous timber apple packing sheds still survive in many small towns. Each apple packing case was made from native timber and on the side of each was pasted a bold and colourful label that identified the individual grower. These labels are lasting and charming examples of industrial folk are and have been preserved by the likes of the Huon Valley Apple & Heritage Museum in Grove. South of Hobart at Woodbridge he Magnus family's nursery grows more than 300 varieties of apple (the amazing figure of 7500 apple cultivars in existence worldwide has been put forward by a number of scholars), most of which are heirloom apples. These varieties fulfilled different purposes – storing, fresh eating, dessert, cooking and cider-making.

The Magnuses cultivate such treasures as the spicy-flavoured 'Catshead' apple with the most enormous fruit, which is an unusual old English cooking apple, and very long and narrow in shape. Tasmania has also bred its own hybrids such as the 'Huonville Crab', which is probably a hybrid between a crab and a cultivated apple. The Magnuses found an old tree growing in Huonville, 'weighed down each year by massive crops of large deep purple crabs which have deep red flesh right to the core'. Not only is the edible fruit the size of a plum, it can also be used for cider. Nursery-owners Karen and Peter Cooper from Mole Creek have recently rediscovered the 'Lemon Pippin' in Tasmania, a multipurpose apple that originated in Europe around 1700, but hadn't been seen in Tassie for decades. It has a large fleshy elongation covering the stalk, which gives it a lemon-like appearance. Its skin is pale yellow, tinged with green, changing to a lemon yellow as it matures, speckled with russet spots.

Clockwise, from top: **A 'Bramley's Seedling' apple is a perfectly espaliered living sculpture; apple 'Cox's Orange Pippin'; looking north over the orchard; pear 'Beurre Bosc'.**

Geraldine and Bret grow a number of heritage apple varieties in their garden including 'Gravenstein' (from Europe in the 1600s), 'Bramley's Seedling' (1809), 'Waltham Abbey Seedling' (1810) and the dessert apple 'Cox's Orange Pippin' (1825). They also like 'newer' varieties like the 'Australian apple', the 'Granny Smith', which came from a seedling found in the Sydney garden of Mrs Thomas Smith around 1860 (an eating apple that Geraldine also uses for cooking because they hold their shape so well). In their orchard on a slope overlooking the Tamar River they have planted nectarines, feijoas, a persimmon, the green gage plum and the prune plum *D'Agen*, with its ovoid fruit as purple-black as night. The orchard is obviously paradise for the Flood's Silver Grey Dorking chooks that enjoy ranging free under the trees.

Nearly everything in the garden is grown from seed by Bret except for the odd punnet of celery or eggplant. He buys his seeds from the Tasmanian seed business, the Lost Seed Company, that specialises in non-hybrid, open-pollinated and heritage vegetable seeds. He saves his own seed of parsnips, peas and beans, however, from year to year. Most seed is sown in large trays in the shadehouse, using bits of old timber as dividers between different plants or varieties. He uses the same bits of silvered hardwood as plant labels, writing in permanent felt marker the vegetable name, sowing date and sometimes any special fertiliser he may have applied before pushing them into the ground. These labels prove a great aid to remembering and evaluating his successes and failures. In the poly-tunnel an electric waterbed heater is used under seedling trays to start seeds as early as July and August for planting into the garden in summer. Sited at the north-west end of the kitchen garden, with a small berry cage containing raspberries and thornless blackberries in between, the shadehouse and poly-tunnel are indoor–outdoor places in which Bret spends many happy hours.

Launceston gets perhaps only half-a-dozen frosts a year, with minimum temperatures of −3° to −4°C. Mild summers normally characterise the climate, but they have been hotter lately – as to whether that's due to a weather cycle or the effect

THE CONMEL COTTAGE GARDEN

1. Tomatoes, capsicum, chilli and basil
2. Herbs, roses
3. Globe artichokes, scarlet runner bean
4. Zucchini, silverbeet and celery with espaliered 'Bramley's Seedling' apple tree
5. Leeks, cucumber and rhubarb
6. Herbs, roses and French lavender
7. Herbs, roses and French lavender
8. Corn
9. Kale and fallow bed with espaliered 'Buerre Bosc' pear tree
10. Bush beans
11. Fallow bed
12. Hedge of Rosa 'Paul Ricault'
13. Potted bay tree
14. Asparagus and silverbeet
15. Carrots, zucchini, climbing beans
16. Strawberries
17. Corn and tomatoes
18. Herbs and roses
19. Rose arbour
20. Privet hedge
21. Shade house
22. Berry cage

of a man-made crisis, Bret is not sure. Good 'normal' annual rainfall at Rosevears is around 600 mm (23.6 inches) but in recent years they have received more like 500 mm (20 inches). Living here, Bret and Geraldine realise just how precious a clean environment is, in particular the health of the rivers that supply their drinking water and water for their garden. The Tamar River is very tidal, more like a salty estuary in the upper reaches at Rosevears, and it is the mighty North and South Esk rivers that supply Tasmanians in the north their drinking and gardening water. At Conmel Cottage an old-fashioned overhead sprinkler waters parts of the kitchen garden (its 'thwack-thwack' sound surely inducing great nostalgia in those gardeners from areas of water restrictions), but Bret prefers to hand-water the remaining areas in the evening. Soaker hoses are used in the raspberry cage and on the trees in the orchard. A revitalising sense of lushness is created by the proximity of the river and the abundance of plants both edible and ornamental.

The vegetable garden at Conmel Cottage receives exceptionally regular love. Bret practices organic gardening 'as much as I can', excepting snail pellets for those pesky gastropods, and glyphosate herbicide on weeds in the gravel paths. He uses pyrethrum for insect control and Dipel, the commercial product of *Bacillus thunbergiana*, for white cabbage moth caterpillars on the brassicas. For some reason, says Bret, the moths don't seem to lay their eggs on the curly kale and the plants form tall blemish-free bushes. (Geraldine likes to steam curly kale's sweet new growth and dress the leaves with lemon before serving.) In Tasmania, as in so many parts of the rest of Australia, the other major pests are introduced European ones: blackbirds, sparrows and rabbits. Sparrows are a menace, particularly with seedlings and strawberries, so the ever-inventive Bret uses wire chook-mesh covered with the smaller-aperture black bird netting to make little bird-proof tunnels to cover seeds like carrots, sown direct into the beds. To ensure their soil remains at peak fertility they use composted 'MooPoo', sheep poo (they'll use over a hundred bags a year), 'Rooster Booster', and blood and bone (which they buy in bulk). Bret swears by potash for strawberries, tomatoes and peas. Pea and wheat straw are used as mulch in this kitchen garden, whereas other local gardeners might use pyrethrum and poppy trash as mulch – the by-products of the local commercial industries.

> 'There is room among the productive plants for the non-productive: "It doesn't have to be totally useful to be in my garden, it can have a beautiful name or be pretty," she declares.'

Bret grows the strawberry variety 'Red Gauntlet' and as it doesn't keep very well he recommends they be eaten as soon as they are ripe, preferably with cream! To protect the berries from the birds, he has constructed four lightweight cages from 16-mm electrical conduit with standard poly-pipe joiners and covered with black bird netting. He doesn't use the plasticulture method of growing strawberries under black plastic, but he has adopted an innovative method of cleaning up the strawberry plants by using a whipper snipper to leave the crowns bald and ready for winter. Bret has many such tricks; his secret to perfect carrots is not to over-thin them, he reckons, as a bit of competition in his very fertile soil seems to help keep them nice and small and straight.

The zucchini 'Costata Romanesco' with a light-green skin and prominent ridges is an unusual and beautiful vegetable of the summer garden. It doesn't suffer from mildew as much as the common varieties such as 'Black Jack' and Bret and Gerry think its creamy coloured flesh has a superior taste and texture. The bell and banana sweet peppers that Bret has grown from seed are planted with common, lemon, purple and Thai basils. (Gerry recommends using the tiny leaves of lemon basil in fruit salad.) Greens are very important in their daily meals: mizuna and rocket add zest to salads of butter crunch, brown mignonette and cos lettuce, and there is also sorrel, silverbeet, perpetual spinach (a type of silverbeet). They

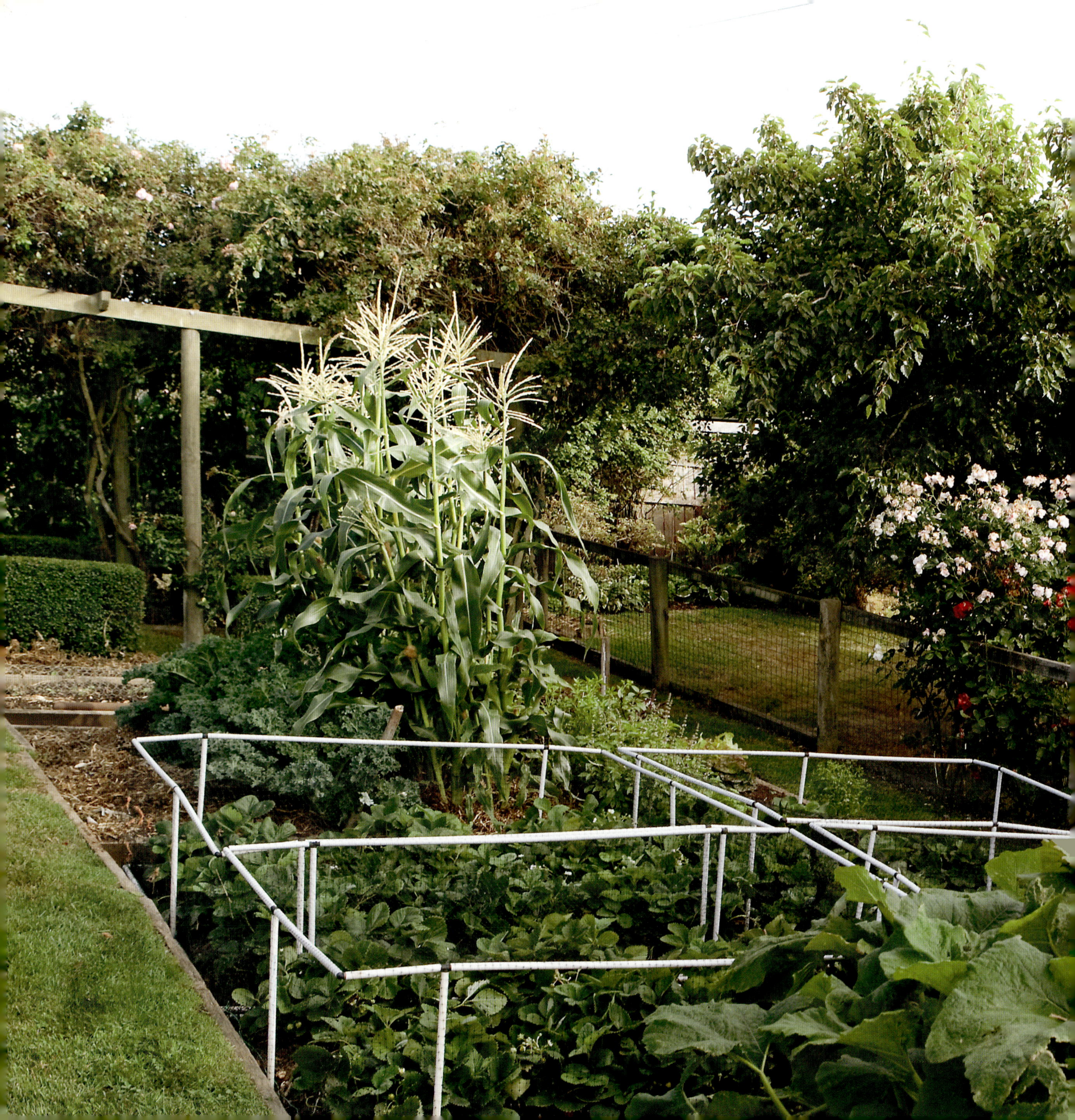

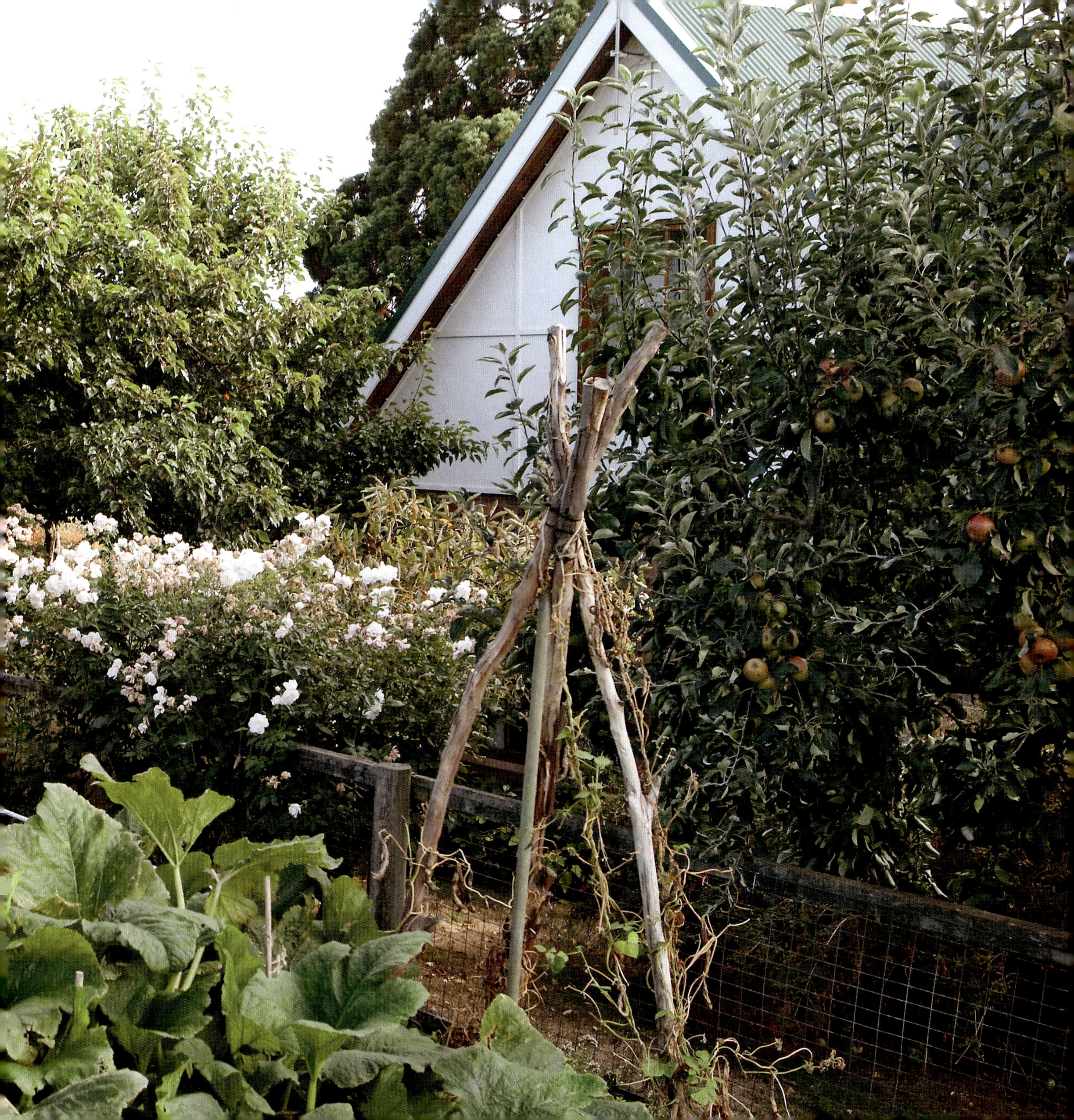

combine the coloured lettuces, baby sorrel and baby spinach with herbs to make their own mesclun mix. Many olde-worlde herbs intermingle with the common sage, thyme and rosemary and in between the vegetables: sweet cicely, lovage, hyssop, wall germander, winter savory and betony – *Stachys officinalis*. Geraldine loves elecampane 'because it has a beautiful name' – in her garden there is room among the productive plants for the non-productive: 'It doesn't have to be totally useful to be in my garden, it can have a beautiful name or be pretty,' she declares.

Due to the short growing season, tomatoes are a summer event that must be planned months in advance. Here, near Launceston, gardeners often don't get tomatoes until mid-February and the plants have been started back in August. Bret has most success with 'Mortgage Lifter', which he thinks tastes fabulous and has beautiful flesh, 'Brandywine' is 'tomato heaven' and the cherry tomato 'Sweet Bite' is a prolific fruiter. Eggplants cannot be planted out into the open garden until December and melons are a complete and utter gamble. Given the frosts, Bret is understandably very proud of his Tahitian lime – which by rights should not be nearly so happy here in Tassie; certainly not bearing fruit the size of lemons like his is doing. His tree just goes to show what creating the right microclimate can accomplish.

The Floods both enjoy their brasiccas and grow the broccoli varieties 'Romanesco', 'Summer Green' and 'Purple Sprouting', as well as mini cauliflowers, swedes and curly kale. Geraldine loves purple cabbages such as the variety 'Red Drumhead' because they are so ornamental: 'Their colours are stunning,' she says. She describes the combination of slate-grey leeks with the purple and yellow Johnny jump-ups growing through them as a 'glorious' addition to the kitchen garden. November is a quiet time in the garden – there are leeks, cabbages and the last of the carrots – as Bret waits for the soil to warm up.

There is plenty to eat through the winter, though, as Bret and Gerry stock their kitchen cupboards full of homemade jams, marmalades and preserves, and their freezer fills with their berries and mulberries to use in cakes and desserts. Bottling seems to be an art less forgotten down south, with many Tasmanian produce gardeners possessing Fowlers Vacola units they actually use. Bret and Gerry are no exception, as they preserve over 200 bottles of fruit a year. 'Putting up' some of a garden's harvest is a traditional practice that tends to become popular all over again at times of economic hardship when people activate the waste-not-want-not larder-stocking 'recession mindset' habits of their parents or grandparents.

Like the Floods, fellow produce gardener and Tamar Valley local (as well as ex-host of ABC1's *Gardening Australia* program) Peter Cundall believes that people *can* survive out of their own gardens. According to Cundall, feeding ourselves is an act of independence and an expression of self-reliance, one that can prove helpful, if not critical, in surviving uncertain financial times. For others, preserving is simply the only way of living independently of the supermarket and getting true flavour from out-of-season fruit and veg. Many local food growers swear by the book *A Year in a Bottle* by Hobart cook and author Sally Wise for bottling inspiration. Such bottling enthusiasts would understand how deeply satisfying and pleasurable popping the top off one of Bret and Gerry's beautiful jars is – far more so than opening a bought tin of pears!

Both the kitchen garden at Conmel Cottage and the Floods' food-growing passion are a wonder to behold. Together Bret and Gerry have created a place where beauty and bounty meet, a working garden that seduces the eye and palate. Not only is it a living tapestry of seed-grown and diverse food plants, its management conveys an intimate understanding of intensive land use and of the climate here – the result of thirty years of loving the one small piece of rural Tasmania.

Pages 110-111: **The Tasmanian climate suits plants of the Rosaceae family perfectly — including strawberries, apples, pears and roses.**
Clockwise, from right: **Tomato 'Purple Russian'; strawberry 'Gauntlet'; Geraldine's beautiful preserves; the rose arbor bisects the kitchen garden; delicious bounty headed for the kitchen.**
Centre: **Bret and Geraldine are passionate about their piece of rural Tasmania.**

GAY BILSON'S KITCHEN GARDEN

Size	400 m²
Climate	Temperate (warm summer, moderately dry winter)
Soil	Sandy, poor
Average annual rainfall	550 mm
Frost	Rare
Water source	Tank, mains water
Irrigation method	Spray and drip irrigation, hand-watering
Compost and fertiliser	Bought and homemade compost, chicken manure
Mulch	Pea and lucerne straw
Biggest challenges	The poor soil and rabbits
Favourite herb	Coriander and curry leaf
Favourite food plant	Eggplant, broad beans and quince

CHAPTER 10
LA HUERTA
Gay Bilson's Country Kitchen Garden

The township of McLaren Flat is where the Adelaide Hills come down to meet the vales, where sharp cliffs of the Fleurieu Peninsula crumble towards the sea like the golden Catalan coastlines in Dali's surrealist paintings. The early-summer rural landscape is all blonde grass, bleached buff and copper and already tinder-dry, chequered by green-black patches of vineyards, and framed by the blue waters of the Gulf of St Vincent and Southern Ocean beyond. This is the *terra firma* into which cook, ex-restaurateur and writer Gay Bilson has chosen to transplant herself. After eighteen years running the Berowra Waters Inn on the Hawkesbury River near Sydney (a restaurant held to be among Australia's best), Gay has few regrets about leaving the brouhaha of the restaurant world behind. She has chosen instead to pursue a life both more peaceful and solitary in the McLaren Vale in which 'everything is DIY' and nourished by much cooking, reading, writing and gardening. Gay was a 'late starter' who came to gardening for the first time in her mid-fifties and since then has been creating an edible garden on the sandy hillside around her mudbrick house. To her pleasure, Gay has found that gardening has added a particular and unexpected type of mindfulness to her daily rituals of living.

Before she even knew whether gardening was going to be for her Gay decided to grow only plants that she could eat – she *had* moved to the country after all. 'I didn't know whether I'd enjoy gardening or not,'[1] she says, but has since decided that gardening, like reading, 'is one of the great activities'. Although she claims not to be a *real* gardener, Gay displays all the attributes of one: a gardener's optimism, and conversely, the anxiety about lack of rain and the condition of her soil, the hatred of rabbits, compulsive seed-saving and long interludes staring out the window at her fruit trees. Gay named her property La Huerta (Spanish for orchard) and has proceeded to plant fruit trees in dedication to individual good friends. On the question of why make a productive garden: Well, to eat of course, but specifically to eat well and seasonally. For Gay, the farmer and author Wendell Berry's 'notion of the "extensive pleasure" of growing to eat is also pivotal'. In growing her own raw ingredients – herbs, fruit and vegetables – the transition from garden to kitchen couldn't be more immediate and their 'processing' prior to their culinary transformation generally consists of nothing more than a quick wash. Says Gay: 'Growing food has certainly taught me the real meaning of "fresh". I take it for granted now but in the beginning I was constantly amazed at how long something picked from one's garden kept its life as opposed to produce in shops.' Take Gay's favourite herbs coriander and curry leaf (*Murraya koenigii*), for example, (vital to the Chinese and Indian food she loves to cook) – no shop-bought coriander lasts more than a day or so in the fridge before it wilts (only to become slimy), and try buying fresh curry leaf in the Willunga supermarket!

Gertrude Stein once wrote that 'A vegetable garden in the beginning looks so promising and then after all little by little it grows nothing but vegetables, nothing, nothing but vegetables.' But this is never true of a kitchen garden where all manner of herbs, fruit and flowers coexist with the veg. In four terraced garden beds on the hillside adjoining her east-facing verandah, Gay cultivates both the flavourful and the 'nutritionally necessary'. Wild rocket, Vietnamese mint, coriander, garlic and borage flourish at the base of a row of maturing plants of 'Oxheart' tomatoes. In the other vegetable bed she has planted sorrel, leeks, Lebanese eggplants, chillies and land cress. Gay has fondness for edibles that readily self-sow like land cress (*Barbarea vulgaris*), which is even more hot and peppery than her wild rocket (the fine divided-leaf form). French sorrel (*Rumex scutantus*) is another one of those weedy-looking edibles that look after themselves, seeding wherever it likes unless deadheaded. A perennial herb that is related to dock, sorrel's lemony chlorophyll sourness (due to its high level of ascorbic acid) make it a lovely addition to scrambled eggs or the basis of an intense and wonderful soup.

Gay adores broad beans (if you have to double shell them, they're too old, she maintains), so she will find a new spot every winter to sow a good-sized patch. Herbs, including rosemary, oregano, a bay tree, Kaffir lime and lemongrass are spread among the fruit trees and garden beds. Even the roses are

The growing/dying cycle of the kitchen garden.
Spent peas and the feathery umbels of seeding dill
behind new growth of globe artichokes and leeks

LA HUERTA

1	Stone wall and proposed pizza oven	8	Kaffir lime	16	Pêche de vigne
2	Quinces (north to south): 'Orange', 'Smyrna', 'Pineapple', 'Van Deman', 'Portugal'	9	Pomegranate 'Azerbaijan'	17	English mulberry
		10	Peach	18	Leeks and globe artichokes
3	Capers, thyme and rugosa roses	11	Bay tree	19	Sorrel, peas, eggplant, bird's eye and jalapeno chillies, capsicums, land cress and lettuce
4	Espaliered quinces (east to west): 'Apple shaped', 'Champion', 'De Bourgeaut'	12	Passionfruit		
		13	Medlar	20	Potted herbs, including curry leaf, and vegetables
5	Fig	14	Trellised apples with table grape at south end		
6	Pomegranate			21	'Oxheart' tomatoes, leeks, wild rocket, coriander and Vietnamese mint
7	Bay hedge	15	Lemon	22	Rosemary, dill and other herbs

edible in Gay's garden – she has planted the white and single-flowered *Rosa rugosa* 'Alba' because their large red-orange hips make beautiful jelly. Gay's gardening style is generally low-interventionist, although she protects young fruit trees from the rabbits using wire guards and nets the apples and grapevine, peach and apricot or else 'the rosellas would take most of the crops'. Growing vegetables and herbs in pots has proven a good way of outsmarting the varmints and Gay has tomatoes, eggplants, strawberries and a curry leaf plant thriving in pots along her verandah.

Although she had intended to grow only edible plants, Gay has also nurtured the existing native plants and grown new trees and shrubs from seed to add to the plantings around the perimeter of her land. The bird life attracted to this habitat gives her great pleasure: 'Superb fairy wrens, the odd, tiny mistletoe bird, grey fantails, willy wagtails, sometimes red-browed finches' but they also make her cranky 'when they steal mulch and scratch up any worm that by some miracle turns up here'. Building up her 'sandpit' of a site has been a huge task. 'I slowly learned how ridiculously sandy the soil is and instead of bringing in huge amounts of good soil and organic matter and starting by making proper beds, I stumbled along and got by by adding more compost as I went in the beds in which I was growing food. All the while the sandy stuff dribbled out of the imperfect beds.' She now says, 'Had I known soil mattered so much when I liked this property and house, I may have changed my mind.'

Along with the major problem of the soil, drought, water restrictions, regular summer heatwaves with temperatures into the forties and multitudes of plant-eating insects (possibly taking refuge from all the pest management in the surrounding vineyards) constitute Gay's major gardening challenges. Gay claims to be an 'inexpert' gardener but in the process of caring for this land she has acquired many new skills as well as knowledge about cultivating native and edible plants. She points out that she also gardens with very little money – she expends her own labour and grows plants from seed and makes compost with which to feed them. Gardening has taught her patience, says Gay, and 'also a sense of responsibility to the plants'. It makes her 'think a lot about whether it is best to nurture the plants that grow well by themselves or pay more attention to those which are doing poorly'.

> **' Gardening has taught her patience, says Gay, and "also a sense of responsibility to the plants".'**

Growing amid carpets of thyme in the warm arms of a stacked-stone wall are large specimens of the caper plant. The caper (*Capparis spinosa*) is a spiny perennial native to the regions surrounding the Mediterranean Sea, where it is found growing wild on hillsides, cliffs, old walls and on rocky coastsides. The plant is best known for its edible flower bud – where would *puttanesca* or tartare sauce be without the caper's distinctive piquant flavour? The immature buds are olive green and usually harvested when they're about the size of a corn kernel and either pickled in salt, or a salt and vinegar solution. In Sicilian and southern Italian cooking, generally the smaller the better when it comes to capers, with those up to 7 mm in size being the most expensive. The buds are followed by gorgeous flowers with white crepe petals and a bunch of long pink stamens. Gay's plants are thriving thanks to her 'impossibly sandy soil' and the long hot days of the McLaren Vale's Mediterranean climate. Perhaps the reason the rabbits leave the plants alone is because capers contain glucocapparin, a defence compound also found in members of the Brassica family and horseradish?

A lemon tree, pomegranates, fig, mulberries and four apple trees planted by the previous owner and trained to a 'Y-trellis' system constitute a portion of Gay's orchard at La Huerta. The apples comprise a divided canopy trained to three horizontal wires – the idea is that the open vase shape and the precise angle of the branches will improve yield and fruit size. Gay planted a peach kernel she was given of a tree that supposedly bears fruit with carmine-coloured flesh, but the sapling is yet to reveal whether it really is the variety 'Black Boy' or the famous *pêche de vigne* (peach of the grapevine). The fruit of 'Black Boy' has furry red-grey skin and the streaky red flesh is richly perfumed and intensely sweet.

In old farm gardens or derelict homesteads with but a single chimney still standing you will likely find gnarled and lichen-encrusted fruit trees. More often than not these will be fruits such as quince, Japanese quince, medlar, loquat, pear, hawthorn, apple and crabapple and their inedible cousins firethorn, cotoneaster and photinia. These edible pomes (a type of accessory fruit where the core constitutes the true fruit) belong to the apple subfamily Maloideae and something in their genetic makeup makes them incredibly hardy, able to survive frost and heat and the low rainfall of temperate Australia. It is their very old-fashioned nature that appeals to Gay; these pome fruits, and their transformation in the kitchen into sweet treats like crumbles, tarts, cakes and jam, or jellies to serve with roast meat, represent something essentially generous. Perhaps they evoke a past in which we imagine people had *time*. Time for baking and preserving, time for visiting and afternoon teas. Perhaps it's a longing for the visits to country cousins we never had, for the grandmother in the Country Women's Association, for an age before computers and takeaway – nostalgia is edible, after all.

The medlar (*Mespilus germanica*) is one of the old-fashioned fruits that Gay loves and she has planted one so she can make jelly from its odd brown pomes. It is an ancient and 'unimproved' species that appears to have entirely escaped the breeding that apples have undergone over hundreds of years (if not a thousand-odd), the cultivation that Michael Pollan calls humankind's 'Dionysian knack – for marrying the wildest fruits of nature to the various desires of culture.'[2] The medlar is edible only when the fruit is 'bletted' – meaning it is overripe and perfumey and on its way to the consistency of grainy jam. Medlars, therefore, aren't a mainstream fruit (the same can be said of persimmons) – the Australian market typically demands crisp and bland vegies (representing healthful and fresh) that have been refrigerated to death, while the extra-ripe, flavoursome and runny are regarded as suspiciously abject. Putrefaction is not permitted in the modern kitchen and the supermarket, although it's fine in the compost bin! As Adam Leith Gollner writes in *The Fruit Hunters*: 'Nature is a feedback loop, from putrefaction to perfection and back again.'[3]

Like the medlar, the quince is a member of the Maloideae subfamily. *Cydonia oblonga* is the queen of fruits and is now the only member of the genus *Cydonia* (the three shrubby quinces – including the one known as the Japanese quince or japonica – previously included in the genus are now classified in *Chaenomeles*). But they are not lonely, these quince trees of Gay's, as she has planted nine varieties of them in her garden. You cannot have too much of a good thing when it comes to quinces! There are about sixteen quince varieties generally available in Australia and Gay grows 'Portugal', 'De Vranja' (early- to mid-season varieties); 'Apple Shaped', 'Champion', 'Orange' and 'Smyrna' (mid-season); 'Fuller's', 'Pineapple', 'De Bourgeaut' (mid–late); and 'Van Deman' (very late). Gay purchased her plants bare-rooted from Keith Robertson at Creswick in Victoria, as he specialises in heritage pear and quince varieties.

Three quince trees have been given some training by Gay's friend Ann, who has espaliered them against the verandah posts – soon they will cast knobbly quince-shaped shadows on the decking. Growing multiple quince varieties like Gay does helps improve fertilisation (although the trees are self-fertile) and having a range of varieties with differing maturity dates can extend the harvesting period over a period of two

Clockwise, from top left: **Caper plants and thyme nestle behind a stone wall; pomegranates have both ornamental flowers and fruit; Gay's vegetable terraces are located right next to her house; furry developing quince fruit; land cress is an enthusiastic self-seeder; the beautiful stamens of the caper flower; Gay and her potted herbs and veg.**
Centre: **Curry leaves.**

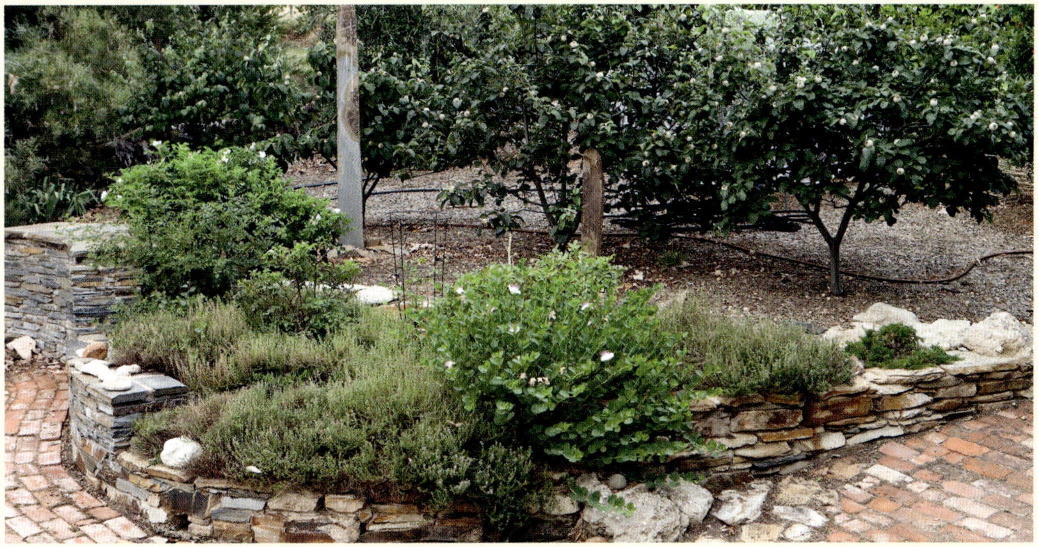
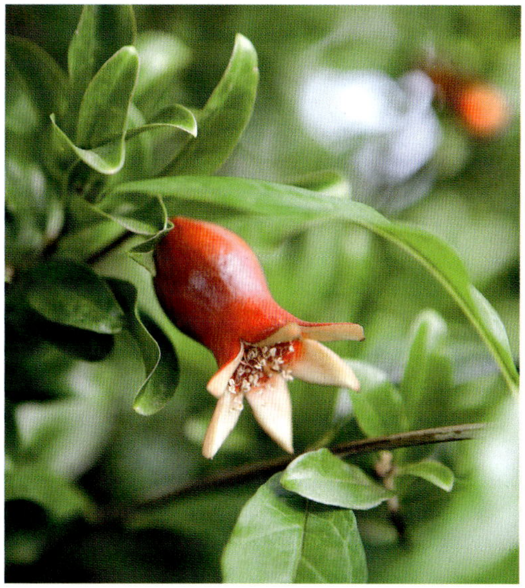
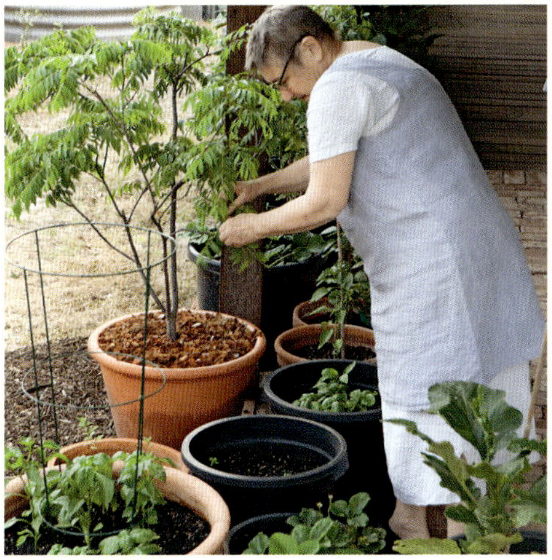
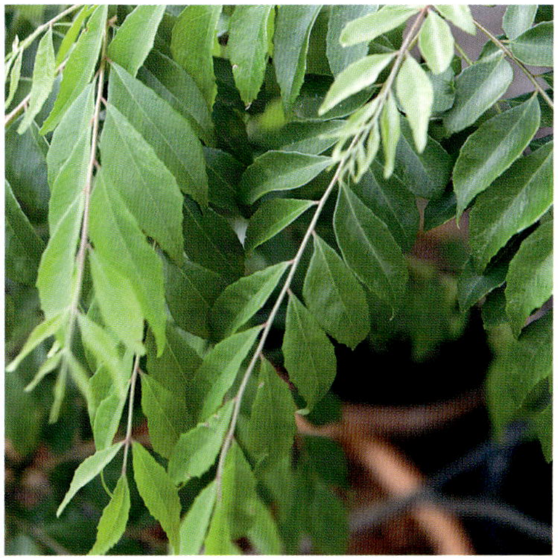
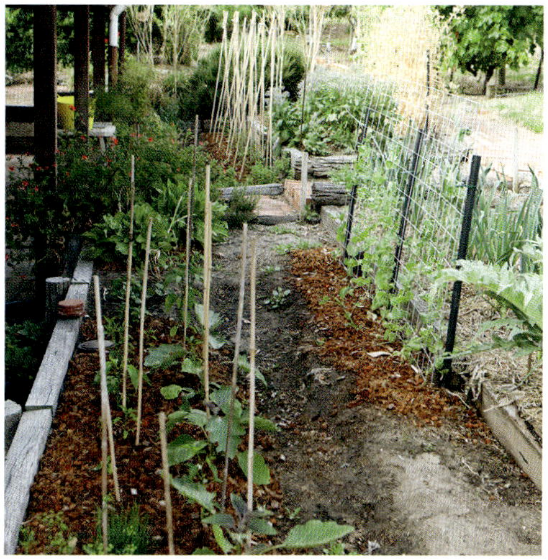
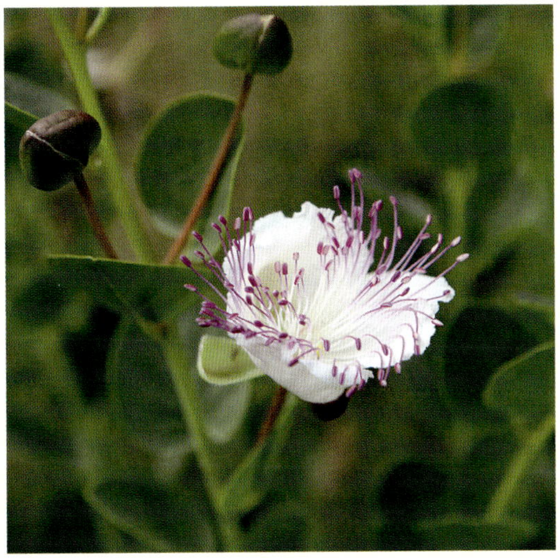
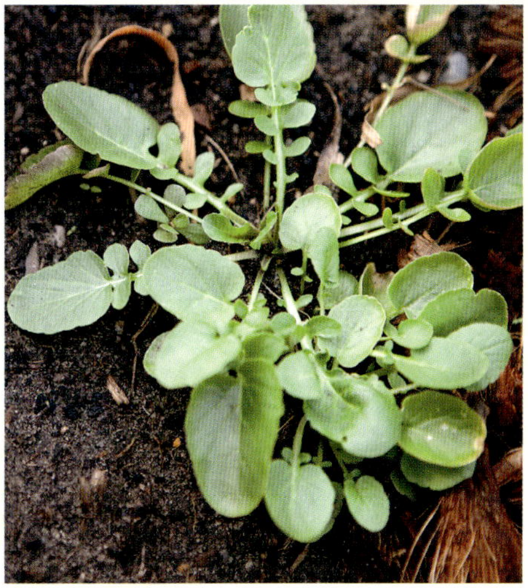
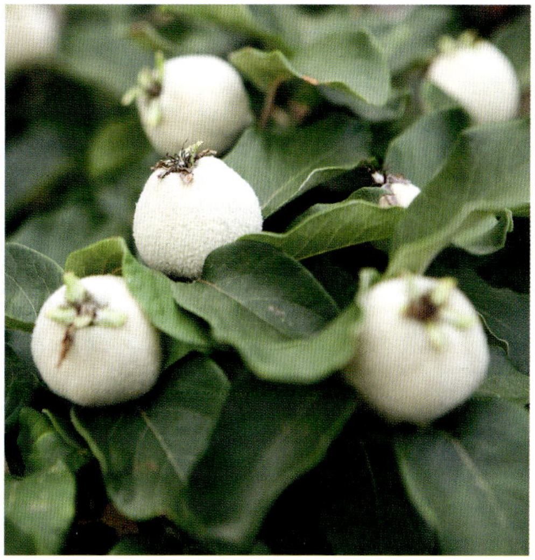

months. Quinces originate from Asia, somewhere deep in the Caucasus region. 'De Vranja' (also known as Berezki) originates from Serbia, and has white flowers and bears longish pear-shaped fruits with pale yellow skin and very aromatic flesh. 'Van Deman' is a Californian variety selected by the great plant breeder Luther Burbank himself in 1900. Its flowers are pale pink and the bright-yellow fruit is large and irregularly shaped, with flesh that cooks to a grit-less pulp that is spicy and aromatic. A close relative of the common quince is the Chinese quince (*Pseudocydonia sinensis*), also a beautiful tree with edible large quince-like fruit and stunning leopard-skin bark like that of a crepe myrtle. It differs from *Cydonia oblonga* primarily in its smaller flowers, more leathery serrated alternate leaves and semi-deciduous habit.

Despite being prone to fungal diseases like quince fleck and to infestation by codling moth, quinces are one of the least fussy fruit trees. They grow in most soils except shallow soils and sands that dry out quickly. Feral trees are often seen growing near creek banks or damp patches in old farm gardens and beside roads, but poorly drained soils are not ideal. Established trees can withstand periods of very wet conditions and also dry conditions, but summer irrigation will help produce good crops. With her quinces increasingly producing an 'embarrassment of plenty', Gay's cooking approaches, she writes, a near 'Persian delirium'. She makes *membrillo* or quince paste, quince jelly, quince with rabbit and star anise, poached quinces with crushed cardamon pods, and her favourite: a chutney of grated quinces with preserved lemon and chilli. 'It is marvellous and I make lots and give it away as well as keep enough until the next season,' she says.

Gay also grows pomegranates, which always seem a natural garden companion for quinces as both fruits (in Western

Top to bottom: **Home-grown rocket makes a Salad Niçoise; Gay has a new appreciation for fresh produce since starting her garden; one day the espalier quinces will cast summer shade over the verandah.**

minds) are steeped in the romance of Middle Eastern cuisine. Quinces and pomegranates easily cross the divide between sweet and savory dishes and cook up well with spices and meat. In Morocco, quince is used in tagines and stuffed with spiced mince and pine nuts, and in Syria, it is cooked in pomegranate

> **'As Gay would have it, a good and delicious meal made from fresh home-grown produce, shared around a table with great conviviality, is a very personal and down-to-earth act of independence.**

paste (*dibs rouman*) with shank meat and kibbeh to make *kibbeh safarjalieh*. Pomegranate molasses is a divine elixir for using in sweet desserts, or with lamb and grilled meats, couscous, vegetables and salad dressings. Gay has planted the red-skinned pomegranate 'Azerbaijan' for its large juicy 'grenades' full of crunchy arils.

In country areas today it is not necessary to grow absolutely everything yourself. Foraging necessitates quite a different attitude towards the rural landscape than that of the culinary tourist seeking to sample olives and olive oil, the seafood, and, of course, the wine for which the McLaren Vale region is famous. Foraging requires local knowledge – as to where the mushrooms grow, where that extra good feral olive tree is located, on which roadsides fennel and the spiky cactus fruit of the Indian fig is to be found. Gay also loves the idea of *gleaning*, and she gleans figs from an especially prolific neighbourhood tree. In Europe, gleaning was for many centuries considered a right and related to the old concept of 'usufruct' (*usufruit* in French) an English word deriving from the Latin expression *usus et fructus*, meaning 'use and enjoyment'. The Old Testament's 'Law of Moses' is regarded as the oldest example of usufruct (and an early idea of welfare), for it required landowners to set aside the edges of their fields in order that the poor and the immigrant might harvest the remainder and avoid starvation. The Mosaic Law also stipulated that 'the owners could not go back through the field a second time in order to harvest more thoroughly'.[4] However, an English legal case in 1788 decided that gleaning was a privilege rather than a right, upholding the primacy of private property and certain greedy farmers over the common good.

As Gay would have it, a good and delicious meal made from fresh home-grown produce, shared around a table with great conviviality, is a very personal and down-to-earth act of independence. It is something that ideally should help reclaim domestic cookery from the pressure of looking like 'restaurant food'. She has written: 'Food is so beholden to commerce, so lacking in independence from the idea of marketing, as opposed to the original definition of "market", that our personal relationship with what we eat seems to have no legitimacy. Yet this is really all there is: the growing and production of food, through to its transformation into dishes in kitchens, is so completely material, so literally down-to-earth, so nutritionally necessary that it defies advertisement.'[5] Conceivably, kitchen gardening is 'keeping food real' and transpires beyond fashion and foodie-ism! With the herbs, fruit and vegetables from her hillside garden Gay is enjoying one very DIY, seasonal and short food chain, which is something both logical and magical all in the one basket.

GILES AND KATE'S KITCHEN GARDEN

Size	300 m²
Climate	Mediterranean
Soil	Sand
Average annual rainfall	860 mm
Frost	No
Water source	Mains, greywater (the washing machine keeps the lawn alive in summer)
Irrigation method	Spray and drip irrigation
Compost and fertiliser	Compost, worm wee and castings, organic fertilisers, some homemade organic fertilisers and 'sand remedy' (a mix of bentonite clay, zeolite and gypsum)
Mulch	Lucerne and pea straw – sugar cane and tree marigold are home-grown for mulch
Biggest challenges	Sand – not sandy soil – just sand! Possums
Favourite herb	Flowering lemongrass
Favourite food plant	Heirloom strawberries 'Kunowase' and 'Cambridge Rival'

CHAPTER 11
EDIBLE GARDENING IN SUBURBAN PERTH

Permaculture practitioners say, 'Eat what you grow where you live,' and this is a philosophy shared by landscape architect and avid gardener, Giles Pickard. In just over two years Giles has transformed the backyard of his and wife Kate's property in suburban Perth into a bounteous garden of vegetables, herbs and fruit trees. In the large north-facing back garden of their rented home Giles has had both the space and sunshine to create an intensively cultivated organic garden from which they live very well indeed. However, being the passionate third-generation gardener that he is, the backyard wasn't enough for him, and he has dug up the front yard too! Giles and Kate are blessed with a wonderful landlord – not all would be so willing for tenants to embark on this kind of backyard blitz (nor welcome their shaggy wolfhound, Jess). While greater self-reliance is one objective of Giles' food production, it is a genuine love of growing things that compels him to garden on a daily basis.

Giles and Kate's backyard is around 300 m² with the main kitchen garden measuring 10 × 11 m. It is a charming mélange of edible plants and flowers – of the pretty intermingled with the useful. Flat-leaf parsley, borage, poppies, calendulas and feverfew all self-seed freely amid the vegetables. Small sculptural 'offerings' in the form of potted plants and found objects are dotted among the herbs and fruit trees. But under all the vegetation there is order – rectangular beds are edged with recycled timber and narrow paths of sawdust lead to all corners of the garden. (The sawdust paths are not only soft underfoot, sawdust is the easiest and cheapest of surfaces to lay.) Snow and podded peas climb tripods made from bamboo as well as quirky re-purposed structures – a metal Ikea furniture frame, for instance! In the spring garden there is rainbow chard, cauliflower and broccoli ready to harvest, a fine array of root vegetables – including beetroot, parsnips, potatoes and carrots, and bumper crops of red onions and garlic on the way. Cherry tomatoes, zucchini and squash are staple summer crops, as are the climbing beans Giles sows to twine up wire netting he has fixed to the western fence. Having such good-looking produce has proven very handy for Kate. As an editor who works for a publishing house, she sometimes needs fresh vegetables to use in her cookbook photo shoots at short notice.

In order to make the most of your available growing space, Giles recommends that you grow high-value annual crops (for example, he advises to grow garlic as it's worth $50 per kg, whereas pumpkin is only $2 per kg) – 'high turnover crops and the things that you love to eat or can't buy like mulberries and heirloom tomatoes'. He grows about 70 per cent of his annual plants from seed, and sources the heirloom varieties that he favours from the Digger's Club and local nurseries. Giles also likes to mix perennials throughout the garden to give his plantings structure – strawberries are used as edging plants, herbs such as apple mint, tansy and oregano compete for space with Warrigal greens underneath the almond tree. Larger perennial food plants include monster globe artichokes, Cape gooseberry, pepinos and a clump of lemongrass that threatens to engulf the rear of the house.

Giles has youth and enthusiasm on his side. Rather than use glyphosate herbicide to kill the couch grass on the proposed site of his vegie garden, he dug the entire area up by hand. Some might call him mad, but so keen was he to get things growing he was prepared to put in the hard physical work to make it all happen. Most of the hard materials used to construct this garden have come from kerbside rubbish collections – one resident's trash is another's treasure, after all. Other modifications have been more immediate – Giles 'forked out' and purchased 15 m³ of compost made locally from Perth's green waste to prepare his garden with. He figured he had neither the time nor the patience, let alone the capacity, to produce enough homemade compost with which to amend his sandy soil. As Giles says, if you don't keep attending to it with compost and the growing roots of plants, your soil will turn back to sand before your very eyes!

A fence to demarcate the vegie garden from the ornamental garden has become redundant as the edibles have escaped outwards to take over the entire block. Citrus trees, a feijoa, plum, goji berry, pomegranate, Chinese jujube and the red and yellow fruiting forms of tamarillo represent a mini-orchard growing in the beds around the lawn. Giles has planted nearly

Giles and Kate get immense pleasure from their kitchen garden

GILES AND KATE'S GARDEN

1. Frog pond and native garden
2. Nursery
3. Shed
4. Chooks under coral tree
5. Compost bays
6. Almond tree with herbs, potted fruit trees and strawberries
7. Pergola
8. Fruiting plants along back fence: Natal plum, fig, goji berry, pear, nectarine and apricot
9. Herbs, flowers, zucchini, berries, passionfruit 'Nellie Kelly'
10. Annual vegetables
11. Potatoes, squash, climbing beans, strawberries, banana passionfruit and navel orange
12. Cape gooseberry, artichoke, sugarcane, Kaffir lime, Jerusalem artichoke, dragon fruit and perpetual spinach
13. Feijoa, strawberry guava, pomegranate, Tahitian lime and yellow tamarillo
14. Panama passionfruit, lemon, Cape gooseberry and jujube
15. Olive, pawpaw, pepinos and red tamarillo
16. Banana
17. Herbs, lemongrass, Indian guava, passionfruit 'Nellie Kelly' and strawberries
18. Herbs and flowers, strawberry guava, plum 'Wilson's Early', globe artichoke, ice-cream bean, goji berry and grapevine

forty different genera of fruit throughout the garden and their provenance ranges from tropical to temperate climes. Perth is not a climate one would normally associate with cultivating amazing strawberries (they originate from high-rainfall deciduous woodlands), but Giles is doing just that. 'Cambridge Rival' and 'Kunowase' are dripping with fruit and the perfume alone of the white fruit of 'Frais des bois', an alpine variety, is divine. Heritage strawberries such as these are almost a thing of the past because their fragility and the fact they do not keep make them commercially unviable. Subtropical fruits include babaco, banana, the unusual 'ice-cream bean tree' (*Inga edulis*), with large pods that contain a white cotton-wool-like pulp that tastes of vanilla ice-cream, and a Brazilian cherry (*Eugenia uniflora*).

The latter, a highly ornamental South American shrub of the Myrtaceae family, is also known as the Surinam cherry or pitanga. The fragrant foliage is bronze-coloured when juvenile, later becoming a glossy deep green. Small white flowers precede decorative multi-segmented fruits that turn dark red when fully ripe. The taste can be tart but they are high in vitamin C and also make a good jelly. (This shrub is not recommended for warm regions with higher rainfall like northern New South Wales and Queensland, where it is a declared weed.) The goji berry or wolfberry (*Lycium barbarum*) is another fruiting shrub that has recently become popular in Australia. The attractive red berries (usually available dried) have long been used in Chinese medicine and have been the subject of much hype about their magical 'superfruit' properties. Being closely related to the noxious weed African boxthorn (*Lycium ferocissimum*) it is no surprise that the goji berry is a tough, suckering, sprawling (and also potentially weedy) shrub. Also hardy yet with much tastier fruit is the Chinese date or jujube (*Zizyphus jujuba*) whose plum-like fruits have apple-flavoured green flesh, although when dried the taste and texture of the jujube is more prune-like.

The Great Aussie Dream once entailed owning a detached house on a 'quarter acre' block with a few fruit trees, lawn, the ubiquitous Hills hoist and a small vegetable plot. Land ownership and gardening have been represented as a symbiotic affair in Australia's history since white settlement. But it shouldn't necessarily follow that those who don't own a house – be they squatters, renters, mobile-home owners or residents of hostels or public housing – are denied a garden. Apart from unwilling landlords, renters who want to grow their own food face a few challenges. Making substantial physical improvements to a property that is not your own, especially if it's a short-term rental,

> ' It shouldn't necessarily follow that those who don't own a house – be they squatters, renters, mobile-home owners or residents of hostels or public housing – are denied a garden.'

will normally be impracticable. Gardens of renters thus tend to be mobile and take the form of pots or easily disassembled garden beds or boxes that can be packed up and moved. When Giles was renting in Melbourne while he was studying at RMIT, he amassed a collection of over 300 potted plants! (Which, of course, had to be transported to Perth on his return.) Giles is open to the idea that there are other kinds of 'garden tenure' beyond the bastion of the owner–occupier garden. Planting a garden like he has done is not an over-capitalisation. It is about living for today and also leaving a living legacy. Giles is optimistic that after he moves on, others will enjoy the fruit trees he has planted. However, spending money on very large and expensive items that you cannot take with you is another matter. Giles puts water tanks and solar panels in this category (despite the fact they can be moved), as they can be expensive to disconnect and transport.

To keep his garden going through Perth's long, dry and hot summers, Giles has utilised both mains water and household greywater. Drip irrigation has helped make his watering more efficient, constant composting preserves the water-holding capacity of the soil, and mulch is used to reduce evaporation. There are no pesticides or snail pellets used in the garden so Giles' pest management has taken the form of a frog pond he has established near the vegie patch. Between rocks and logs

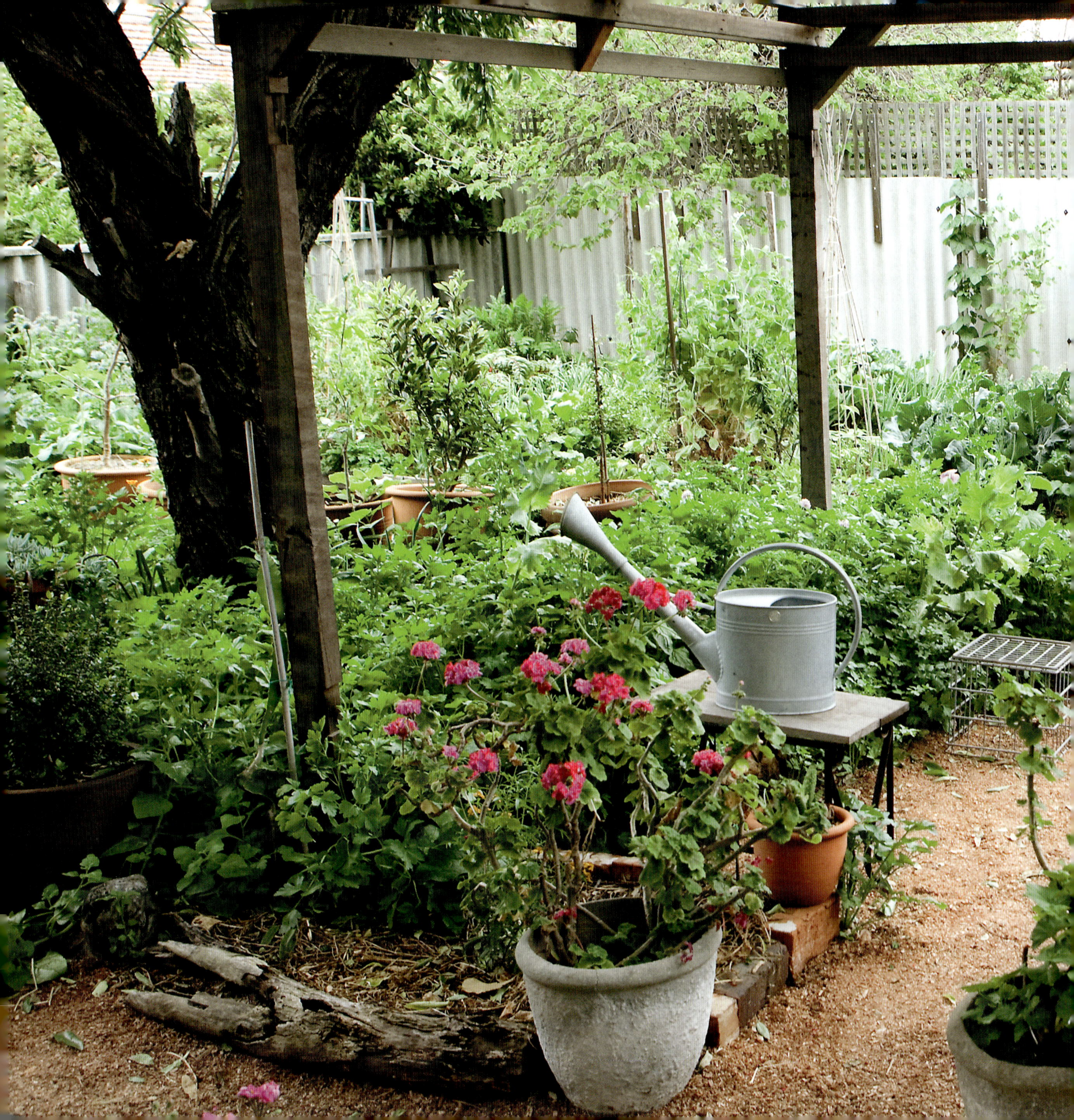

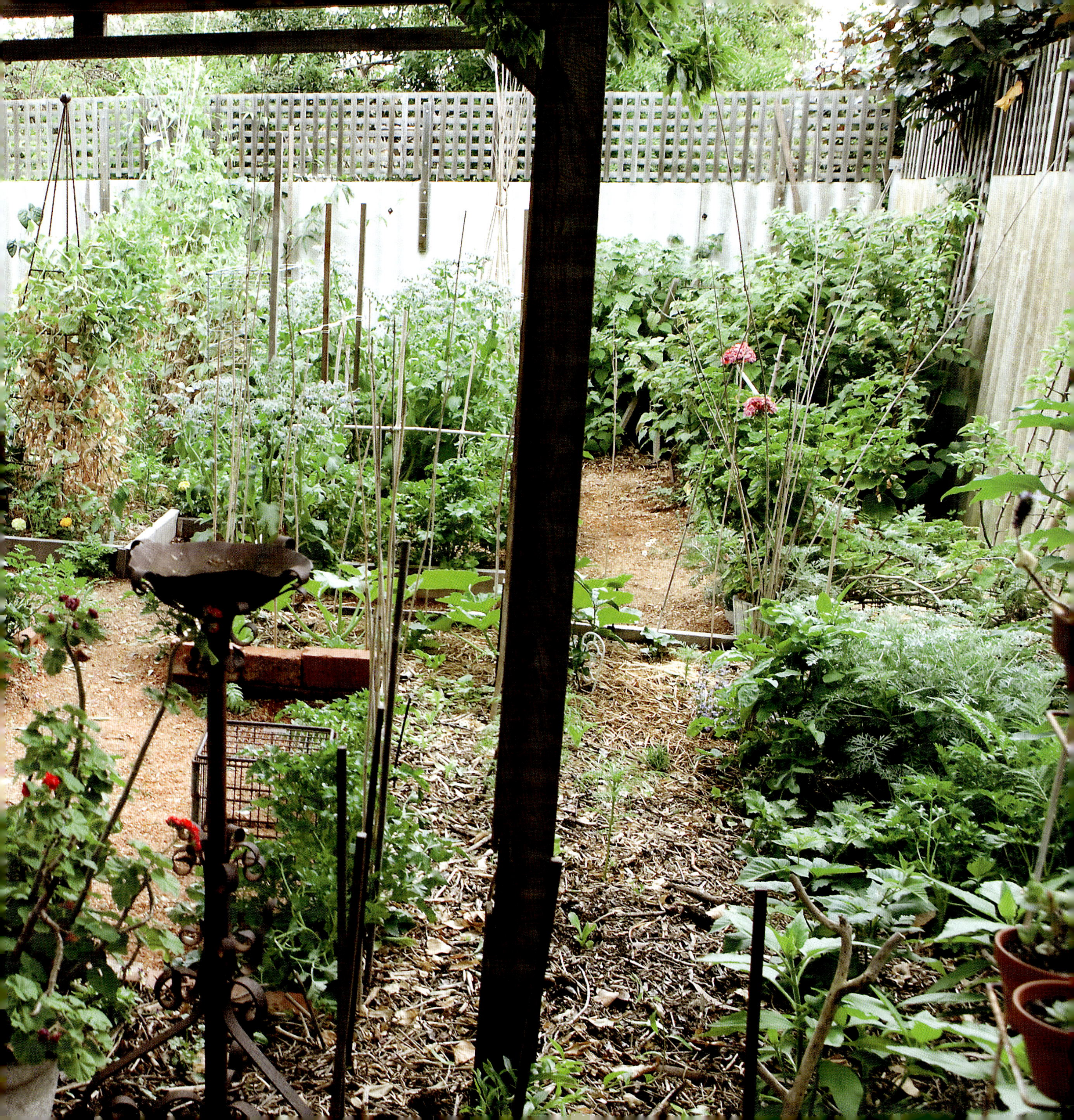

Previous pages: **Giles and Kate's garden shows that renting is no barrier to having a beautiful and sustainable productive garden.**
Clockwise, from top left: **Strawberry 'Frais des bois'; the sculptural and edible globe artichoke; thriving vegies attest to Giles' improvement of the sandy Perth soil; the unkillable pepino; Jess, the wolfhound cross; ruby chard; the frog pond.**

he has planted indigenous aquatic and marginal species like *Lepidosperma gladiatum* and *Centella asiatica*. Giles anticipates that this tiny patch of habitat will attract the insect- and arthropod-eating motorbike frogs and slender tree frogs to the greater vicinity of the backyard. Bobtail lizards, a lumpier, scalier version of the eastern blue-tongue, are regular visitors and welcomed for predating insects, snails and those very pesky slaters, but not for their taste for strawberries!

It was in his late teens that Giles became interested in environmental conservation issues. A period of nearly five years of activism soon followed, when he became involved in blockading the logging of old-growth forests throughout the south-west and at Walpole, near Denmark in southern Western Australia. This region has five endemic trees: karri, jarrah, marri and three species of tingle, all of them giants of the forest. The red tingle trees (*Eucalyptus jacksonii*) – the world's only buttressed eucalyptus – grow in a 6000-ha area around Walpole and nowhere else on earth. Giles sees the south-west eco-region as one of Western Australia's greatest assets and believes it's senseless not to safeguard its future. In recent years his involvement in conservation has involved research undertaken for his degree, particularly in the area of climate change and mitigating its impact on urban communities through changing our urban land-use practices.

These days, with his dreadlocks gone, and him being in a challenging career, Giles' eco-intervention has taken a rather more serene, if no less subversive form: he has dug up half of his front lawn and replaced it with vegetables. Giles was inspired by an American garden book with a difference entitled *Edible Estates: Attack on the Front Lawn*. The book was the result of a project instigated by artist and architect Fritz Haeg, which involved digging up the hallowed ground of American front lawns in suburban housing estates and creating productive gardens. Haeg envisions a suburban landscape where 'The banal lifeless space of uniform grass in front of the house will be replaced with the chaotic abundance of biodiversity.'[1] The lawn itself has become a moral issue, Haeg argues. All that water, fertiliser and chemicals expended on vast shaved monocultures produces no tangible benefit, no thing, apart from homogeneous, resource-guzzling, 'neighbours-keep-off' space. In this context, Haeg posits creating a productive front garden as a political act, 'a small and modest intervention on our streets', a food garden that can nonetheless 'have a radical effect on the life of a family, how they spend their time and relate to the environment, whom they see, and how they eat'.[2]

With their first baby on the way, Giles has even greater plans for feeding the family beautiful produce from their own edible estate. The new front vegetable garden is a simple rectangular bed edged with bricks in which he has planted strawberries, sweet corn and climbing beans. It has proven quite a drawcard for neighbours: 'From gardening out the front I have begun to meet the people that live in my street, share tips on gardening, stories of other gardens in the street and have enjoyed just talking to people about urban food production, or "my vegie garden", as I prefer to call it,' says Giles. 'I have also learnt about the history of the neighbourhood from some of the older residents and hear appreciation for my efforts from those that have watched it grow on their walk to the shops.' The nature strip has also received the Giles treatment, being mulched and planted with local kangaroo paws, saltbush, indigenous grasses and the twining shrub *Chorizema cordatum* with its irrepressible pink and orange pea flowers. (The artist Lin Onus once told how his son as a child used to think the words to our national anthem included 'Our land abounds in nature strips' – which is a delightful mondegreen that's both true and ironic at the same time!)

Giles is by no means an anti-lawn food-growing survivalist who thinks all grass should be banished. Lawn has great social and cultural significance – who doesn't love a nap, picnic or a ball game on smooth verdant lawn? But food growing in urban areas, or urban agriculture, is increasingly important for our future cities, Giles says. How exactly are we to grow food locally when peri-urban food production is in decline and food has to be transported vast distances to the suburbs where most Australians live? Especially when house sizes are increasing yet block sizes are getting smaller? Not to mention when owning a home is but a dream for many, and when there is immense competition for the public land potentially available for community gardens? We need to grow food where we live and work. But we don't have to grow everything ourselves – food-growing neighbourhoods can provide a wider network of exchange and cooperation, and an opportunity for resource-sharing and waste-recycling on a larger and more efficient scale.

Giles is lucky to have so much space, as well as enough direct sunshine (at least six hours is required to grow a wide range of vegetables) and clean uncontaminated soil. Finding enough space in the suburbs to grow food is an obvious problem, especially for those who live in flats and apartments. For many, gardening in containers may be the only way to grow food and flowers in small areas, or upon existing concrete or paved surfaces. Annual vegetables require containers that are at least 30 cm deep – pots, polystyrene boxes, old laundry troughs or baby baths can be used. Fruit trees, shrubs and berries can also be grown in pots, half-wine barrels, old fruit crates, wheelie bins – anything that is non-toxic, allows water to drain freely and holds at least 50 cm of soil.

Alternative types of 'garden tenure' for urban food gardeners include renting individual plots in community/allotment gardens or joining or developing a communal garden. 'Guerrilla gardens', on the other hand, are created without any agreement. Giles has encountered many unconventional urban land uses in his role as a council landscape architect. Unused and uncared-for land (whether private, crown land or land belonging to other authorities) is seen as an opportunity for growing food by 'vegeplante vigilantes': on nature strips, reserves adjoining railway lines and creeks, land around derelict houses, laneways and even cemeteries! There are alternatives to clandestine gardening, though – guerrilla gardening has the potential to 'evolve into something more than just those without resources gardening on their own'.[3] Asking landowners' permission may well bear fruit – local churches or community centres could prove amenable to hosting a community garden. On council-owned land, working with local government to initiate community gardens may prove more successful over the long term than guerrilla activities. The more community gardening organisations can work with councils to put urban agriculture and community gardens into council land-use policies, the more stable these projects will ultimately be.[4] Only sustained campaigning for food-growing land will garner prime local sites for community gardens rather than the 'dregs' – old tip sites, land under power lines – that no one else wants and councils cannot sell.

> **'Why use your own and the sun's energy to grow grass you can't eat when you can have baskets full of white strawberries, green peas and freshly dug potatoes?'**

Giles' personal enjoyment of 'garden interventions' does not usually conflict with his professional awareness of the reasons councils are risk-averse. The main issues he has come across in regard to urban agriculture (whether legal or illicit) are pollution; pest control (vermin such as rats and mice); neighbours spraying chemicals; watering (accessing mains water given water restrictions, and also storing enough rainwater); nutrient run-off into waterways and groundwater; and, with guerrilla gardens, there is the issue of legal liabilities – especially public liability. Polluted or contaminated soil is potentially hazardous for food gardeners. Lead and other heavy metals, industrial chemicals, fuels, pesticides and asbestos are all more common in urban soils than we'd like to think. Guerrilla and home gardeners alike need to be aware of the potential for contamination of the plants they eat and the importance of getting soil tested (a process that can be quite expensive) before embarking on digging and planting. If unsure, it is preferable to garden above ground level in pots and tubs so as to avoid contact with the existing soil.

Giles' edible estate sets a marvellous example that should inspire us to mow less and garden more. Why use your own and the sun's energy to grow grass you can't eat when you can have baskets full of white strawberries, green peas and freshly dug potatoes? Gardeners all over the nation are being more creative about growing food in their backyards, front yards, on balconies, nature strips and unused local land. Giles is particularly enthused that through urban food growing city people are getting to 'play, learn, explore, grow and share within the landscape in which we all live'.

Unlike the fruit trees Giles has planted in the ground, the potted trees will go with him and Kate when they move house

ANDREA EVANS' KITCHEN GARDEN

Size	30 × 10 m (300 m^2)
Climate	Mediterranean
Soil	Local soil is sandy loam
Average annual rainfall	735 mm
Frost	No
Water source	Dam water
Irrigation method	Micro-spray irrigation and hand-watering
Compost and fertiliser	Homemade compost, mushroom compost
Mulch	Compost
Biggest challenges	To pick everything!
Favourite herb	Parsley
Favourite food plant	Rocket and lettuce

CHAPTER 12
VILLA LETTISIER'S WALLED KITCHEN GARDEN

Flinders is a small seaside town located on the Mornington Peninsula, Victoria, the boot-shaped promontory at the southern extremity of Port Phillip Bay that protects the bay from the open waters of Bass Strait. The whole region, known locally as 'the Peninsula', has increasingly become a favourite retreat for Melbournians from the madness of city life. If Portsea and Sorrento constitute Victoria's Riviera, then Flinders, situated on the Western Port side of the Peninsula, is possibly its Monte Argentario. Beautiful rolling hills terminate in windswept cliffs and gleaming beaches that fringe the waters of Westernport. The maritime climate also makes it a most appealing destination – not only does the Peninsula receive far more rain than the metropolitan area thanks to favourable ocean/weather systems (the average annual rainfall is 735 mm), its average summer temperatures are also much lower than Melbourne's.

Over the last thirty years a thriving food culture has emerged in the region with small producers specialising in high-value crops. The neighbouring Boneo and nearby Tyabb are mini food bowls and the entire Peninsula now has enough vineyards, olive groves, organic beef producers, market gardens and venison, avocado, berry, cherry and boutique cheese farms to keep both locals and tourists well provided for.

It is no wonder that Andrea Evans and her late husband, Ron, chose to purchase their bayside Flinders property back in 1994. The 200-degree views of the Western Port coastline are breathtaking and reason enough to want to build a home here. Today, paddocks roll away in three directions from the hilltop villa they built together, while a large garden lies to the north. Along the kilometre-long driveway stand huge gnarled specimens of Monterey cypress (*Cupressus macrocarpa*). These living sculptures evoke the indigenous coastal tea-trees (*Leptospermum laevigatum*) whose dark-silver twisted trunks and silver-green foliage are naturally wind-pruned into cloud shapes like oversized bonsai. Andrea is a self-declared Italophile, who has fallen deeply and passionately in love with Italy over her many visits there – with the food, people, architecture and the gardens. The design of the house (by interior designer John Coote) thus came to be based upon Renaissance architect Andrea Palladio's Villa Almerico-Capra (Villa Rotonda), which is regarded as the epitome of the classicist Italian country house. The garden too was conceived in the Italian style and contains all the plants of the Mediterranean palette: box, olives, citrus, iris, lavender, silver-foliaged shrubs, pots of pelargoniums and lots of clipped hedges.

Ron and Andrea approached Melbourne garden designer Paul Bangay to create a fabulous setting for their new villa. Ten years on, the formal garden succeeds in anchoring the house to the earth and manifests the sense of scale and proportion Bangay is renowned for. The house and garden, as with the great Renaissance gardens, are an integrated entity – the Italian inspiration is obvious and has been joyfully realised in the course of Andrea and Paul's collaboration. Axes are fundamental, as is a strict geometry of forms and the symmetry of the rectilinear plan. Borrowing on ancient traditions, the long approach to the house takes in three garden rooms before reaching the forecourt. Hedges, use of statuary and garden rooms enclosed by either solid walls or hedges: all are utilised in this hilltop landscape. In this windy environment walled gardens are an obvious way of creating pleasant and calm outdoor spaces, and Andrea's productive garden is no exception. The kitchen garden is a *giardino segreto* (enclosed garden) behind ochre walls on the east side of the house, a short walk from the kitchen. Through tall timber gates, up a flight of steps and the surprise is revealed: a formal kitchen garden full of edible delights. The *giardino segreto* is a space that is both protected and protecting, a place for gardening or simply contemplation. With walls of solid masonry backed by a taller hedge of Leyland cypress (*Cupressocyparis leylandii*), one could be busy gardening or reading a book and no one would suspect you were there.

Inside the kitchen garden a path of pebbles and square pavers takes you down a long pear walk that flanks rectangular garden beds. Twelve pairs of pears make a living tunnel, an irresistible *allée*, which invites you to stroll its length. The pear variety is the 'Williams', which is thought to date from around

The *allée* of 'Williams' pears is just one lovely feature inside this secret kitchen garden

1770, originating in the yard of an English schoolmaster. It became known as the 'Williams' after a nurseryman later acquired the variety, named it after himself and introduced it to the rest of England. (Although the pear's true name is said to be *Williams' Bon Chretien* – Williams' good Christian – it is confusingly known as the 'Bartlett' pear in the US.) The trees have been espaliered in the classic four tiers style, planted 2 m apart and trained to a steel skeleton of an arbour. Pears are particularly suited to such culture and are tough and long-lived. In early spring the structure is enveloped in pure white blossoms and in autumn, the ripe pears turn a soft yellow and dangle in their masses just above head height. The bounty keeps Andrea and everyone she knows in pears for weeks on end – both for eating fresh and for poaching.

From the main axis, four paths enable access to each of the four garden beds that are enclosed by neat hedges of box. These bays terminate in metal seats behind which 'Meyer' lemons have been trained against the western wall. The lush green lemon trees are so productive they could supply lemons to every fish-and-chip shop on the Mornington Peninsula! Inside the garden beds diagonal hedges further divide the space into triangular-shaped beds. A hedge of curry plant (*Helichrysum italicum*) in the first bed alternates with English lavender in the next and so on. Andrea loves the spicy smell of the curry plant's foliage as she works in the garden. 'Apple obelisks' mark the centre of each bed – 2-m-high metal pyramids with 'Jonathan' apples trained upon and through the steel framework. The obelisks, the pear walk, box hedges, lemons and enclosing garden walls form the bones of the garden, the ever-present year-long structure. The effect is not precious, however; it's not like a mini-Villandry potager where the removal of any one edible annual species would spoil the whole effect. Like oversized bento boxes, the box-rimmed triangles of dark soil contain a variety of edible treats. That the whole garden is so beautifully maintained is testament to the many hours a week that Andrea spends working here.

All winter long Andrea harvests the most perfect broccoli. Whether it's the maritime climate or the distance from any other gardens, very few pests bother Andrea's vegetables. Maybe it's just too darn windy for cabbage moths! Spring is snow peas on small metal tripods, broad beans, spinach and silverbeet, glaucous cabbages and the fattest spears of asparagus

> **'Small signs made of slate with names written in chalk – human, rather than plant – mark different plantings and indicate the proprietorship of each of Andrea's eight grandchildren.'**

I've ever seen (perhaps it's the variety so rudely named 'Fat Bastard'?) The silver foliage of garlic and globe artichokes contrast beautifully with the bright-green new growth of the box hedging. Pink ranunculi and orange calendulas add bright spots of colour to the mass of spring foliage. Seedlings of black kale (*Laciniato*, *Nero de Toscana* or *Cavallo nero*) are a new addition – Andrea is spoilt for choice in the nursery department in having the home of the Digger's Club nearby at Dromana. Here, from the historic property Heronswood, the headquarters of the heirloom vegie movement, owner Clive Blazey has popularised a plethora of unusual and almost-forgotten varieties such as the Tuscan kale, purple carrots, black tomatoes and striped eggplants since the early 1980s.

In October Andrea plants bush beans, basil and tomatoes ('Grosse Lisse' and 'Apollo'). Cos lettuce and wild rocket are two of her favourite salad greens, so there's plenty of those. Her enormous rhubarb was originally given to her by friend John Kennedy, a gardener and footballer, and much to her delight her rhubarb plants vastly outperform his! Potatoes, onions and beetroots thrive in the magnificent well-drained soil that is dark with organic matter. (Because the kitchen garden is raised well above the natural soil level, soil was brought in during construction and has been continually enriched with compost made onsite from garden prunings, leaves

VILLA LETTISIER'S WALLED KITCHEN GARDEN

1. Pear walk
2. Box hedging
3. Espaliered 'Meyer' lemon
4. Leyland cypress hedge
5. Tomatoes
6. Beans
7. Cabbage
8. Ranunculi
9. 'Jonathan' apple on metal obelisks
10. Beetroot and cos lettuce
11. Beans
12. Garlic and Tuscan kale
13. Potatoes and rhubarb
14. Spinach
15. Onions
16. Broccoli
17. Globe artichokes and asparagus
18. Silverbeet
19. Cos lettuce
20. Broad beans
21. Snow peas
22. Cutting flowers

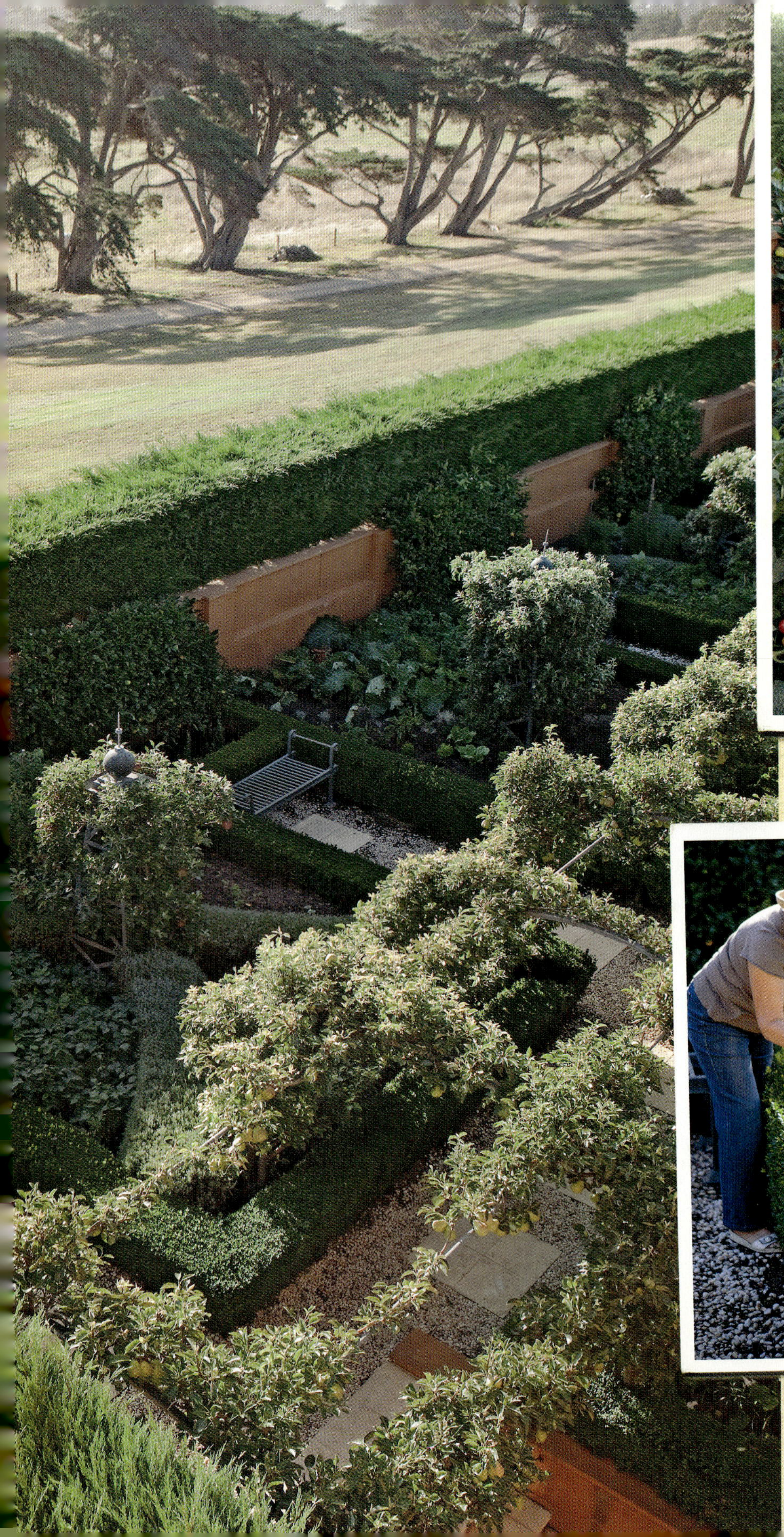

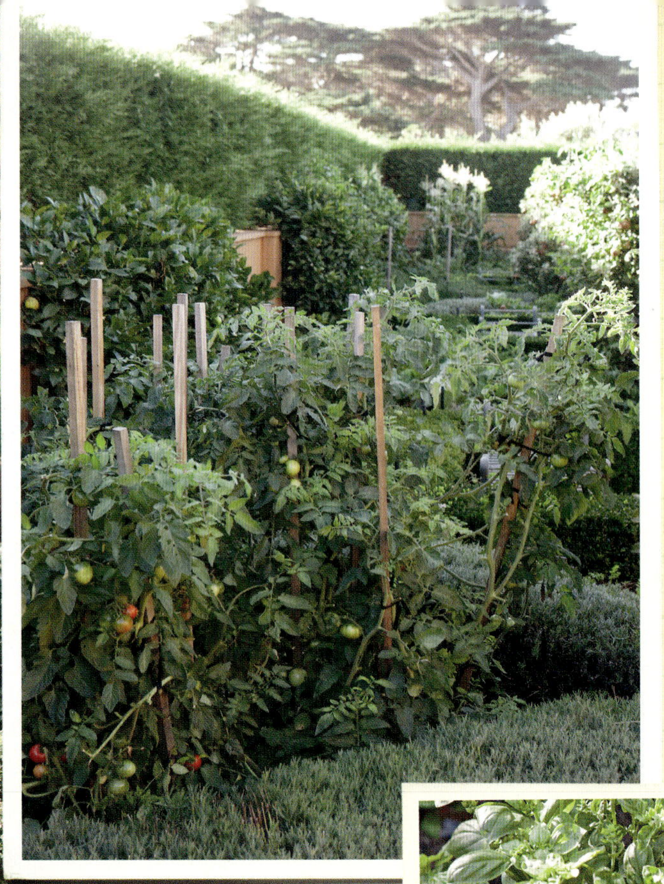

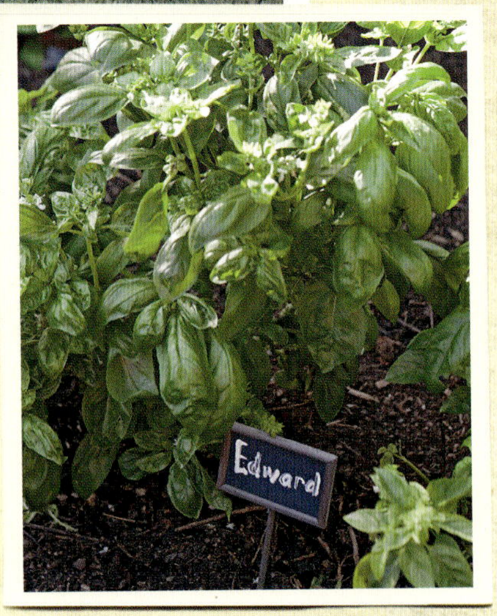
Edward

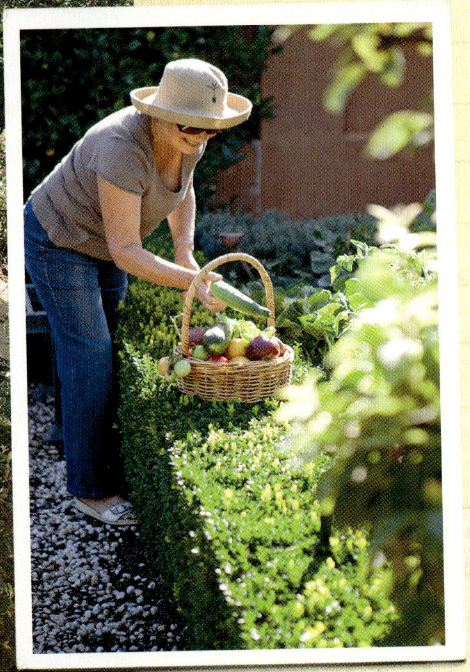

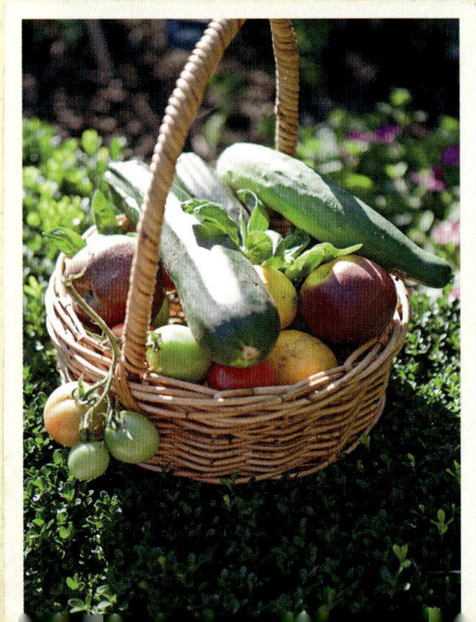

and kitchen scraps.) Small signs made of slate with names written in chalk – human, rather than plant – mark different plantings and indicate the proprietorship of each of Andrea's eight grandchildren. Each grandchild has a plot planted with what vegetables they like to eat. Katie likes beans and Tom snow peas. A passionfruit vine planted at the behest of her eldest grandchild at age ten (now eighteen) has only just been removed. The kids always come and check on 'their' bit of garden when they visit.

Come summer and the kitchen garden is an especially gorgeous sight. The lavender hedges are in flower, revealing their diagonal 'cross' pattern in violet blooms. It is no wonder that the English word paradise comes from an old Iranian term *pairi-daeza*, originating from the word for walled (enclosure) – from *pairi-* 'around', and *-diz* to 'create/make'. It has been a dry time here in paradise, though – over the previous decade of below-average rain each subsequent summer has seen the water level in the four dams on the property (from which the garden is watered) keep falling. The Peninsula has been far more fortunate with rainfall than many areas of Victoria, however, and the dams here are full once again and the garden has survived.

While the Mornington Peninsula has a history of food production, it hasn't always boasted such a diversity of enterprises as it does today. Farming emerged in the late 1830s as squatters began to move into the hinterland, but fishing and vegetable and fruit growing remained the primary pursuits. Lime-burning, quarrying, logging and gold diggings further transformed and denuded the traditional lands of the Boonwurung nation. During Melbourne's goldrush of the 1850s over a hundred Chinese lived at Flinders Beach, fishing and establishing market gardens among the tea-trees and moonah. Due to the immigration tax levied at the ports in Melbourne apparently quite a number of Chinese immigrants used to jump ship at Flinders.[1] Until as late as the 1970s the Peninsula was peppered with orchards, mainly apple and pear, and still possessed many remnant areas of bushland and their unique vegetation communities. Back then, the local demographic was far less wealthy. Now retirees, weekenders and increasingly, people undertaking a life-changing 'seachange', are all eager to experience the delights that the area has to offer.

Edible plants feature elsewhere in this Flinders garden. Across the forecourt from the kitchen garden is a matching garden room containing the swimming pool. Food plants even make their way into this ultra-formal space, this time in the form of fig trees. The figs are grown behind low hedges of box and trained against all four walls – over 45 delicious linear metres of figs! A sweet summer treat indeed – they say you should eat mango in the bath, so why not figs in the pool? Olive trees are an important feature in the main garden, pruned into standards pairs off the main driveway axis. Hedged olive trees have also been established as windbreaks by Andrea's gardener Jeremy Tuxen. In between the trees and the exterior gardens walls, Jeremy has created long flower borders using tough flowering and foliage plants. Underneath the olives he's planted the evergreen shrub known as the Natal plum. The oval pink fruit has delicious if slightly tart pink flesh tasting like a cross between a cherry, wild plum and cranberry. (Its skin and seeds are edible and the fruits preserve well as jams and chutneys and can be frozen, dried or bottled.) The five-petalled white flowers resemble those of the tree gardenia (*Gardenia thunbergii*) and are quite fragrant on warm nights. This *Carissa* species is native to South Africa, to the KwaZulu-Natal and Eastern Cape coastlines, where it is commonly called the 'large num-num'. As its provenance suggests, the plants require excellent drainage, love the heat, withstand drought, wind and salt spray. Their sharp spines mean the Natal plum makes an effectively spiky hedge (that can reach 2 m high), and is best

Clockwise, from top left: **The rolling landscape of Flinders outside the walled garden; the walls and hedges are essential to stop the wind; one of Andrea's grandchildren's garden plot; produce to eat and share; harvesting is pure pleasure.**

pruned with heavy-duty gloves on and not planted in areas of high pedestrian use. Propagation is via cuttings as the flowers are supposedly sterile.

The Natal plum, along with the caper bush (*Capparis spinosa*) and Australian natives such as pigface (*Carpobrotus rossii*), seaberry saltbush (*Rhagodia candolleana*), bower spinach (*Tetragonia implexicoma*) and coast beard heath (*Leucopogon parviflorus*) constitute some of the toughest edible plants for coastal conditions in southern Australia. The coast wattle *Acacia sophorae*, indigenous to the area, has edible seeds (these were harvested when green and steamed in the pod) that formed an important part of the diet of the indigenous people of Victoria and Tasmania. In the northern hemisphere, sea kale (*Crambe maritima*) and samphire (rock samphire – *Crithmum maritimum* and marsh samphire – *Salicornia* sp.) are at home among dunes, estuaries and salt water, as is that plant from the very ocean itself – seaweed.

In Palladio's time the *villa rustica* was an estate built to house extensive farms within their boundaries. There were typically vegetable and herbal gardens, an orchard, fishponds, servant buildings, barns, stables, poultry and rabbit pens, areas for winemaking and oil production, ovens and wells located inside the main enclosure. Palladio broke with tradition with Villa Rotonda in unharnessing it from agricultural purposes, building a *villa urbana* for a retiring priest who wished to enjoy the locale and prospect of Vicenza without all the rural responsibilities. Andrea's villa is similarly not part of a working farm but the way the property's lovely old dairy has been incorporated into the main axis at the end of the garden (as if there's a ley line between the centre of the new building and that of the corrugated-iron dairy, linking the exotic and classical with the local and vernacular) references the property's farming history.

Andrea shares her love of both Palladian architecture and of vegetable gardening with the unlikely figure of Thomas Jefferson, the third president of the United States (1801–09).

(Of course, I am not suggesting that Andrea has anything other than these passions in common with the slave-owning president!) Jefferson's home Monticello in Charlottesville, Virginia, was a paean to Palladian design. Jefferson designed his home himself, which, like Andrea's villa, featured a central cupola and porticos like miniature temple-fronts. In addition, he also had a wonderful vegetable garden set among beautiful gardens. (While Jefferson's vegie plot was over 300 m long, Andrea's kitchen garden is a more modest 30 m.) His passion for vegetables is legendary, and as well as introducing a plethora of vegetables to America (he is credited with introducing Brussels sprouts, eggplant, cauliflower, and broccoli), he used his garden as a laboratory where he trialled over 250 different varieties of vegetable. As he wrote in 1811: 'I have often thought that if heaven had given me choice of my position and calling, it should have been on a rich spot of earth, well watered, and near a good market for the productions of the garden. No occupation is so delightful to me as the culture of the earth and no culture comparable to that of the garden.'[2]

Fresh fruit, vegetables and salads are the *raison d'etre* of Andrea's produce gardening. Cooking is one of her great pleasures – for Andrea, it is about using beautiful and fresh ingredients and sharing meals and time with family. She will usually head back to her Melbourne home on a Sunday night with the boot of her car full of garden produce to be shared with her children and friends. For Andrea the Peninsula truly is a gourmet destination – it certainly beats a visit to the supermarket any day!

Domestic gardens perform many functions – they are private landscapes for personal expression in which nature is the essence and the focus; sanctuaries for rest and restoration; play spaces for kids and grandchildren; sites of recreation and hard physical work; and places that elicit memories and in which memorials to loved ones are placed or planted. That Andrea's garden fulfils all of these functions in addition to the growing of food is quite simply a wonderful thing.

Clockwise from top left: **The garden measures 30 m in length and consists of four rectangular beds, each divided into four triangles by hedges of lavender and curry plant; you step up into the enclosed garden; the swimming pool is surrounded on four sides by figs – heaven!; ripe 'Williams' pears.**

LEONIE'S KITCHEN GARDEN

Size	200 m²
Climate	Tropical savannah
Soil	Shallow brown clay
Average annual rainfall	1750 mm
Frost	None
Water source	Bore water
Irrigation method	Spray irrigation
Compost and fertiliser	Homemade liquid fertiliser, cane toad compost, aged chook poo, compost
Mulch	Bush litter, lemongrass, hay, grass clippings, cover crops like peanuts and lab lab bean
Biggest challenges	Termites, seven months without rain in the Dry season, monsoonal rains, chewing insects and increasingly mites during the hot Dry time
Favourite herb	Pepper – Leonie adds it to everything
Favourite food plant	Pawpaw because it is so versatile – being able to be used as a fruit, vegetable, tenderiser and a medicine

Malabar Nightshade (White)

CHAPTER 13
LEONIE NORRINGTON'S TROPICAL FOOD GARDEN

Having been born in Darwin and the author of the excellent gardening book *Tropical Food Gardens*, you'd expect that Leonie Norrington knows a thing or two about growing food in the Northern Territory. Although she calls herself 'the world's laziest gardener', a walk around her productive garden, 50 km south of Darwin, shows that this is far from true. Leonie is, in fact, a clever gardener – one who likes her garden to develop from a low labour to high-reward ratio, and wouldn't we all? Her garden is remarkably productive and adapted to unique challenges – take the fundamental fact of the tropical climate: its Dry and Wet seasons necessitate a real gardening binarism. Add to that cyclones, feral pigs, termites and all manner of destructive insects. In Leonie's brand of 'survival of the fittest' organic gardening, she uses climate-adapted methods like permanent plantings, perennial crops, mixed plantings, cover crops, lots of compost and tonnes of mulch in order to reduce labour, feed and preserve her soil, and ensure a dependable and delicious bounty.

'Your vegetable garden should be a jungle,'[1] writes Leonie. Jungle vegetable gardening is unfussy food growing as opposed to the kind of over-tilled regimental-produce gardening (where a tapestry of monocultures grows side by side) celebrated in the northern hemisphere gardening books of yesteryear. Leonie is also an acclaimed children's author, and I can't help but think of the eponymous English gardener Mr McGregor in Beatrix Potter's *The Tale of Peter Rabbit*, and how, gardening in that manner in Darwin, he'd be one starving Pom in no time!

The mythology of 'the Territory' conjures a harsh and beautiful landscape that inevitably shapes the people who live in it – a place where the men are tough and the women are tougher. The emphasis on 'wildness' and 'wilderness' in the discourse of white settlement in the Northern Territory is perhaps stronger than that of any other Australian state. The history of gardening up here is one of remote cattle-station gardeners struggling to make their homes cool and green and townies struggling to make their backyards attractive, with both all the while trying to feed themselves. In the nineteenth century, horticulture in Darwin was preoccupied with economic gardening and plant acclimatisation, and it wasn't until last century that more attention was given to ornamental and civic gardens. Of course the city's collective garden-making began all over again after Cyclone Tracy decimated the landscape, buildings, trees and gardens in 1974.

Leonie came to gardening out of necessity – she was a 1970s hippie with a dream of living off the land, and who needed to feed a family of five on nothing. Her knowledge has been acquired through trial and error over her horticultural journey, and has also been handed down by her late grandmother Eve, a legendary local gardener, born and bred in the tropics. A native of Far North Queensland, Eve lived in Papua New Guinea until just after World War II, before settling in Darwin. Grandma Eve 'grew food plants with a passion', writes Leonie in *Tropical Food Gardens*. 'She befriended the local Chinese market gardeners and swapped seeds and advice. She secreted plants out of government trials in her bra. She built food gardens around all the shacks and army camps she lived in, and until she died forced advice, cuttings and her passion for growing food on everyone she met.'[2] With a grandma like Eve, Leonie really had no option but to become herself a passionate grower of food! Eve would surely be proud that Leonie is spreading her inherited knowledge to an audience of millions on national TV in her role as a presenter on the ABC1's *Gardening Australia*.

Leonie and husband Alan's self-built stone house is set among a shady tangle of native and exotic trees, the green foliage of ferns and shrubs interspersed with rusty sculptures of salvaged farm equipment. The kitchen garden is a stone's throw from the house, and occupies an enclosed area of about 6 × 10 m as well as a number of un-enclosed beds clustered close by. This enclosed garden structure was made from recycled 100-mm rural-grade polypipe secured to the ground on each side and curved over and joined in the middle to make a series of six arches. Crop netting was then stretched over the entire structure. This cage is essential given the abundant wildlife: possums, bandicoots, flying foxes, rats, sulphur-crested cockatoos and scrub fowl (which look like mini cassowaries). Other unlucky Northern Territory gardeners might also have to deal with feral buffalo, pigs or even brumbies tracking through their properties!

Clockwise, from above: **Leonie's jungle; not only is she a great gardener, Leonie is also an author and a presenter on ABC1's** *Gardening Australia*; **fresh tumeric; verandah living.**
Following page: **The enclosed vegie garden measures 6 x 10 m and keeps Leonie's food plants safe from flying foxes, scrub fowl and feral pigs.**

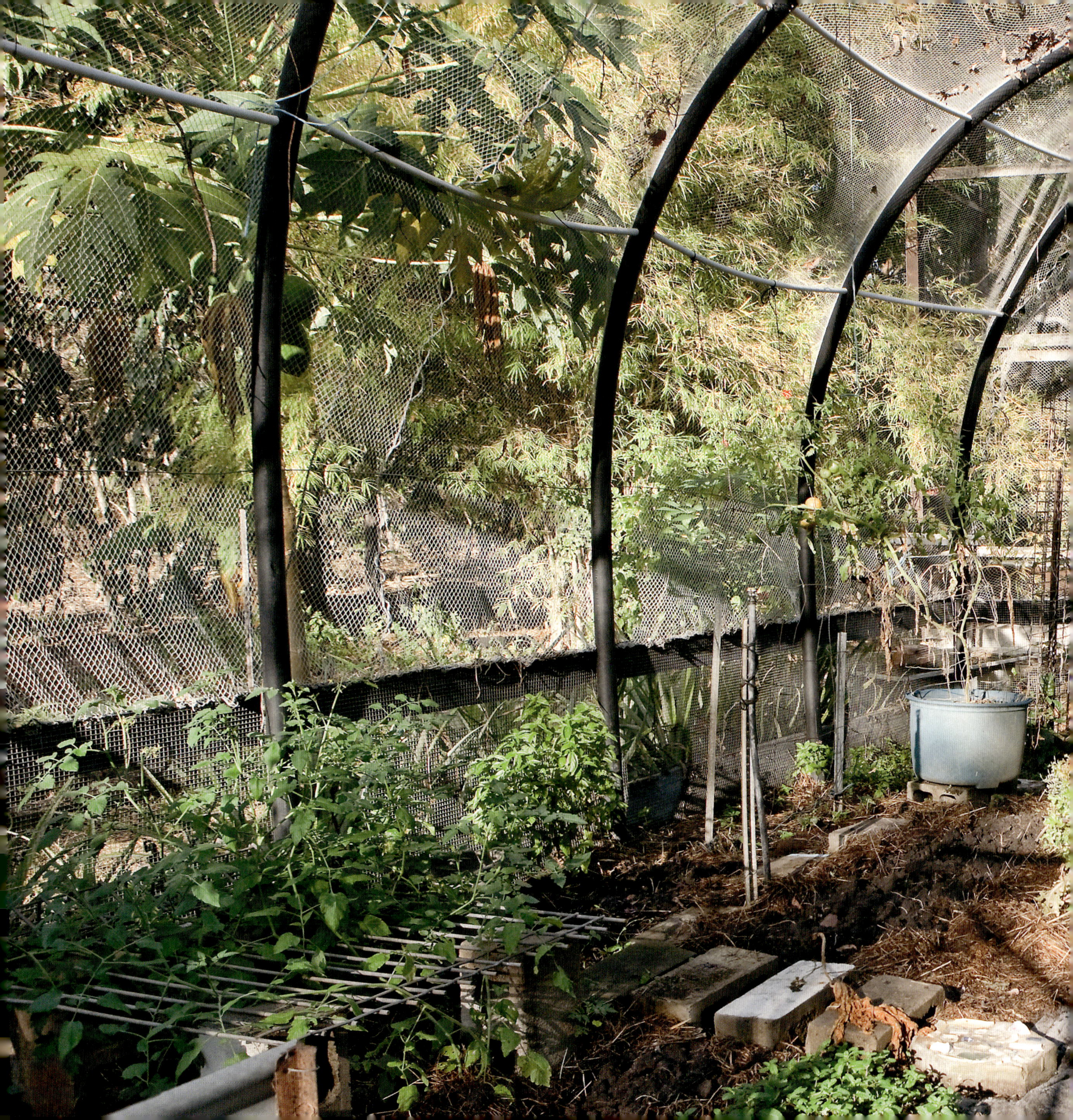

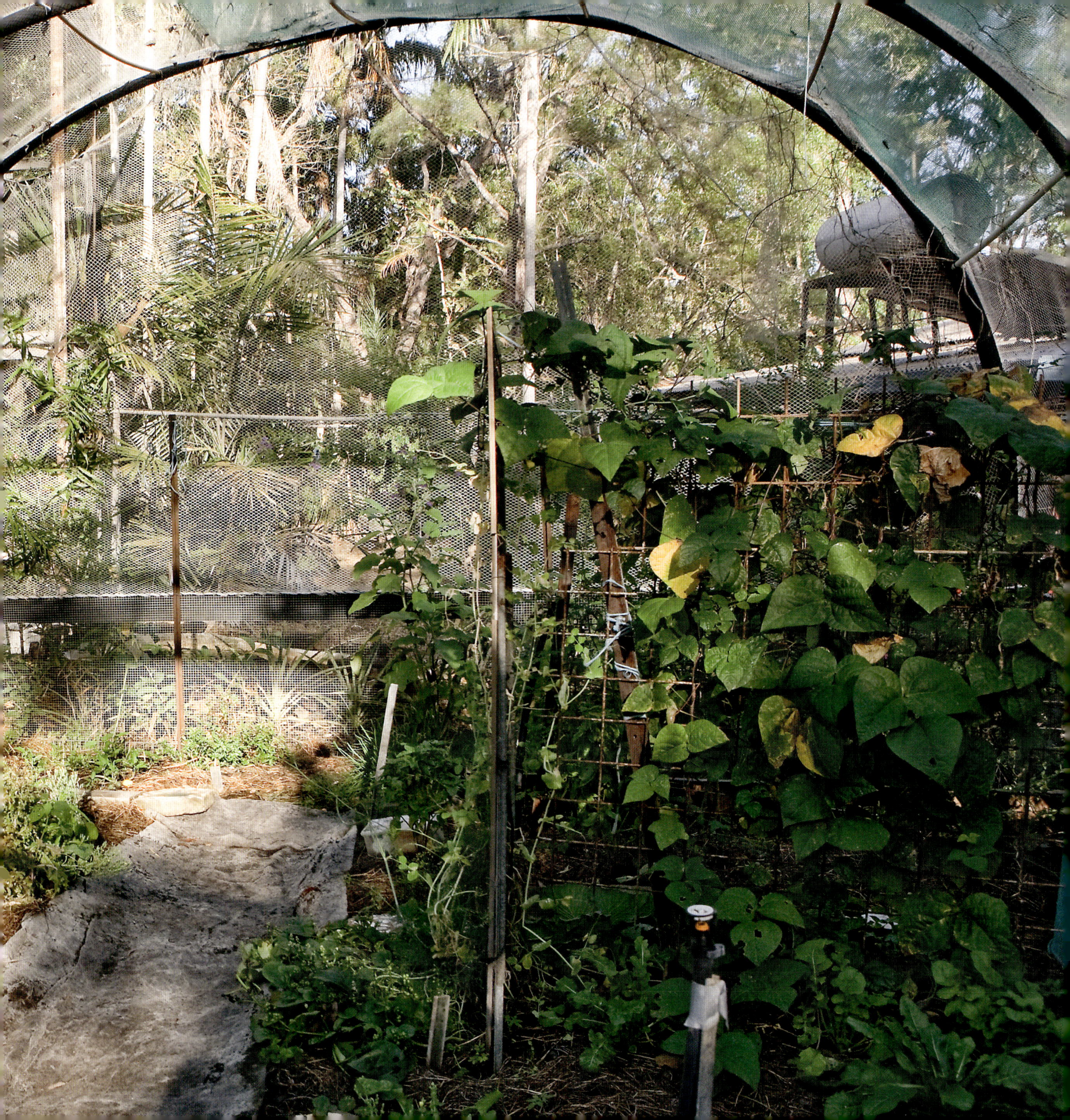

LEONIE NORRINGTON'S TROPICAL FOOD GARDEN

1	Basil	10	True pandanus
2	Kang kong and coriander	11	Ginger and galangal
3	Eggplants	12	Water chestnut and native waterlily in pond
4	Climbing beans	13	Pumpkins and lemongrass, lime and mulberry
5	Salad greens	14	Nursery area
6	Corn	15	Bananas and pawpaws
7	White sweetpotato	16	Wet season chook run
8	Cucumber	17	Dry season chook run
9	Tomatoes	18	Kaffir lime and bamboo

In addition to the hungry megafauna there are the insects – termites are a menace, as are ants that steal your corn seeds from the vegie beds (necessitating their being propagated first in trays). It's an intensively cultivated space where food plants are the focus and only an occasional weedy orange cosmos pops its pretty head up. In the enclosed garden Leonie has used a geotextile – a long-lasting synthetic fabric employed for erosion control – on her paths, which still allows water to permeate but smothers weeds. The produce garden is watered with bore water via sprinklers and, along with the small area of lawn and selected trees, is the only garden area to receive water over the long Dry season.

You wouldn't think that with an annual rainfall of around 1750 mm, water would be an issue in tropical Darwin. Up here, where the sun passes through the zenith twice during the solar year, there are two 'whitefella' seasons – the Dry season, from April through to September; and the Wet season from October through to March. The Dry season has high temperatures of 32°C with no rain for up to eight months at a time. In the Wet, Darwin's rain falls over four months with highs of 38°C and lows of 22°C, compounded by 98 per cent humidity. The local Larrakia people recognise six seasons: late March and April is the end of the Wet season; late April to August is the Dry season; September, October is the hot dry season; the 'Build-up' is from late October to December; and late December and January is the breaking of the Wet. January, February and March is the Wet season proper, while February and March is the 'Knock-em down' storm season.

Despite the huge rainfall, Darwin is not immune from issues of water supply. Its water comes from the Darwin River dam as well as aquifers. But this underground water is not an infinite resource, and the rate of development in the city and suburbs is a big danger to these reserves. Little rainwater harvesting in tanks goes on up here – the paradox is that although there is so much rain, the Dry is so long that it is simply impossible or impossibly expensive to capture enough of it to last over more than six months of no rain.

In addition to one mango tree (the neighbouring properties around here are mango farms) Leonie grows the 'Darwin lime' – an incredibly tough and thorny citrus – a mulberry, a fig, the yellow tropical guava (*Psidium guajava*), a tamarind tree and pawpaws, which are eaten green, cooked as a vegetable or used raw (grated in salads) as well as ripe – either fresh or dried. Leonie uses home-grown bananas like a staple food, eating them fresh and cooked, and she also freezes them or dries them in a dehydrator. With all the travel she's had to do in recent years she has reduced her orchard to the bare minimum. Her vegies and herbs, however, are abundant and thriving. The aromatic Mediterranean herbs like oregano and thyme (which don't enjoy the tropical humidity) are grown in the garden or in pots on the paving near the house. Basil, on the other hand, thrives. There is every herb you might desire for fantastic curries: ginger, galangal, curry leaf, Kaffir lime, Vietnamese mint and, of course, lemongrass. Turmeric is grown in an old washing machine tub so as not to lose its rhizomes. There is the true culinary pandanas, which is a common ingredient in sweet Indonesian rice desserts. Parsley and coriander are grown from seed in polystyrene boxes.

> 'In the Wet season plants can literally grow before your eyes and the bush goes completely berserk.'

If Leonie should ever need cinnamon or pepper and vanilla beans, a friend with a productive garden nearby grows all three. Her neighbour grows pepper (*Piper nigrum*), a tropical vine, on a purpose-built timber frame and the vanilla vine – in fact, an orchid – scrambles up trees and through ginger plants. Even his outdoor dunny has a vanilla vine growing over it! Vanilla is a labour-intensive plant in that it requires hand pollination at night in the absence of the moth that pollinates it in the jungles of Brazil, where it originates, but considering the cost of vanilla beans, it may be worth it.

In the Wet season plants can literally grow before your eyes and the bush goes completely berserk. Rot, fungal diseases

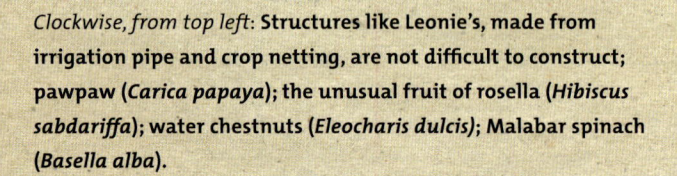

Clockwise, from top left: **Structures like Leonie's, made from irrigation pipe and crop netting, are not difficult to construct; pawpaw (*Carica papaya*); the unusual fruit of rosella (*Hibiscus sabdariffa*); water chestnuts (*Eleocharis dulcis*); Malabar spinach (*Basella alba*).**

and pests that thrive and breed in warm, moist conditions are dangers to the vegie garden at this time of year. The Wet-season list of plants includes beans, pumpkin, bamboo shoots and rosella, sweetpotato and wing beans. A wider range of vegetables enjoy the Dry – especially those from cool or southern climates, which she calls 'princess vegetables'. Early in the Dry season Leonie cultivates a variety of these: beetroot, tatsoi, bok choy, lettuce, cabbage, spring onion and snow peas – an old variety grown by Chinese gardeners in Darwin that she obtained from a friend. Corn, cucumber, white sweetpotato, rockmelon, watermelon, zucchini and squash all do very well in the Dry. Chilli plants and eggplants grow into 1.5-m-high monster bushes and Leonie finds the yellow currant tomato handed down to her from Grandma Eve particularly hardy.

Greens such as malabar spinach, sweet leaf (*Sauropus androgynus*) and kang kong (*Ipomea aquatica*) are used frequently by Leonie. Kang kong is a semi-aquatic tropical relative of sweetpotato and morning glory, and is Leonie's favourite green. It's a pleasant-tasting and nutritious leafy vegetable that can be grown in both the Wet and Dry seasons. It is cultivated extensively in South-East Asia and used in all manner of stir-fries and soup and noodle dishes. In the garden here it is grown in a plastic-lined trench as it loves wet feet. Edible water plants also thrive in a small pond in a sunny position outside the main enclosed garden. The Chinese water chestnut is the corm of the sedge-like *Eleocharis dulcis* (there are many edible native species, though – *E. acuta* is endemic to southern Australia) that shares the pond with the beautiful native waterlily, *Nymphaea violacea*. The waterlily, whose local name is *Dambilinggwa*, has a number of edible parts – the ripe seeds, raw stems and the long rhizomes that are harvested at the end of the Dry season when the water dries up. Leonie recommends the roots roasted or fried with garlic. The traditional waterlily cake is made by grinding the ripe seeds between stones into a paste, then forming it into little dampers that are baked in hot coals.

Leonie knew from an early age that there is food growing outside of the vegie-garden fence right there in the tropical savannah. Leonie's books for children celebrate the wonders of the natural world and the bush, and the people and cultures of the Northern Territory. They convey her deep understanding of the bush and the sense of custodianship, taught to her from childhood by her Aboriginal friends. Tropical savannah constitutes about a quarter of mainland Australia's land area. Much of it is Aboriginal land, and a very large proportion of its population is Aboriginal. The region where Leonie lives is the traditional land of the Larrakia people. It has very high levels of biodiversity – it's an amazing ecosystem, shaped over millennia by fire, flood and rain. Characterised by an open canopy of Darwin stringybark (*Eucalyptus tetrodonta*) and Darwin woollybutt (*E. miniata*) with cocky apple (*Planchonia careya*), billy goat plum (*Terminalia ferdinandiana*) and spiral pandanus (*Pandanus spiralis*), the sand palm (*Livistona humilis*), green plum (*Buchanania obovata*) and the beautiful semi-deciduous cycad *Cycas armstrongii*, a living fossil, in the mid-storey. The under-storey is made up of dense grasses like spear grass. All the uses – food, medicine, tools – of the plant species here are known by the Larrakia and are fundamental to their culture. Just one of the multitude of local bushfood plants is the yam *Dioscorea transversa*, whose position is marked above ground by its climbing stems with heart-shaped leaves clambering up the trees for the sky. The yams are harvested when the vine dies off in the Dry and can be boiled or roasted like sweetpotato and potato. Another is the billy goat plum tree that grows to 10 m high and bears its 3–4-cm-long pale green fruit from March to June. It was recently added to the list of 'native super-foods' because vitamin C makes up 5 per cent of the weight of the fruit, which is a hundred times more than the concentration in oranges!

It is hard for a southern gardener like me to comprehend the climate – especially the rate of nutrient leaching and of decomposition in the Wet, and the extreme evaporation and months without rain in the Dry. Leonie has developed a bit of a mulch mantra – she says it is absolutely essential up here to cover the soil or else lose its nutrients and structure through the powerful action of heavy and prolonged monsoonal rain.

Organic mulches like hay, lemongrass or even lawn clippings are valuable, she says, as are aged manures and living cover crops like peanuts, cow peas and Wynn cassia (*Chamaecrista rotundifolia*). Mulch, dead or alive, keeps soil temperatures down and encourages soil macro-invertebrates such as earthworms as well as microbes and bacteria that recycle nutrients and carbon in soils. Their activities increase soil porosity, which is critical to the infiltration of water and to making nutrients available to plants.

Like the weather, termites are a fact of life here – they will eat your trees from the inside out before you even realise they're there. Leonie finds she has to move her cassava plants every season in order to prevent the termites getting to them. She has come to realise that having the bush around your productive garden is ultimately beneficial – it creates habitat for predators like insect-eating bats, frogs, spiders, birds and lizards, increases competition for the big destructive termites from other termite species, increases beneficial predator insect populations and greater biodiversity in general.

Leonie's wonderful sense of humour is illustrated by two signature gardening methods – a liquid fertiliser mixture dubbed 'Super Dead Shit', and cane toad compost. 'Super Dead Shit' was invented by a friend and involves submerging a bag of chook-poo or dead animals in a large drum of water. It's stinky but totally fantastic for the soil says Leonie. (However, due to the potential risk of pathogens like *Salmonella*, it should only be used well in advance of planting food crops.) Leonie and family go collecting the cane toad, the scourge of the tropics and one of Australia's worst ever pests. Introduced into Queensland in 1935 to control sugar cane pests, cane toads are one of the world's hundred-worst invasive species. They poison native amphibians, reptiles and mammals, and eat beneficial insects. They are currently spreading at a rate of 30–50 km per year in the Northern Territory. War has been declared on *Bufo marinus*, but cane toads are covered by animal welfare laws and the recommended humane method of exterminating them is by putting them in the fridge and then in the freezer. 'Cane toads grow great bananas,' says Leonie, 'simply dig a hole, put in your dead frozen cane toads, some soil, the plant, and backfill – easy!'

Growing your own food requires really only a small amount of time and labour compared to regular shopping at the supermarket, believes Leonie. And she and Alan are highly self-sufficient – Alan makes bread, is a dedicated fisherman and hunts the occasional buffalo and wild pig. Their Isa Brown chooks lay all year round in their two residences – they have a chook yard for each of the seasons. In the Wet-season yard they live among large clumps of the multipurpose lemongrass. In the Dry-season yard Leonie makes a green chook feeder – she grows orange sweetpotatoes under an old car roof-rack that lets the chooks eat the green tops but protects the tubers below. There's not a helluva lot this couple needs from the supermarket, although an organic grocer in Darwin suburbs supplies the things Leonie doesn't grow in any one season, like carrots and onions. One of her tricks is to minimise a glut of produce by growing the right amount of the things she uses frequently, and fertilising less so as to only 'grow what you need – as there are only so many bananas and eggplants you can eat!'

There is evidently a lovely community of gardeners in the Northern Territory, committed to their amazing natural environment as well as to making gardens within it and producing food from it. Who would ever choose to watch TV with all the ecological entertainment to be found up here in the tropics: plants, animals, birds, reptiles and insects, not to mention the incredible weather and storms, and all the fishing and gardening to be done? But then they might miss seeing Leonie on *Gardening Australia*, and forego a regular dose of her wonderful gardening common sense and delightful enthusiasm.

Clockwise, from top left: **Leonie propagates many of her plants; kang kong (*Ipomea aquatica*); the seedpods of the tamarind tree; chillies grow year round in the Northern Territory climate; the fruit of the pepper vine; bananas; Leonie inspects a turmeric rhizome; lemongrass (*Cymbopogon citratus*).**
Centre: **The 'white' sweet potato has pale yellow flesh.**

VEGETABLE	Depth of Sowing	METHOD OF SOWING	Days to Emergence
Parsley		Direct in drills	15 - 20

JOSH BYRNE'S KITCHEN GARDEN

Size	Property: 300 m^2
	Garden: 60 m^2
Climate	Mediterranean
Soil	Sandy
Average annual rainfall	860 mm
Frost	No
Water source	Greywater, rainwater tanks, mains water
Irrigation method	Drip irrigation
Compost and fertiliser	Homemade compost and worm castings, pelletised manure, rock minerals, fish emulsion and seaweed solution
Mulch	Shredded lupins and pea straw for vegies and fruit trees, aged shredded tree prunings for natives
Biggest challenges	Sandy alkaline soil
	Hot, dry summer
Favourite herb	Sweet basil and coriander
Favourite food plant	Asian greens (pak choy, bok choy and tatsoi), grapes and figs

CHAPTER 14
JOSH BYRNE'S SUSTAINABLE BACKYARD

Environmental scientist, green gardener and author, Josh Byrne is known to the nation's gardeners primarily through his role as the Perth-based presenter of ABC1's *Gardening Australia*. It is always reassuring to learn that our experts practise what they preach, and in Josh's case, sustainability is no made-for-TV green-wash but an ethos both lived and pursued. His own backyard in the seaside city of Fremantle is a great example of his commitment to sustainable living. Here, Josh has not only created a decked living area with pizza oven, BBQ, outdoor kitchen and storage that incorporates a laundry and clothesline, he's also built a separate studio (that can function as a home office or guest room), installed storage for 8500 L of rainwater and a greywater system, and established a productive garden containing vegetable beds, fruit trees, chooks, compost bins and a worm farm. All this is squeezed into an area of just 6.5 × 25 m – there obviously is no space allocated to lawn or a swimming pool on this intensively utilised property!

Instead, there is an outdoor room that Josh, partner Kellie and baby Oliver use all year round and a garden that provides food throughout the seasons: fruit, herbs, greens and a number of carefully chosen seasonal vegetables. (When space is limited it really makes you sort the things you truly 'can't do without' from the desired yet non-essential.) Over the last four years the garden's creation has been documented on *Gardening Australia*, and shown viewers how Josh has integrated elements of permaculture design as well as how he has cleverly addressed the challenges of Fremantle's extreme climate and conditions.

Gardening was something Josh became interested in during his early years. Born in Esperance on the south coast of Western Australia, he spent his childhood among some of the most biodiverse bushland in all of Australia. Known as the South-west Botanical Province, the region is a flora 'hotspot' with around 53 per cent of its species occurring nowhere else on the planet. Josh's horticultural interests have developed very much in symbiosis with his environmental ones. He created his first vegetable garden at age fourteen and had a gardening maintenance round by eighteen. Josh studied Environmental Science at Murdoch University in Perth, where he met Kellie, an ecologist who shares his commitment to conserving Western Australia's unique natural environment. As an undergraduate living in rental properties and working as a gardener, Josh continued to practice hands-on what he was learning at uni by creating both ornamental and productive gardens. His share-households wanted to eat cheaply as well as locally to reduce their ecological impact. For Josh, it was also important that his food be grown organically so as to benefit both his own and the environment's health. He cites the absence of chemicals or synthetic fertilisers, reduced pollution, reduced waste going to landfill, and food that has not travelled thousands of miles before being consumed, as just some of the reasons he grows his own at home following organic methods. Flavour is, of course, the other great reason: 'Once you have tasted vegetables picked only minutes before you eat them, you will never look back,'[1] writes Josh in his book *The Green Gardener*.

Following some key building work (luckily their landlords are family friends and were happy to have them improve the property), Josh and Kellie were able to begin on their latest garden. With only 60 m² of open space to play with for food production, this north-facing rear garden needed to be carefully designed. A path of reused brick connects the deck to the building at the rear, and allows access to the vegetable garden beds – one rectangular garden bed at ground level and one 3 × 1.5-m raised corrugated steel bed. In winter Josh grows Chinese cabbage, celery, broad beans, leeks and broccoli, while pak choy, bok choy and tatsoi provide ample greens for stir-fries. In the spring the raised bed contains lettuces – green cos and the frilly red 'Lollo Rosso' – and perhaps carrots, spring onions and silverbeet. Herbs and mixed salad greens are year-round necessities and are staples that Josh and Kellie certainly don't want to have to buy. With summer approaching, these are joined by cucumbers, basil and bush beans. This season Josh has also planted the climbing beans 'Purple King', 'Blue Lake' and borlotti to climb teepees made of locally sourced stakes. Cherry tomatoes as well as 'Beefsteak' and 'Roma' varieties, and eggplants 'Bonica', 'Japanese Long' and the Lebanese type

Josh's Fremantle backyard with its deck, vegetables, chooks, water tanks and studio. Could anything more be fitted into this 6.5 × 25 m space?

JOSH BYRNE'S SUSTAINABLE BACKYARD

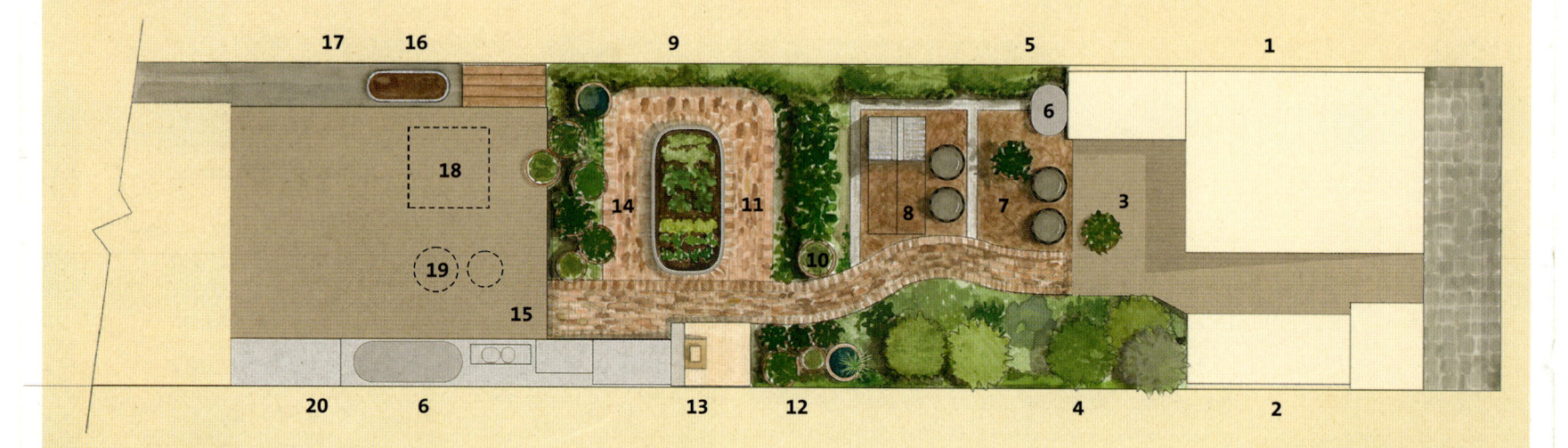

1. Studio (home office/guest room)
2. Outdoor bath and shower
3. Deck
4. Ornamental shrubs, companion plants, pomegranate and feijoa
5. Corrugated steel water tank
6. Potted fig 'Jenny Smith Blue'
7. Compost bins
8. Chooks
9. Trellised fruit trees
10. Climbing beans
11. Raised bed for annual vegetables
12. Potted bay and kaffir lime trees, potted tomatoes and eggplants, aquatic pots and grapevines on fence
13. Pizza oven and outdoor kitchen
14. Pot collection of herbs and berries
15. Deck
16. Worm farm
17. Potting bench
18. Tank underneath deck
19. Greywater system
20. Laundry

are being grown in pots and growbags filled with potting mix and compost. Beans, tomatoes and eggplants are their favourite summer vegetables and, says Josh, will provide enough for three or four meals a week over the summer months.

Deciduous fruit trees – including an apricot, nectarine, plum, apple and pear – are located around the garden's perimeter in narrow beds and are trained to grow flat against the fence. The height of the trees is maintained at about 2.4 m in order to enable easy harvest and prevent their shading the rest of the garden. On the east fence Josh has planted grapevines including the popular table grapes 'Sultana' and 'Red Globe' – which bears bunches of large red grapes in mid- to late February. The single fig tree planted in a pot at the north end of the garden is an early variety with beautiful purple-blue-skinned fruit and dark pink flesh named 'Jenny Smith Blue'. In a small yard like this an edible borrowed landscape is also a wonderful thing – next door is an established mulberry tree ('Hick's Fancy') that bears prolific amounts of the delicious red-black berries in October to December.

A collection of different-sized pots (some raised off the ground) help give a three-dimensional aspect to the space and contain a large variety of herbs. There are many different mints and thymes, as well as sage, chives, parsley, oregano, Thai basil, a bay and a Kaffir lime tree. Taller growing herbs like rosemary and companion plants surround the pots at ground level. The potted herbs couldn't be more handy for the pizza oven and for BBQ cooking, especially over the warmer months when, as Josh says, they 'live out here'. Pot culture also suits strawberries and blueberries – which are quite happy in hanging baskets. Josh has filled other pots with water and these contain pygmy perch and edible aquatic plants such as Lebanese cress (*Aethionema cordifolium*), taro, kang kong and water chestnut (*Eleocharis dulcis*) – the corms of which make a delicious addition to vegetable stir-fries. A feijoa, olive and pomegranate are thriving in the ground amid hardy shrubs like buddleia, *Salvia microphylla* and scented-leaf pelargoniums – which may not be edible but are pretty and attract bees and butterflies for pollination.

Josh has used materials that are recycled, salvaged or have low embodied energy wherever possible in building the deck, outdoor kitchen and studio, both to minimise environmental

> **'The potted herbs couldn't be more handy for the pizza oven and for BBQ cooking, especially over the warmer months when, as Josh says, they "live out here".'**

impact and to save money. At the rear of the garden the studio has been constructed with salvaged timber floors, windows and doors to encompass a heritage-listed out-house. The brick pizza oven was built from recycled bricks by a local friend. The corrugated-steel tanks were chosen because not only do they look good, they also have a fairly low environmental impact. Even simple things can save energy in the home – Josh designed the deck to be open to the west to allow the famous cooling south-westerly breeze known as the 'Fremantle Doctor' to blow in of an afternoon. Similarly, a gap between the deck and house roof lets hot air escape from the deck area. As well as clever design, there are playful elements in the garden, too. Rendered walls painted vivid pink add a sense of vibrancy, as do artworks that hang above the outdoor kitchen bench in the form of painted-tile installations by Josh's stepfather.

Perth has the triple whammy of sandy soil, a true Mediterranean climate where there is little if any summer rainfall, and extreme summer heat. The city lies at latitude 33°S on the south-west of the continent; to the west is the Indian Ocean and the low coastal escarpment of the Darling Range is to the city's east. The average annual rainfall is around 860 mm, which is relatively high (compared to arid-zone Alice Springs with 280 mm or even parts of cool temperate Tasmania with 600 mm) with the months of May to October being the wettest (744 mm), and December to January the driest (36 mm). The winter rain is thanks to the miraculous 'Leeuwin Current', a stream of warm tropical water that flows southward, parallel to the landmass, and is strongest in autumn and winter. Yet the classic 'summer dry' climate means there is no rain to harvest and store in small urban water tanks over the hottest months. To make matters even more difficult, the south-west of Western Australia has experienced a 10 per cent decline in average rainfall over the last twenty-five years. Stage 1 water restrictions came into place in Perth in 2004 and by 2009 permanent Stage 4 restrictions were in force, limiting sprinkler use with mains water to two rostered days a week. (Prior to the 2004 water restrictions, about 50 per cent of all water used by Perth households was on their gardens and swimming pools – an average of 700 L per day.)[2] Yet still people garden!

> **'Perth will run out of its available sustainable natural water resources by 2015 if nothing is done to slow usage rates. Josh has taken domestic water conservation and the reduction of his 'water footprint' to a new level.'**

There are many environmentally friendly gardening and design strategies for dealing with the limitations of climate. In designing his garden, Josh first of all grouped plants according to their water needs: moderate-use fruit trees and shrubs are grown in ground-level beds and are watered with greywater, whereas high-water-requirement vegetables are grown in the two vegetable beds and in the pots, and are watered by tank water with mains back-up. This hydro-zoning is the first step in designing a more water-efficient garden. Secondly, all the garden beds and pots are serviced using drip irrigation, which is more efficient than sprays. The greywater is delivered via a 16-mm lilac drip line with high flow (8 L per hour) clog-resistant drippers. The rainwater (with mains water as back-up) is supplied to the vegetables by regular 16-mm drip line with 4 L per hour drippers. Pots are irrigated with adjustable pot drippers. Thirdly, Josh chooses his food plants not only according to the space available, but also in relation to their water requirements and seasonal nature. 'Water guzzlers' like celery and pak choy are therefore planted in autumn to grow over winter and only the summer-hardy vegetables like eggplants and tomatoes are planted to grow through the heat.

Josh has installed various tanks for storing rainwater to use on the vegies and herbs, as well as supplying water to the toilet and washing machine. Two corrugated-steel tanks together hold 3000 L and there are two underground poly tanks beneath the deck totalling 5500 L. These catch run-off from 100 per cent of the roof catchment. In order to fit the tank under the deck Josh excavated the local sand to a depth of 2.5 m. Also hidden underneath is the greywater system – a direct-diversion 'non-treatment' type system (which means the greywater cannot, in accordance with the Western Australian Department of Health regulations, be stored for more than 24 hours) comprising concrete sedimentation and pump-out tanks and a filter.

It is amazing to consider that there is no *new* water being made on Earth – that the only water we have is already in existence since the planet's hydrological cycle is a closed system – thus the amount of water in the hydrosphere is constant. Only 3 per cent of the world's water is fresh, 68.7 per cent of that is ice and snow, 30.1 per cent is ground water and a mere 0.3 per cent of fresh water is held in rivers, lakes and reservoirs. Josh is adamant that West Australians (indeed, all of us) need to conserve the state's limited drinking water supplies and stop relying solely on mains water for gardening. Rainwater and greywater for domestic irrigation as well as toilet flushing are the way to go. A 2002 study by the University of Western Australia found that Perth will run out of its available sustainable natural water resources by 2015 if nothing is done to slow usage rates. Josh has taken domestic water conservation and the reduction of his 'water footprint' to a new level. His research and interest in water conservation has been the catalyst for establishing his

Clockwise, from top: **Josh grows food plants in an assortment of containers: vegies in the raised bed, herbs in pots and berries in hanging baskets; the irrigation system with USB data loggers; four compost bins are needed in this household and garden; the underground deck tank holds 3500 L of water.**

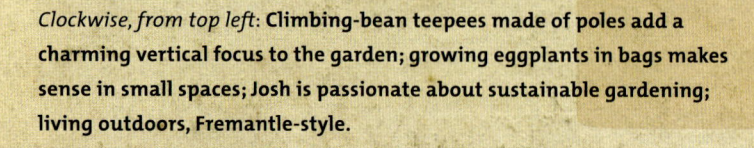

Clockwise, from top left: **Climbing-bean teepees made of poles add a charming vertical focus to the garden; growing eggplants in bags makes sense in small spaces; Josh is passionate about sustainable gardening; living outdoors, Fremantle-style.**

own garden as a kind of prototype. Josh is definitely a 'water nerd' who gets satisfaction from knowing the precise details of how much of what water gets used where! Such knowledge is an industry necessity these days; only by tracking the flow of water and collecting the data – in this case via data-logging meters (which he downloads on to his computer) – will Josh collect information that is immensely valuable in his design business, and to pass on to the gardening community via publications, talks and TV.

Despite the problems with water, the biggest challenge here is actually the sandy soil, says Josh – it's like gardening on the beach! Fremantle – the traditional land of the Nyungar people who knew it as *Walyalup* – is a fragile ecology of sand over a series of limestone hills. 'Freo' has been a port town almost since white settlement and its early landscape was marked by warehouses, shipping-related commerce, workers' housing and also stabling for the horses that worked the port. It is a testament to just how sandy Fremantle is, and the local gardeners' need for organic matter that, as historian Andrea Gaynor points out in her wonderful book *Harvest of the Suburbs*, Fremantle Council was still selling nightsoil to gardeners as late as 1908.[3] Sandy soils have little or no structure, are usually free draining and low in nutrients. The grains of sand have no 'glue' – sand is devoid of the clay particles and organic particles that bind the large mineral fractions together to form aggregates, which in turn creates soil structure.

The physical characteristics of soils can be changed with good management, however. There are a number of steps to making sandy soils productive for vegetable growing. Firstly, Josh's advice is to overcome the hydrophobic (or water-repelling) nature of sandy soils. Josh likes to use an organic, humus-based wetting agent rather than the detergent-based surfactant-type product in order to maintain 'wetability'. Then, he incorporates compost – with Fremantle's sand it is imperative to keep adding organic matter. Josh warns that garden beds should 'never be left empty or rain and irrigation will leech them back to sand' and he therefore also recommends sowing a green manure crop over winter. Without access to clay, compost is the best way to improve the water-holding capacity of sand. As well as increasing soil fertility and microbial activity, organic matter creates soil structure by adding the essential aggregating 'glue' to turn sand into soil, and also functions as a water-absorbing sponge. Next, Josh adds rock minerals in either dust or pellet form. (These come in a range of supplement combinations; zeolites, in particular, can act as a water moderator, adsorbing up to 55 per cent of their weight in water and slowly releasing it under plant demand.) Finally, he mulches the garden with an organic mulch like pea straw or shredded lupins. Mulch is absolutely essential as Perth experiences around 8 mm of daily evaporation during summer.

Apart from seaweed solution and fish emulsion, Josh makes his own fertilisers to use on his soil and keep his food plants thriving (and in doing so he reduces the amount of waste going into his wheelie bin and thus his carbon footprint). The chooks, compost bins and worm farm all convert house and garden waste into plant food. Weeds and leaves from the garden as well as kitchen scraps are fed to the two bantam Rhode Island Red chooks housed in a mobile 'A-frame' pen. The worm farm adjoining the deck is inspired – it's an old bathtub enclosed within a timber frame with a timber lid that doubles as an extra bench. Anything that the worms and chooks won't eat goes into the black plastic compost bins. Having four small bins is ideal for urban gardens. Providing your carbon/nitrogen ratio is good and your 'lasagne' of different compost materials is adequate – by the time you fill the fourth bin, the contents of the first bin should be nice and decomposed.

With advocates of sustainability like Josh creating gardens adapted to such tough local conditions, the west coast is leading the way in gardening for the changing climate. We are, it seems, finally beginning to realise that suburbia has a significant potential to provide its own water, energy and food. Josh's home demonstrates the potential for suburban rain-water harvesting and greywater reuse to enable households to grow some of their own food, as well as recycling their organic waste. Josh's backyard is green and attractive, tactile and edible, scented and colourful – an oasis in the Fremantle sand.

FRANK'S KITCHEN GARDEN

Size	20 × 25 m (500 m²)
Climate	Subtropical
Soil	Improved clay
Average annual rainfall	750 mm
Frost	No
Water source	Fitzroy River
Irrigation method	Drip irrigation and hand-watering
Compost and fertiliser	Composted chook manure, cow manure, liquid seaweed plant conditioner
Mulch	Grass hay, composted manure
Biggest challenges	Fruit fly
Favourite herb	Lemon basil
Favourite food plant	Zucchini 'Tromboncini', watermelon 'Moon and Stars'

CHAPTER 15
KITCHEN GARDENING IN CAPRICORNIA

Being the beef capital of Australia, Rockhampton is better known for its Santa Getrudis, Brafords and Bos indicus than for its gardens. Blessed with Australia's second-largest river system and endless sunshine, it is perhaps surprising that there is not a large local horticultural industry. (There is cotton farming at nearby Emerald, sugarcane at Bundaberg in the south and at tropical Mackay, further north, but little actual crop or fruit growing in Rocky itself.) Still, as the Rockhampton Botanic Gardens demonstrate, the climate supports a botanical diversity of plants from all of the world's warm zones – banyan trees from India, cycads from South Africa and palms from the Caribbean.

The gardens were established in 1869 when 96 acres (39 ha) of grazing land on the western slopes of the Athelstane Range was set aside for a botanical garden. While the Acclimatisation Society of Queensland responsible for the garden was interested in economic botany, I'm sure they recognised the new settlement needed more than just grass, dust and cattle – that a city was made liveable by thriving plants and gardens. In this region, deep shade and green lawns are important climate-modifiers that make the considerable heat, glare and humidity of the summer months more bearable. Food plants and ornamental flowers, on the other hand, sate the tastebuds and the eye – and are things that are just as important as shade trees and lawns, as many gardeners in central and outback Queensland would agree. Such gardeners are a special breed who think nothing of a 400-km drive to visit an open garden – after all, isolation is a mindset as much as it is a geographical reality.

These are all things that local gardener and teacher, Frank, understands well. Born and bred in Rocky, Frank has been gardening since childhood. His garden of the last fifteen years is established on a steep south-facing slope in urban Rockhampton. The garden, he says, shows that it 'is possible to have a kitchen garden in our climate and for the garden to be moderately attractive'. This is quite an understatement, for his garden is the most delightful mix of flowers in shades of purple, red, yellow and orange; abundant green foliage; the air is scented with jasmine and the pennyroyal crushed underfoot. When Frank and his wife Jenny bought the old Queenslander in 1994, the block was covered in poinciana and palm trees, and the only fruit tree was a single mulberry. Now, having purchased an adjoining block of land, every bit of available space is filled with edible and useful plants: they grow in the ground, in raised hay-bale beds, polystyrene boxes, colourful plastic tubs, tractor tyres and in pots. This garden is choc-a-bloc with plants.

The Rockhampton climate is classified as subtropical and the city is situated on the Tropic of Capricorn, but it exists in a sort of in-between zone: it is not coastal, being 40 km up the Fitzroy River (on which it depends for water), yet neither is it properly inland, meaning that it can get cyclones. It is hotter and drier than both Brisbane and Cairns, but situated too far south to experience regular monsoons. It is not a place you'd expect to find azaleas growing among heat-loving flowering shrubs from South America but they are flourishing in Frank's front garden! Like many parts of central Queensland, Rockhampton's average annual rainfall has steadily declined over the past 100 years. In 1900 it received around 1000 mm, but in recent years it is closer to 750 mm. Locals say that there is no distinct Wet and Dry season any more: spring temperatures are much higher than they used to be, and there have been periods of up to eight months without rain. It is not irrational to regard this as the warming and drying effect of climate change, and not merely a meteorological trend.

They do say the grass is always greener on the other side, and Rockhampton is too tropical for growing garlic, kale, Brussels sprouts and most stone fruit, but it's a perfect climate for snake beans, galangal and pawpaws. The southern aspect of Frank's garden means that some areas are shaded in winter but receive the full force of the sun's rays in summer. The heat is the determining factor in what will survive in the productive garden. With average high temperatures around 36°C in summer, Frank usually needs to water leafy crops twice a day, but sometimes three times. Frank can, however, successfully grow root crops like eschalots and beetroot as well as bulb fennel and coles such as cabbage, broccoli and cauliflower in winter.

Frank's kitchen garden is a charming mix of flowers, fruit trees, herbs and vegetables

FRANK'S GARDEN

1	Pond	9	Globe artichokes, snow peas on trellis gate	17	Carambola tree
2	Sitting area	10	Pawpaw, dragon fruit, salvaged boat	18	Lime tree
3	Hay-bale garden with potatoes, cabbage, eschallots, eggplants, fennel	11	Hay-bale bed	19	Corn, tomatoes, zucchini and macadamia and jaboticaba trees
4	Herbs, sunflowers	12	Herbs	20	Coconut palms
5	Arbour and seat	13	Citrus trees	21	Barbados cherry
6	Herbs	14	Native mulberry	22	Black mulberry
7	Arbour with 'Malabar' spinach and grape 'Flame'	15	Juju tree	23	Curry leaf and olive trees
8	Chook run	16	Ginger, tumeric, arrowroot, salvias and white mulberry		

The summer heat doesn't stop the Solanaceae family: yellow cherry tomatoes, numerous bushes of chillies, capsicums and eggplants including the varieties 'Snowy', 'Little Finger' and the stunning purple-and-white striped 'Listada di Gandia' thrive. Frank says he grows approximately eighty-four different herbs, thirty-six (mostly heirloom) vegetables, twenty-seven different fruit trees and nine edible flowers. Perennial food plants include pepper vine, Malabar spinach, potatoes (which are grown in 'potato bags' and in hay-bale beds), arrowroot and rainbow chard. Seeds of mesclun salad mix and cos lettuce are sown regularly so the family will have a constant supply of salad greens. There is thyme, oregano, basil 'Limelight' with unusual frilly leaves, sorrel, parsley, chervil, sage, dill and rosemary. Asian herbs include Vietnamese mint, ginger, Kaffir lime tree and turmeric. In the damp soil around the pond and waterfall, Lebanese cress (*Aethionema cordifolium*) – a leafy shade-loving herb that tastes like celery and cucumber – is spreading as a groundcover. It is just as well that Jenny and Frank are committed foodies with all this produce erupting from the garden. Cooking from the garden is part of the family's daily routine, with old favourites as well as vegies being tried for the first time, all on the menu.

Frank tries to use local materials in his garden and the by-products of the local beef industry are readily available. Ordinary grass hay makes do as mulch in his kitchen garden (lucerne hay is very expensive up here) and Frank uses rotted cow manure from the Rockhampton abattoir for filling and topping up his garden beds. This is in addition to the composted litter from the family's lovely chooks (two Rhode Island Reds, one Dark-Barred Plymouth Rock and two buff-coloured Wyandottes). Frank grows much of his produce from seed, enjoying the range of heirloom varieties now available by mail order. One treasured Italian heirloom is zucchini 'Tromboncini'. Tromboncini has pale-green fruit that terminate in a bulbous lump resembling the bell on a trombone – giving the zucchini its name. They can be trained up a trellis or allowed to ramble over the ground, and while they can reach 1 m long, they are best picked much smaller. Frank loves their flavour as well as the fact that they store so well.

His other favourite is a watermelon with red flesh and a dark-green skin marked with many small yellow dots and one large spot resembling the night sky, named 'Moon and Stars'. The story of this beautiful watermelon is a common one: heirloom plant disappears from the market in the twentieth century because of commercial forces only to be 'rediscovered' because some gardener or entire village has been happily growing them all along. The melon was called 'Sun, Moon and Stars' when it was introduced in the United States in 1926 by Peter Henderson & Company, and it was sold by a number of seed companies in the 30s. According to writer Amy Goldman in her book *Melons for the Passionate Grower*, the 'Moon and Stars' melon was thought extinct until 1981, when the co-founder of Seed Savers Exchange, Kent Whealy, was contacted by a woman from Missouri who had been growing the melon for years. The watermelon quickly became the 'poster child of the heirloom seed movement'. When it was introduced into Australia by the Digger's Club in the 1990s, Frank planted it with his school students and produced an incredible crop of melons weighing in at around 13 kg each.

> **' Frank's garden is bursting at the fences with a veritable fruit salad of trees . . . It is just as well that Jenny and Frank are committed foodies with all this produce erupting from the garden.'**

Frank's garden is bursting at the fences with a veritable fruit salad of trees. Citrus trees form a glossy green mantle across the hillside kitchen garden. Lemonade trees, navel and 'Valencia' oranges, a mandarin, lemon, pink grapefruit and a Tahitian lime keep the family in juice, fruit and marmalade for months on end. Elsewhere in the garden Frank has planted a curry leaf tree, a macadamia, coconut palms, avocados, a black sapote (*Diospyros digyna*) and a carambola or star fruit tree (*Averrhoa carambola*).

Clockwise, from top left: **Ruby chard and dianthus grow happily in an old wheelbarrow; tomatoes grown in colourful plastic trugs; 'teapotted' herbs; Lebanese cress (*Aethionema cordifolium*) enjoys a damp spot in the garden; black sapote fruit.**

Frank's favourite tree is the Barbados cherry (*Malpighia glabra*), an evergreen with graceful arching branches and small pink flowers. It bears tart red fruits that are full of seeds and extremely high in vitamin C, almost all year long.

Other unusual fruit include the slow-growing jaboticaba with black berries growing straight from the trunk and the extraordinary climbing cactus that is the pitaya or dragon fruit. With its huge white cactus flowers followed by fluorescent pink knobbly fruits and white flesh dotted with black seeds, the dragon fruit is the epitome of exotic. The flavour is sweet and refreshing, and there are now self-pollinating selections bred in Vietnam where the fruit is grown commercially. Such fruity treasures are the subject of Adam Leith Gollner's book *The Fruit Hunters*, in which he describes a Willy Wonka-like world of crazy fruits and horticultural obsession, where although 'a select few species dominate international trade, our whole planet is brimming with fruits that are inaccessible, ignored and even forbidden'.[1] Which makes you wonder just how cosmopolitan the Australian fruit-growing scene is . . . perhaps not very, due in part to the 'biosecurity risk' that imported fruit plant species pose to our horticultural industry, and partly because we have yet to realise the potential bounty of our own native fruits.

Frank also grows fruit trees more common to temperate climes: two olive trees (which only produce when there is a very cold winter), a 'Brown Turkey' fig and dwarf white peaches. These are 'low chill' peach varieties bred to fruit in the subtropics without the number of chilling requirement hours needed to trigger fruit formation. But, Frank complains, he has only had a handful of peaches since planting the trees – not because of the heat and drought, but due to that most ruinous and hated of all produce garden pests: the fruit fly and its maggots! There are few insects that cause more damage to fruiting plants than the Queensland fruit fly *Bactrocera tryoni* (QFF). It is one of the world's worst horticultural pests as it attacks a wide range of plants, diminishing production and making fruit inedible. Not surprisingly, it has huge consequences for local and international trade. The female fly lays white banana-shaped eggs into a ripening fruit. (Among the only fruits that don't host the Queensland fruit fly are those of coffee, choko, olive and monstera.) The 5–10-mm long larvae emerge soon after – they eat their way towards the centre of the fruit with cutting jaws that help to tear the fruit into pieces small enough to swallow. The larval activity promotes rotting of the fruit, and while it may look perfect from the outside, it is putrid on the inside. Parts of Queensland, New South Wales, the Northern Territory and the eastern corner of Victoria are permanently infested by QFF. Growers work hard to maintain QFF-free zones and it is no wonder we're prohibited from taking fruit across the border into Victoria.

Frank's pest policy is one of 'exclusion and confusion'. Exclusion involves putting special paper bags over young fruit to exclude fruit flies as the fruit ripens. The exclusion bags have proved a labour-intensive but chemical-free way of actually getting some fruit! The fact that they increase the sooty mould on the oranges and lemons is a small price to pay. Frank prefers to generally 'confuse' insect pests through the sheer diversity of his plantings. He practises some companion planting with plants being grown specifically to either deter pest insects or to attract beneficial ones like predators or pollinators. The garden is one nectar-rich patch of over a hundred flowering plants: herbs, petunias, alyssum, lobelias, foxgloves and tropical vines. Salvias originating from South America do particularly well in the Rockhampton climate, being tolerant of both the heat and humidity. Frank grows the common pineapple sage, the dazzlingly red scarlet sage (*Salvia splendens*), *S.* 'Black Knight' with its purple-black calyxes and purple corollas, the deep pink *S.* 'Wendy's Wish' and the yellow *S. madrensis*. The magenta-purple *S. iodantha* blooms from autumn to summer, and is especially beautiful growing in combination with purple larkspurs and a little yellow sunflower that Frank found beside the road near Emerald. Many of the salvias self-seed readily here and seem as at home among the edibles in Rockhampton as if in the mountains of Guatemala or Brazil.

Not only is Frank's garden attractive as well as edible, it is an ongoing experiment in edible garden construction methods. His techniques are informed by his being involved in sustainability education, his understanding of the natural environment, and a dislike of waste. Over millennia humans have learnt to modify the physical environment in order to grow vegetables. Given certain resources and techniques we know we can cool or warm the soil, beat frost, advance or extend the growing season and grow plants outside their normal climatic range using windbreaks and hot beds of manure to glasshouses and heated walled gardens to today's fully climate-controlled poly-tunnels.

With climate change, Frank predicts that the future of home produce gardening may well involve making garden beds out of materials that will conserve water and insulate the soil, perhaps erected underneath a sun-filtering canopy. European-style kitchen gardens still tend to dominate our vegetable garden design schema. It could therefore prove rewarding to think more creatively about other means of constructing vegetable beds for intensive backyard food production. There are 'no dig' gardens, soil-less hydroponic gardens, 'wicking bed' vegie gardens (plastic-lined beds that are watered from a reservoir below the growing medium), aquaponic systems that involve running nutrient-rich water from fish tanks through vegetable beds and back again, and various possible combinations of these. All make the traditional rectangular bed constructed at ground level look slightly medieval. Non-European produce gardens have a long history and much to teach us – take the ancient Mexican system of raised beds known as *chinampas*, where, in marshy areas and shallow lakes, land was reclaimed by piling mud dredged from the lake bottom into mounds. With their sides reinforced with branches and timber, the *chinampas* would stand about 50 cm above water level and serve as the garden plots in which people like the Maya grew their crops. That they are still used in Mexico today is testament to their effectiveness.

Frank likes to use bales of hay to create raised 'no dig' beds. The cellulose breaks down in contact with soil, water and microbes, creating rich compost as the bales decompose and as earthworms feeding on the organic matter leave behind their castings. The soil inside the hay bales also tends to be cooler and moister than that in the beds out in the open ground. He grows lettuces in old polystyrene boxes as the boxes help keep the soil cool and can easily be moved into the shade. Recycling is a big part of Frank's gardening practice. There are great finds to be had at the local depot – take the star pickets and pool-fencing panels that enclose the garden. A galvanised wire gate found underneath a burnt-down building makes a perfect climbing frame for snow peas, and old metal wheelbarrows and even a salvaged wooden boat now contain edible plants. In the steepest part at the bottom of the garden Frank has used car and tractor tyres to retain soil so that he can plant yet more food in this inaccessible spot. Double-layer tyres grow corn and zucchini and triple-stacked tyres contain tomatoes. Tyres are stable and durable – they don't rot. The very qualities that make them an environmental nightmare ensure their suitability for building garden beds or even houses – take the famous 'earthship' dwellings that have walls built from tyres packed with earth. As for their safety, tyres do contain minute amounts of certain heavy metals, but the theory goes that if the tyres are in good condition the compounds are tightly bonded within the actual rubber and should not leach into the soil or waterways.

Frank feels his move to sustainable gardening is a natural progression that comes out of decades of making gardens, tending plants and improving the soil. His philosophy is to use no poisons, do no harm and eat well from his garden, and if this makes him a 'greenie', then so be it. In fact, he would like to see the government introduce 'incentives for people to grow food and look after the soil'. Government support for backyard farming could have the practical benefit of increased access to fresh fruit and veg within local neighbourhoods, and ideally improve community and environmental health. Imagine if such radical talk led to widespread community action – it could bring about a revolution in the suburbs and towns of the nation! Starting with Rockhampton, Frank may find that spreading the word, like compost, can prove enormously productive.

Frank is an ardent recycler and his edible plants flourish in a variety of containers.

PANSHANGER'S KITCHEN GARDEN

Size	800 m²
Climate	Cool temperate (mild summer)
Soil	'Panshanger sand'
Average annual rainfall	610 mm
Frost	Yes
Water source	River water
Irrigation method	Spray irrigation and hand-watering
Compost and fertiliser	Composted food scraps and plant material, sheep manure, seaweed emulsion, green manure
Mulch	Lucerne hay
Biggest challenges	Slugs and snails
Favourite herb	Parsley
Favourite food plant	Leek

CHAPTER 16
PANSHANGER
Self-sufficient Gardening on an Historic Tasmanian Farm

The 1835 lithograph *Panshanger, The seat of Joseph Archer, Esqr., county of Cornwall, Vandieman's [sic] Land*[1] (based on an original drawing by William Thomas Lyttleton) depicts the most bucolic of landscapes, the epitome of the picturesque: contented cattle and horses graze on pastures at the edge of the gleaming Lake River among a few well-spaced European-looking trees. At the crest of the hill squats the homestead's new stone mansion with its grand Grecian revival façade and four-pillared portico. From its wide stone terrace a lawn sweeps down to the Lake River; on the left are a round pigeon tower and farm buildings with the blue hills of the Western Tiers mountain range beyond. Lyttleton's image gives no hint of an island marked by the brutality of its early years of the penal system and the genocide of its indigenous people, nor of its extraordinary wilderness. It is the artist's (a retired soldier and neighbouring settler) ideal landscape, which was a mini-England transplanted to the antipodes – productive and safe, encapsulating Anthony Trollope's famous description: 'Everything in Tasmania is more English than is England herself.' (The state was renamed in 1856.)

The land depicted in the print was among some 5500 acres (2228 ha) taken up by Joseph Archer (1795–1853) in the 1820s and named *Panshanger*. (The name means the hillside resting place of the god Pan.) Joseph was one of four sons of miller William Archer of Hertford, all four of whom were free settlers who took up land grants in the Longford region. All four men went on to establish large and prosperous estates in Tasmania – the best known of which are Panshanger, Woolmers and Brickendon. All are important in the colonial history of the state and in its transition from isolated and beleaguered British colony to successful pastoral economy. Today, Panshanger is no less pastoral; just as the objective of generations of Archers was working the land, so too has it been the focus of the Mills family since it was purchased by George Mill's grandfather Thomas for his son Charles in 1908.

The Longford region of northern Tasmania, with its dependable river systems, is evidently very productive country if Maree Mills' two vegetable gardens are anything to go by.

In Maree's case, the answer to the question: 'Where does my food come from?' is a simple one: 'From down the garden path'. When Maree arrived at Panshanger as a new bride in 1975 there was little garden as such – it was a lovely park-like landscape with many mature trees (including stone pines, elms and oaks planted in the 1820s). It is therefore quite amazing to comprehend the 8 ha (20 acres) of garden she has created, not to mention maintained, over three decades. She and her husband George run Panshanger as a mixed farming property where they grow wool, cattle, poppies, potatoes, oats, garlic, barley, fava beans and lucerne. While the farm is not by any means remote – being only thirty-five minutes from Launceston and two hours from Hobart – the Mills' are pretty independent from the supermarket and greengrocer thanks to Maree's gardening endeavours. Through growing and eating a wonderful diversity of fruits and vegetables that thrive in the soil and cool climate here, Maree has co-created the shortest of food chains, one in which she is both primary producer and consumer.

Maree has a bigger 'foodshed' than most produce gardeners, having not one but two kitchen gardens. They cover an area of about 800 m² and their productivity is impressive – they really comprise a farm within a farm. (She is the most hands-on of gardeners, but she does get some help to maintain the extensive gardens here at Panshanger.) Her first vegetable garden – known as the 'bottom garden' – is a short and beautiful walk down the garden path through a wooded landscape of elms and laurels. It has that very workmanlike no-nonsense grid layout of every serious farm vegie garden I've ever seen (although cutting flowers in the form of big colourful dahlias grow around the perimeter). It comprises a fruit-cage structure measuring 20 m long × 20 m wide and had been built originally by Maree's father-in-law for his treasured strawberries. Mr Mills was a strawberry lover who used to fumigate the soil every year (probably with methyl bromide, which was widely used as a soil sterilant) between replanting the newly fumigated soil with fresh strawberry plants. Maree quickly put an end to this questionable practice and the garden is now exceptionally healthy, the shrubs and roses full of blue wrens and grey fantails, insects and butterflies.

Clockwise, from top: **Rows of broccoli, garlic chives and leeks inside the garden enclosure; Maree's 'bottom garden' is set within beautiful surrounds; the Tasmanian pastoral property depicted in an 1835 lithograph.**

Clockwise, from top: **Maree's 'bottom garden' was built as a fruit cage for her father-in-law's beloved strawberries; black kale; does Tasmania produce Australia's best raspberries?; perfect soil and a cool climate suit carrots just fine.**

A commitment to gardening without toxic pesticides means that Maree deals with insect pests such as infestations of harlequin bugs on the raspberries and tomatoes and of caterpillars of the cabbage white butterfly on the brassicas using pyrethrum spray. Bicarb soda is employed as a spray for powdery mildew on zucchini, peas and roses. In the rest of the garden Maree has a variety of feathered and furry visitors to contend with, including wallabies, bandicoots, rats and cockatoos, but it is the possum that does the most damage to trees and flowers. While possums are not her favourite native fauna, Maree's love of Tasmania's bush is unwavering. The environmental degradation of the state concerns her immensely, most especially the loss of its forests for woodchips. 'Our self-destructive tendency to destroy the very resources on which we depend for clean air, water and food is short-sighted and unsustainable,' says Maree.

The vegetable garden has a neat grid of beds and the earth paths are laid simply with straw. The edge of the beds has been cut into the ground and the soil is slightly mounded to aid drainage. Maree grows vegetables here that require a bit more space like pumpkins and corn. This is her 'late garden', for it is more exposed to early frost than her 'top garden', meaning she cannot plant out tender plants like beans until later in the season, but it is also sunnier than her garden up near the house. Summer heralds strawberries, 'Golden Nugget' pumpkins and corn. Black kale or *Cavallo nero*, as they call it in Tuscany, has long crinkly leaves the colour of blue-grey slate, and looks beautiful growing among the orange flowers of the pumpkin vines. This particular brassica can live for a couple of seasons, forming mini-palm trees to 1.5 m high. It is traditionally used in minestrone soup with the leaves being picked individually from the stem and the tough mid-rib usually removed before cooking. Carrots, parsnips and cauliflowers are other favourite winter vegies. In late spring, gooseberries, blackcurrants and the spring-fruiting form of raspberries are a sweet bounty after a cold and frosty winter.

Maree's garden epitomises rural produce gardens the country over; she has access to the things that we city gardeners envy: lots of space and great quantities of animal manures and mulches. The soil here is known as Panshanger sand – it has taken Maree years to build it up into the rich dark-brown earth in which her plants thrive. A combination of home-grown lucerne hay (either spoilt bales or good hay off the second cut if she's lucky), green manure (fava beans, lupins, oats and barley), dried seaweed flakes, seaweed concentrate, blood and bone, the occasional dressing of dolomite and sheep poo cleaned out from under the shearing shed with a front-end loader, have been the secrets to her food-growing success. The vegie cage is a twentieth-century structure; it mightn't have a solid roof or walls but it's become a familiar motif within the rural landscape and is

> 'The environmental degradation of the state concerns her immensely, most especially the loss of its forests for woodchips. 'Our self-destructive tendency to destroy the very resources on which we depend is short-sighted and unsustainable,' says Maree.

as classic a vernacular farm building as the Australian shearing shed, chook shed or meathouse. The availability and increasing affordability of woven wire netting from the late 1800s onwards enabled these utilitarian structures, which, in protecting a household's fruit and vegetables from wildlife, presumably increased yields. As pretty and aesthetically lovely as the French-style potager might be, the much younger traditional design of the Aussie vegie garden has a delightful charm all of its own.

Behind the enclosed kitchen garden is a levy bank originally built to protect the cottage and garden from flooding from the Lake River, the river on which the productivity of this farm and others in the region depends. Panshanger's water is pumped from the river – a tributary of the Macquarie, which in turn joins the South Esk – via a pumping station installed in 1860. The dry seasons of recent years have taken a toll on the farm

PANSHANGER'S KITCHEN GARDEN

1. Asparagus
2. Rhubarb, globe and Jerusalem artichokes
3. Tomato 'cupboard'
4. Capsicum and parsley
5. Capsicum and basil
6. Raspberries
7. Assorted herbs
8. Youngberries, lettuce, nasturtiums, spinach and kale
9. Jostaberries and a cherry tree
10. Clipped hedge shrubs
11. Zucchini, climbing beans and 'Golden Nugget' pumpkins
12. Broccoli, spinach, carrot, celery
13. Beetroot, cucumber, zucchini, lettuce and oregano
14. Garlic chives, broccoli, silverbeet and cauliflower
15. Oregano, leeks, climbing beans and lemon thyme
16. Bush beans, carrots, sweet corn
17. Chives and climbing beans
18. Grapevines

and the garden, which Maree keeps irrigated using overhead sprinklers. A good year's rainfall in the region was 914 mm (36 inches); an average year's – 610 mm (24 inches); but in recent years it has been around 356–432 mm (14–17 inches). 'I think it's probably a cycle,' says Maree with an optimism born of living through droughts before as well as from reading Panshanger's farm records that document the weather back to the turn of the nineteenth century. Maree has observed that frosts 'seem to go with the dry cycle' and can be 'quite devastating,' she says, having recently lost quinces, stone fruits, apples and pears to a late October frost. Sometimes they'll have light frosts in summer, and when more serious ones occur in mid-March, that puts an end to all the heat-loving annual vegetables.

> **'Maree spends from three to five hours in her garden most days . . . she gets on with the job of making food happen.'**

Maree's 'top vegetable garden' is a mere 30 m from her kitchen door. Outside the enclosed vegie garden roses abound, a mature fig tree leans against the old brick wall of the courtyard, and eating grapes are ripening in a cage of their own. This kitchen garden constitutes a more modern replica of her bottom garden except it has paths surfaced with blue metal gravel, rectangular beds edged with split pine logs and it is covered with synthetic bird netting rather than metal wire. Inside, there is yet more corn, pushing against the roof of the cage and more lettuce, but there is much more besides: garlic chives, beetroots bursting out of the ground, cucumber, an unknown purple variety of garlic, zucchini, globe artichokes and a large bed of asparagus. In one bed the white-flowered and delicious 'Lazy Housewife' bean scrambles up a trellis. Maree doesn't take the easy way out with her beans: she saves her seeds and those of peas each season instead of buying them.

Maree cultivates the varieties of food plants she knows will perform: she grows the basics that she and her family like to eat and that grow well, rather than fashionable heirlooms or the latest hybrid. She would really rather be gardening than cooking, and spends from three to five hours in her garden most days. In the indomitable way of someone from a farming family, Maree gets on with the job of making food happen. The cycles of the kitchen garden – the germination of seeds, growth of leaves, ripening of fruit, composting of spent plants – in this ultra-managed landscape are not sentimentalised but cherished all the same. Maree's favourite vegetable is the leek and she uses them regularly in soups, stir-fries and when cooking with zucchini. 'Dessert fruits' in the form of rhubarb, autumn-fruiting raspberries, young berries and jostaberries – which are a cross between a gooseberry and a black currant – flourish in this kitchen garden. Jostaberry fruits look like giant black currants the size of marbles and the plants form a thornless shrub about 1 m high. Excess raspberries, young berries and jostaberries are frozen, along with strawberries, corn and tomatoes. In winter Maree can then make jam as she needs it from the frozen berries and sauce from the tomatoes. She also bottles her stone fruit, stores pumpkins for eating over winter and gives surplus vegetables and fruit to her family, staff, church fetes and neighbours.

Because of the short growing season and danger of early frost, Maree has created an ingenious structure within the covered garden that looks rather like a 'tomato cupboard' – a three-sided timber frame covered in plastic. Due to the prevailing north-westerly winds the open side faces east. Tied to their individual stakes, her tomatoes bear massive bunches of fruit and reach a height of 6 ft (1.8 m). Maree grows some less common tomato varieties: 'Cyndal', 'Super Roma' and 'Mamma Mia'. 'Stupice' (pronounced STOO-peach-ka) is a Polish heirloom variety that produces loads of small, salad-sized tomatoes and flourishes in the cooler weather of late spring and early summer. The early season Norwegian tomato 'Imur Prior Beta' is another unusual variety – it was developed to fruit in Norway's short season and cool temperatures. The breeding program began with seeds that came from high-altitude areas in Chile; another example of how important it is to preserve

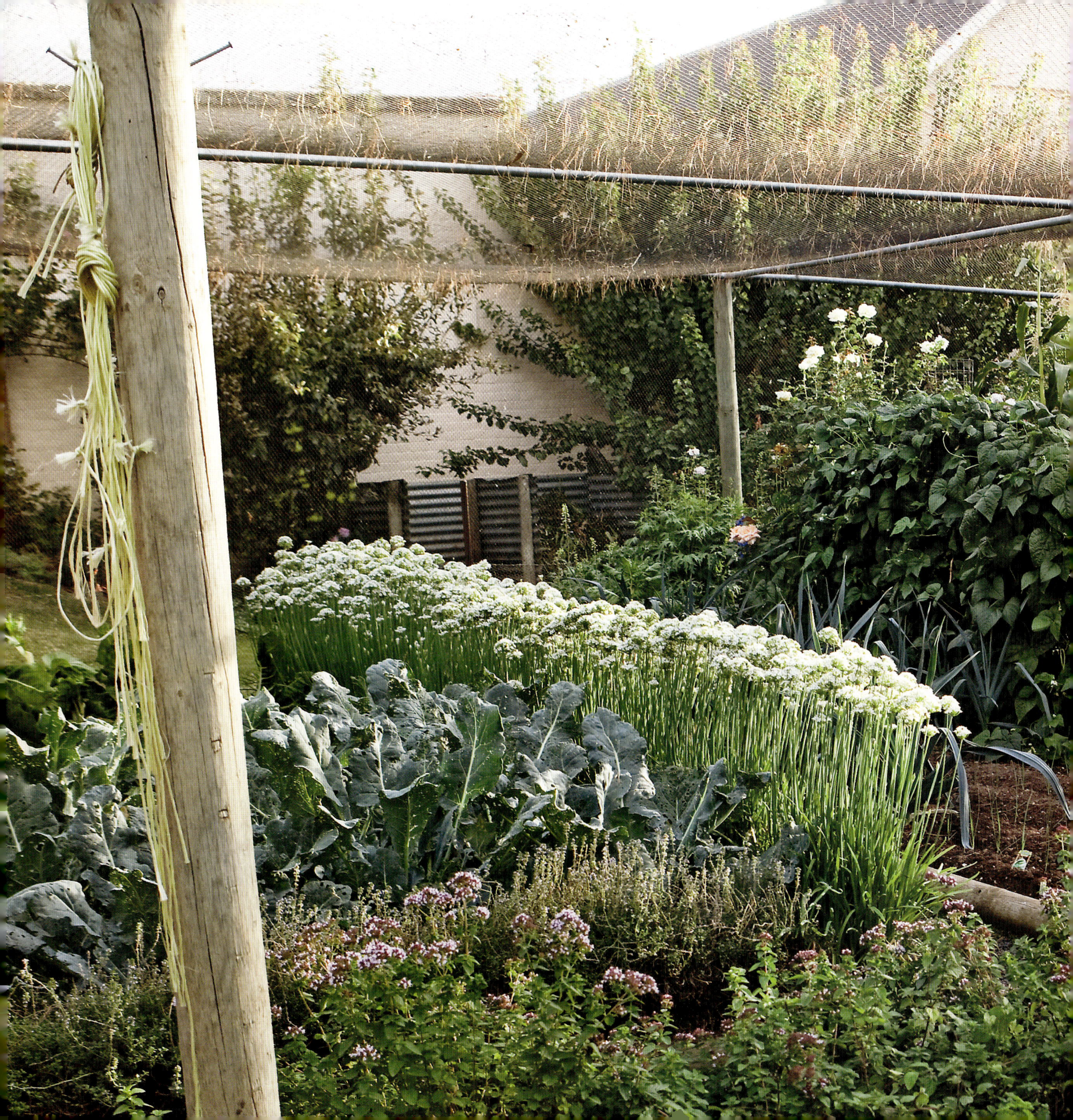

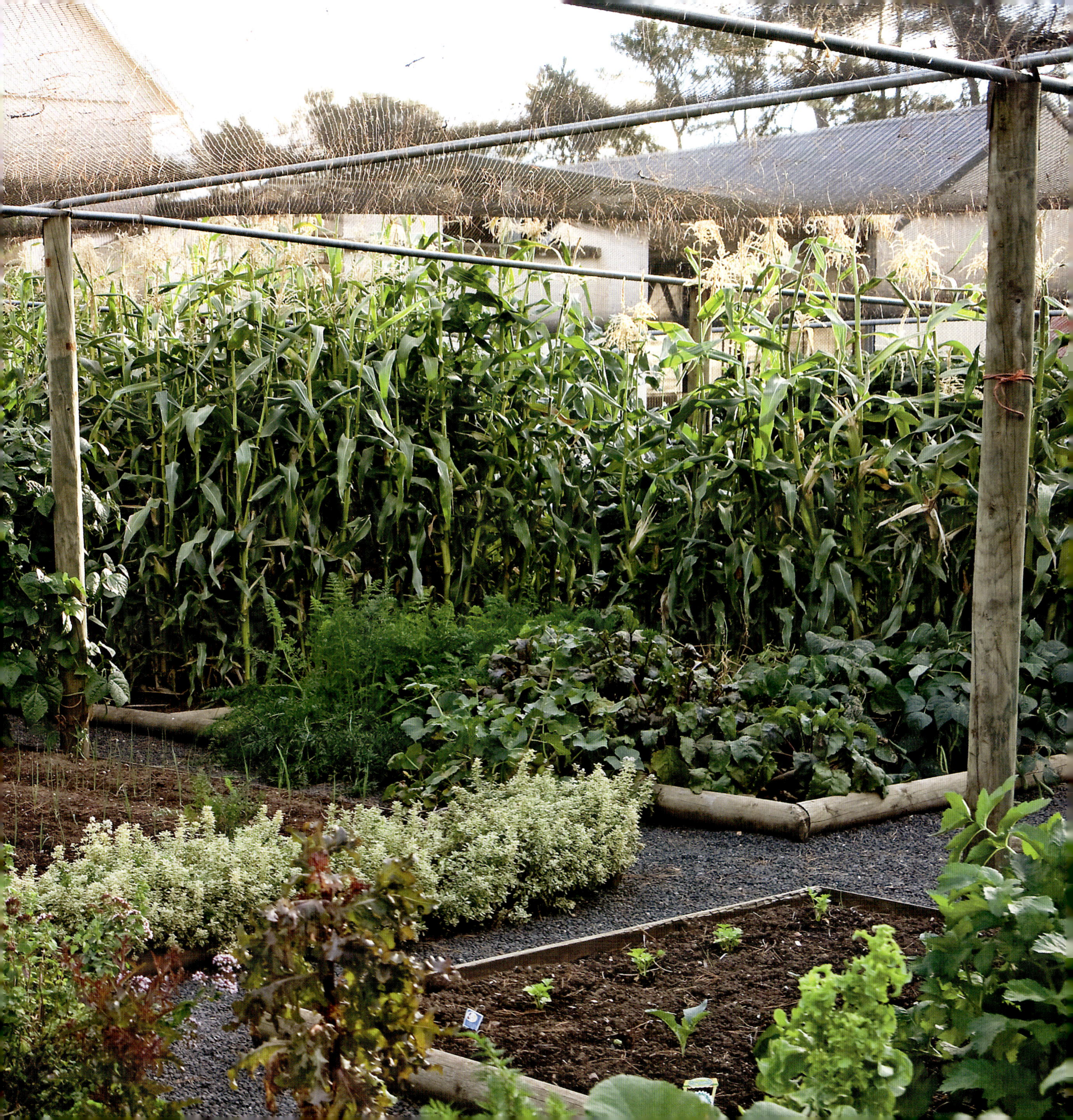

heritage food plants for their unique germplasm as well as for the food security of the people who traditionally grow them.

Panshanger was settled at a time when over 80 per cent of the adult population of Van Diemen's Land either were, or had been, convicts. Panshanger would have begun operating with assigned convict labour, but its workforce was increasingly made up of free labourers well before transportation ended in 1853. Joseph Archer was an active opponent of transportation, although, paradoxically it would seem, the convict records reveal him to have been a hard master. Archer is recorded in 1830 as sentencing his assigned servant John Douglas to six months' hard labour in irons for the theft of a single bushel of potatoes.[2] One non-convict labourer was Charles Wills who was head gardener at Panshanger from 1855 until his death in 1874. Charles was sponsored out to Van Diemen's Land by George Meredith, a well-known settler grazier (father-in-law and uncle of the noted artist and writer Louisa Anne Meredith), and he lived most of his married life with his family in the gardener's cottage on the estate. As well as maintaining the grounds, Charles would have been responsible for helping to feed around forty people living on the property.

Charles Wills was what was known as a 'clean potato' in the slang of the day – meaning he'd never been a convict. The vernacular expression perhaps suggests just how important potatoes were not only in the settlers' diet, which was very much one of meat (salt pork and beef as well as mutton) and damper, but in supplementing the rations of convicts and labourers. Much was written in praise of the potato throughout the British Empire: 'In reference to the kitchen garden, amongst the first of all roots in the vegetable world, the potato may be said to take the lead; this is cultivated in Tasmania with the most complete success'[3] enthused Henry Widowson in 1829. From the 1840s north-west Van Diemen's Land was a major producer of potatoes – *Solanum tuberosum* was perfect carbo-loaded survival food. Potatoes also became an excellent cash crop for the region's farmers as they exported them to feed Melbourne's booming gold-rush population. To return to a present-day potato story, Maree grows the butter-fleshed 'Dutch Cream' potatoes in her kitchen garden, which are one of her favourites, and her husband George has been heard to say that her Dutch Creams taste better than his 'Russet Burbanks' out in the paddock.

Scurvy, known colloquially as 'Barcoo rot' (a disease caused by vitamin C deficiency), was still common in pastoral and convict diets of the 1800s despite the numerous leafy green esculents listed by Tasmanian seed catalogues of the day. It was not commonly thought that the indigenous or endemic plants of Van Diemen's Land had much sustenance to offer the colonists. As visiting nurseryman and botanist James Backhouse wrote in 1835: 'The eatable fruits of Van Diemen's Land are not worthy of comparison with the commonest English fruits: they rank in value nearly in the following order . . .' and yet he then went on to list a dozen edible native plants, including *Solanum laciniatum*: kangaroo apple; *Astroloma humifusum*: native cranberry; and *Correa alba*: Cape Barren Tea.[4] Enculturated in European farming practices and ill-equipped for the conditions, the settlers often struggled to survive.

The Mills, more than most people, understand what American writer Wendell Berry meant when he wrote that 'Eating is an agricultural act' and Maree's relationship with food is an uncomplicated one, owing precisely to the fact the she is the person who grows her food. She considers edible gardening the most rewarding of physical connections to the natural world and wishes others could enjoy its daily rituals and pleasures. 'I feel quite sad that the general public have lost the skill to produce their own food, does not know the satisfaction that goes with it and the resulting health advantages,' says Maree. With Panshanger's farm supplying food to state, national and international markets, and Maree's vegetable garden covering the home one, the Mills are most certainly upholding northern Tasmania's claims on being the new Australian food bowl.

Pages 186–187: **Kitchen gardening perfection at Panshanger.** *Clockwise, from right:* **Maree's 'tomato cupboard' allows her to extend the tomato-growing season in her cool frosty climate; asparagus; the entry gate to the 'top garden' at Panshanger; the heirloom 'Lazy Housewife' bean.**

ARMANDO AND MARIA'S KITCHEN GARDEN

Size	Property: 32 × 41.5 m (1328 m^2)
Climate	Mediterranean
Soil	Sandy loam
Average annual rainfall	520 mm
Frost	No
Water source	Mains, tank and bore water
Irrigation method	Micro-spray irrigation and hand-watering
Compost and fertiliser	Compost and sheep manure
Mulch	Composted manure, grass clippings
Biggest challenges	Taking holidays – who will feed the rabbits?
Favourite herb	Parsley and rosemary
Favourite food plant	Apples, figs and nectarines

CHAPTER 17
PARADISE IN SOUTH AUSTRALIA
Armando and Maria's Garden

Perhaps no one appreciates 'plenty' in the form of good home-grown food quite in the same way than those who have endured deprivation or hunger. 'Hard times' are no cliché – war, poverty and displacement are the real experience of many migrants and refugees. The memory of loss and the impact of dislocated identities persists and often has multi-generational impact. This is regardless of whether the transnational shift was recent or in decades past, and whether or not the individuals now feel accepted in their adopted community. It's ironic that many an émigré since 1788 was told that Australia was 'Paradise' on earth, only to find it anything but – even Hell had better food! But in the case of Armando and Maria Matteucci, Paradise has literally transpired as a result of their migrating here from Italy. Since 1963 the Matteuccis have made their life together in a suburb of Adelaide with the wonderful name of Paradise. Here, in their bit of Paradise – a double-sized block with a solid brick home, huge vegetable garden and small orchard – not only is the food always abundant but their children and grandchildren live close by. Armando is the constant gardener and Maria the constant cook, the fruit and vegetables are plentiful, the meat tender, the wine sweet and the cupboards and cellar are full.

Armando and Maria came to Australia in 1951, part of the second-wave post-World-War-II migration, via an assisted passage scheme with Italy established that same year. After the war migrants from Italy, Greece, Malta, Croatia and Turkey were included in a national intake that had previously been dominated by citizens of the British Isles. Ten-year-old Maria came with her family, and the nineteen-year-old Armando sailed out alone. He remembers his few weeks at infamous Bonegilla well, before going on to fulfil the two years of work required by assisted migration. Fruit picking in Renmark, grape picking in Mildura, cane cutting in Queensland, potato harvesting in Colac, Victoria – you name it, Armando's labour has helped to gather it. Still, the money was good, allowing him to establish the trucking business that brought him to Adelaide where he met the lovely Maria in 1960. Coincidentally, both Maria and Armando came from the Marche (MAHR-kay) region in the central western area of Italy between the Apennines and the Adriatic Sea. Even more amazingly, both were from the town of Ascoli Piceno (inland about halfway between Ancona and Pescara) – it was meant to be! Their families were from a highly self-sufficient farming community and that connection to land has also been sustained here in Australia. Maria's father became a celery-grower in Adelaide, so she too knows the labour involved in food production.

All is ordered and productive in Armando's garden, which isn't to say there are no flowers – there are dark-purple stocks, potted pink and red geraniums and zygocactus (*Schlumbergera* spp.) in hanging baskets – but the focus is definitely on those plants you can eat. The garden resembles a small farm, with the serious trappings of horticultural endeavour as well as egg and meat production with chooks and rabbits. Beyond the house are numerous sheds, the hutches housing their meat rabbits and the chook run – the entire block measures over 1300 m^2, or a third of an acre. The chequerboard geometry of contrasting foliage and differing row directions makes Armando's *orto* look like a miniature Italian market garden. (Like those developed so successfully on the urban fringe, especially from the 1950s on, that supplied Adelaide's local market with all manner of herbs, fruit and veg.) Narrow paths of recycled bricks and pavers dissect soil the colour of good milk chocolate: a well-drained sandy loam with gravel aggregates that has been improved by Armando through years of love and compost.

Certain edible plants have 'permanent' status in the garden here – obviously the fruit trees and grapevines, perennial herbs such as rosemary and oregano, but also greens like lettuce and silverbeet. No individual food plant occupies as much space over the course of any year as artichokes, tomatoes and broad beans do, followed closely by root vegetables (carrots, beetroot, onions and potatoes), greens like endive and canola and coles: including walking-stick cabbage, cabbage and broccoli. *Carciofi* (artichokes) herald the arrival of spring. Armando cultivates an early purple-headed variety that fruits from mid-August and another form that crops into October. These artichokes – essentially perennial thistles – occupy about 50 m^2 of land

Clockwise, from top: Armando's garden has the chequerboard geometry of a traditional *orto*; canola flowers and a serious crop of garlic in the spring garden; the broad bean crop.

around the north-eastern corner of the backyard. Almond, olive, peach and mandarin trees emerge out of their silver sea of thistle-like leaves. After fruiting, Armando will cut the entire crop to the ground and remove the older plants, leaving the young suckers room to grow in the coming year.

> 'An alchemy of factors is responsible for Armando's perfect tomatoes: perhaps it's the climate, the five-year rotation he follows to avoid a build up of pests and disease, or is it his home-made compost?'

Along with lentils, peas and chickpeas, it is estimated that broad beans became part of the eastern Mediterranean diet in around 6000 BC or earlier. In Italy, broad beans are traditionally sown on 2 November, which is All Souls Day, whereas here in the temperate zones of southern Australia they are usually sown between April and July, as they grow through the cooler weather. Also known as *fave* (the Italian word for broad bean), Armando's crop inhabits a bed of 5 × 5 m and is contained by upright stakes tied to horizontal bars with lengths of willow (recycling is an advanced art form in many an Italian's garden). Using osiers or willow branches is a traditional practice in rural Europe. The basket willow (*Salix viminalis*) in Armando's front garden is coppiced mercilessly in winter to resemble a tree sculpture, providing him with armfuls of branches to use as ties and also promoting long growth the next year. The willow ties are used for restraining all manner of plants and look far more attractive than baling twine, plastic ties or pantyhose, and – unlike those materials – are fully biodegradable. Maria and Armando will dry some of their *fave*, and eat the rest fresh in *antipasto*, mashed as a dip and eaten simply on their own. To double-shell broad beans is surely an expression of true love for those you are cooking for, but it is amazing how speedy you can become at it! In addition to *fave* Armando grows *lupini* or lupins, more commonly seen in Australia as ornamentals or escapee weeds on farms and in bushland. They have soft felted leaves and their mauve and white racemes produce pods like smaller *fave*. Maria dries the buff-coloured seeds for later use (as a snack, with the shelling being done on the spot). They will need to be boiled for ten minutes then soaked in water for a couple of weeks to leach out the bitter alkaloids before being cooked and then preserved in jars of brine.

In late September, along with seedlings of beans and cucumbers, Armando plants out his tomatoes. There are two separate beds for tomatoes – one for the Roma-type varieties Maria uses for making sauce, and another for those that are eaten fresh. An alchemy of factors is responsible for Armando's perfect tomatoes: perhaps it's the climate, the five-year rotation he follows to avoid a build up of pests and disease, or is it his home-made compost? This is made in a large pit dug into the ground into which go the food scraps, rabbit and chook manure, garden prunings and dead annual plants. When it has decomposed to a crumbly organic matter, Armando digs it into the soil wherever he grows his major food plants, using it to plant new seedlings or to top-dress the artichokes. The Mattueccis also prefer to use no chemical sprays in their garden unless they have a really bad infestation. Generally, the intensive polyculture and the many hours of care this ultra-managed garden receives is the key to its health. Armando also raises most of his plants from seed – some seed he has saved himself, some bought from Eden Seeds in Queensland. (A poly-tunnel is useful for starting seedlings, but even more so for growing and ripening tomatoes through winter.) A productive garden like this, with its onsite waste and nutrient recycling, thrifty reuse of materials and low-inputs (it does not rely on many external and non-sustainable purchases from nurseries), can definitely, as historian Andrea Gaynor suggests, contribute to 'a more cyclical, sustainable, urban metabolism'.[1]

Spring is a wonderful time to visit Armando's garden – there is tender beetroot, garlic, leek, carrots and celery in the vegie beds, and in the orchard there is *nespole* (loquat) – one of the earliest spring fruits. Its sweet, mild-flavoured oval fruit is under-appreciated by Anglo-Australians but beloved by Greek

ARMANDO AND MARIA'S GARDEN

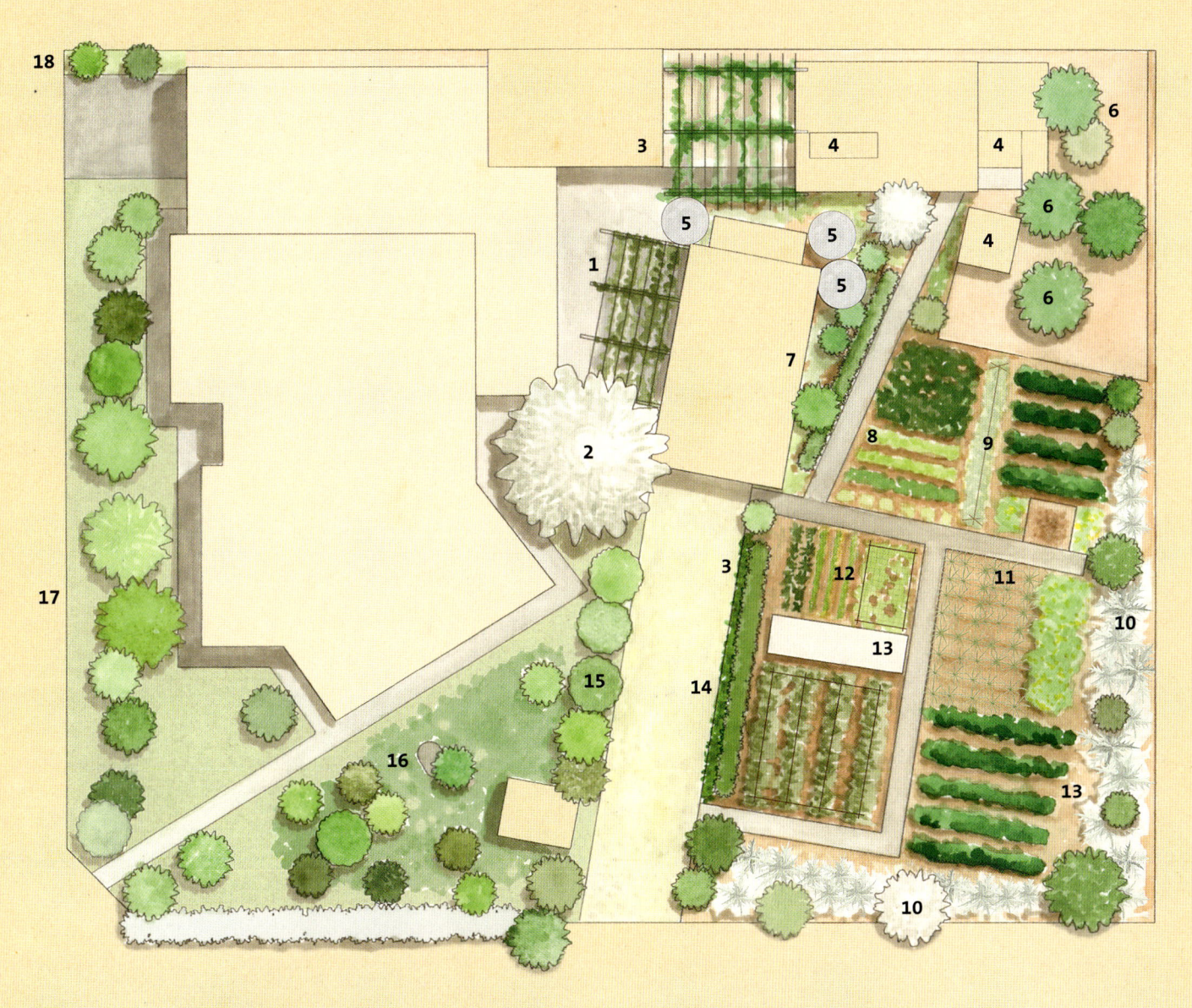

1. Kiwifruit on pergola
2. Olive tree
3. Grapevine
4. Rabbits
5. Water tank
6. Fig
7. Persimmon, orange and blood orange trees and a rosemary hedge
8. Cabbage, potatoes, beans and celery
9. Paste tomatoes and peas
10. Artichokes and fruit trees
11. Leeks, garlic and canola
12. Cucumber, carrot, beetroot, onion and broad beans
13. Tomatoes
14. Lupins and silverbeet
15. Fruit trees: peach, nectarine, loquat and apple
16. Lucerne growing underneath apple, peach, apricot, pear, nectarine and plum trees
17. Orange, persimmon, nectarine, pear, basket willow, apricot, walnut, plum and feijoa trees
18. Peach and lemon trees

and Italians. Originating in southern China, loquats are tough and attractive evergreen trees and deserve to be more widely grown. Summer means a feast of cucumbers, beans, onions and potatoes as well as the ubiquitous basil and tomatoes – the first of which will be picked before Christmas. By late February there are eggplants, capsicums and chillies. This is an extremely busy time as it's when Maria fires up her 'copper' to preserve the ripe tomatoes in a large army of glass jars and bottles.

Armando's nostalgia for his homeland is qualified – while cultural tradition is important and his birthplace is an essential part of his identity, he says he is quite happy to never see snow again! Ascoli Piceno is mountainous and very cold in winter, whereas Adelaide's climate suits him beautifully – even the customary weeks of summer temperatures in the very high thirties don't slow him down. The city of Adelaide itself has an average rainfall of around 520 mm compounded by little humidity and high evaporation rates in summer. The rainfall is highly seasonal – in recent times summer rainfall has been negligible, meaning that good winter rainfall between May and October is even more vital. The city's dependence on the struggling Murray River is also reaching the point of crisis – the river's increasing salinity may soon see Adelaideans buying bottled water to drink and cook with! Stage 3 water restrictions are operational here, which means dripper systems and hand-held hoses can be used to water gardens for a maximum of three hours on only two specific days a week. In this context Armando's food garden would simply not exist without his water tanks and bore. Watering is via micro-sprays on grapevines and some fruit trees and the rest is by hand. It is daily work for the very early mornings and late evenings during the heat of summer.

The narrow front garden features fruit trees: peach, apricot, plum, pear, persimmon and lemon. Under the apple, apricot and peach on the southern side of the house Armando grows lucerne for feeding the rabbits. Although lucerne is a pasture, fodder, cash crop and an important part of agricultural land management, it is also fantastic for the home garden. Being a deep-rooted perennial, it helps to break up the structure of clay soils, reaching deep into the subsoil (making lucerne ideal for preparing a site for a new garden). The flowers attract beneficial insects and, as they're leguminous, the plants fix nitrogen in the soil. Established lucerne crops can also help lower the pH of limey soils to a more ideal range – given the naturally alkaline soil here it makes an excellent acidifying cover crop under the fruit trees. What a pity that lucerne is not more drought-tolerant as it makes the best garden mulch of all!

'Even the chook run has fruit trees inside it – three figs are growing happily inside the fence, no doubt benefiting from the chicken manure and the hens' constant predation of pests.'

Even the chook run has fruit trees inside it – three figs are growing happily inside the fence, no doubt benefiting from the chicken manure and the hens' constant predation of pests. Like his other soft summer fruits, Armando nets the fig trees to exclude the birds. Autumn, however, is the peak season for fruit in the garden: in March and April the grapes are ripening – both eating and winemaking varieties. Trellised grapes make an important structural feature in the garden and are perfectly pruned on both vertical and horizontal frames. (Recycled steel water pipe is Armando's material of choice.) Grapevines on pergolas are the most pleasant edifice – they allow space for living underneath while growing above one's head, are cool and shady in summer, yet they let the light through sculptural bare stems in winter. They are tough, quick growing, long-lived and provide shade and dessert in one! They give leaves as well as fruit and wine, and are far more beautiful than shade cloth or an umbrella. The weekend required to prune the vines during winter is more than worth it. Green roofs may be fashionable these days – but trellised grapes make wonderful green ceilings!

Le Marche is known for its dry white wine *Verdicchio*, as well

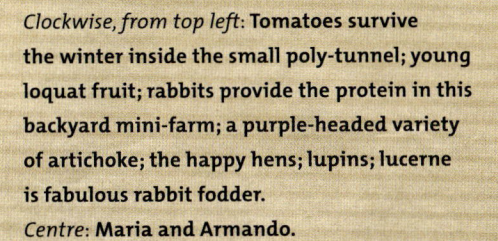

Clockwise, from top left: **Tomatoes** survive the winter inside the small poly-tunnel; young loquat fruit; rabbits provide the protein in this backyard mini-farm; a purple-headed variety of artichoke; the happy hens; lupins; lucerne is fabulous rabbit fodder.
Centre: **Maria and Armando.**

Top to bottom: **Chicory is a favourite bitter green in the Matteucci household; Armando in the cellar he dug himself; Maria's superb bottled fruit and vegetables.**

as *Rosso Conero*, made from the 'Montepulciano' grape, and the sparkling red *Vernaccia di Serrapetrona*, but here in Paradise, Armando's backyard *vitocultura* makes use of what is readily available – a combination of home-grown and bought grapes from the market. (Winemaking in the Adelaide Plains has a significant Italian heritage, with Sangiovese, Moscato and Pinot Grigio among the first of the Italian varietals to be produced in the region, and Italian winemakers have been integral in developing the industry in South Australia.) As well as a light red, Armando makes a lovely sweet wine, a *vino dolce*, that is delightful with some of Maria's sugar-coated biscuits that are themselves made with the sweet wine. His flagons are stored in the cellar he excavated himself – with its walls lined with bottles and jars, it is a cavern of sufficiency hidden beneath yet another of his sheds.

From late autumn into winter feijoas (pineapple guava) and walnuts begin to fall to the ground, and the kiwifruit and persimmons aren't far behind. At this time of year the olives are ready for harvesting (there are three trees in the garden), the *arance sanguigna* are turning orange and *cachi* hang on bare boughs into the winter until they achieve their lovely gelatinous consistency. Winter vegetables include peas, cabbage, turnip and *finocchio* – fennel. Armando says his secret to nice fat fennel bulbs is to transplant the young seedlings, even if you have already germinated them directly in a garden bed. There are green rows of chicory (*Chicorium intybus*), a biannual with long, bitter green leaves used in salads or cooking. The long taproot can also be blanched and used in food dishes. In the past, including during food rationing in World War II, the roots were dried and roasted for a coffee substitute (there are still nineteenth-century chicory kilns to be found around the Australian countryside). Endive is also a chicory (*Cichorium endiva*) with attractive serrated curly leaves, and Maria uses both this and chicory raw in *insalata verde*, as well as blanched and then sautéed with garlic and olive oil as a side dish. Both are useful frost-hardy greens that are little-grown these days, probably because of their very bitterness. Like dandelion leaves, they are rich in antioxidants and incredibly good for us.

Now that both Armando and Maria have retired (although Armando has a local gardening job), they are busier than ever. The division of roles is harmonious in this happy partnership; Armando is the gardener, winemaker and in-house butcher; Maria is the pasta-making, pickling and preserving superwoman. Cooking in Le Marche is deeply rooted in tradition. The province is famous for its *brodetto*, *porchetta al forno* and *vincisgrassi* – the Marche version of lasagne, made with chicken livers, chicken or pork, mushrooms, truffles and prosciutto. As food writer Patrizia Passigli says of the region's cooks: 'they all have in common a kind of mania that is exclusive to the *Marchigiani* – a fixation for stuffing. Everything is diligently stuffed, from chickens to pecorino *ravioli*, from cauliflower to olives'.[2] Stuffed olives are a *Marchigiani* specialty and Maria's version is a quail-egg-size oval delight, a delicious and labour-intensive dish comprising large pitted green olives filled with minced chicken and beef, then dipped in flour, egg and breadcrumbs, and fried in vegetable oil.

The many sheds contain all kinds of treasures; in one stands a wooden barrel containing Maria's maturing *aceto* – the vinegar made from their wine – in another, Maria's preserving copper. Maria jokes that Italians might spend up big on home kitchen renovations yet will still do all their cooking out the back in the old *cantina*! In the cellar there are rows of her preserves, including the tomato *passata* and olives as well as jars of stone fruit and of capsicum strips, fennel segments and artichoke hearts – the vegetables are pickled in a light vinegar that doesn't overwhelm their essential flavour. Maria makes salt-dried olives layering salt and fruit, preserves ripe black olives in brine and green olives in a solution using 20 g of caustic soda to 1 L of water. The green olives are an essential ingredient of a favourite *Marchigiani* rabbit recipe – Maria takes a jointed rabbit (their own, of course), stews it with wine, olives and garlic, rosemary and parsley, and cooks it slowly.

There is inherent optimism in the planting of a garden. As South Australian author, gardener and fellow migrant Lolo Houbein writes: 'Think of your garden as your paradise and paradise will emerge within a few years.'[3] And so it has emerged for Armando and Maria. It is testament to the couple's generosity that they are so happy to share their piece of Paradise with hundreds of visitors on Open Garden Days. Urban eco-warriors, foodie gardeners, retirees, families and young couples: the Matteuccis are not bemused by their attention and eagerness to learn. If Maria and Armando inspire others to grow and cook their own fruit and vegetables, that's wonderful – but food production is not rocket science. It is human tradition – in their case, it's the antithesis of cultural amnesia – and also immensely satisfying. Who'd want to eat supermarket food when you can have a garden? *Paradiso l'orto nella città!*

MARR GROUNDS' KITCHEN GARDEN

Size	700 m²
Climate	Temperate coastal
Soil	Clay
Average annual rainfall	700 mm
Frost	No
Water source	Dam water
Irrigation method	Drip irrigation
Compost and fertiliser	Composted food scraps and plant material, blood and bone
Mulch	Pea straw
Biggest challenges	The initial soil improvement, wildlife, especially birds
Favourite herb	Chives
Favourite food plant	Asparagus

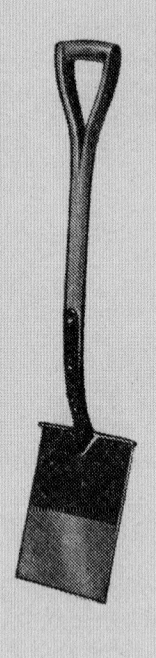

CHAPTER 18
A GARDEN OF PLENTY ON THE SAPPHIRE COAST

It would appear serendipitous that retired environmental sculptor and designer Marr Grounds – with his vision for a sustainable house and garden – has settled in the rural paradise that is the 'Sapphire Coast'. This region on the New South Wales south coast is not only beautiful but the climate's lovely, which is especially good if, like Grounds, you are hoping to grow much of your own food and live self-sufficiently. Marr has lived in the area for twenty years, his first home with his daughter Marina being an idyllic coastal property among the banksia and bangalay trees. During the last ten years, though, he has resided slightly further inland where he has built two houses, a studio and a garden in which virtually everything is productive. The lovely garden at Narra Bukulla, as the property is named (an Aboriginal phrase for 'black stump'), is an example of edible landscaping at its most creative and is a truly rose- and petunia-free zone.

In terms of ecology and topography the area around and within the Mimosa Rocks National Park has a little bit of everything one might wish for: coast, bush, hills and rivers. The vegetation diversity is remarkably significant despite intensive logging and dairying in the vicinity from the 1840s until the 1950s. There's spotted gum (*Corymbia maculata*) forest with its understorey of cycad-like burrawangs (*Macrozamia communis*), pockets of warm temperate rainforest, heathland, wet and dry sclerophyll forest, and grassy forest and woodland too. The coastline is fringed with freshwater systems, estuarine communities and paperbark swamps. The wetlands and lagoons are the habitat of oysters and the nursery grounds of prawns and a range of fish species. A rich hunting ground indeed – as demonstrated by the many shell middens that form the archaeological remains of the Yuin people's occupation.

As much as Marr loves the region, though, as far as horticulture goes his own land is 'pretty ordinary' he says, putting it politely. In creating a garden here Marr has succeeded in overcoming unforgiving soil conditions – hungry ground, with clay over rock – 'soil' is not the word he'd use! He now feels enormously satisfied with the fact that no soil or compost was bought onto the site, but created over three years through rigorous composting *in situ*. Green manures and pea straw were employed in this process, as was plenty of hard work. Following a concept plan by Sue Barnsley Design, with construction by landscape architect Robyn Barlow, the place has been transformed over ten years. Thanks to an overarching environmental design ideology, however, it remains the very antithesis of an 'instant garden'.

While at first the house appears uncompromisingly contemporary, it is in fact highly liveable and is the product of collaboration between the owner and architect, Tone Wheeler. The house is a plural structure of two self-contained buildings and this is reflected in the design of the garden – the two garden wings lie on the east–west axis divided by the central double driveway, with the house and a covered walkway to the north. The east and west gardens are mirrored symmetrically: both have linear garden beds running parallel with the house, both have the same layout of raised island beds and steel pergolas, and even a little cooking plate rests on the log retaining wall. What is notable about this garden is a design synthesis of aesthetic goals and function, yet at the same time certain key distinctions are maintained. The north-facing dwelling marks the 'bush' from 'garden' on the south – it is the line between built and unimproved space. Marr wanted the disparity between exotic and bush made clear, not softened with planting that borrows from the broader landscape.

North of the house are the transpiration beds for the greywater and septic system from the house, which are planted with indigenous species of reeds. At the bottom of a gentle slope lies the dam, which, says Marr, is 'integral to the site'. As well as providing water for the garden, the sparkling interplay of light and water – the reflection of sky and tree trunks – afforded by the dam's surface is dynamic and enhances the 'ordinary bush block'. To the south, all is produce-driven and utilitarian.

Clockwise, from top left: **The garden is divided into two 'wings' running east–west parallel to the house; 10 m of asparagus; one of the amazing entry-sculptures to the garden; the north-facing enclosed vegetable garden.**

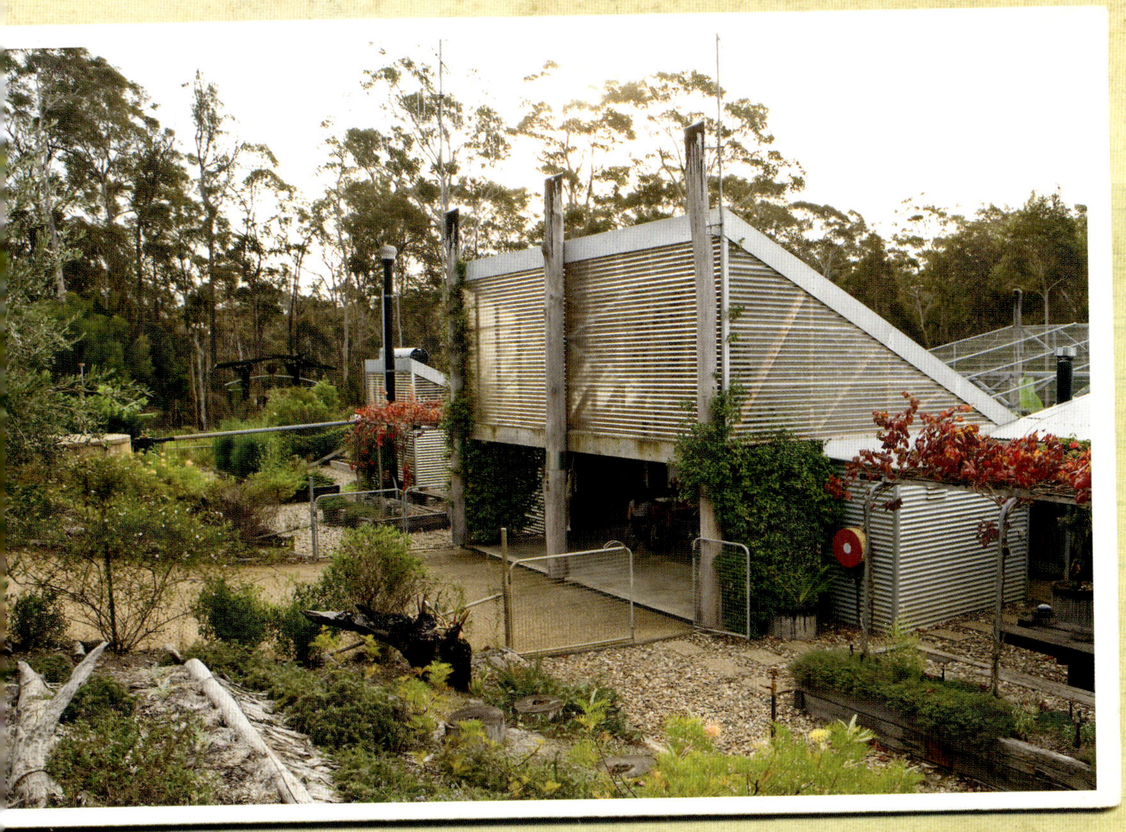

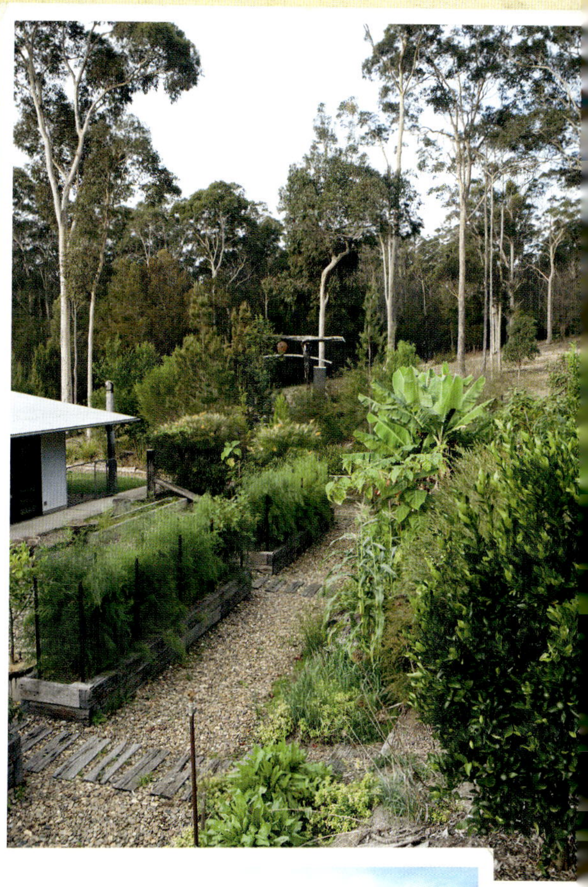

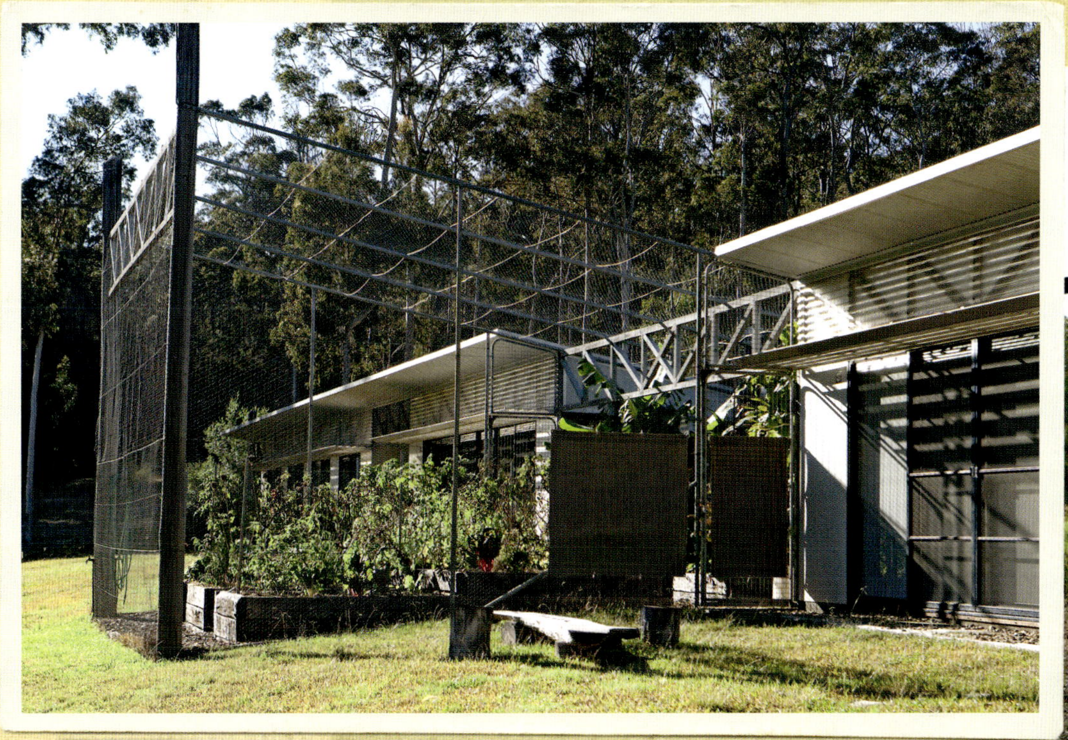

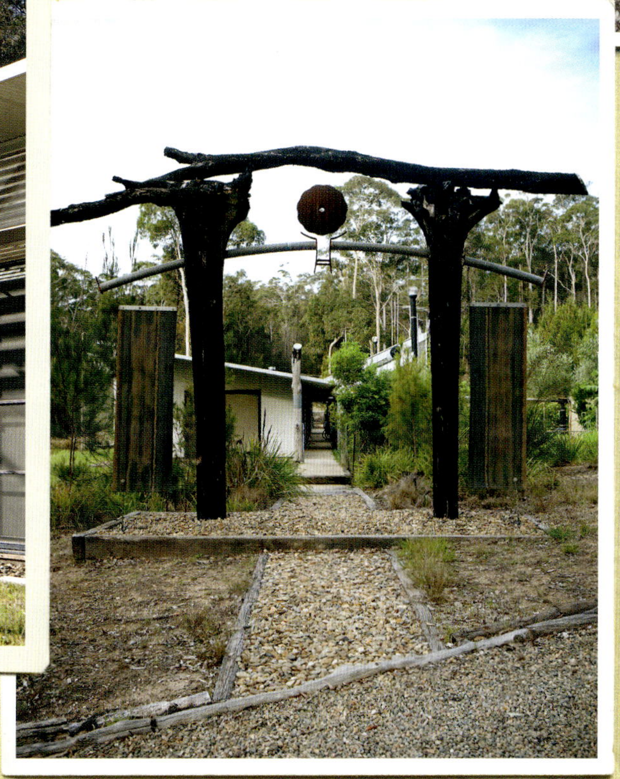

Here are the photovoltaic panels that enable the property to sell electricity back to the grid and the exhaust stacks that initially vented the composting toilets (since modified to a septic system). This is the visual candour of self-sufficiency – all the systems for living are in plain view: water, compost, power, septic. It could be termed a 'bush brutalist' aesthetic, perhaps: one that arguably manifests in the house, with its clean lines, as quite masculine – even blokey.

The hard materials used in the garden's construction are simple and low-tech – broomed concrete, exposed aggregate, concrete water tanks, corrugated iron, bush poles, pebbles, galvanised steel, old concrete pipes, rabbit-netting, recycled timber and other objects. They are plain, unpretentious materials that blend in with the surrounding forest. Materials equally familiar within the rural context and similarly embodied with the vernacular are used by Marr to create his sculptures. Massive twin installations in the form of blackened tree trunks adorned with giant metal gongs serve as gateways to the home space. The impression is one of Shinto temple meets Jurassic Park/ Aussie-land-art. In fact, if there was ever an antipodean answer to Charles Jencks' 'Garden of cosmic speculation' in Scotland, Narra Bukulla, with its celebration of the black stump, could be it.

The proportions of the gateways are based on the natural formula of the Golden Mean (or Golden Ratio or Section) represented by the Greek letter *phi* ϕ (1.618 . . .); Charles Jencks, no doubt, would thoroughly approve. 'I wanna be a landscape architect when I grow up,' drawls the Californian-born octagenarian, half seriously. Timber and stone are Marr's materials of choice, but found objects are happily employed – his readymades might include termite mounds, discarded rubber thongs or old houseboats. Both environmental and ephemeral sculptures by Marr, but also by artist friends like Tony Trembath and Richard Moffat, are a feature of the property. As even the immaculately stacked wood piles attest, this is the place of someone who sees beauty in order and pattern, and in the patterns to be found in the natural world.

Both inside and outside the kitchen garden fence principles of permaculture are generally abided by. All garden and kitchen waste is composted or fed to the worm farm, insecticides are avoided and little is brought on site – perhaps a couple of large bales of pea straw a season. The climate here (the garden is 1 km from the ocean) is ideal for a wide range of plants, from

> **' As even the immaculately stacked wood piles attest, this is the place of someone who sees beauty in order and pattern, and in the patterns to be found in the natural world.'**

those requiring a chill factor like apples to the subtropical babaco. While Marr rarely achieves tomatoes by Christmas, there are avocados, berries, beans and cucumber. A tangle of herbs – oregano, chives, thyme, tarragon and lemongrass – cover the sloping banks of the kitchen garden and leave little room for weeds to take hold. Textures and tones are subtle in this garden, dependent on leaf shape, size and colour. There is a multiplicity of greens and greys, though – the deep green of the Kaffir limes, verdant grassy-green bananas, lime-green herbs, grey-green of olive leaves and culinary sage. Small flashes of colour are provided by nasturtiums and the flowers of other herbs, fruit and vegetables rather than bedding plants or herbaceous perennials. *Grevillea* 'Peaches and Cream', one of the few showy flowers in the garden, attracts honeyeaters and eastern spinebills and is delightful planted among lemon verbena, purple heliotrope and silver shocks of artichokes. The garden proves that permaculture can be pretty and not, as some would have it, just pretty messy.

Marr essentially 'lives out of the garden' at Narra Bukulla. Never being one to do things by the book, he doesn't cook from recipes but prefers to eat vegetables from the garden raw or lightly steamed and to dress salads with lime or lemon juice and olive oil. With such good fresh produce he figures you don't need to fiddle around with it much. Each season has its own special bounty: spring heralds a feast of asparagus worthy of a festival.

Simple materials were used to construct this productive garden: sleepers for the raised beds, concrete pipes as pots, all surrounded by a sea of pebbles

MARR GROUNDS' GARDEN

1. Fruit cage
2. Pergolas with raised beds of herbs
3. Sloping bank of herbs and edibles
4. Olive trees, globe artichokes and herbs
5. Avocados, Kaffir lime, lemongrass
6. Tamarillo, citrus and banana
7. Sweetpotatoes, chillies, herbs
8. Asparagus
9. Citrus in concrete pipes
10. Ponds
11. Strawberries and herbs
12. Lettuce, carrot, broccoli
13. Tomatoes, shallots, beetroot
14. Tomatoes, lettuce, silverbeet
15. Banana, monstera, ornamental foliage plants

Have you ever grown enough asparagus to make yourself and your friends truly sick of eating it? Imagine not one but three asparagus beds measuring 5 m long – 15 delicious metres in mid-spring! In December, luscious red orbs of strawberries hang over the sides of the raised vegie beds. In January, peaches, nectarines, mulberries and beans and the passionfruit are ripening. Unlike more southerly areas of mainland eastern Australia that receive most of their rainfall in winter and spring, the south-east coast of New South Wales receives its rainfall in February thanks to prevailing north-east to south-east winds that deliver moist air to the coastal fringe; and the region's driest months occur during autumn and winter.

Around Easter, cantaloupe and chillies are ready. In late autumn, olives festoon branches and are snatched by cheeky currawongs, king parrots and bower birds. Spinach and peas are planted to replace tomatoes, the tendrils of sweetpotatoes begin to sneak over their beds, and feijoas litter the ground beneath grey-green bushes. In many respects the garden has achieved a self-perpetuating equilibrium. The river-pebble paths provide an ideal growing medium – lettuce and herbs of all kinds germinate readily among the cool stones. Winter is all soft mists and skies, and the beautiful smell of damp bush and wood smoke. Then there is rhubarb, greens, herbs and plenty of citrus: tangelos, oranges and mandarins. Marr likes the ageing foliage of the asparagus and its cut-back is left until the very last minute.

Anyone who has tried to produce a crop in the bush knows it means excluding wildlife, both native and introduced. The northern cleavage between the two building pavilions forms a green room roofed with steel beams and wire netting. Here, large-leaved plants furnish a sense of tropical abundance: there is a sexy medley of taro, banana, tamarillos, silverbeet and babaco. Babaco is a hybrid of the papaya or pawpaw, and is native to the cool, subtropical and highland zones of Ecuador. It is thought to be a naturally occurring hybrid of *Vasconcellea stipulata* and *V. pubescens*. Babaco is a fascinating plant in that it is sterile – the flowers, which rise from every leaf axil, are all female and the fruits set parthenocarpically, meaning there are no seeds present within the fruit. Propagation is therefore

Top: **Raised vegie beds, enclosed by galvanised wire netting.**
Below: **Grevillea 'Peaches and Cream' is one of the few inedible plants in Marr's garden.**

from softwood cuttings. It has unusual five-sided fruits that can grow up to 30 cm in length. The juicy flesh is effervescent, with a light tingly flavour that gives it its other name – 'champagne fruit'. It is often described as tasting like a mix of strawberries, pineapple and pawpaw. Babaco has a texture similar to pear – it can be a little bland due to its low sugar content, but it has a nice acidity. *Cordyline stricta* and other ornamentals have snuck their way in to this garden zone to help avoid the bare look after the big winter cut-back. *Monstera deliciosa* is both evergreen and edible, however. The 'fruit salad plant's weird knobbly cones are tutti-frutti tasting – like pineapple crossed with banana passionfruit – and, as with tamarillos and feijoas, can be an 'acquired taste'. Also known as the 'Swiss cheese plant', monstera is a climbing relative of the philodendron from the jungles of Mexico and Guatemala, and much tougher than its huge fleshy leaves would suggest – it even fruits in Hobart.

Above the house a whimsical fruit cage constructed from chicken-wire, fencing wire and poles is based on a structure created by Marr's father, architect Sir Roy Grounds. The fruit cage – named *Barn II* – references Roy's idiosyncratic 1966 *Barn* (a teepee structure built on a nearby headland made of logs and with a sod roof) in its exact dimensions. *Barn II* encircles the soft fruit that the local birdlife and marsupials would otherwise devour: peaches, apples, nectarines, a mulberry, plums and raspberries. Varieties include red and 'Golden Delicious' apples, 'Santa Rosa' plums, pear 'Packham's Triumph', and nashi 'Winter Cole'. Red clover grows as a nitrogen-fixing groundcover under the fruit trees, while blueberries and strawberries are mulched with the needles of the local black sheoke, *Allocasuarina littoralis*.

Ornamental grapevines are grown over curved galvanised metal pergolas adjoining the house. The vines shade timber tables and benches in the warm months, and share their pots – concrete pipe off-cuts – with cucumbers and herbs over the summer. In long ponds, reminiscent of horse troughs complete with plastic floats, native nardoo drifts its clover-like leaves. Ornamental, non-edible plants have crept in here alongside the main axis of the house, including the chef's cap correa – a most well-behaved glossy-leaved native shrub. A bed of the pretty white-flowered *Libertia paniculata* had to go, however, when the local blacksnakes (finding the house in their path to the dam) began sheltering there. Now the pretty ground-covering native violet *Viola banksii* gives a lower profile edge to the ponds.

While he wouldn't be so rude as to say so, the gardener at Narra Bukulla, Artie Piekalns, has one very idiosyncratic client in Marr Grounds. Not many clients offer such a varied program of interesting and unusual projects. Artie possesses a deep understanding of the seasonal requirements of this kitchen garden. Maintenance has decreased as ground-covering herbs have established; weeding is reduced but the seasonal sowing, pruning and mulching continue. As the shelter belts of she-oaks grow, the garden's microclimate will change, and plants such as the avocado trees will begin to really thrive. Artie and Marr will now often share a punnet of seedlings between them and avoid the over-abundance that inevitably happens when planting vegetables with abandon.

Happily, what may have begun as 'a project' and a prototype in sustainable building design is now much more than a successfully autonomous and award-winning dwelling – it's a home. The pleasure of the garden, says Marr, lies in sharing it – harvested produce is given to friends and neighbours and shared with the gardeners. Harvesting and then cooking and eating with family is another love. Marr's sculptures emerge from the forest floor seemingly without effort – as naturally as the local termite mounds. One month there is a boat up a tree; another, a trio of blackened tree-trunks roots to the sky, and meanwhile, back at headquarters, the edible harvest continues.

Clockwise, from top left: **Tamarillos; the gate to the fruit cage; Marr's amazing fruit cage; with the birds excluded, Marr is able to grow all manner of fruit; oranges growing in a concrete pipe pot; one of the many sculptures to be found on the property; red chillies; even sub-tropical plants flourish in this enclosed north-facing garden.**

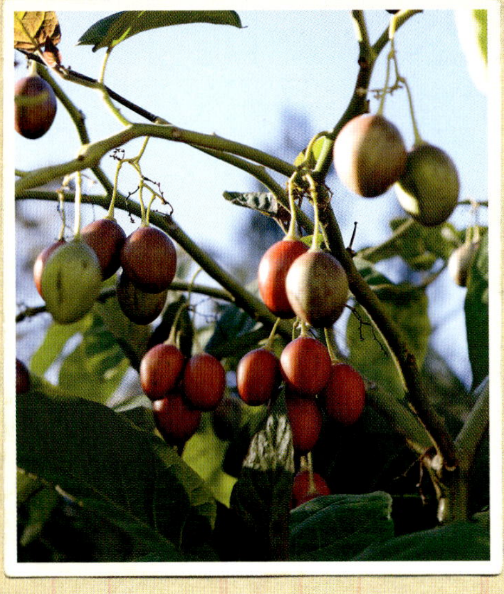

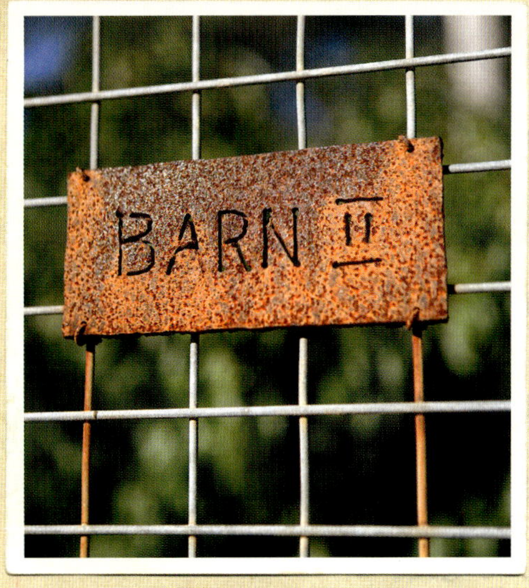
BARN II

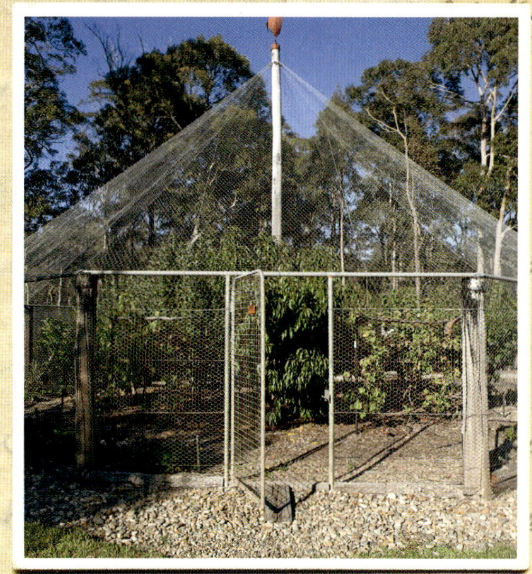

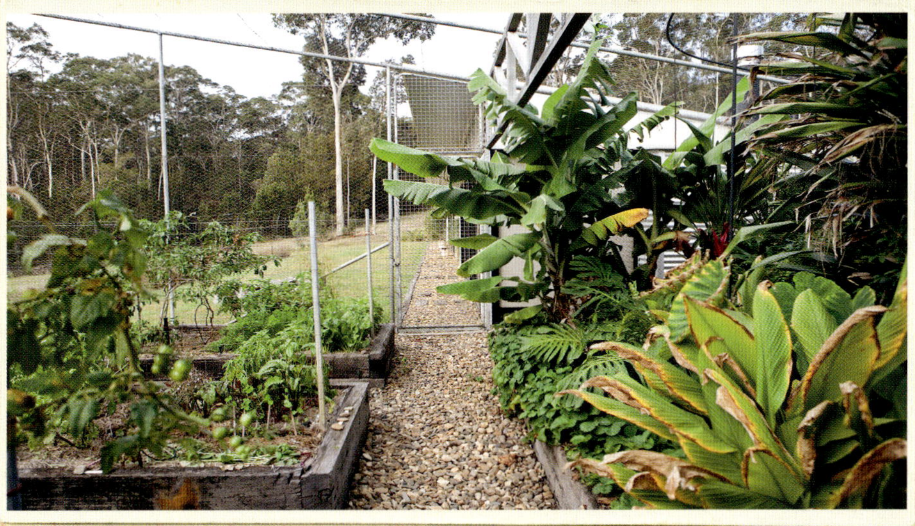

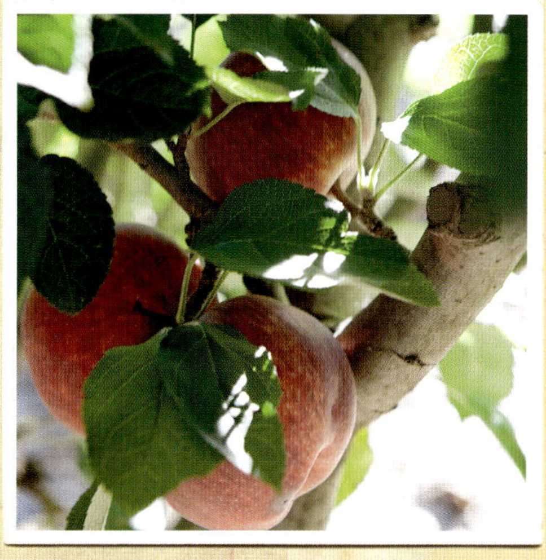

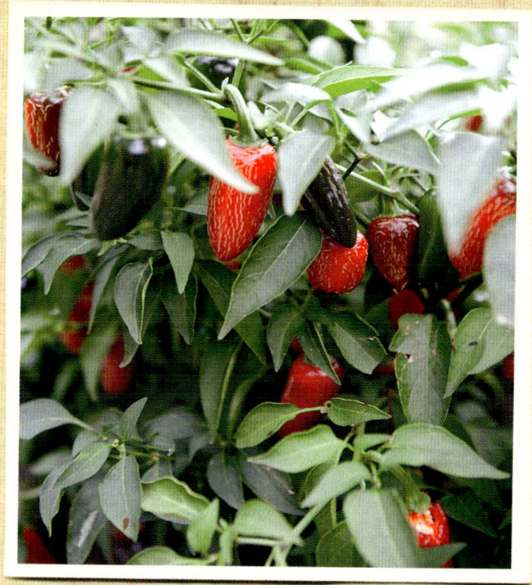

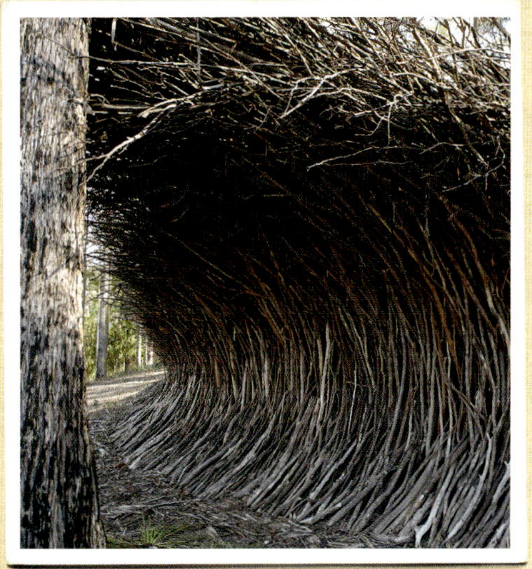

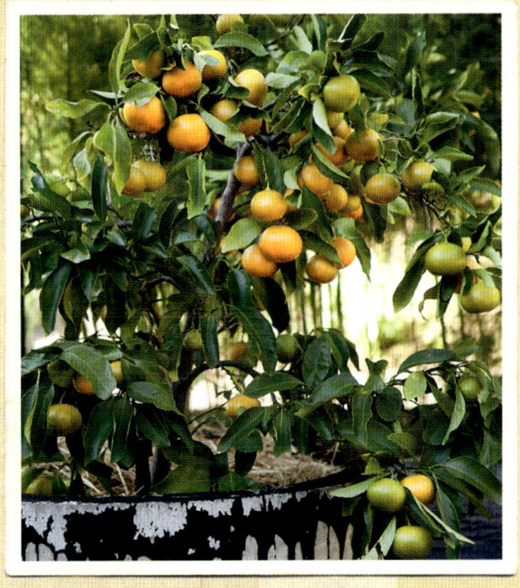

FOOTNOTES

INTRODUCTION
1. Frank Finedon, *The Australian Kitchen Garden*, George Robertson & Co., Melbourne, 1897, Preface.

THE BENEFITS OF A KITCHEN GARDEN
1. Andrew Campbell, *Paddock to Plate: Food, Farming & Victoria's Progress to Sustainability*, The Future Food and Farm Project Background Paper, Australian Conservation Foundation, Melbourne, 2008, p.vi.
2. Paul Holper and Simon Torok, *Climate Change: What you can do about it*, Pan Macmillan, Sydney, p. 53.
3. Green manure means a crop that will be incorporated into the topsoil so that it will decompose and consequently feed both the soil and the new, usually different, crop. Green manure plants can be legumes (plants in the family *Fabaceae*, which includes peas and beans) such as clover, mung beans and peas; grasses such as wheat or barley; or broadleaf species like mustard, canola and sunflowers.
4. Organisation for Economic Cooperation and Development, *OECD environmental indicators 2004*, OECD Environment Directorate, Paris, p. 22.
5. John Quiggin, 'Urban water supply in Australia: the option of diverting water from irrigation. *Public Policy*, 1:14–22. 2006.
6. Australian Bureau of Statistics. *Home production of selected foodstuffs, Australia, year ended April 1992*, Catalogue no. 7111.0
7. *Australian Food Statistics 2008*, Australian Government Department of Agriculture, Fisheries and Forestry, Canberra, 2009, pp.157–159.
8. National Nutrition Survey in Australia was conducted from February 1995 to March 1996 by the ABS (ABS, 1995).
9. Emily Morgan, F*ruit and vegetable consumption and waste in Australia: Recommendations towards a food supply system framework that will deliver healthy food in a sustainable way*, Vic Health, 2009, p. 6.
10. Michael Pollan, *The Botany of Desire: A plant's-eye view of the world*, Bloomsbury, London, 2003, p. 197.

CHAPTER 1
1. Australian Bureau of Statistics. *Home production of selected foodstuffs, Australia, year ended April 1992*, Catalogue no. 7111.0
2. *List of esculent vegetables and pott herbs cultivated in the Botanic Gardens, Sydney, December 1827*, Manuscript ledger compiled by Charles Fraser, Historic Houses Trust, Sydney, NSW.
3. Barbara Santich, 'Tomatoes in Nineteenth–Century Australian Gardens And Kitchens', in *The Changing Rural Landscape . . . Gardens, Vineyards, Forests*, Australian Garden History Society 20th Annual National Conference, Mount Gambier, SA, 5th–7th November 1999, pp. 66–70.
4. Stefano de Pieri, www.visitvictoria.com

CHAPTER 2
1. Denise Gadd, 'Pick of the crop', *Sydney Morning Herald*, 30 January, 2008.
2. L. Head, P. Muir & E. Hampel, 'Australian backyard gardens and the journey of migration', (in) *Geographical Review*, July 2004, 94, 3, p.346.
3. Michael Pollan, *The omnivore's dilemma: a natural history of four meals*, Penguin Press, New York, 2006, p. 296.

CHAPTER 3
1. Sunday Reed to Jean Langley, November 1972, Langley Papers, in Burke, Janine, *The Heart Garden*, Random House, NSW, Australia, 2004, p. 382.
2. Food Production by Suburb Type, Melbourne, 1941, 'Income and Poverty in Melbourne, 1941–42', Melbourne University Social Survey, in A. Gaynor, *Harvest of the suburbs: an environmental history of growing food in Australian cities*, Crawley, W.A., UWA Press, 2006, p. 102.
3. J. Langley, 'The Kitchen Garden', in *Heide Park and Gallery*, [Booklet designed and compiled by Maudie Palmer], Heide Park and Gallery, Bulleen, Vic., 1981.
4. Sunday Reed to Guy Smith, 20 July 1981, Reed Papers, State Library of Victoria.
5. Janine Burke, *The Heart Garden*, Random House, NSW, Australia, 2004, p. 161.
6. 'My Space: Nick Harrison' Interview by Andrew Stephens, *The Age*, 12 January 2008.
7. Ibid.
8. Sunday Reed to Jean Langley, November 1972, Langley Papers, in Burke, Janine, *The Heart Garden*, Random House, NSW, Australia, 2004, p. 382.

CHAPTER 4
1. Rosalind Creasy 'My House in the Garden' in *Edible Estates: Attack on the Front Lawn*, Fritz Haeg, p. 40.
2. Karen Sutherland, 'An edible eden' in *Green Garden and Home*, first edition of *Backyard & Garden Design Ideas*, Universal Magazines, North Ryde, NSW, 2008 p. 10.
3. www.edibleedendesign.com.

CHAPTER 5

1. *Gardening Australia* episode 27, 2008, ABC 1.
2. Michael Pollan, 'Why bother?' in *The New York Times Magazine*, 20 April, 2008.
3. Jeremy Coleby-Williams, 'Four Questions about sustainable living', 1 March 2008, www.bellis.info.
4. *Gardening Australia* episode 27, 2008, ABC1.

CHAPTER 6

1. *The Australian*, George Williams, Sydney, N.S.W, 13 January, 1830. (W. C. Wentworth was co-founder and co-proprietor of the newspaper).
2. Edward A. K. Higginbotham, *Historic Houses Trust of New South Wales; Report on the archaeological investigation of the kitchen garden at Vaucluse House, Vaucluse, N.S.W.*, Historic Houses Trust, Sydney, July, 1999.
3. Carol Liston, *Sarah Wentworth: Mistress of Vaucluse*, Historic Houses Trust of New South Wales, Glebe, N.S.W., 1988, p. 78.
4. J.C. Loudon, *An encyclopaedia of gardening: comprising the theory and practice of horticulture, floriculture, arboriculture, and landscape gardening . . .*, Longman, London, 1859, p. 754.
5. J.C. Loudon, *An encyclopaedia of agriculture . . .*, 3rd edition, Printed for Longman, Rees, Orme, Brown, Green, and Longman, London, 1835, p. 461.
6. Seeds were later distributed from Kew elsewhere and plants were grown at Napoleon and Josephine's French chateau Malmaison and were illustrated by Belgian botanical artist, Redouté in 1803. Bennett, J. F., Stevenson, G., *The Royal South Australian Almanack and general directory for 1840: being bissextile of leap year, calculated for the meridian of Adelaide* [compiled by J.F. Bennett] 1840, p. 52.
7. J. H. Maiden, *The useful native plants of Australia*, Trubner, London, 1889, pp. 62–3. (in) Philip A. Clarke, *Aboriginal Plant Collectors: Botanists and Australian Aboriginal People in the Nineteenth Century*, Rosenberg Publishing, Kenthurst, NSW, 2008, p. 31.
8. Michael Pollan, *The Botany of Desire: A plant's-eye view of the world*, Bloomsbury, London, 2003, p. 17.
9. William Cobbett, *The English Gardener . . .*, London, 1833, p. 127.
10. J. F. Bennett & G. Stevenson, op. cit., p. 28.
11. Sarah Wentworth to Thomasine Fisher, 20 December 1861, Wenworth Papers, ML A868, p. 115, Mitchell Library, SLNSW.
12. W. C. Wentworth, *A statistical, historical, and political description of the colony of New South Wales, and its dependent settlements in Van Diemen's Land: With a particular enumeration of the advantages which these colonies offer for emigration, a demonstration of their superiority in many respects over those possessed by the United States of America; and a word of advice to emigrants.* 2nd Edition, G. & W. B. Whittaker, London, 1820, p. 129.

CHAPTER 7

1. Anne Latreille, *Garden of a Lifetime: Dame Elisabeth Murdoch at Cruden Farm*, Macmillan, Sydney, 2007, p. 89.

CHAPTER 8

1. Australian Conservation Foundation: www.acfonline.org.au/consumptionatlas/. See also 'Household environmental pressure from consumption: an Australian environmental atlas' (2007) Dey, C., Berger, C., Foran, B., Foran, M., Joske, R., Lenzen, M., Sydney University Press, http://hdl.handle.net/2123/2104.
2. Ibid.
3. *Alice Springs Backyard Vegie Garden Companion*, 2007, Brock, Collins, Brisbin, et al., Northern Territory, Australia, p. 50.

CHAPTER 9

1. J. Larkcom, *Creative Vegetable Gardening*, Mitchell Beazley, London, 1997, p. 17.
2. See A. McConnell, & N. Servant, *The history and heritage of the Tasmanian apple industry: a profile*, Queen Victoria Museum and Art Gallery, Launceston, Tasmania, 1999.

CHAPTER 10

1. Compass, ABC TV, September 9, 2009
2. Michael Pollan, *The Botany of Desire: A plant's-eye view of the world*, Bloomsbury, London, 2003, p. 61.
3. Adam Leith Gollner, *The Fruit Hunters: a story of nature, adventure, commerce and obsession*, Scribner, New York, 2008, p. 103.
4. Paul Cox and Scott Rae, *Bioethics: A Christian Approach in a Pluralistic Age*, Wm. B. Eerdmans Publishing Co., Michigan, USA, 1999, p. 25–6.
5. Gay Bilson, 'Buyer's Market', *The Monthly*, December 2007–January 2008, No. 30, www.themonthly.com.au.

CHAPTER 11

1. Fritz Haeg (a project by) *Edible Estates: Attack on the Front Lawn*, Metropolis Books, Distributed Art Publishers, Inc., New York, 2008, p. 22.
2. Ibid. p. 27.
3. Tom McGuire in 'Guerrilla gardening: Renters, eco-activists make the most of pocket spaces that can yield big results' by Rosemary Ponnekanti, www.divineearthgp.com.
4. David Campbell, *Entrepreneurial community gardens: growing food, skills, jobs and communities*, University of California, Oakland, California, 1999, p. 26.

CHAPTER 12

1. Hunter Rogers, 'The Early History of the Mornington Peninsula', Hallcraft Printers, Melbourne, 1968, p. 75.
2. Letter to Mr. Peale, 20 August, 1811, *The Writings of Thomas Jefferson: Being his autobiography, correspondence, reports, messages, addresses, and other writings, official and private*, Vol. VI. ed. by H.A. Washington, Taylor & Maury, Washington D.C., 1854, p. 6.

CHAPTER 13

1. Leonie Norrington, *Tropical Food Gardens: A guide to growing fruit, herbs and vegetables in tropical and sub-tropical climates*, Bloomings Books, Melbourne, Australia, 2003 edn., p. 132.
2. Ibid., p. 4.

CHAPTER 14

1. Josh Byrne, *The Green Gardener*, Viking, Penguin Group, Camberwell, Australia, 2006, p. 77.
2. This is ex-house use for single-residential households with an average occupancy rate of 3.35 persons. Michael Loh & Peter Coghlan, *Domestic Water Use Study in Perth, Western Australia, 1998–2001*, Water Corporation, Perth, Australia, 2003, p. 9.
3. Andrea Gaynor, *Harvest of the suburbs: an environmental history of growing food in Australian cities*, UWA Press, Crawley, Western Australia, 2006, p. 24.

CHAPTER 15

1. Adam Leith Gollner, *The Fruit Hunters: a story of nature, adventure, commerce and obsession*, Scribner, New York, 2008, p. 6.

CHAPTER 16

1. William Thomas Lyttleton, *Panshanger, The seat of Joseph Archer, Esqr., County of Cornwall, Vandiemen's Land*, 1835, two-colour lithograph with added hand colouring, 54 × 66 cm, Allport Library and Museum of Fine Arts, Tasmania.
2. Bruce Hindmarsh (in) R. Dare, (ed.) *Food Power and Community*, Wakefield Press, 1999, p. 170.
3. H. Widowson, *Present State of Van Diemen's Land: Comprising an Account of Its Agricultural Capabilities, with Observations on the Present State of Farming, &c. &c. Pursued in that Colony: and Other Important Matters Connected with Emigration . . .*, S. Robinson, London, 1829, p. 170.
4. J.C. Loudon, *The Gardener's Magazine*, Vol. XI. 1835, Printed for Longman, Rees, Orme, Brown, Green, and Longman, London, p. 338.

CHAPTER 17

1. Andrea Gaynor, *Harvest of the suburbs: an environmental history of growing food in Australian cities*, UWA Press, Crawley, W. A., 2006, p. 193.
2. Lorenza De'Medici, *Italy the Beautiful Cookbook: Authentic Recipes From The Regions of Italy*, Sunshine Books, Australian edition, Social Club Book Supplies, Collingwood, Victoria, 1990, p. 120.
3. Lolo Houbein, *One Magic Square: Grow Your Own Food On One Square Metre*, Wakefield Press, Kent Town, South Australia, 2008, p. 224.

PLANT LIST FOR THE KITCHEN GARDEN

(T) – Tropical areas
(ST) – Subtropical areas

Hedging plants – deciduous
Lemon verbena
Pomegranate
Japanese quince
Hazelnut
Rose
Raspberry

Hedging plants – evergreen
Bay
Chilean guava
Citrus
Coffee
Feijoa
Jaboticaba
Lemon myrtle
Myrtle
Natal plum
Olive
Rosemary
Strawberry guava
Tea camellia

Perennial edging plants
Chives
Garlic chives
Parsley
Society garlic
Strawberry
Thyme

Annual edging plants
African marigold
Calendula
Pansy
Viola

Trees for standardising
Apple
Bay
Citrus
Gooseberry
Medlar
Olive
Pear

Plants for espalier
Apple
Apricot
Cherry
Citrus
Fig
Gooseberry
Pear
Plum
Quince

Edible flowers
Anise hyssop
Bee balm
Borage
Calendula
Citrus blossom
Daylily
English lavender
Nasturtium
Pansy
Roses
Salvia patens
Sunflower
Viola
Violet
Zucchini

Potentially weedy plants of the kitchen garden – beware!
Amaranth
Asparagus
Borage
Brazilian cherry
Cape gooseberry
Coffee
Curry tree (T and ST areas)
Sorrel
Goji berry
Horseradish
Jerusalem artichoke
Mint
Nasturtium
Orach
Yellow guava
Winged yam

Purple flowers
Chives
Echinacea
Garlic
Lavender
Viola
Yarrow

Blue flowers
Borage
Chicory
Radicchio

White flowers
Camomile
Dianthus
Feverfew
Garlic chives
Strawberry

Red flowers
Daylily
Nasturtium
Scarlet runner bean
Broad bean (crimson flowered)

Orange or yellow flowers
African marigold
Calendula
Jerusalem artichoke
Nasturtium
Okra
Sunflower
Yacón

Tall flowers
Ginger
Jerusalem artichoke
Russian garlic
Sunflower
Yacón

Feathery foliage
Carrot
Chervil
Dill
Fennel – bronze and Florence
Tansy
Yarrow

Red and purple foliage
Amaranth
Beetroot 'Bulls Blood'
Bronze fennel
Brussels sprouts 'Ruby'
Purple basil
Purple sage
Red cabbage
Red kale
Red mustard

Red orach
Red perilla
Red cos lettuce
Radicchio 'Treviso'
Lettuce 'Lollo Rosso'
Lettuce 'Red Oakleaf'
Lettuce 'Rouge d'Hiver'
Ruby chard/silverbeet –
   red-leaved form

Grey and silver foliage
Cardoon
Cape gooseberry
Globe artichoke
Sage
Sea kale

Blue/grey foliage
Black kale
Broccoli
Cabbage 'January King'
Kohlrabi
Leek

Golden foliage
Gold-leaved feverfew
Golden oregano
Golden elder
Golden purslane

'Cut and come again' plants for harvesting more than once
Broccoli
Broccolini
Chervil
Chicory
Cornsalad
Endive
Kale
Mizuna
Mibuna
Mesclun mix salad greens
Mustard greens
Loose-leaf-type lettuces
Rocket
Silverbeet
Spinach
Watercress

Perennial food plants
Arrowroot
Artichoke
Asparagus
Bamboo
Cassava (ST – T)
Celery stem taro (ST – T)
Chinese water chestnut
Cranberry
Globe artichoke
Goji berry
Horseradish
Jerusalem artichoke
Kang kong (ST – T)
Malabar spinach (ST – T)
Oca
Pepino
Rhubarb

Sacred lotus (T)
Sea kale
Silverbeet
Sorrel
Sweet potato
Taro (ST – T)
Warrigal greens
Water chestnut
Watercress
Welsh onion
Yacón

Perennial herbs
Chives
Curry leaf
Garlic chives
Galangal
Ginger
Kaffir lime
Lemongrass (ST – T)
Lemon balm
Lovage
Mint
Oregano
Perennial basil
Rosemary
Sage
Saffron
Sorrel
Thyme
Turmeric
Vietnamese mint

Annual herbs
Basil
Chervil
Coriander
Lemongrass (annual in cool areas)
Perilla
Thai basil

Annual climbing plants for growing over structures
Climbing bean
Malabar spinach
Cucumber
Hyacinth bean (ST – T)
Pea
Pumpkin
Snake bean (ST – T)
Snow pea

Perennial climbing plants and vines
Air potato (ST – T)
Grapes
Hops
Kiwifruit/Chinese gooseberry
Dessert kiwi
Passionfruit – banana, black, 'Panama'
   (ST – T) and granadilla (T)
Seven-year bean
Vanilla bean (T)
Winged yam (ST – T)

Plants with unusual fruit/veg
Beetroot 'Golden'
Brussels sprouts 'Ruby'
Carrot 'Purple King'

Carrot 'White Belgian'
Cauliflower 'Purple Cape'
Cucumber 'African horned'
Cucumber 'Lemon'
Dragon fruit
Eggplant 'Rosa Bianca'
Pea 'Purple-podded Dutch'
Pea 'Golden podded'
Pumpkin 'Turk's Turban'
Rainbow chard
Rosella
Finger lime

Kids' favourites
Apple
Apricot
Blueberry
Carrot
Cherry tomato
Mulberry
Passionfruit
Pea
Potato
Strawberry
Strawberry guava
Watermelon

Shade-tolerant food plants
These plants will tolerate partial shade.
Celery
Chervil
Chicory
Chives
Cornsalad
Dill
Ginger
Kale
Kang kong
Lettuce
Malabar spinach
Mint
Mizuna
Mustard greens
Radish
Rhubarb
Salad burnet
Sorrel
Spinach
Silverbeet
Vietnamese mint
Warrigal greens

Tough food plants for dry conditions*
Caper
Carob
Cape gooseberry
Chinotto
Choko
Desert lime
Fig
Goji berry
Jujube
Loquat
Mediterranean herbs
Mulberry – white and black
Natal plum
Pineapple
Pomegranate
Quandong
Winged yam

*all plants require watering during establishment

Trees for the kitchen garden
Apple
Apricot
Babaco (ST – T)
Banana (ST – T)
Bay
Cherry
Coffee
Crab apple
Curry leaf
Fig
Grapefruit
Kaffir lime
Kumquat
Lemon
Lime
Loquat
Nectarine
Orange
Mandarin
Medlar
Mulberry (dwarf)
Olive
Pawpaw (ST – T)
Peach
Pear
Persimmon
Pomegranate
Plum
Quince
Strawberry guava
Tamarillo

RESOURCES

BOOKS

Asian Herbs and Vegetables: How to Identify, Grow and Use Them in Australia by Penny Woodward, Hyland House Publishing, Flemington, Victoria, 2000.

The Australian Fruit and Vegetable Garden by Clive Blazey and Jane Varkulevicius, Digger's Club, Dromana, Vic, 2006.

Backyard Self-sufficiency by Jackie French, Completely revised 2nd edition, Aird Books, Flemington, Victoria, 2009.

Citrus: A Guide to Organic Management, Propagation, Pruning, Pest Control and Harvesting by Allen Gilbert, Hyland House Publishing, Flemington, Victoria, 2007.

The Complete Book of Fruit Growing in Australia by Louis Glowinski, Lothian, Port Melbourne, 1997.

Creative Vegetable Gardening by Joy Larkcom, Mitchell Beazley, London, 1997.

Fabulous Food from Every Small Garden, Mary Horsfall, CSIRO Publishing, Collingwood, Vic., 2009.

Good Gardens with Less Water by Kevin Handreck, CSIRO Publishing, Collingwood, Vic., 2008.

The Green Gardener by Josh Byrne, Viking, Penguin Group, Camberwell, Australia, 2006.

The Nut Grower's Guide: The Complete Handbook for Producers and Hobbyists by Jennifer Wilkinson, CSIRO Publishing, Collingwood, Vic., 2005.

One Magic Square: Grow Your Own Food On One Square Metre, Lolo Houbein, Wakefield Press, Kent Town, South Australia, 2008.

The Practical Australian Gardener by Peter Cundall, Penguin Books, Camberwell, Vic., 2007.

Tropical Food Gardens: A Guide to Growing Fruit, Herbs and Vegetables in Tropical and Sub-tropical Climates by Leonie Norrington with illustrations by Colwyn Campbell, Bloomings, Hawthorn, Vic., 2001.

Water Not Down The Drain: A Guide to Using Rainwater and Greywater at Home by Stuart McQuire, Alternative Technology Association, Melbourne, Vic., 2008.

FOOD GROWING AND GARDENING RESOURCES ON THE INTERNET

ABC1's *Gardening Australia* Website
www.abc.net.au/gardening

Australian City Farms & Community Gardens Network
www.communitygarden.org.au

Biodynamic Agricultural Association of Australia (BDAAA)
www.demeter.org.au

Biodynamic Agriculture Australia
www.biodynamics.net.au

City Food Growers
www.cityfoodgrowers.com.au

Earth Garden
www.earthgarden.com.au

Organic Federation of Australia (OFA)
www.ofa.org.au

Permablitz
www.permablitz.net

Rare Fruit Council of Australia
www.rarefruitaustralia.org

Rare Fruit Society of South Australia
www.rarefruit-sa.org.au

The Garden Clubs of Australia Inc.
www.gardenclubs.org.au

The Food Forest – Permaculture Farm and Learning Centre
www.foodforest.com.au

The Permaculture Research Institute of Australia
www.permaculture.org.au

The National Association for Sustainable Agriculture, Australia (NASAA)
www.nasaa.com.au

Sustainable Gardening Australia (SGA)
www.sgaonline.com.au

Stephanie Alexander Kitchen Garden Foundation
www.kitchengardenfoundation.org.au

The Seed Savers' Network
www.seedsavers.net

WATER, GREYWATER AND COMPOSTING RESOURCES

Bokashi Bins
www.bokashi.com.au

Environment Protection
Authority of Victoria
www.epa.vic.gov.au

Environment Protection Authority
of Queensland
www.epa.qld.gov.au

Environment Protection Authority
of South Australia
www.epa.sa.gov.au

Environmental Protection Authority
of Western Australia
www.epa.wa.gov.au

Lanfax Laboratories
An independent lab with lists of
detergent ingredients.
www.lanfaxlabs.com.au

Reln compost and worm bins
www.reln.com.au

Sustainable Gardening Australia (SGA)
www.sgaonline.com.au

Water saving information for the
home, garden, school and workplace.
www.savewater.com.au

SEED COMPANIES

Eden Seeds
M.S. 905, Lower Beechmont QLD 4211
(07) 5533 1107
www.edenseeds.com.au

Green Harvest Organic
Gardening Supplies
PO Box 92, Maleny QLD 4552
(07) 5435 2699
www.greenharvest.com.au

Greenpatch Organic Seeds
109 Old Bar Road,
Glenthorne NSW, 2430
(02) 6551 4240
www.greenpatchseeds.com.au

New Gippsland Seeds & Bulbs
120 Lewis Road, Silvan VIC 3795
(03) 9737 9560; 1800 887 732
www.newgipps.com.au

Phoenix Seeds
Channel Highway, Snug TAS 7054
(03) 6267 9663

Select Organic
M.S. 905, Lower Beechmont QLD 4211
(07) 5533 1177
www.selectorganic.com.au

The Diggers Club
Heronswood, Dromana, and the
Garden of St Erth, Blackwood VIC
(03) 5984 7900
www.diggers.com.au

The Lost Seed
PO Box 321, Sheffield TAS 7306
(03) 6491 1000
www.thelostseed.com.au

FRUIT TREE COMPANIES

Daley's Fruit Tree Nursery
36 Daley's Lane, Geneva
via Kyogle NSW 2474
(02) 6632 1441
www.daleysfruit.com.au

Fleming's Nurseries
PO Box 1, Monbulk VIC 3793
(03) 9756 6105
www.flemings.com.au

Heritage Fruit Trees
PO Box 35, Beaufort VIC 3373
(03) 5349 2949
www.heritagefruittrees.com.au

Perry's Fruit & Nut Nursery
Kangarilla Road, McLaren Flat SA
5171
(08) 8383 0268
www.perrysfruitnursery.com.au

Strzelecki Heritage Apples
1699 Korumburra-Warragul Rd,
Strzelecki VIC 3950
(03) 5659 5242

Stun'sail Boom River Nursery
Kangaroo Island SA 5223
(08) 8559 7264
www.appletrees.com.au

The Diggers Club
(see listing under Seed
companies above)

Woodbridge Fruit Trees
PO Box 95, Woodbridge TAS 7162
www.woodbridgefruittrees.com.au

Yalca Fruit Trees
602 Tyacks Road, Yalca VIC 3637
www.yalcafruittrees.com.au

BIBLIOGRAPHY

Abraham, A. B., Gaballa, S., *Food Miles in Australia: A Preliminary Study*, CERES Community Environment Park, Brunswick, Victoria, 2007.

Anthony, D., *The Ornamental Vegetable Garden*, Warwick Publishing, Toronto and Los Angeles, 1998.

Ashley, B., Hollows, J., Jones, S., & Taylor, B., *Food and Cultural Studies*, Routledge, London, 2004.

Atkinson, James, Fraser, Charles, Mansfield, Ralph, Howe, Robert, *Australian almanack, for the year of our Lord 1832: being bissextile, or leap year; and the second of the reign of His Most gracious Majesty King William the Fourth / published under the sanction and patronage of His Excellency Major-General Richard Bourke*, Sydney, Ralph Mansfield, Gazette Office, for the executors of Robert Howe, 1832.

Bennett, J. F. & Stevenson, G., *The Royal South Australian Almanack and general directory for 1840: being bissextile of leap year, calculated for the meridian of Adelaide*, Printed and published by Robert Thomas and Co., Adelaide, 1840.

Bilson, Gay, *On Digestion*, Melbourne University Publishing, Carlton, Vic., 2008.

Bilson, G., *Plenty: Digressions on Food*, Penguin Group, Camberwell, Victoria, 2007.

Blackman, Barbara, *Glass after Glass: Autobiographical Reflections*, Penguin Books Ltd, Ringwood, Victoria, Australia, 1997.

Bravery, Suzanne, 'Fruit & vegetables in colonial New South Wales', in *Australian Garden History: Journal of the Australian Garden History Society*, Vol. 11, no. 5 March/April, 2000, pp. 10–15.

Bravery, S., 'The reconstruction of the kitchen garden at Vaucluse House', in *Australian Garden History: Journal of the Australian Garden History Society*, Vol. 11, no. 5 March/April, 2000, pp. 16–20.

Broadbent, Dr. James, *The Australian Colonial House Architecture and Society in New South Wales 1788–1842*.

Burke, Janine, *The Heart Garden*, Random House, NSW, Australia, 2004.

Byrne, Josh, *The Green Gardener*, Viking, Penguin Group, Camberwell, Australia, 2006.

Campbell, Andrew, *Paddock to Plate: Policy Propositions for Sustaining Food & Farming Systems*, The Future Food and Farm Project Propositions Paper, Australian Conservation Foundation, Melbourne, 2009.

The Changing Rural Landscape: Gardens, Vineyards, Forests, Proceedings of the 20th Annual National Conference, Mount Gambier, South Australia, 5–7 October, 1999, Australian Garden History Society, South Yarra, Vic., 2000.

Clarke, P. A., *Aboriginal Plant Collectors: Botanists and Australian Aboriginal People in the Nineteenth Century*, Rosenberg Publishing, Kenthurst, NSW, 2008.

Clarson, W., *Kitchen Garden and Cottager's Manual: A Reliable Guide to Garden Management and to the Culture of Culinary Crops for the Table*, A.H. Massina & Co., Melbourne, 1886.

Dare, R., (ed.) *Food Power and Community*, Wakefield Press, Kent Town, South Australia, 1999.

Edible Estates: Attack on the Front Lawn (A project by Fritz Haeg), Metropolis Books, Distributed Art Publishers, Inc., New York, 2008.

Finedon, F., *The Australian Kitchen Garden*, George Robertson & Co., Melbourne, 1897.

Ford, G., 'Neil Douglas, a personal search for a paradise garden: Bayswater, 1925/1958', *Australian Garden History*, v.8 no.1 July/Aug 1996, pp. 5–7.

Gaynor, Andrea, *Harvest of the Suburbs: an Environmental History of Growing Food in Australian Cities*, UWA Press, Crawley, W.A., 2006.

Gollner, Adam Leith, *The Fruit Hunters: A Story of Nature, Adventure, Commerce and Obsession*, Scribner, New York, 2008.

Griffin, R., & Hughes, J., eds. *Vaucluse House: A History & Guide*, Historic Houses Trust of New South Wales, The Mint, Sydney, N.S.W., 2006.

Head, L., Muir, P., and Hampel, E., 'Australian backyard gardens and the journey of migration', *Geographical Review*, July 2004, 94, 3, pp. 326–347.

Heide Park and Gallery, [Booklet designed and compiled by Maudie Palmer], Heide Park and Gallery, Bulleen, Vic., 1981.

Heuzenroeder, A., *Barossa Food*, Wakefield Press, Kent Town, South Australia, 1999.

Higginbotham, Edward A. K., *Historic Houses Trust of New South Wales; Report on the Archaeological Investigation of the Kitchen Garden at Vaucluse House, Vaucluse, N.S.W.*, Historic Houses Trust, Sydney, July 1999.

Holmes, K., Martin, S. K., & Mirmohamadi, K., *Reading the Garden: The Settlement of Australia*, Melbourne University Publishing, Carlton, Vic., 2008.

Houbein, Lolo, *One Magic Square: Grow Your Own Food On One Square Metre*, Wakefield Press, Kent Town, South Australia, 2008.

Huntley, Rebecca, *Eating Between the Lines: Food & Equality in Australia*, Black Inc., Melbourne, 2008.

Langley, Jean, 'The Kitchen Garden', in *Heide Park and Gallery*, [Booklet designed and compiled by Maudie Palmer], Heide Park and Gallery, Bulleen, Vic., 1981.

Larkcom, J., *Creative Vegetable Gardening*, Mitchell Beazley, London, 1997.

Latreille, Anne, *Garden of a Lifetime: Dame Elisabeth Murdoch at Cruden Farm*, Macmillan, Sydney, 2007.

Liston, Carol, *Sarah Wentworth: Mistress of Vaucluse*, Historic Houses Trust of New South Wales, Glebe, N.S.W., 1988.

Loudon, J.C., *An encyclopaedia of agriculture: comprising the theory and practice of the valuation, transfer, laying out, improvement, and management of landed property, and the cultivation and economy of the animal and vegetable productions of agriculture, including all the latest improvements, a general history of agriculture in all countries, and a statistical view of its present state, with suggestions for its*

Loudon, J.C., *future progress in the British Isles*, 3rd edition, Printed for Longman, Rees, Orme, Brown, Green, and Longman, London, 1835.

Loudon, J.C., *Encyclopaedia of cottage, farm, and villa architecture and furniture*; with an introduction by Eric Mercer, Shaftesbury, Donhead, 2000. Originally published: London: Longman, Brown, Green and Longmans, 1846.

Loudon, J.C., *An encyclopaedia of gardening: comprising the theory and practice of horticulture, floriculture, arboriculture, and landscape gardening . . .*, Longman, London, 1859.

Low, T., 'Anyone for "Spinage"?' *Australian Natural History*, 23: 1989, pp. 108–109.

Low, T., *Wild Food Plants of Australia*, Angus & Robertson, North Ryde, N.S.W., 1991.

McEwin, G., *The South Australian Vigneron and Gardener's Manual*, Adelaide, 1843.

Meredith, L. A., *Notes and sketches of New South Wales during a residence in the colony from 1839 to 1844*, Ure Smith in association with the National Trust of Australia (N.S.W.), Sydney, 1973. First published, London: John Murray, 1844.

Mollison, B., and Holmgrem, D., *Permaculture One: A Perennial Agricultural System for Human Settlements*, Corgi Books, Melbourne, 1978.

Morgan, E., *Fruit and Vegetable Consumption and Waste in Australia: Recommendations Towards a Food Supply System Framework that will Deliver Healthy Food in a Sustainable Way,* Vic Health, Carlton South, Vic., 2009.

Norrington, Leonie, *Tropical Food Gardens: A Guide to Growing Fruit, Herbs and Vegetables in Tropical and Sub-tropical Climates*, Bloomings Books, Melbourne, Australia, 2003.

Pollan, Michael, *In Defence of Food: The Myth of Nutrition and the Pleasures of Eating*, Allen Lane, Penguin Books, London, 2008.

Pollan, M., *Second Nature: A Gardener's Education*, Bloomsbury, London, 1996.

Pollan, M., *The Botany of Desire: A Plant's-eye View of the World*, Bloomsbury, London, 2003.

Pollan, M., *The Omnivore's Dilemma: A Natural History of Four Meals*, Penguin Press, New York, 2006.

Reed Papers, State Library of Victoria.

Shepherd, T., *Lectures on Landscape Gardening in Australia*, William McGarvie, Sydney, 1836.

Thompson, R., *The gardener's assistant, practical and scientific: a guide to the formation and management of the kitchen, fruit, and flower garden, and the cultivation of conservatory, green-house, and stove plants, with a copious calendar of gardening operations*, Blackie & Son, London, 1859.

Vilmorin-Andrieux et cie. *Album de cliches: containing the illustrations published in the different books and catalogues of Vilmorin-Andrieux & Cie* [trade catalogue], Vilmorin-Andrieux & Cie., Paris, 1883.

Wentworth, W.C., *A statistical, historical, and political description of the colony of New South Wales, and its dependent settlements in Van Diemen's Land: With a particular enumeration of the advantages which these colonies offer for emigration, a demonstration of their superiority in many respects over those possessed by the United States of America; and a word of advice to emigrants*. 2nd Edition, G. & W. B. Whittaker, London, 1820.

Widowson, H., *Present State of Van Diemen's Land: Comprising an Account of Its Agricultural Capabilities, with Observations on the Present State of Farming, &c. &c. Pursued in that Colony: and Other Important Matters Connected with Emigration . . .*, S. Robinson, London, 1829.

PHOTOGRAPHIC CREDITS

Page 46: lemon balm – from *Vilmorin-Andrieux et cie. Album de cliches*: containing the illustrations published in the different books and catalogues of Vilmorin-Andrieux & Cie [trade catalogue], Vilmorin-Andrieux & Cie., Paris, 1883; Page 56: pea – Vilmorin; Page 67: sea kale, oyster plant and cardoon – Vilmorin; Page 69: *Vaucluse*, 1851, oil on canvas by GE Peacock (Ref: ML 236) Mitchell Library, State Library of New South Wales; Page 125: Wilmots Late Scarlet Strawberry from *Pomona Londinensis . . .* William Hooker, (1779-1832), London, 1818. State Library of Victoria, Rare Books Collection; Page 146: Malabar spinach – Vilmorin; Page 181: Panshanger lithograph – Louis Haghe, (1806–1885), *Penshanger, the seat of Joseph Archer, Esqr., county of Cornwall, Vandieman's Land [picture]*, London : Day & Haghe, lithrs. to the King, [ca.1835] 1 print : lithograph, hand col; 21.2 x 51 cm. nla.pic-an8866004 National Library of Australia.

ACKNOWLEDGEMENTS

Foremost, thanks to Duré Dara for the gift of Louisa Jones' *Kitchen Gardens of France*, which inspired this book. My immense gratitude to Ingrid Ohlsson and Julie Gibbs of Penguin Books for giving me the chance to produce a beautiful book on my favourite subject. Simon Griffiths is an absolute pleasure to work with and understands my love of books, plants and dogs perfectly. And of course, thank you to Saskia Adams for putting my book proposal on Ingrid's desk in the first place, as well as for being the wonderful editor that she is. Danie Pout's design is so lovely I could cry. Thanks also to my 'inhouse design girl', Laura Thomas.

My sincere thanks also go to all of the garden owners and garden managers in this book. What a generous bunch of people you all are! Neil Robertson, Cassie Johnstone and Sarah von Bibra at Australia's Open Garden Scheme were of great assistance in helping me find gardens to visit and write about. Also the AOGS State Coordinators of Tasmania, Queensland and South Australia. Thanks to David Martin, Sandra Nobes, Margaret Cooper and Juliet Flesch. To Megan Utter, Philip Stray, Belinda Cant, Jela Ivankovic-Waters and Frances Saunders for reading particular chapters. Mary Trigger and Sustainable Gardening Australia. Louise Foletta for her watercolour advice. Nick Harrison, Elizabeth Peck, Guy Smith, Dugald Noyes and Kendrah Morgan regarding the kitchen gardens at Heide. Geoff Miers and Dave Albrecht in Alice Springs. Scott Carlin at HHT. Jane Dennithorne, James Matthews and Mac McVeigh for keeping my own garden alive while I was writing about other peoples'! Chris and Tina Foster for all the minding of my beloved dog Inka. Lastly, to all my produce-gardening friends for their feedback and answers to my vegie-growing questions!

And an extra big thanks to my partner Philip for visiting so many of the gardens with me and being such a wonderful sounding-board for this project over the last two years.

Small Chinese Turban Gourd (⅙ natural size).

INDEX

Adelaide, SA 196
African horned cucumber (kiwano) 95
Alice Springs Seed Savers Network 95
allotment gardens 134
'Ampelon' Sunraysia garden, Gol Gol, NSW 12–21
apple *(Malus domestica)* 19, 104, 107, 140
aquaponics 55, 176
Archer, Joseph 180, 188
Armando and Maria Matteucci's garden, Paradise, Adelaide, SA 190–9
arrowroot *(Canna edulis)* 63
artichokes 192, 194
arugula ('wild rocket') *(Eruca sativa)* 19, 30
asparagus *(Asparagus officinalis)* 95, 140, 204, 207
avocado 19

babaco ('champagne fruit') *(Vasconcellea x heilbornii)* 207–8
bananas *(Musa* spp.) 60, 153
Bangay, Paul 138
Banks, Sir Joseph 73
Barbados cherry *(Malpighia glabra)* 175
beans
    broad beans *(Vicia faba)* 24, 116, 194
    heirloom bush bean 53
'Bellis' sustainable garden, Brisbane, Qld 56–65
Bernstein, Gerard 78–89
Berry, Wendell 116, 188
billy goat plum *(Terminalia ferdinandiana)* 155
Bilson, Gay 114–23
biocides 5–6
birds 84, 87, 109, 119
blackwater 10, 64
Blazey, Clive 140

The Botany of Desire 104
bottling 112
bower spinach *(Tetragonia implexicoma)* 144
Brazilian cherry *(Eugenia uniflora)* 129
Brock, Chris and Helen 90–101
Brocks' locavore garden, Alice Springs, NT 90–101
Brussels sprouts *(Brassica oleracea)* 17
Burbank, Luther 122
Burke, Janine 41
bush tomato *(Solanum centrale)* 100
bushfood 65, 100–1
Byrne, Josh 158–67

cabbage *(Brassica oleracea)* 17, 63, 95, 112
cabbage white butterfly 183
Campbell, Susan 77
cane toads *(Bufo marinus)* 156
capers *(Capparis spinosa)* 119, 144
carbon footprint 5, 167
carrots *(Daucus carota)* 24, 109
cat's ear *(Hypochoeris radicata)* 30
celery stem taro *(Colocasia esculenta)* 64, 65
Chaffey brothers 14
chervil *(Anthriscus cerefolium)* 41
chicory *(Cichorium intybus)* 30, 73, 198
children
    'free range' omnivores 97
    fresh produce and health 10
    school kitchen gardens 10, 97
Chilean hazelnut *(Gevuina avellana)* 53
Chinese date *(Zizyphus jujuba)* 129
Chinese gooseberries (kiwifruit) 27
Chinese quince *(Pseudocydonia sinensis)* 122
climate change 2, 20, 74, 170, 176
cocoyam *(Xanthosoma sagittifolium)* 64–5
Coleby Williams, Jeremy 56–65
coltsfoot *(Tussilago farfara)* 37

community gardens 134
companion planting 24, 175
The Complete Book of Edible Landscaping 48
compost 7, 126, 156, 167, 194
    kitchen scraps 29
    mushroom 17
'Conmel Cottage', Tamar Valley, Tas. 102–113
Creasy, Rosalind 48
Cretan dittany *(Origanum dictamnus)* 50
crop factor 8
crop rotation 19, 24, 53
'Cruden Farm', Langwarrin, Vic. 80
Cundall, Peter 7, 112
curry leaf *(Murraya koenigii)* 65, 116
curry plant *(Helichrysum italicum)* 140

Darwin, NT 148, 153
'Darwin lime' 153
Dawe, Chris 14, 17
desert soils 95
Digger's Club, Dromana, Vic. 17, 73, 84, 126, 140, 173
dragon fruit (pitaya) *(Hylocereus* spp.) 175
drip irrigation 10, 20, 95, 100, 129, 164
Dry season 63, 153, 155, 170
Dymiotis, Markos 22–31

eco-intervention 133
ecological footprint 5, 29, 92
Eden Seeds 73, 194
edible borrowed landscape 163
Edible Estates: Attack on the Front Lawn 133
edible landscaping 48, 55
edible water plants 155, 163
edible weeds 27, 30, 64
eelworms 100
eggplant (Solanum spp.) 20, 27, 112
elecampane *(Inula helenium)* 37, 112

endive *(Cichorium endiva)* 63, 198
erosion control 87, 153
espaliered trees 19, 48, 50, 104, 140
Evans, Andrea and Ron 136–45

famine foods 64
'farmscaping' 87
feijoa *(Acca sellowiana)* 48, 50, 53, 198
fennel *(Foeniculum vulgare var. azoricum)* 198
fertilisers
    green manure 7, 58, 60, 100, 183
    organic 6–7
    synthetic 6
    'worm juice' 7
fig *(Ficus smyrna)* 19, 27, 143, 163, 196
Flood, Geraldine and Bret 102–113
foraging 123
Frank and Jenny's garden, Rockhampton, Qld 168–77
Fremantle, WA 167
French sorrel *(Rumex scutantus)* 116
frog pond 129, 133
frosts 17, 185
fruit cage 180, 208
fruit dehydrator 55
fruit fly 175
The Fruit Hunters 120, 175
fruit salad plant *(Monstera deliciosa)* 54, 208
fruit trees 10
    and birds 84, 87
    deciduous 163
    espaliered 104
    grafted stock 24
    netting 19

Gamble, Sally 78–89
'garden tenure' 129, 133, 134
Gardening Australia (TV) 58, 112, 148, 156, 160

garlic (*Allium sativum*) 27, 126
Gaynor, Andrea 167, 194
genetic diversity of crops 7
genetic engineering 7
giant agave (*Agave americana*) 87
giardino segreto 138
Giles and Kate Pickard's suburban
    garden, Perth, WA 124–35
gleaning 123
global warming 64, 74
globe artichoke (*Cynara scolymus*) 19
goji berry (wolfberry) (*Lycium
    barbarum*) 129
Gollner, Adam Leith 120, 175
grape (*Vitis* spp.)
    juice 29
    syrup 29
    table 19, 163
    vine leaves 24
    for wine 19, 29, 196, 198
grasshoppers 100
Gray, David 68, 73
The Green Gardener 160
green manure 7, 58, 60, 100, 183
greywater 10, 53, 64, 164, 202
Grounds, Marr 200–209
growing from seed 7–8, 107
guava
    Chilean guava (*Ugni molinae*) 53
    pineapple guava (*Acca sellowiana*)
        48, 50, 53
    strawberry guava (*Psidium littorale
        var. longipes*) 53–4
    tropical guava (*Psidium guajava*) 53
'guerilla gardens' 134

habitat restoration 87
Haeg, Fritz 133
Harvest of the Suburbs 167
Heide kitchen gardens,
    Bulleen, Vic. 32–45
heirloom movement
    seeds and plants 7–8, 42, 48, 53, 63,
        95, 107, 126, 133, 140, 173, 185, 188

in US 48
hemlock (*Conium maculatum*) 37
herbs 19, 126
    in Mediterranean diet 27
    in pots 163
    see also specific herbs
heritage plants see heirloom movement
'Heronswood', Dromana, Vic. 140
Historic Houses Trust of NSW 68, 77
A History of Kitchen Gardening 77
Houbein, Lolo 199
huauzontle (*Chenopodium berlandieri*
    syn. *C. nuttalliae*) 64
Huon Valley Apple & Heritage
    Museum, Tas. 107
hybrids 8
hydroponics 176
hydro-zoning 164

ice-cream bean tree (*Inga edulis*) 129
Indian fig (*Opuntia ficus-indica*) 73
irrigation (drip) 10, 20, 95, 100, 129, 164

jaboticaba (*Myrciaria cauliflora*) 175
jam melon (citron) (*Citrullus lanatus
    var. citroides*) 74
Jefferson, Thomas 144
Jeffs, Naomi 73, 74, 77
Josh Byrne's sustainable backyard,
    Fremantle, WA 158–67
jostaberries 185

kale (*Brassica oleracea*)
    black kale 140, 183
    curly kale 109
kang kong (*Ipomoea aquatica*) 155, 163
Karen Sutherland's urban Eden,
    Pascoe Vale, Vic. 46–55
kitchen garden
    benefits of 5–11
    cycles 185
    defining 1–2
    French 34
    sustainability 2

konkleberry (*Carissa lanceolata*) 100

'La Huerta', McLaren Flat, Adelaide
    Hills, SA 114–23
land cress (*Barbarea vulgaris*) 116
landlords and garden-making 126,
    129, 160
Langley, Jean 34, 37
Launceston, Tas. 107, 109
lawns 63, 133
leaf amaranth 30
Lebanese cress (*Aethionema
    cordifolium*) 163, 173
lemon (*Citrus limon*) 17, 19, 48, 140
Leonie Norrington's tropical food
    garden, Darwin, NT 146–57
lettuce 17, 63
locavores 60, 90–101
loquats (*Eriobotrya japonica*) 194, 196
'low input' edible plants 53
lucerne 173, 183, 196
Lúcuma tree (*Pouteria lucuma*) 53
lupins 194

mangel-wurzel (*Beta vulgaris*) 60
'Marangy' walled kitchen garden,
    Benalla, Vic. 78–89
Markos' Mediterranean-style
    backyard, Hampton, Vic. 22–31
Matteucci, Armando and Maria 190–9
medlar (*Mespilus germanica*) 120
mescal 87
microclimates 50, 63, 80, 112, 208
midyim berries (*Austromyrtus dulcis*)
    50, 65
Mills, Maree and George 178–89
Mills, Margot and Dennis 12–21
Mimosa Rocks National Park, NSW 202
Mornington Peninsula, Vic. 138, 143, 144
mulberries (*Morus* spp.) 92, 163
mulch 63, 95, 155–6, 167, 173
    sandwich mulching 6
    sheet-mulching 20
mulga (*Acacia aneura*) 100

muntries (*Kunzea pomifera*) 50
Murdoch, Dame Elisabeth 80
Murray–Darling basin 14, 19–20
myrtle
    aniseed myrtle (*Backhousia anisata*) 50
    cinnamon myrtle
        (*Backhousia myrtifolia*) 50
    lemon-scented myrtle
        (*Backhousia citriodora*) 50

naranjilla (*Solanum quitoense*) 54
'Narra Bukulla', Sapphire Coast, NSW
    200–209
Natal plum (*Carissa macrocarpa*) 64,
    143–4
native finger lime (*Citrus australasica*)
    50
native lemongrass (*Cymbopogon
    ambiguus*) 100
native waterlily (*Nymphaea violacea*) 155
nature strips 133, 134
nematodes 100
nitrogen fertilisers 6
no-dig beds 6, 176
Norrington, Leonie 146–57
Northern Territory 92, 148, 155, 156
Noyes, Dugald 42, 45

olives (*Olea europaea*)
    grafted stock 24
    harvesting 88, 198
    preserving 29–30, 199
    stuffing 199
    trees as windbreak 143
oranges (*Citrus sinensis*) 19, 48
over-watering 100

Palestinian radish 64
Palladio, Andrea 138, 144
'Panshanger', Longford, Tas. 178–89
peaches 74, 175
Peak Oil 5, 58
pears (*Pyrus* spp.) 19, 138, 140
peas (*Pisum sativum*) 60, 63, 126

pepino *(Solanum muricatum)* 54
pepper *(Piper nigrum)* 153
Permablitz 1
permaculture 126, 204
persimmon *(Diospyros kaki)* 120, 198
Perth, WA 129, 163–4
Peruvian ground apple (yacón) 54
pest control 5–6, 29, 100, 109, 183
    frog pond 129, 133
    see also specific pests
phosphate fertilisers 6
Pickard, Giles and Kate 124–35
pigface *(Carpobrotus rossi)* 144
pineapples *(Ananas comosus)* 60, 74
pine oil 6
poison hemlock *(Conium maculatum)* 37
Pollan, Michael 11, 58, 73, 104, 120
poly-tunnels 107, 176, 194
pome fruits 120
pomegranate *(Punica granatum)* 84, 122–3
Poole, Jeff 56–65
possums 183
potato *(Solanum tuberosum)* 17, 24, 42, 188
potted plants 50, 119, 129, 134, 163, 164
preserving 112, 199
pumpkin *(Curcurbita* spp.) 17, 42, 183
    'Turk's Turban' 73
purslane (Portulaca oleracea) 27, 30

quandong *(Santalum acuminatum)* 100–1
Queensland fruit fly 175
quince *(Cydonia oblonga)* 120, 122, 123

rabbits
    breeding 95, 97, 196, 199
    as pests 119
raised beds 80, 84, 97, 140, 160, 176
'real food' 11
recycled materials 126, 163
    tyres 176
Reed, Sunday and John 32–45

Reid, Barrett 41, 42
rental property gardens 126, 129, 160
rock minerals 167
Rockhampton, Qld 170
Rockhampton Botanic Gardens 170
rosemary 'Blue Lagoon' 48
Rosevears, Tas. 104, 109
rough (bush) lemon *(Citrus jambhiri)* 73
ruby saltbush *(Enchylaea tomentosa)* 100

saffron crocus *(Crocus sativus)* 50
sage *(Salvia)*
    S. 'Black Knight' 175
    S. *fruticosa* 27
    S. *guaranitica* 42
    S. *iodantha* 175
    S. *madrensis* 175
    S. *splendens* (scarlet sage) 175
    S. 'Wendy's Wish' 175
samphire
    marsh *(Salicornia* sp.) 144
    rock *(Crithmum maritimum)* 144
sandy soils 119, 163, 167, 183
Santich, Barbara 17
school gardens 10, 97
sea kale *(Crambe maritima)* 144
seaberry saltbush *(Rhagodia candolleana)* 144
seed, growing from 7–8, 126
Seed Savers Exchange 173
Seed Savers' Network 63
Smith, Guy 41
society garlic *(Tulbaghia violacea)* 50
soil
    acidification 6
    contaminated 24, 60, 134
    pH 100
    porosity 156
    rehabilitation 58, 60, 63
    testing 134
strawberries *(Fragaria* sp.) 109, 126, 129, 163, 180, 208
subtropical fruits 129

sugarcane straw 20, 63
Sunraysia region 14, 19
Sutherland, Karen 46–55
sweet leaf *(Sauropus androgynus)* 155
sweet peppers 109
sweet potato *(Ipomoea batatas)* 58
swine-cress *(Lepidium didymum)* 64
synthetic fertilisers 6

Tahitian lime 112
termites 156
tomato *(Solanum lycopersicum)* 17, 30, 63, 112, 185, 188, 194, 196
'tomato cupboard' 185
Tropical Food Gardens 148

usufruct 123

vanilla grass *(Hierochloe odorata)* 50
vanilla vine 153
'Vaucluse House' colonial kitchen garden, Sydney, NSW 66–77
vegetables
    crop factor 8
    health benefits 10, 11
    per capita consumption 10
vegetable cage 148, 183
vermiculture 7, 167
'Villa Lettisier' walled kitchen garden, Flinders, Vic. 136–45

walled gardens 80
Walling, Edna 80
Warrigal greens *(Tetragonia tetragonioides)* 48, 50, 64, 73
wartime gardens 37
water 2
    blackwater 10, 64
    bore 100, 153
    'embodied' 8
    estimating needs 8
    greywater 10, 53, 64, 164, 202
    Murray–Darling controversy 14, 19–20

    stormwater 63
water chestnut *(Eleocharis dulcis)* 155, 163
'water footprint' 8, 164
water restrictions 8, 27, 45, 164
water tanks 8, 29, 45, 153, 164
water-for-food ratio ('water intensity') 8
waterlilies 155
watermelon 'Moon and Stars' *(Citrullus* spp.) 173
weeds
    control 6
    edible 27, 30, 64
Wentworth, Sarah 68, 70, 74
Wentworth, William Charles 68, 70, 74
Wet season 63–4, 153, 155, 170
'wicking beds' 10, 176
wild foods 53
Wilson, Edward O. 2
Wise, Sally 112
witchetty bush *(Acacia kempeana)* 100
worm farm 7, 167
'worm juice' 7

yam *(Dioscorea transversa)* 155
A Year in a Bottle 112

zucchini *(Curcurbita pepo* var. *melopepo)* 109, 173

LANTERN

Published by the Penguin Group
Penguin Group (Australia)
707 Collins Street, Melbourne, Victoria 3008, Australia
(a division of Pearson Australia Group Pty Ltd)
Penguin Group (USA) Inc.
375 Hudson Street, New York, New York 10014, USA
Penguin Group (Canada)
90 Eglinton Avenue East, Suite 700, Toronto, Canada ON M4P 2Y3
(a division of Pearson Penguin Canada Inc.)
Penguin Books Ltd
80 Strand, London WC2R 0RL England
Penguin Ireland
25 St Stephen's Green, Dublin 2, Ireland
(a division of Penguin Books Ltd)
Penguin Books India Pvt Ltd
11 Community Centre, Panchsheel Park, New Delhi – 110 017, India
Penguin Group (NZ)
67 Apollo Drive, Rosedale, North Shore 0632, New Zealand
(a division of Pearson New Zealand Ltd)
Penguin Books (South Africa) (Pty) Ltd
24 Sturdee Avenue, Rosebank, Johannesburg 2196, South Africa

Penguin Books Ltd, Registered Offices: 80 Strand, London, WC2R 0RL, England

First published by Penguin Group (Australia), 2011
This paperback edition was published by Penguin Group (Australia), 2012

3 5 7 9 10 8 6 4 2

Copyright © Kate Herd and Simon Griffiths 2011

The moral right of the author has been asserted

All rights reserved. Without limiting the rights under copyright reserved above, no part of this publication may be reproduced, stored in or introduced into a retrieval system, or transmitted, in any form or by any means (electronic, mechanical, photocopying, recording or otherwise), without the prior written permission of both the copyright owner and the above publisher of this book.

Design by Danie Pout Design © Penguin Group (Australia)
Cover design © Penguin Group (Australia)
Design coordination by Laura Thomas
Cover photograph by Simon Griffiths
All internal photographs are by Simon Griffiths, except those listed on page 219
Pages iv–v: The intensively worked kitchen garden at 'Panshanger', Tasmania
Author photograph by Ponch Hawkes
Typeset in FF Scala by Post Pre-press Group, Brisbane, Queensland
Colour reproduction by Splitting Image Colour Studio Pty Ltd, Clayton, Victoria
Printed and bound in China by Imago Productions

National Library of Australia
Cataloguing-in-Publication data:

Herd, Kate.
Kitchen Gardens of Australia / Kate Herd; Simon Griffiths
9781921383427 (pbk.)

635.0994

penguin.com.au

Patient Number
360993

Kay Morrison

ORIGINAL WRITING

© 2010 Kay Morrison

All rights reserved. No part of this publication may be reproduced in any form or by any means—graphic, electronic or mechanical, including photocopying, recording, taping or information storage and retrieval systems—without the prior written permission of the author.

978-1-908024-07-7

A CIP catalogue for this book is available from the National Library.

Published by ORIGINAL WRITING LTD., Dublin, 2010.

Printed by CAHILL PRINTERS LIMITED, Dublin.

I would like to thank Darren for letting me write this story about him, I hope I have done him justice, and told the story as he would himself, in a truthful and honest manner.

Introduction

Hi, my name is Kay, and I have been trying very hard to get this short book written for many years. It happens to be a true account of my son Darren's extraordinary experience in a major Dublin hospital, and how we fought for his life. This was after a dreadful mistake was made, and not followed up on, to the extent of him nearly loosing his life. He never dreamt in a million years that he would have to go through anything like this torture, and neither did we. This is not another story about a person getting cancer and recovering, its much more; its an endurance test. It was very difficult writing this account and recalling all the dreadful details, so I stopped writing it many times. I finally finished it, as I felt it had to be told. A few of my family were too young to know what went on, so this will help them also.

It's sad in places, and I have tried to remember the happy times as well, and some of the mad times, so I hope you enjoy reading this amazing story of what happened, and how we all came through it.

How does some family's get through life without ever encountering major sickness? Although we have six children, the most we ever had to rush to a hospital with was when they broke their arms. I remember lifting one of my daugh-

PATIENT NUMBER 360993

ters down from a tall wall out our back garden, warning her that she was in danger of falling. She went out to the front garden to play, fell off the low wall, and broke her arm. On another occasion when we were having a street party ,our second son fell out of a tree, and broke his arm badly. He had to be rushed to hospital, and got great care to repair his arm. These were very stressful times, but in each case we had total confidence in the treatment that they received in our local hospital. I would not like to put any doubt into anyone's mind about care that they are about to receive in any hospital, as the majority of care and nursing is excellent. I myself have had some very good treatment in this hospital, so it leaves me feeling a little bit of a traitor having to write this story, but someone has to do it! Doctors and nurses work extremely hard to ensure that patients receive the best of care. It was just our bad luck that we encountered trouble, and nothing prepared us for the drama that lay ahead for all of us.

I have changed the Doctors names to protect the Guilty!

Kay

Chapter One

Let me first tell you a little bit about our children. I had a miscarriage at sixteen weeks on our first child, which was devastating because we were both so looking forward to becoming parents for the first time. I had continued to work in a laundry which was in a home for the elderly, and I should not have been pulling large bags of laundry around. I had discovered I was pregnant, but denied it to the nun when she had suspected this, and asked me. I was so young that I did not understand. I was afraid I would lose my job. So Darren is our first-born child. He is the eldest of six. We were married two years before he arrived, and we could not wait to be parents. He was born on the 17th March 1972, a bouncing nine pounds ten ounces baby, and a beautiful present for us for St. Patrick's Day. We were living in a house in Sandycove at the time, which is a beautiful scenic area. It over-looks the harbour, and is very close to Dun Laoghaire, south county Dublin, Ireland. We were living right beside a beautiful park, with flowering plants all year long, and I brought Darren there nearly every day. The swings and the slide in the play-park were there freely to use, and every now and then you could hear the trains passing. Imagine living right beside this large park, so this was our own garden, it was brilliant.

I would push Darren there, and then lift him out as he really loved to toddle around freely. He was a very good child, (well, most of the time) as were all of his siblings. Our next son Johnny was born the next year, so they were great company for one another. Then a couple of years later, our first daughter Catherine was born. They certainly kept us busy running around after them, so it was great to live near Dun-Laoghaire, and to get the fresh sea air as well. We had the famous Teddy's ice-cream shop just around the corner from us, and if we had the money, we would treat the children and ourselves to an ice-cream cone while walking in the park. As the family grew, I applied for a larger house, preferably with a bathroom, (I never had a bathroom before) and when I was nearly due our fourth child Anthony, we were so excited to move into a newly built house a few miles away in Achill Road, Loughlinstown, County Dublin. It was a lovely house, huge compared to the small one in Dun Laoghaire. It was like a mansion to me, as I was so used to having a scullery for a kitchen, and two small rooms. I had my first bathroom; we only ever had a basin to wash in before this. I loved buying all the new bits of furniture for the new house, three bedrooms at last!

I had my second daughter Fiona a few years later in Loughlinstown Hospital, and our last child Richard, was born seven years later. A large family, by anyone's standards!

So Darren is the eldest of our large brood, four boys and two girls.

It was here in Loughlinstown that our family were reared, without any outstanding problems. We had good neighbours and all the children in the area were brought up together. So when communions and conformations, and later Debs, and 21st birthdays came about, there were many children celebrating together. Rearing children back then in the 70's and the 80's was so much different than it is today. The most trouble they got into was hitting a football into some neighbour's window, or throwing stones. (Well maybe the odd orchard was robbed) They were always chastised, and we got on with it. They also had great Grandmothers, and Granddads to keep a close eye on them and guide them. After completing primary school in the local area, all of our children went to Cabinteely Community School, a brilliant school, I would recommend it to anyone, and they all did well through it.

Darren went to work part time whilst still at school. He walked up to the office in Dun-Laoghaire Shopping Centre and asked the manager was there any jobs going for him. There wasn't, but because the manager was so impressed by Darren's cheekiness, he developed a job for him. It was when he completed his leaving cert ,that he went on to work as a maintenance man for Dun Laoghaire Shopping Centre full time.

I don't remember him being sick, just the usual childhood illnesses and colds and flu.

The years passed...........

"Hi honey I'm home", was Darren's cheerful call every night as he returned home from work. He was hardly ever in bad form, and kept everyone smiling with his witty humour. This was the norm in our house, and we were well accustomed to it. Ever since he was young, he has had many friends, and kept himself busy with his leisure activities. He loves music, and he and his friends were involved with the local ventures. As a matter of fact he was also a strong trusted venture Scout leader. This brought him away on many weekends with a loaded down back-pack to exciting destinations in all weathers. When he would return home, he would fill us in on all that had gone on with him and his friends (well nearly all). They would gather in our house and the laughter and music would cheer us all up. I would often dance around the room with them, much to the embarrassment of the family, but I would enjoy the music. Johnny is only a year younger, and was a keen football player, but when they got together with Catherine, Anthony, Fiona, and Richard, you couldn't hear yourself think with all the noise and music! It was great for Richard being the youngest, to be reared with all his brothers and sisters, and their friends and all the activities that went with it. We seemed to have a lovely normal family life, all ticking along nicely, the usual fights and arguments, and laughter as well. But it was all about to change.

Chapter Two

Something strange happened to Darren whilst he was out walking the pier with Lisa his lovely girlfriend at the time. He suddenly got a dreadful pain in his tummy, and fell to the ground. Lisa thought he was just messing around, and as soon as he got up the pain had disappeared. There was no explanation for this, and he didn't report this to our doctor. This was the first sign that something was wrong. I remember his friend Declan telling me that Darren had a dizzy spell while they were out walking the hills with the scouts, and he fell down one of the hills. When I heard about this I advised him to go to our doctor. But when he did, it was put down to him growing so tall, six foot three inches tall to be exact, and he was advised to take things easier when he stood up. This we believed, nothing else crossed our minds! He never complained about anything, and just got on with his life of working, and having a laugh with his friends. Everything was good…too good!

In April of 1991, Darren came home from work complaining of severe back pain. It wasn't like him to complain, and I thought he might have strained himself in his work as a maintenance manager in Dun Laoghaire Shopping Centre. He had no energy, and always collapsed into a comfortable chair when he got home. We all thought that this was normal after a hard day's work in the centre, as there was always so much to do down there. But his symptoms got worse over the following few days, and he returned home from work some days a little weak and looking pale. The pain was now also starting in his tummy, and we advised him to call into St. Michael's Hospital in Dun- Laoghaire, to ask their advice (You could do that then without first going to your doctor for a letter). We were getting concerned now, and I was looking up his symptoms in medical books. His temperature was fluctuating up to 104 degrees, indicating an illness somewhere.

So after work the next night he made a visit to the hospital on his own. The doctor on duty examined him, and advised him to rest at home for three days. He said he thought it could be a kidney infection, and gave him a note excusing him from his work. All my feelings contradicted this, and I instantly knew it could be much worse. Darren was never sick, so this was so strange. He did rest as much as possible, but when he wasn't any better after a few days, it was back to the hospital, and he was put on a course of antibiotics.

But he still got worse. He always complained of feeling weak, no energy, and he was in constant pain. It was obvious to anyone that the antibiotics were not working.

We got up one morning to find him collapsed on the bathroom floor, so it was all systems go. We rushed him down to the local hospital in his Dad's car. The same doctor just happened to be passing by, and took one look at Darren. It was strange the way that happened and he told his Dad to bring him straight downstairs to the A & E department immediately. It was obvious that more tests would have to be done, and quick!

Even in so much pain, one of the doctors had Darren jumping up and down, to try to establish what the problem was. When he could not do this, they realized how sick he was and gave him a bed to lie down on. The doctor wanted to send him home, as he could not see anything too serious, but we insisted that there was something wrong, and told the doctor about how he was so sick at home, and how he was showing no signs of getting better. I felt I had to convince them, and they were the doctors. (Looking back now, this was the start of our convincing the doctors for years to come). After a few hours of tests and x- rays, the doctor admitted him, and revised his symptoms. It was then that they found blood in his urine and they decided to follow up on this and do an ultra-sound scan. This unfortunately showed up an abnormality, and the doctor rang me to say they were doing an emergency operation. We returned to the hospital just in time to wish Darren good luck as he was been wheeled into the hospital lift to bring him up to the operating theatre. We were glad then that they were taking his pain seriously! At first they thought it was a burst appendix to have him in this condition, but after further investigation they soon discovered that the problem was much worse. The diagnosis was a large tumour, and it was attached to other organs. This unfortunately was found in Darren's pelvis. It was a terrible shock to the whole family. Our nightmare had come true and we were all now caught up in a life changing situation.

We were at home now waiting on news when eight hours later, a doctor rang us to say that the operation was

PATIENT NUMBER 360993

over, unfortunately they could not remove the tumour, but Darren was in recovery and was very sick. We were glad the operation was over, but felt confused and frightened. We cried our eyes out, I didn't want my son having a tumour and we certainly did not want to hear this news. The doctor said he would speak to us the next day to try and explain the situation to us.

Here was a young nineteen year old man, who was in the prime of his life, in a serious way.

His Dad and I met the doctor the next day in the corridor of the hospital, and that's where he told us that the tumour was malignant; an unusual tumour for a young man to get in his pelvis. It was called a Euwings sarcoma. I had never heard of this tumour, but I soon discovered that it was a cancer that usually grows in bones, or soft tissue, but can occur in any part of the body. It is very serious. It usually presents itself in early childhood, and mostly in boys. So now Darren would need months of treatment, and specialist care. At least he was in a very good hospital, and it wasn't too far away from us, so we could easily visit him.

The doctor who operated on Darren was a top consultant, and we put our faith in him. Because the tumour was so large, it was interfering with his normal functions, and a tube had to be inserted to relieve the urine. Darren was kept as comfortable as possible and he was given morphine to relieve the pain. This was the start of a long stay in hospital.

I remember listening to him talking to friends who had called in to see him. They asked him how he was, and he said he was fine, "At least it is not cancer" We realised he was in denial, one of the stages he was to go through. He would get cross with me also and tell me to leave. The Sister -in-charge would comfort me in the corridor. She explained to me that this was a well expected way for people to react, when faced with such a shock to their system. It was a gruelling time and then he had to face chemotherapy and radiotherapy to attempt to shrink the tumour. Darren was extremely sick at this time and was so brave. But there was no other way around this nightmare; I wished it upon myself instead. All his family could visit him and his workmates from the shopping centre also called to visit him, with some of the women leaving upset. His nanny was distraught, because in her day if you mentioned the word cancer you were finished. I tried to explain to her that in these times that is not the case, as there has been so many new treatments developed over the years, that everybody that develops cancer has a good chance of beating it, especially if it is caught in time. She calmed down a little then, but she continued to pray for him for years. If we visited her she would have a candle lighting on her mantelpiece on front of holy pictures. "That's for Darren" she would say.

After a few months, He was then transferred into a top major Dublin hospital, where his condition was monitored, and his treatment was continued. Darren was given his own little room, with his own bathroom attached, but he was so sick on the chemotherapy; he spent a lot of the time in there. The treatment was so fierce, that he soon lost all of his hair. Most days he could not even talk to us, but he was just grateful we were there. We never missed a day's visit, as his condition could change from day to day.

As this was all new to us, I remember joining the library in Dun-Laoghaire, and leaving with arms full of medical books. I'm sure people thought I was some sort of nurse or doctor, but it was the only way to try to get some information on cancer related issues. This helped me a lot to understand all the jargon you hear in hospitals and it helped me in the years to follow also. To this day I love to read medical books, but of course now you can Google any queries you may have, it's so simple. If you haven't got a computer you can slip in to any book shop and have a sneaky look at the medical books on the shelf.

Chapter Three

Four months passed very slowly, and September approached. Darren had remained in the hospital for all this time, and after all his suffering, it was now time to have the tumour removed at last. With all the intensive treatment, it had eventually shrunk down to a size that could be operated on at last. Masses were said and everyone was involved with praying and wishing Darren a speedy recovery. Family, friends, the local priest and the whole parish were involved. We even had the nearby convent of nuns offering up their prayers for him. Mr. Mathews performed the major operation to remove the tumour, and after many hours we heard that it all went very well. Darren got tender loving care from the staff of the hospital at this time. He recovered very slowly, and after a few months it was decided to treat Darren with another course of chemotherapy just to be on the safe side, so he again lost the little bit of hair he had managed to grow.

He got home after a few weeks, but it was heartbreaking to see him so sick for so long. His life consisted of sleeping and watching telly, and eating little.

After a while, an ambulance bus collected him and brought him in to the brilliant St. Luke's hospital in Rathgar Dublin. This was a top cancer treating hospital and at least ten miles away. (I knew this hospital, as my Mother had treatment there many years before). I was not allowed to go with Darren as the bus was full with other patients. He had his radium treatment there. This was very hard on him, sometimes burning his back, but it had to be done to ensure the tumour didn't return. He never complained! With the special nursing he received, he got stronger every week. It was a slow process, but he managed to begin to move slowly but surely around the house. His brothers, sisters, friends and girlfriend Lisa were great in helping him in his recovery and we sort of got some normality back in all our lives. We hoped to put it all behind us and look forward to the future.

January arrived, and we all celebrated to see Darren fit enough to return to work, a day he thought he'd never see. His job had always been held open for him, and he enjoyed working there also. He had many friends waiting for his return to the Shopping Centre in Dun Laoghaire, and his managers Michael and Peter, (R. I. P.) were so nice. They had always kept in touch with us, enquiring about his health. I sometimes called in to the office to keep them informed. Darren took life a little easier now and slowly got his energy back. Before long, he was getting on with his life as we knew he would, a little slower perhaps, but he did it and made us all proud.

Chapter Four

One year later, just as we were all putting the experience of the previous year behind us all, a doctor at the Dublin hospital sent Darren a letter stating that it was again time for tests to be carried out and a review laparoscopy was necessary. The reason for this was to see if the dreaded tumour was returning or not. This was the first time he was told of this new keyhole approach to surgery. It was the last thing he needed… It was supposed to be the greatest single advance in surgical practice in fifty years. The laparoscopy is carried out with the help of a computer chip, a television and a camera. This allows the surgeon to see inside the body's cavity, by means of a small surgical telescope or laparoscope It is a two dimensional image. The surgeon can move the scope around a large area of the body and the camera will transfer images that are relayed on a screen. The surgical procedure is then performed using specially designed instruments, which are introduced into the body through small openings. An incision is made near your belly button, and carbon dioxide is pumped through the tube to inflate your abdomen so the surgeon can see your organs more clearly. It's usually done under general anaesthetic.

The surgical wounds are therefore small, and there should be minimal blood loss, and recovery is supposed to be rapid.

The expected length of stay for this procedure is about one or two days stay in hospital.

It's terrible now looking back and remembering how we totally believed this information we were given. It was so new to us all. Maybe they believed what they told us, who knows. They should have added that if nobody pierces any of your inners, there is a good chance that you will get home after two days... (Give me open surgery anytime!)

We do know that this type of operation was first performed in 1988, to remove a gallbladder, and it was successful. But that might be, they still forgot to mention that there was the possibility of major risks.

Because Darren had had two major abdominal operations before, he might have dense adhesions in his stomach cavity, and would not be suitable for a laparoscopy. In them years, doctors were trained on simulators and on dead meat, which does not bleed. It is somewhat different on humans.

Chapter Five

When the 23rd of June 1992 arrived, Darren was nervous and would have preferred to go to work rather than face the uncertainty of not knowing what was about to happen. Little did he know that his endurance test was about to begin.

The details of what happened will be etched in my memory forever.

John, his Dad, drove Darren reluctantly into the hospital at 8.30am, and he was admitted to St. Marks Day ward to be prepared for the laparoscopy. He did not want to go. It was as if he had been forewarned about what was about to happen. He actually said to me that he was thinking of cancelling the operation and going to work instead! But he went in anyway. I waved him off.

We watched the clock, as we were told that he would probably be ready to be collected at around 5pm. That would allow for the procedure and the recovery and his Dad was on standby to collect him.

We spent the next few hours phoning the hospital and leeching on to any information we could extract from the nurses. With each hour that ticked by we innocently thought it was all behind him. Alarm bells rang when, in anticipation, we rang the hospital and when we inquired if Darren was ready to come home we were told to ring back at 6pm as Darren was not recovering as he should.

He was complaining of pain, and vomiting. It was then that we were informed that he had to be transferred to the main hospital ward, namely St. Teresa's.

On hearing this, his Dad and I drove in immediately. We were concerned now, and didn't know what to expect. We thought that maybe because of his medical history, Darren was taking longer to recover from the anaesthetic than other patients. Besides, doctors know best, don't they? We put all our trust in the doctors, we had no choice.

When we entered the ward and first set eyes on Darren, it was obvious to anyone that he was in a lot of pain and quite sick. He was a terrible colour, sort of jaundiced and he could not move. Our hearts sank. He was very distressed and complaining of an excruciating pain that was radiating up to his left shoulder. This was obviously aggravated by breathing. Although he was given the painkiller Voltarol, and the nurses gave him a hot pack to his shoulder, he remained in pain constantly. His stomach was enlarged also and we noted this. It was a shock to us, as the last thing we were expecting was to see Darren in so much agony. We thought this was all behind him.

We both inquired at the nurse's station about how the operation went, and we tried to get some explanation for the pain that Darren was obviously in. But we were told that when a person has a laparoscopy, the abdomen is inflated with carbon dioxide, to allow the surgeon more access to the organs, which we already knew, but they said maybe this was the cause of all the discomfort that Darren was experiencing .We now know that most of it should be removed from the patient before the operation is completed. We believed this information when we were told it at the time and we hoped that by the next day the situation would have improved greatly and that we would have Darren home with us. Why the doctors didn't have a high degree of suspicion I will never know!

But no, his condition deteriorated in the next four days and panic began to set in to both him and ourselves and we were getting no answers at all. He still looked terrible. We would sit and try to talk to him and listen when he tried to tell us how much pain he was in. You just had to look at his face to see the agony he was in.

By the second day we had suspected that something dreadful had happened on the 23rd of June at that laparoscopy operation. But nobody could tell us what had happened and trying to convince the doctors of our suspicions was totally useless. There was no explanation for what went wrong and no one was listening to us. The standard of note keeping leaves a lot to be desired, especially during the crucial first week of his admission.

For example there are no entries at all for the first and second postoperative days and on the third and forth days there are none by the doctor's team, only by the intern on call. I wonder why? Have they gone missing? Yes they have.

Darren was only seen twice by a senior doctor during the four postoperative days, once by Mr. Savelle and once by Mr. Mathews (we only found this out a few years later when we read notes on the nurse's charts). We were nearly tempted to take his charts home to look at them in detail, but we could not. John would say to me "Is there anyone looking, I think I will take the charts". But we never had the nerve. We often said later that it was a pity we didn't!

You certainly didn't need any medical experience to see that Darren needed prompt treatment now, but he was not getting it, as much as we tried. We went in some days to see Darren been escorted up and down the corridor, mostly held up by the nurses. Mr. Mathews had ordered the nurses to do so and I believe that he well knew that Darren was not up to it. It was like dragging a sack of potatoes up and down the corridor. He was always much worse when he returned to his bed and always told us he was in dreadful pain. He just wanted to rest in his bed and not to be dragged up and down a long corridor!

We cried a lot, and asked a lot of questions, sometimes going nearly hysterical but getting nowhere. I had never heard of this happening to other parents before this, or since. Although people are speaking out now more freely about mistakes made in hospitals, a lot is still hidden. What attracted such bad luck to us, I will never get an answer to. The nurses didn't know what to say to us and I believe they tried their best to get some answers for us, but to no avail. Our world was falling apart again and we were desperate for answers. We wished we could take Darren home with us, where we believed he would have been safer and besides, I had a young family at home also. I wanted to talk with Mr. Mathews, but where was Mr. Mathews?

Even the nurses could not contact him sometimes. I remember standing out in the corridor of the hospital, listening to the nurses on the phone, and waiting on him to answer his bleep to maybe come and help us all.

We would be listening to other people's accounts of their loved ones getting worse and dying. We also got to know other parents in there when we would sit in the day room for a rest. If they were in trouble, we all shared it. People awaiting news of loved ones would either sleep on Buxton chairs, or would just sit up and talk all night. We would all dread when the door of the waiting room would open and a doctor would come in grim faced to talk to relatives.

We stayed in the hospital as long as we could every day, not getting any answers. This was very hard to organize with such a young family to care for but we managed somehow, with great help. Richard our youngest was only three years old then, so his sisters and brothers looked after him while we were at the hospital. Sometimes his aunts would be good enough to take him. We will be forever grateful for all their help. The neighbours kept a close eye on the house for us as well. There wasn't much housework done in those first few weeks, just the basic needs to get us through. The situation also caused a great strain on our relationship and sometimes we were so stressed that we would argue. I would run out for a bus to get me in to the hospital instead of waiting for a lift from my husband John. The children would be sent after me, running up the road to tell me to wait on a lift, but I would walk faster away. I didn't want to know. But waiting for buses was dreadful in all weathers so I would give in and take the lift home! I never learnt to drive and this was no time to even think of it either.

This was a major Dublin hospital, with an international reputation for skill and care, but it didn't live up to its reputation this time as far as we were concerned.

At one time Darren asked Mr. Mathews himself, what went wrong at the time of the operation, but the doctor was rude to him. He didn't give him any explanation at all and even wrote a note to dismiss him out of the hospital, even though he knew that Darren could not move from the bed! (I have kept this note for future reference). His team were no better than him, I wonder what would have happened if just one of them had spoken up? It would have taken just one and it would have meant so much to all of us. Darren would have been saved years of pain and stress. Just as well that Darren was able to speak up to the doctor and the team to tell them and us, that in fact he could not move and felt extremely sore and not fit to leave the hospital at all.

So he remained where he was and he was so right to speak up to them! We were losing our faith in doctors now.

Chapter Six

We went in to find Darren passing blood on the 26th June. We asked to speak to Mr. Mathews, but of course he could not be contacted. Another doctor eventually came to see him and gave some excuse for this blood loss, only the nurses and us seemed concerned. Even though we requested an explanation, we didn't get any. There was no doctors to be seen anywhere. Imagine in such a drastic situation, and no doctor could tell us what was happening. We felt that everything that could go wrong did go wrong.

We were hours there, but eventually had to go home. We always rang the sister in charge to enquire how he was doing before we went to bed. You could not rest if you didn't ring to get some information.

When we walked into the ward the next day, we were horrified to see that Darren's pajamas bottoms were destroyed with blood. He informed us that he had passed a large amount into the commode. This had been going on all morning, and we had no idea. The nurses were very concerned now and were monitoring the situation. We now insisted on seeing a doctor. We were feeling sick and very alone. Darren could only speak in whispers, and he told me he felt he was dying. His body was hurting so much.

His Dad cried outside the office, and all the staff knew how upset we were. Looking back now, the poor nurses must have hated us coming to the office expecting them to have answers for us; they could see us getting more and more upset. The only reason we asked them was because we could not get a doctor to talk to us. Oh God, it was happening again, except this time we didn't know why. Hadn't he suffered enough with his cancer and all the suffering that went with it?

"Hello Mrs and Mr Morrison, step into my office. So we can talk in private."

At last, maybe now we would get some explanation!

It was Dr. Savelle, senior register to Mr Mathews. He had also assisted at the operation, so would have information for us. The nurses called him up to talk to us at our request.

"We have some good news, and some bad news. First I will give you the good news.

There was no evidence of the dreaded tumour, much to our surprise, but the bad news is that, we did some amount of damage whilst looking for the tumour. We had to pull your son around a bit, and push organs out of the way."

He went on to tell us that there was a pool of blood in Darren's abdomen, and that, according to him it would do him no harm. It would eventually be absorbed into his system.

I found this explanation a little hard to believe, and I asked the question, "What would happen if this blood became infected?"

The doctor told us it was highly unlikely that this would happen, and besides, they would know, as Darren would develop a high temperature! He must have thought that we were totally ignorant of anything medical!

We returned home to see to our other five children and try to reassure them that their brother was going to be ok. On our return to the hospital that night, Darren's temperature was up.

His Dad blew his top, and went to the nurse's station. He demanded to be put through to Dr. Saville.

He told him that we did not believe what we were told previously, and made it clear to him that we felt we were been treated like imbeciles. We were two very upset parents that were now desperate to get help for their seriously ill son. It was a race against time, but we didn't have time. No one was willing to help us. It was a nightmare!

If any of my children got very sick at home, the first sensible thing to do would be to rush them into hospital, here we had a case where our son was in hospital, but not getting the treatment he desperately needed.

Would this happen in other countries, or is it just an Irish thing? Would it have been allowed to happen if he had gone private? No, I don't think so. Because of having cancer Darren could not get private insurance, so he had to go public. To this day he still cannot get health insurance!

I understand now that when it was obvious that Darren had major problems after the operation, the proper treatment would have been to operate in the normal way, to patch up the damage to the bowel that was obviously done at the time of the laparoscopy. This was what you would expect to happen if anything went wrong after an operation.

Unfortunately, this did not happen, and it led to Darren being eventually septic throughout. This has gone on to ruin his life; the damage that this has caused is incomprehensible, and seems to be everlasting.

We were told that the two suppositories that Darren was given caused the bleeding. This account was given to us by no other than Dr. Saville, when he finally came to see us. But in reality, we were not told of the Clostridia and E. coli in his blood cultures, which pointed clearly to the large bowel as a source of infection. That is where these organisms are normally present in the body. Finding them in the blood is usually evidence of bowel injury! So now Darren was left with a life-threatening complication. The so called pool of blood he talked about was really his bowel leaking out!

I wrote down our conversation, and continued to do so each day we went in. The days became repetitive, but never boring. We were on a mission to get help for our son, and I needed to be pointed in the right direction.

I also decided to go to the top and write to the minister for health Mr. Brendan Howlin. I voiced my concerns around Keyhole surgery, and the use of it on patients who have had previous operations, and may have adhesions. Also I pointed out that doctors should not operate using this method unless they are properly trained. After a while he wrote back to me to say he had received my letter, and would look in to it. I never heard any more from him.

Darren now had to have chest X-rays, and ultrasound scans, which showed up, as we were led to believe, "A pool of blood" in his abdomen. He was also now on antibiotics, but despite this, he continued to deteriorate before our very eyes. He could not even sit up any more.

His tummy was very swollen, and we wanted to know why, but getting no answers. At one stage it was suggested by a nurse who knew us well, that because the pain relief voltaral was not working, his Dad or I had somehow put it into Darren's mind that it would not. It was far from Voltarol he needed, try a good doctor! It was hurtful to hear this, as we felt that she was somehow blaming us for this whole situation. We wondered if many more felt like this.

We were advised by Dr. Saville, to go down to see Mr. Mathews in his Out Patients Department. At this stage I think he guessed that we would not stop until we got answers. He had assisted at the operation; he knew the answers but was not willing to give them to us. It was like passing the buck. So, if that's what we had to do, so be it! We went down immediately to the out-patient department hanging onto each other for support. Imagine having to do this, he should have made it his duty to come and see us!

We marched nervously by the waiting queue in the Out Patients Department, and they watched in annoyance as we went before them and knocked on the door, with great anticipation. We were thinking that maybe now we would get some answers to help Darren. On the outside we looked strong and angry, but on the inside we were shaking, not knowing if we were supposed to be barging in to a consulting room. Would we be thrown out? Would they throw Darren out? Did we even care?

One of the nurses answered our loud knock on the door. We asked her could we please talk to Mr. Mathews, and told her who we were. After a few whispered words to the doctor, she brought us in.

To say he was not pleased to see us would be an understatement! But we stood our ground. We told him that we were anxious to know what exactly happened at the operation. His reply was....

"Nothing went wrong, and you are harassing me by asking me all these questions, now just let us continue treating your son Darren, and stop asking questions"

I know that he had to insert the instruments at a different angle, due to Darren's previous operations, and the adhesions that they caused, but he said he was not aware of any bleeding from Darren. According to him, everyone passes blood after any operation. He also denied that he was bleeped on the previous Saturday. He repeated over and over again, that if anything had gone wrong he would have told us (Like when?). Looking back I should have told him that if he hadn't noticed that something had gone wrong, try a different job!

We questioned why Darren was so sick, and if he was going to be all right. And, by the way, why was he not able to get out of his bed?

Mr. Mathews lost his temper, jumped up, and shook his fist into John's face.

He told us to leave, so naturally a row erupted. At this, John and I actually spoke back to him. We voiced our concern about Darren's deterioration, and asked him why he could not tell us what the hell happened. It was the least he could have done! Mr. Mathews told us that indeed he would pull out of Darren's treatment if we continued to ask questions and harass him. At one point John actually asked him did he want to step outside and have it out like a man!

I felt like saying to him "Your services are no longer required, take a hike,

Cheerio", but of course I didn't. The reason I didn't was because I had never heard of this happening to anyone before, and I would not be sure of the consequences. It was amazing to see his team been so loyal, at the risk of a person's life under threat. They gathered around him, like politicians around their leader, ready to defend him no matter what. Why can't they speak up when they suspect that all is not well with a patient? Would they treat their own children in this manner? I don't think so. The consultants are not Gods! It's a terrible thought that these young doctors would go on to practice this learned behavior on other unsuspecting patients in the near future. So we left without getting any answers. Anyway, if we had not left then, there was a good chance that security would have been called for us, and we would have been thrown out! The doctor was arrogant and rude, and the team were no better, they never gave us one word of encouragement, but I was expecting this. It was what we were getting quickly used to! This unnatural world of hospitals and stress was beginning to be the norm.

We actually laughed when we found ourselves outside the consultant's room, and needing some fresh air, as my blood pressure had suddenly gone up. The shock of the whole thing, had we really gone in there? Had we really at last spoken up to doctors who previously we would never have dreamt of speaking our mind to, out of respect for them? But we still had no answers! Who would believe what we had just gone through? I looked at the queuing crowd waiting their turn to go in to this consultant, and I actually felt sorry for them.

Yes, the fight was well and truly on. "OK, if that's the way the doctor wanted to treat us, with no respect and leaving us totally in the dark, so be it"

After a few minutes we went up to the ward to Darren, and excitedly reported what had just happened downstairs, word by word. We then repeated it to the nurses. They could not believe what we told them, and said that it was indeed them, and not us, who were harassing the doctor and his team, to no avail. This was a first, as I had never before heard nurses talking like this before. It was very brave of them to admit this information to us.

We had always known that the nurses were concerned about the treatment that Darren was receiving, but their hands were tied as to how to rectify the situation that they were in. It is always hard for nurses to speak out against doctors, because of their supposed superiority. To this day that has not changed, although maybe they are braver now, I don't know.

Chapter Seven

On the 30th June, we rang up the hospital, only to be told that Darren was very sick and vomiting large amounts of terrible fluid very frequently. The nurse said he was in very bad form. I believe that Mr. Mathews was in with his team, and appeared to be more concerned now. Was this because they knew that we were asking questions and knew too much?

By the time I got in to visit him, Darren had tubes inserted into his nose, draining the contents of his tummy directly into a bag. I noticed that this was a brown/green colour. He continued to vomit while I was there, and he was still on antibiotics. (And he wasn't meant to be sick) Considering he was only supposed to remain in hospital for a few hours originally, this was ridiculous.

He continued to receive drugs intravenously. He couldn't talk much, and we were shocked to notice when the sheets moved, that his tummy had a mysterious large brown stain which had appeared on the side of his tummy. It must have measured about twelve inches by twelve inches, and this was supposed to be the blood that was left inside him after the keyhole surgery! The colour was just under his skin, and you could not miss it. We had never seen anything like it. I was very suspicious of this explanation that this was supposed to be blood left inside him, because surly it could not be this colour. I found out much later that this was indeed the bowel leaking out, just as I suspected!

It didn't take a medical person to tell you that this was totally wrong. We told anyone who would listen to us about this, but as usual we were told not to worry about it. "No, don't worry", our son is gradually fading on front of our eyes yet we were told, "Don't worry".

Darren was very miserable, and needed assistance to wash and change him, and we felt so helpless. He had to fast for a C.T. scan the next day. After the scan, a drainage catheter was inserted, and an amount of fluid was removed from his tummy for investigation. I was told by Mr. Mathews that the results were indeed all clear, which turned out to be a lie.

1st July... I went to leave the hospital with a heavy heart. His Dad and I were getting depressed watching Darren deteriorating in front of our eyes, and not able to help him. We didn't know who to turn to. The nurses knew us all by now, and they could see us getting very down over the situation. On many nights they used their skill as only nurses can do, to calm John down. They stopped him hurting his fists on their walls. He would take out his frustration on the nearest wall, and punch it, usually regretting his actions afterwards, and placing his sore fists under his armpits for comfort. They did not want the other patients upset either. We were so close to losing Darren, all because the doctors were not willing to help him. This was so unreal.

It was then that a Sister in charge approached me and requested to talk to me in private. She took me aside in the corridor. The reason she wanted to help us was because her own mother had gone through something similar. The information she gave me didn't surprise me, but I welcomed her honesty anyway.

She then told me that Darren was been neglected, and that all the nurses were indeed asking Mr. Mathews to do more for Darren to save his life, but it wasn't happening. She informed me that this doctor in charge of Darren's case had indeed taken the sample from that brown stain on the wrong side. (And none of his poor team noticed)

She knew that Darren was septic throughout, and was seriously ill. She advised me to change over doctors. Only for her honesty I don't know what would have happened. I would not have known which way to turn, and I would be writing a different story now. She was our angel.

I needed permission from Mr. Mathews to change over care to a different doctor. It was as we suspected a case of unsatisfactory standard of care. Neglect in the highest degree!

*"*The key to beating peritonitis is prompt treatment by doctors. If appendicitis or a burst appendix is causing it, the appendix is removed. Another common cause is a hole in the bowel causing faecal contents to infect the abdomen. It is necessary to operate, remove the diseased bowel and join the healthy bowel together. Left untreated, these organisms multiply and the bowel stops working.*

PATIENT NUMBER 360993

The organisms can also enter the blood stream, causing a potentially fatal infection."
(Medical journalist Dr. Ellis Downes)

Before I left the hospital the nurses tried to contact Mr. Mathews for me, but as usual there was no answer from his bleep. So as soon as I got home I tried to contact Mr. Mathews, to get his permission to change over as quickly as possible, but I couldn't get through to him.

An hour later, he rang me. He said he had heard that I was looking to contact him, and wondered why.

He pretended to be concerned now and he just wanted to tell me that indeed the test that he carried out on Darren came back clear, and that he did not have any infection. I could not believe what I was hearing. I was shaking, and could not understand why he was denying everything! At this late stage he was still not willing to help our family. I contradicted this information that he was now giving me, and told him that I was told that Darren had a very bad infection, and was very sick. He was shocked to hear this. We exchanged words, and I tried to remain calm and cool, which was very hard when talking to a Consultant, and trying to stand your ground.

I asked him nicely to give us permission to change over to Mr. Howard. He asked me who gave me my information, but I told him if he could not give me any information, then I could not give him any information. He also asked me why I would think that Mr. Howard would be any better than him. I answered by saying that maybe Mr. Howard would save Darren's life, as he deserved it, and that's what we desperately needed now. He had no answer to that.

He knew quite well about Darren's rather complex previous history, as well as what was now happening, as he was the doctor who had removed the large tumour the year before. (We were very grateful to him at that time) so he should have considered straight away giving him a good chance of recovery. In the end he gave me permission to change over to a different doctor. I had to put it in writing straight away.

We celebrated with the family, and felt that at last we were doing something constructive to help Darren. I remember that it was a Friday, and we celebrated by ordering in a simple thing like a take-away meal for the lot of us for our dinner. We were happy, excited about what we had just done, and we felt optimistic for the first time in ages. We left Catherine and Johnny, and Anthony to mind the rest of the family, Fiona and Richard, and we headed into the hospital. They were doing a fantastic job of babysitting and keeping the house together. My sisters and brothers, and neighbours were on standby also, if needed.

This day was the turning point. We rushed into the hospital and we told the Sister -in -charge what had gone on. She made a phone call from her office, and after a short while we met a beautiful doctor called Mr. John Ray. He was the Senior Registrar to Mr. Howard. I handed him my letter that I had quickly written. We pleaded with him to help us, and he came into the ward to meet Darren for the first time. I said to him "Mr. Ray, this is our son, please help us"

We left the ward while he examined him, and after a quarter of an hour, he came out and told us that Darren was a very sick person, and would be lucky to recover from all this. I knew that he was very sick, but at least now we had a doctor actually admitting this!

Darren was losing his breath when he spoke, but he did manage a smile for us when we told him the good news that he had a new doctor looking after him.

The relief was written all over his face, and ours. As soon as Mr. Howard and his great team took over, they continued to give Darren the best of attention and medical treatment, and we now had hope at last. The whole team were fantastic, and they took a genuine interest in Darren's health. The relief to us all was unimaginable.

According to the four hourly charts for the 2nd July, Darren's temperature reached a maximum of 38.7. Degrees, and his pulse rate a maximum of 130 beats a minute, but he was well monitored. The nurses told us that Mr. Mathews often stopped at Darren's room, and peeped through the little glass window in the door, just to see if he was still there, and they all knew this.

Fri. 3rdJuly...Darren was now having blood transfusions and a drip up for intravenous antibiotics, and also drainage tubes coming from his body. He wasn't looking too good at all. He continued to have visitors; his own brothers and sisters loved coming in to see him, also his elderly

Grandmother. His aunties, family, and Lisa his girlfriend never failed to visit and have a laugh with him. Some of his scout friends came in also.

Sometimes we had to step in and stop people from visiting, when Darren was too sick for visitors. I was all over the place sometimes. I also felt bad that I was neglecting my friends and some family members, especially my eldest sister Ann. I didn't get to see her for months, but I knew she would understand. I was trying to ring everyone to keep them informed about the situation, and also trying not to alarm his grandmother, so had to force a smile on my face when I visited her.

She would study my face, to see if I was lying when I told her he was coming along nicely, thanks to her prayers.

Sat.4th July... He was very down in himself, and his temperature was up. His pain control was changed, but he continued to complain about tummy ache. His temperature rose, and his pulse rate was 156 beats a minute.

All we could do was pray.

Chapter Eight

Sun. 5th July... We were asleep when the phone rang at 6.30am.......John ran down to answer it, and I followed.

It was the hospital to say that Darren was bleeding very badly, and had vomited up one and a half litres of blood. They requested us to come in as soon as we could, as he needed us in with him. It was a haemorrhage from his tummy, and had started around 4am. the doctors were trying to get on top of the problem, but to no avail. I knew what we might be facing, but yet I didn't want to face it. We went into slow motion, and could not hurry... There seemed so much to plan before we went in. We woke up the eldest two, and told them that we had to leave. This was a taste of what people go through in tragedies, and we certainly did not know what we were about to face.

When we arrived in at 7am, the place was eerily silent, except for the fact that we could hear Darren violently vomiting up blood, and the team of doctors were frantically surrounding him. They were trying all they could to help him.

An emergency situation was now in progress, and from his own bed. I was surprised as I was expecting Darren to be removed from his own ward and placed in I.C.U. The situation was so bad that they could not move him out of his bed. There was just a screen around his bed in the ward, and a sea of white coats surrounded him.

Our nightmare was now coming through. What was going to happen?

Darren had at least fifteen pints of blood pumped in to him intravenously as fast as they could, to try to replace the copious amount he was vomiting up.

They had the bed raised up at the bottom, and needles inserted into his toes and hands. The nurses and doctors were literally pumping the blood in with their hands, to try to cope with the loss, but it was coming out just as fast as they were putting it in to him. Nurses stood there beside the bed doing their job of keeping the sick-bowl under his chin, and then running to empty it when it was full of blood. It was very traumatic for even trained nurses to have to do this. The doctors were fantastic that morning; it was just as hard for them, as for us to witness this. They saved his life, and they were guided by Mr. Howard over the phone. I am so grateful to them for that.

Darren was drained of colour, and looked very frightened.

I sat amongst all this mayhem, and held his hand. He said to me "Mammy, I'm dying" I told him that no, he was strong, he wasn't going anywhere, and he would get over this dreadful situation that he was now in. I think I mentioned something about how he was a scout leader, and had to be strong. I had no intention of leaving the ward so the doctors worked around me. I think they were glad we were there anyway, and I like to think that Darren calmed down a little bit because he knew we were there. I held his hand throughout all of this.

His Dad could not stay in the ward too long to look at him suffering, and in this situation, so stood frantically outside the door. The other patients must have also had a terrible morning listening to all of this. The doctors and nurses were fantastic in this situation.

When Mr. Howard came in at nine a.m., he said he had no option but to operate immediately. Darren was wheeled away from us very quickly up to the operating theatre, and his eerie screams echoed down the busy corridors. We stood there in total shock not knowing if we would ever see him again.

Mr. Howard operated shortly after, and we waited in the waiting room. We cried with frustrating, not knowing what was to come. All we could hear now was silence. My sister Patricia, and her husband Kevin, (R.I.P.), came in to stay with us. My other sister Mary took Richard to her house for the day. Eventually, three hours later, and what seemed like an eternity, Mr. Howard came into the waiting room to see us.

Darren was over the operation, but he was very critical. The doctor had found Darren's stomach grossly distended with clotted blood secondary to active bleeding from an acute ulcer in the curve of his stomach. He was found to have an infected haematoma, and a large abscess secondary to a pin hole perforation of the sigmoid colon. The colon was densely adhered to the scars of previous operations. The doctor stopped the bleeding and also patched up the perforated colon. (I read all of this years later when I read his report of the operation, so that's where I got all of this jargon). We were told by the doctor that it was obvious that this perforation had occurred on the 23rd June, the day of the laparoscopy, possibly after carbon dioxide insufflations before the laparoscopy operation. He actually admitted this to me when I asked him.

The doctor told us he was not sure if the bowel would hold, as it was reduced to a very delicate state, like tissue paper is how he described it. Time would tell. Looking back now, it was so unfair for that doctor to have to operate on such a complicated case, due to one of his own colleague's botched work! It would have been so less complicated if the right course of action had been taken on the 23rd June.

We went in to I.C.U, to see Darren. He was on morphine and highly sedated. He looked so bad, and didn't know that we were there. We went home to organize the house and when we returned to hospital at 6.30pm, he was awake and was able to talk to us. He remained critical.

Mon.6th July... Darren was very sick, and needed a lot of attention. He was on oxygen and morphine. He was in a bad mood, and told us all off. The drugs were having a bad effect on him, and he hated having all these blood tests! Later on, he was shifted out of I.C.U, and had to have a chest X-ray.

Tue 7th July... Darren was a little worse today, he got many injections for the pain, and the doctors were attending on him. They told us he was recovering nicely, but slowly.

Wed 8th July...We were all in with him today, but he wasn't able for us. He was very quiet, and it hurt him to talk. There was some fluid on his lungs, and his breathing was affected. Darren had to fast that night for an ultrasound in the morning. He had received liquid food to start off with, he looked depressed, and we went home depressed also.

Thurs 9th July...The doctors decided to give Darren his own box that he presses to control his pain with morphine. As the pain increased, he was able to press a button. This was a great help, and it gave Darren a little boost.
Professor Farrell, who was the cancer specialist, came in to tell us all that the news was good; there was definitely no sign of the tumour returning. Thank God. This was great news, and it came at a good time also. We needed all the cheering up we could get. But the situation that Darren was now in was all for nothing so. But it was good news.

Fri.10th July...Darren had some fluid drained from his lung, which made him better enough to have some yoghurt and tea.

Sat 11th July...His Temperature up today to 103 degrees, and we could not get a conversation out of Darren today. It was obvious he was in a lot of pain.

Sun.12th July...We all helped him walk down the corridor; it was great to see him moving a little anyway. His girlfriend Lisa was great, and all his aunts and uncles came in to visit him. Even his elderly grand-mother managed to come in, and she was so relieved to see him well looked after. Between his brothers and sisters, and even his head teacher from years past, there were a good lot of us to give him support.

His breathing was still bad, and a vicious circle developed, bowel breakdown leading to further sepsis.

More scans were done, as the doctors were worried about an abscess. It ended up that the abscess was about a foot long down his left side, and a smaller one on his right side. A catheter was inserted under ultrasound guidance, and a large amount of fluid was drained from it, no wonder he was in so much pain.

Chapter Nine

Tue. 14th July... Draining still going on. This was dreadful! The drain was through his nose, but it was a necessity, and he hated it.

Wed. 15th July... Darren received three pints of blood, and is still in the same situation as yesterday. He is receiving antibiotics, and the morphine he is receiving is keeping him somewhat sane.

Thurs. 16th July... I went in to speak to his doctor, while he was down having another scan done. He informed me that due to part of Darren's bowel being infected, he may have to undergo another operation tomorrow. We were all devastated. Darren looked bad, and was getting weaker. Thank God that a top doctor would be operating, so we had to put our faith in him. Even the nurses said they were sorry to hear this news.

17th July... His operation took seven hours, and we paced the floor at home for that duration. The other children needed us also, especially Richard as he was only three. Just as well we had a good family to look after him.
Finally, we went in to visit Darren. He was now back in I.C.U. He was totally sedated, and on a ventilator He still had some fluid on his lungs, and he had tubes coming from everywhere.

A small amount of his bowel had to be removed, and the rest repaired.

18th July... The nurses were slowly reducing the amount of sedatives, and he knew we were there. He could not talk, so he communicated through shaky hand-written notes. One of them read "Get this tube out of my mouth, I feel claustrophobic". Another note he wrote to the nurses said, "Where is my Mother, is she gone home?" The doctors told us that the situation could not be any worse.

Lisa continued to visit Darren every day, and she was just as upset as we were. She would sit there holding his hand, and talking him through it. There was nothing any of us could do, just be there for him I suppose.

A lot of prayers were needed now, so we asked the parish priest to mention this at mass each morning. As a matter of fact, people from far and near were praying, even in other countries. The feeling of helplessness we felt was indescribable!

19th July... The ventilator was off him, thank God. He was in better form, which makes us all feel better. By night visit we were all tired. We had to go home to the rest of the family.

Darren was religious, and loved to get presents of various medals from friends and relations. He used to keep this special one in the top pocket of his pyjamas. He had received it from a lovely old lady he had met, called Mrs.

Heffernan. Panic set in this day when he realised he had left the medal in the top pocket, and he sent it down to the laundry room in the hospital, after they had taken the pyjamas off him to wash it. Well we helped them search for it high and low, to no avail. Darren got upset over this. We got him another one but it wasn't the same. I often wondered who Darren was staring at on the wall beside his bed. He stared with the most puzzled expression on his face; I had never seen that look before or since. He appeared very frightened and puzzled. Was it Padre Pio coming personally to meet him, after all the prayers we prayed to him? Darren took my hand and told me he was in a lot of pain, and he was scared. He didn't want us to go, so we waited until he fell asleep. The wound was open now, and surgically packed. His Dad was very upset; we have no control over the situation at all. So we have to put our trust in these doctors. They were great doctors.

20th July... Darren was out of I.C.U. His temperature was a little down now. He was receiving blood today to help him; also lots of different drips were up. This improvement was welcome, so we calmed down a little. We were visiting the canteen and drinking a lot of tea and coffee, it kept us going, and the few snatched sandwiches replaced dinners.

This was a different world we were living in, but it was quickly beginning to be the norm with us. If there was any benefit from it at all, it was that I lost about a stone in weight with all the running up those hospital stairs, and not eating properly.

I tried to avoid the lifts as much as possible, because on one occasion I was stuck in one of them. A porter and another patient were also with me, and he tried to calm me down. When the lift door opened all we could see was half of the floor. We closed the door again and he pressed the button to go up. We went down to the basement. I was in bits, and I would have needed a double brandy by the time I got out. The family had a good laugh, but that finished me with those lifts!

22nd July. Darren walked with some aid, slowly down the corridor.

He was delighted, and as it was my birthday, we had a laugh together. He had managed to get me a card, and it was a lovely surprise.

For the following week, Darren got the best of treatment, and he even managed to sit out on a chair for a little while. We brought him up to the waiting room, just for a short while. We watched television together, and mixed with other patients. He was very weak, but he tried his best to carry on. His temperature continued to fluctuate up and down.

He was eventually put in an ordinary ward, so now all the family could visit him.

29th July... We were staying half a day now, trying to comfort Darren.

While I was there, we were just chatting away when I noticed bowel contents leaking from his tummy wound onto the bandages.

I ran to the nurse's station to inform them. The doctor was called, and I spoke to him outside the ward. Yes, another operation was needed. Oh no! Darren was not strong enough for another operation, but he needed it urgently. I phoned home to tell them, and then went out to get the bus home, I couldn't talk.

That night, the doctor phoned us to tell us that the operation was over. He didn't need to put a stoma bag on, but Darren's stomach will have to remain open, to repair any other leaks that might occur. He made an appointment to see us next day.

We keep in touch with family and friends; it is the only thing to keep us sane, talking to others. We got to know other parents who were visiting their loved ones in the hospital, and we supported each other at times. One of the young patients died from M.R.S.A She was only about sixteen. We comforted her parents in the hall, and we cried with them. I then went in to Darren. He stared at me and asked me what was wrong. I did not want to tell him in case it worried him that this was possible in a hospital, to die of something else apart from what you went in with. He was scared and thought I had been crying after getting bad news about him, so I told him in the end.

It would have been extremely hard to keep the house in order, if it wasn't for Johnny, Catherine, Anthony, Fiona, and family members.

I even remember Maisie my next door neighbour coming in and taking all my washing into her house, and sometimes she would carry in a large pie for us, it was magic, she was so thoughtful. Another good neighbour Sadie always dropped in cakes for all of us and gave us great support. A very good neighbour called James came over and cut our grass for us, without us even suggesting it. That's the way the neighbours were. They were all so kind and thoughtful. We often enjoyed a drink together and enjoyed a chat.

Mr. Howard met us in his out-patient's department. He seemed to be pleased how the operation went, and he had to explain a lot of medical terms to us. He told us that Darren was too sedated to even know that the operation was over, but he is smiling away at everyone. He had a small cubical, and even had his own television in I.C.U. We must scrub up before we enter.

31st July... Darren is in more trouble, He's back up in the theatre, being operated on by the great Mr. Ray this time, an excellent doctor. He was having more patches put on his bowel. He was very tired, and wanted to sleep. Just as well! The sister told us it was better if we didn't see him. We went in anyway. He was so sedated that it was like looking at someone suspended in time. We went home very upset. How much more can he take? Half of his bowel must be gone by now.

Chapter Ten

Sat 1st August... It's our wedding anniversary, and we spent it at the hospital. This is the day that Darren should be going away on his holiday with his brothers, instead of fighting for his life. Surrounded by oxygen masks, he's facing the operating theatre again, for another procedure. At this stage I have lost count of the many operations that he has had!

The hospital have put him into a small ward, and supplied a nurse to sit with him all the time. She monitored his situation all the time. Will this next operation be the last operation for him?

We went out for a drink to the local, to celebrate our anniversary and to catch up on all of our neighbours.

2nd August... We awoke to screaming, and smoke everywhere. I jumped out of the bed and looked out the window. The house next door was on fire. There was so much fire that it lit up the front of our house. The house quickly burnt to the ground, and tragically we lost two of our neighbours. I was one of the first out on the road, and I remember I screamed with one of the girls who lived in the house, I was screaming at her to get the children out, but they were not sleeping there that night. I also knew that the louder I screamed, the other neighbours would wake up and come out. It all happened in a matter of minutes; there was nothing any of us could do. The people who died tragically were a mother and her beautiful daughter, who were our neighbours for years. The whole road was in an uproar. We were all screaming and upset. Our house was totally destroyed by smoke damage. John ran back in to disconnect the cylinder of gas from the cooker in the kitchen. He threw it out the back door. Then he closed all the windows, as he thought this would keep the smoke out. But what he didn't know was that the attic of our house was beginning to catch fire, and the smoke was bellowing in. When the fire-brigade arrived, the firemen checked that we were all out, and then they opened our windows to let the smoke out!

We spent the night on the road in our night gear, as did all of our neighbours. We had grabbed Richard in a blanket, and John and I got all the rest of the family out. We were in shock. We inhaled smoke, so we had to receive treatment in an ambulance on our street. One of our neighbours Terry brought us in to her house for a cup of welcome tea, and somewhere to sit down. We were all still in our night-clothes when the dawn broke.

Our neighbours were brilliant. They followed us back into our house the next morning at day break. Each one of them carried buckets and mops, and began the task of helping us clean up the mess. The house was reeking of dense smoke, and even if you went outside for some air that was just as bad. We noticed that because the bushes out the back yard held all the smoke, all the birds stopped visiting us. That went on for months until the rain finally washed away the smell, and we finally got our birds back.

I never felt the same way about the house after the fire. There was evidence everywhere you looked, and I wasn't in the humour to do much.

The neighbours took down all our curtains to wash them, and took our washing out to their houses. Our carpets, lino, paint work, were destroyed. We also had to throw out all the children's toys. I also had to discard some of our smoke-damaged clothes and shoes. We needed this like a hole in the head! I thought to myself someone up there is taking the piss! But still, we were all ok.

The smell of smoke was unbearable, but we had to stay beside the phone.

Our lives fell apart. I was trying to keep the house as clean as possible, and now we were destroyed. The fact that we had lost two neighbours, in such a drastic way and I was waiting on news from the hospital was just unbelievable.

We went into the hospital, leaving the destroyed house open for air. There wasn't anything worth robbing anyway. We smelled of fire and smoke. It was up our noses, and in our lungs, and we tasted it constantly. I felt sick.

I asked the doctor if I should tell Darren about the fire and losing our neighbours, but he advised against it. The doctor had seen it on the news.

We were not allowed to see Darren for a while, as he was having his bandages changed. To do this, he had to have a drug called Hypnovel. He would go through the procedure, but would not remember a thing afterwards. Sometimes Darren would come out with a string of curses to the doctor, not knowing what he was saying, but they would laugh because they knew that he would be mortified if he knew what he was saying. We would be told later by the nurses what had gone on. Just as well the doctors had a good sense of humour!

We spoke to Mr. Ray, and he advised us to go home and rest.

We went back at 6:30pm. The Parish Priest came in also to talk to Darren and he stayed for a while with him to see how he was coping.

Darren looked dreadful. He wouldn't talk to us. He was sick and depressed and in no humour for visitors. He was having another operation tomorrow. Oh God! Words fail me. We went home to our stinking house. I scrubbed away to get my frustration out. We only had one bedroom that was fit to sleep in, but somehow we all managed. I remember saying at the time that if I ever got over this I would never complain about a bit of dust again.

John was cracking up. He would be depressed from the moment he got up, and he cried a lot.

Something was keeping me strong, and I tried not to get upset in the hospital. I had found an inner strength I didn't know I had. I tried not to cry in front of the children, but in the privacy of my bedroom I did. I remember one night in particular, I was walking around late at night, and I passed Darren's room. I realised that no matter how much we wished him home, it could not be. I cried like a banshee.

Looking back now I realise what the rest of the family must have gone through. I hope I listened to their troubles.

Did they even tell me how they were feeling? How did I respond? I don't remember. I hope they managed between themselves.

The only counseling we were getting was from family and friends.

3rd Aug... John and I went in to see Mr. Ray, the doctor in charge. We didn't speak on the journey in.

First we peeped into Darren's room. He was moaning, and then screaming. I placed my hand on his arm, he whispered to me not to touch him, or the bed. The slightest touch was agony for him. I noticed he now had the horrible colostomy bag that he was dreading having. The head male nurse who was looking after him told me that the highest amount of pain-killing drugs had now been given to him, but it was obvious that it was not enough in this case.

Darren was in a sweat, and seemed to have lost so much weight overnight; there was a different look about him now. It was unbelievable. We looked at one another. Why was he looking so bad? I actually questioned myself how long it was since I had seen my own son.

The doctor called us into the back office. He looked serious.

Chapter Eleven

He said he wanted to tell me personally, that he thought that Darren was struggling to live. He was in a bad way, and it didn't look good. We were to prepare ourselves for the worst. He gently told me that his body was showing signs of giving up. This all shows up in blood tests as well as other tests. He could not possibly take any more punishment. Darren had taken enough.

We listened, and I thanked him for been so honest with us. I calmly asked him to inform Mr. Mathews. After all, it was his fault that our son was in this condition! I wanted him to know personally what we were going through. He said he would, and I believed him at that moment that he would do so. Whether he ever did or not I will never know. The doctors seemed just as upset as we were, as they all knew Darren well by now.

Darren was so very critical.

While we were talking, we could still hear Darren moaning loudly in great pain, it was heartbreaking.

Mr. Ray inquired if that was indeed Darren he could hear, and when it was confirmed to him by the nurses that it was, he told me he could not let him suffer so much. He ordered an injection to be given. This put Darren into a deep sleep.

PATIENT NUMBER 360993

We waited for a long while, and then had to go home late into the night.

We cried all the way home.

My sisters were there waiting for us, as they knew the situation.

Tue 4th August… The next 24 hours are crucial….but, miraculously he's still alive.

Wed 5th August… The next few days went by with hospital visits twice a day. We did not tell Darren's grandmother how bad he was, as she worried so much about him. So it was very hard to disguise our feelings when we were in her company. As soon as we went to visit her the first words were always "How is Darren", I would answer that he was grand, and improving. It was easier than upsetting her and us. I found it very hard to talk about it to anyone. But she would still study my face carefully, to see if I was telling her the truth or not.

The poor kids hardly got a look in, but we tried our best. We didn't have a best any more.

Sometimes I stayed for the whole day, and would have conversations with other visitors in the waiting room. We were kept going with tea from the canteen. And because we were well known now, sometimes we were offered sandwiches. And as for Lisa, I don't know how she managed. We would leave Darren, and sit downstairs every night, just to give them some time on their own. Then we would drive her home, sometimes upset.

On a number of occasions we bumped into Mr. Mathews in the corridor and he would try to say hello. This would cause ructions. On this particular day John and I passed that doctor in the entrance hall where he was standing having a conversation with one of his colleagues, smiling away, appearing not to have a worry in the world. He said hello to us, waving as he did so. Immediately John stopped in his tracks. He swished around and marched back to him and told him in no uncertain terms, never to try to have a conversation with us again. He was ordered never to try to even say hello to us again, as it was his fault that our son was so sick. I think the doctor knew by John's face that he was serious. The desk-porter in the hall told us later that he thought he was going to witness a fist fight between the doctor and John. So any other time that doctor spotted us walking through the corridor, he would look the other way. I don't think I ever relaxed going through the hallway again after that... Just in case he ever did try to say hello, but he never did after that! He was the last person we wanted to see. I tried to speak to John every day to try to hold his temper, and calm him down, if the two of them happen to cross paths.

Darren was unconscious a lot of the time, due to the drugs he was on, and I was glad, because it was the only time he was out of pain.

He was receiving tender loving care, and I never gave up hope.

We were always there for him, and trying to reassure him that everything would be alright. We were always quick to point out to staff if we noticed anything going wrong with his wounds.

We were quickly able to notice wounds turning septic, or on another occasion, I contradicted the doctor when they could not see the jaundice setting in. He had said "No not at all, it's the light in the ward"

When I went in the very next day, I was told that Darren had jaundice. But sure, I already knew that. I think I missed my profession.

The rest of the world was sitting at home watching the Olympics, while we got snatched moments in the hospital waiting room. It was a welcomed distraction that helped us to put in some of the day, and I loved it. It also gave us something to talk about to other relations besides sickness. I also loved to watch quiz programmes of any sort, especially ones that we could all join in with.

We enjoyed talking to other visitors, as it took our minds off our own worries.

My sister Rosaleen and her husband Dennis came home to visit from Scotland, and it was great for us all. They stayed for a few days in our house, and came in with us each day to visit.

Darren's blood was improving, and another operation was talked about.

He got tired very easily, so it was only short visits allowed.

Lisa, John and I went home at ten every night. On a few occasions, the hospital porter came up to tell us the visiting hours were up, but we took no notice, and refused to budge. Why should we? We didn't ask for our son to be damaged, so if we wanted to stay, we did, and if he needs us we were there for him. You could not do that today, security is much stricter. That's the way I would want it, to be stricter, but not for visitors of seriously ill patients, who naturally should be allowed to stay longer. But I am going back a few years.

My sisters and brothers clubbed together to buy a little portable television, and Darren loved it. It made such a difference to his life. He used to mark out his programmes for the day. He also got a loan of a video player. So now we could buy him videos to watch as well. His friends also brought him in some of theirs. So he had a grand set-up altogether, and all he was short of was his beloved budgies from home! He bred budgies, and when he was younger his friends would call him the bird man.

We had the television cable installed in his room, and it helped others afterwards. Each time he was moved to a different room we would get a man in to install cable television.

In spite of this, of course it wasn't what a young man of his age would want; Darren still told us that he was missing home.

My brother Pat, and my late sister in law, Helen, brought in the Padre Pio blessed glove, and it was placed on his tummy. It was then actually passed around other patients, before it was brought back to the Monks, in Frier Street Dublin. We blessed ourselves as well. Religion plays a major part in your life when you find yourself in trouble, I went into churches more now than ever before. There are a couple of small chapels in the hospital, and I remember going into one. I approached the alter saying my usual prayers. Then I got cross. I said out loud for anyone to hear, "Don't you dare take my son from us, DON'T YOU DARE". I was feeling upset and angry at the world, and God. I guess he listened to me.

I now had the courage to tell Darren that there was another operation planned for him, He was shocked but understood.

Chapter Twelve

The doctors contacted a psychiatrist to talk to Darren. We were glad as we recognised that Darren needed to talk about his worries and fears to someone else, rather than his family.

He hid a lot of his emotions and distress from us, so this was a great chance for him to open up to someone else. When she did come to visit, she thought he was managing well, but she didn't ask him much. We could all see that he wasn't managing well, even the doctors could tell that. I don't know where she got her training from. So it was a waste of time.

No one could say when this next operation was to be, not even the doctor.

We would stand out in the corridor as soon as we were told that the doctors were on their rounds. I'm sure they must have dreaded seen us there as we always asked about the operation because we wanted to get Darren out of there. But of course they could not give us an answer because his bowel would have to heal more, and he would have to get a lot stronger before any operation would or could be attempted. But as the months were going in fast, we were losing patience. But still we stood outside the ward, week after week, waiting to see the doctors.

30th Aug…A nasty rash had developed on his side and back. Blood tests were carried out, and unfortunately a young intern was sent into the room to take his blood.

We waited outside the room to give them privacy, then we heard an unmerciful scream coming from the little room, it was from Darren. The nurse who was in the nurse's station ran in. She then ran back to her nurse's station to ring for another doctor. We could hear her frantically requesting assistance. We soon found out that this is what happened:

Instead of going to the right side of the bed, the young doctor had stretched across the bed to take the blood test. He had slipped, and his hand had gone onto Darren's open stomach, causing unknown damage, and also causing Darren to scream in shock. It was a genuine mistake. Another more senior doctor came up and he was not too pleased with the young intern. We could hear him raising his voice and shouting at the intern. Darren had to be brought to the operating theatre as an emergency, but luckily enough, no damage was done.

In the meantime, John ran around the hospital looking for the young intern. Thank God he didn't find him! There was no reasoning with John, he had had enough. He went down lifts, up lifts, raced around the corridors, but could not find this intern. Just as well! At this stage he would have done jail for him.

The nurses had to try to calm John down, as he hit his fists against the walls with his frustration of it all. Besides, he was disturbing the other patients. He would not listen to me, he was gone beyond that.

For weeks later John would look out of the ward door still hoping to catch sight of that intern, and it would cause a row between us, as it wasn't helping matters. Darren got a great laugh from his Dad's behaviour though.

All hell would break out if Mr. Mathews happened to go by, or Dr. Saville.

This amused Darren. As it was the only bit of excitement that he would see! He would say to me "Move out of the way Mam and let me see, I don't want to miss anything" John would stand there with his hands on his hips, giving dirty looks to any doctor that looked like he might be on Mr. Mathews team. Even innocent young doctors just going down the corridor would be on the receiving end of John's temper. Looking back now, they must have all thought he was mad!

Sept...We tried to keep Darren amused, while we had the long wait for his next operation. To keep all our sanity intact, we played cards a lot, simple games like snap or house, or maybe poker (A lot of cheating went on between us, and sometimes we let Darren win, other times we were just out to win ourselves) We used to bet small amounts of money on the card games, just to liven things up a bit. To stop boredom setting in we watched all the afternoon programmes together that we would never dream of watching otherwise. Like Home and Away, Antiques Road Show, Blockbusters and the likes. I even got him listening to Phil Collins, my favorite singer. The nurses and doctors often walked into his small room and Darren would be singing out in his best voice "In the air tonight" his favorite music on his walkman with ear-phones, not realizing that anyone was listening. They got a great laugh from this. I knew that when he would eventually get home that he would be on his karaoke machine a lot of the time.

He often asked the nurses and doctors to pose for photos, another new hobby of his! It was a great form of amusement for him. His Uncle Tony and Aunt Rita travelled up from Galway often to visit, and to give their support. They brought books and games for him. It was great to see them, and they would promise him a holiday down in Galway as soon as he was better.

Unfortunately, Darren continued to have panic attacks. On one occasion, he tore the sheets off his bed, and threw things around his room. He was sedated then. His girlfriend Lisa phoned me to tell me, and we had to drop everything and go in.

The doctors had to arrange a skin specialist to visit him, because his back was in a dreadful state from lying down in his bed. He also prescribed zinc for his hands. He had developed an allergy to latex, which caused its own problems. This did not exist in him before he went in, and this has continued through the years. Even if we have children's balloons in the house he breaks out in a rash.

Oct 1st... Darren had a new type of tube inserted to drain excess fluid; it was called a Shirley wound drain. It was not used often in this hospital, and it seemed to work.

The team took photos of his tummy, for a conference, which was to be held soon in the hospital.

On the 16th October, he was passing blood, and a urine test was done. His temperature was up also. The doctors kept a close eye on him. Another new needle was put in his arm.

Oct 23rd...We had to visit twice, as Darren was in distress. He had a very bad experience up in the theatre. They tried to insert a new line into his neck in his senses. He had a local anesthetic, but felt the lady pulling at him, as she looked for the vein. The needle was about six inches long, to reach the main vein.

He asked her to stop, but she would not. She told him to shut up and be quiet, and let her get on with it. So he went through a grueling time.

After three attempts, Darren screamed the theatre down, and I believe the doctors could hear him in other theatres.

She finally abandoned the attempt to find the jugular vein, and Darren was sent back to his room in distress.

Chapter Thirteen

We were so angry to hear about this that we requested to meet this person, this head anaesthetist. Cathy was her name.

When she arrived, she informed us that Darren was screaming even before they inserted the needle. But we pointed out that that proves how terrified he was, and she should have listened to him. We said it was more like a concentration camp than a hospital.

He had to have general anaesthetic the next morning. They discovered that the major vein that they were looking for was well hidden in his neck. And they never found it. For some strange reason, they thought there was one jugular vein instead of two, which was very strange at the time, because everyone should have two.

30th Oct... The stomoligest visited him, and fitted a bag over his stomach. He was very sore, but morphine was then increased for the pain.

Sun.1st Nov... Darren was asleep, and not well. His temperature is up to 104 degrees. The doctors took his line out at 8 o'clock this morning, guessing that this was probably the main cause.

Lisa's parents came in to visit also. We always had a good laugh with them, and we were glad of their support.

There was a blood infection going on, but it didn't last long.

The next night his boss Michael came in to surprise him and that was great! There were smiles and laughter all around, as we recalled all the antics that were going on in the Shopping Centre. He always brightened up to hear news of his old job, and his work-mates.

We got a surprise phone call from the nurse's station. The nurses and the porter pushed Darren's bed out of his room, and over to their phone. Now he could phone us, and also get out of his room, even for a few minutes. (Nobody had mobiles then)

It was a very emotional time, and Darren said he felt very strange. It did him the world of good. He had been in his little ward on his own for months, without been able to leave once, and it was getting him down. So this was a great idea from the staff. Joe, the orderly, was very good to Darren. He would bring him in the newspaper every day, and stay for a little chat. He would also help me push Darren's bed, with Darren in it, over to the sink, when we started washing his hair. It took a bit of maneuvering, but we managed somehow. We would have a laugh with shampoo and water going everywhere. But he always managed to look grand afterwards. It was a great distraction as well. I would go home knackered though!

Darren could not stand up on his own, and still needed help to do all of this including shaving Etc, but we were getting used to it now. He always tried to keep the good side out and would have a laugh with the staff.

Tue. 10th Nov... I went up to our own doctor, with John. I requested to be referred for some counseling, and he wrote me a letter for the same hospital. I was to make an appointment with Professor Wigan. John got some tablets also, instead of counseling.

We were asked on a number of occasions what we felt about this whole situation that we found ourselves in. I remember one particular social worker asking me to step outside the ward door to discuss this with me. I was reluctant to disclose my true feelings, but he knew how we were feeling about the whole lot of it! Besides, I did not know where, or in what department, my answers would turn up.

When I went in to make an appointment with this Professor Wigan, his secretary told me that there was no way I would be able to see this doctor for months, as he was booked up. But I left my details anyway. The next morning, the hospital rang and offered me an appointment for the very next day. I was surprised to say the least!

After discussing this with a 'friend', she advised me not to keep my appointment, as it was possible that they were going to record me, for future reference. I suspect this was to get my opinion about how Darren had been treated at the hospital. I never got to know if this was true or not as I went in the next day and cancelled my appointment. I counseled myself instead.

We became accustomed to the hospital, and all that went with it, the clatter of trolleys, the smiling faces of the nurses, the crying of some of the patients and their family members, and mostly happy smiling patients. The lovely dinner ladies, the nice doctors (and the not so nice ones) the bed pans, the smell that lingered with you even when you left the hospital, (and that was only me!) dressing gowns, slippers, and white coats fluttering past you, like swans down the corridors.

It was John's birthday, and we all sang happy birthday to him. Darren gave him a card.

More tubes were inserted to remove bile. Darren was not pleased, but put up with it. After a couple of weeks, his brother brought him in a new modern camera as a present from Spain. All his friends had bought it between them, because Darren should have been with them on the holiday. This was a lovely surprise, and he cheered up a lot. The parish priest Fr. Hastings, dropped in also, and we all had a good laugh. We were glad of his continues support.

The shopping centre staff where he worked were beginning to come in now, as they knew that he was improving. This was a tonic. He loved to hear all the gossip that he was missing, and looked forward to the day when he would return to work with them.

My brother Pat arranged for a healing priest to come in. He was from Blackrock College. He was a lovely man, and made us all feel much better. He gave us all some hope for the future and we hung on to every word he said. We had gone down that road of looking up healers. We spent time comparing them, and reading up on them. We could not afford to throw money away on people who claimed to heal every illness, but we were intrigued. This priest from the college was the perfect man for the job. He was gentle and kind and we were so pleased to see him walking in. He gave us all a great boost. We also discussed the possibility of us all going to Lourdes whenever Darren got out of hospital. It hasn't happened yet, but we still talk about it every now and again. Loads of his friends and family have gone there to say a prayer for him, but I would love to go with him. Maybe sometime.

Chapter Fourteen

Tue Oct 18th ... Darren had a panic attack. He was feeling claustrophobic in the small room that he was confined to. He felt that he was losing it altogether.

If only he could get up off his bed and walk around for awhile, but this was impossible. He needed complete rest. But his young mind could not rest. His nose was blocked from the tube, and he could not breathe properly.

I talked to his doctor about the situation. He prescribed a sedative and things improved.

As part of his survival package, a few weeks later, Darren started to go down to the P.E. room and gym. We were trilled! The staff there taught him how to do leg exercises, and attempted to get him fit again, with great results. He needed this for his mental health also, and you could see the change in him. He enjoyed these visits, his daily physiotherapy sessions got him out of his room. Darren was very dizzy when he sat up first; his body was so used to lying down, so it all had to be done very slowly. The girls were very patient with him, and he would slowly walk along the bars, holding on for dear life! This eventually built up his confidence and helped him to walk again. We were allowed to follow him down, and enjoyed watching him getting stronger by the day. It was so much better than sitting up in the stuffy ward.

We began to wheel Darren down in a wheelchair to the church with us, and the coffee shop, where the family would have hot chocolate and sandwiches most days. He really enjoyed this distraction, and anything that made him feel normal was welcome. But through all of this, Darren still had a sense of humour, and many times we would exchange jokes. These he would repeat to the nurses, he loved to try to make them laugh! Thank God he had given up smoking a couple of years earlier, or we would have had to push him out to the door to have a smoke!

His dad was not so lucky; he went back on the smokes after been off them for fifteen years!

Darren was in bed because his stoma bag had burst, and he was waiting on the stomoligest to come and replace it. Besides this, he is coming along nicely. We asked would there be any chance he could come home for Christmas.

He was getting a little down lately, and sometimes had a good cry. But we always tried to cheer him up, and mostly he would cheer us up. The weeks were turning into months, with no sign of an end to it. We made sure that he had a visitor every day, and if no one could get in to the night visit I felt terrible. Darren developed an interest in cookery from the thousands of magazines he had read over the months. We even bought him cookery books. It kept him going, planning meals he was going to cook for the family when he was home and well. He was becoming a conasure in Chinese chicken dishes, lamb, and beef, and he had collected dozens of recipes by the time he came home.

He did keep that promise, and we have had some beautiful meals in his house since he has come home. He even makes his own pork scratchings.

He was coming on in the gym room, getting a little stronger every day, which was a great boost to his morale. The staff were excellent with him and had great patience.

Wed 25th Nov…Lisa's graduation, it made Darren sad to have to miss it, but what could he do, she brought in photos for him instead.

There was more infection in his T.P.N. line, so he had to have it removed.

1st.Dec… He was not looking forward to the new T.P.N. line been put in, but it had to be done.

They brought him up to the theatre to do the procedure. He had it in his arm instead, so now he had one on each arm.

He got an infection in his neck wound, that took another antibiotic to clear up, but he was fine afterwards.

I know this story is beginning to sound like a complete comedy of errors and it is hard to recall it all, but it actually happened this way.

18th Dec… Different doctors came in to see him to give their opinion on his condition; it seems to be a mystery to them why he was getting so many infections. Nothing major showed up, so they came to the conclusion that his body was just giving up, he was on anti-sickness injections all the time. He cried a lot.

With all the medication, he started to recover again, and in the meantime we were busy getting ready for Christmas, and not knowing if he would be home to us or not.

24th Dec… I asked Mr. Ray what were the chances of Darren coming home for just a while, if only for Christmas day, as we knew that if he didn't, we all would not enjoy Christmas. He said if he could arrange it he would.

True to his word, he arranged for an ambulance to collect Darren from the hospital early on Christmas morning and return him back to the hospital Christmas night. This was a great risk to take, as he was so sick. But the doctor knew how much it meant to us, and Darren. We were delighted, it meant everything to us. It would be great mentally for him. We did not have the time to shop properly for Christmas presents that year, so we just got small presents for everyone and nobody minded.

Chapter Fifteen

Christmas day... It was so exciting. We put up banners stating "Welcome home" outside our house. We didn't have to tell all the neighbours, as they were out watching for him also. I rushed around the place cleaning up, as I wanted to have a nice tidy home for Darren to come back to. It was months since he had seen his home; it was such a great treat to be having him home for Christmas day.

We excitingly kept a close eye on the clock, and down the road, where we knew he would be coming up. The crowds gathered outside the house very quickly, as word spread about his homecoming. Cars were quickly pulling up outside as relations were trying to get here before Darren did. There was a lot of rushing around, and excitement. This was not a bit like any other Christmas day, it was just something else!

Eventually we saw the ambulance slowly making its way up the winding road to our house. I was never so glad to see an ambulance. The driver put on his siren and flashing lights as he made his way up to the top of the road to turn. It was so exciting. I had a music-system set up in the garden to play at top volume "Tie a yellow ribbon round the old oak tree", so I ran out to put it on, great timing! To great applause and cheering from everyone, Darren was lifted out from the ambulance. It was great having him home, if only for a few hours. It was well over a year since he was home, and his eyes lit up. The road was full of cars as all his family, cousins, friends, and the neighbours, came to the house to make it a great day.

We tried to enjoy ourselves as much as we could, with laughter and singing, and neighbours coming and going, shaking his hand just to show how delighted they were to see him recovering. Everyone seemed to know the situation that we were in and came to make it as enjoyable as possible. It was the only Christmas that we didn't worry about the dinner! The family were trilled and delighted to have Darren home. It was so wonderful that we did not want it to end, but of course it had to. We will never forget that Christmas! Years later, neighbours still recall that wonderful Christmas day, and the unusual way we all spent it.

Then the ambulance came back to collect him, and there wasn't a dry eye in the house. But at least our dream had come true. That's all we wanted. We waved him off, and then cried as he was taken back to the hospital at eight o'clock on Christmas night. It was a risk worth taking and I am glad we did.

We settled down to watch another repeat on the television, with the rest of the family, including my elderly Mother-in law. It was great then to have some neighbours dropping in to see how we were all coping and to share a drink. I believe there was a good atmosphere in the hospital on Christmas night, so it was not all bad going back in to them. They had their own celebrations.

When we went in the next day, the doctor told us he had no regrets for letting Darren home for a few hours on Christmas day and he had heard all about it from the nurses and Darren.

I wrote this poem for our local magazine......

PATIENT NUMBER 360993

HOMECOMING

You were gone so long,
We missed you.
Your presence or lack of it,
Was noticed.
Hospitals stays are usually short,
Yours went on and on,
We missed you.
Long hours spent travelling,
Buses, trains, automobiles,
Anything to get there,
Just to see you,
Had to see you.
Family unit broken,
Words unspoken, said…..
Why you? What did we do?
To have you suffer as you did.
But wait… you're improving.
The morning comes, excitement grows.
Flags, banners stating,
"Welcome home"
Crowds gather in anticipation, we rush around,
Preparing your homecoming.
Here you come! Cameras flash, music,
Tears flow, never want to let you go,
It's what you've been longing for,
Your homecoming.

He continued to have Sundays home with us, and that would pep him up for the rest of the week. His week consisted of the usual, pain, leaks, repairs, and needles and drips.

16th Feb... The day of the operation we were all waiting for. Darren went down to the theatre at 2 o'clock and we went in at 8 o'clock, he was in I.C.U.

All over, no bag on his side the bowel was together at last. Everything went well, Thank God. The worst was behind him.

The next day he was back in his own room in the hospital. He felt very sore. A skin graft was mentioned for a later date. He was not a bit well for a good few weeks, and didn't want to talk to anyone. If he did talk to us he was cross.

The bowel leaked, and had to be repaired a few times more. In the following weeks.

March....Another operation, to disconnect the bowel again, as it was leaking. He had a bag connected to the part coming out of the stoma.

He slept a lot after that.

We talked of his 21st birthday that was coming up on St. Patrick's Day, and that made him smile. This great event was to be celebrated at the hospital, so we discussed it with the Sisters in charge. They agreed with us that we could not let the day go by without some sort of celebration. So it was arranged that we would take over the waiting room up in St. Teresa's ward, for St. Patrick's Day. It wasn't what he had ever visualised for his big birthday, but it was the only solution at that time, and we were glad of it. We rang all of his friends and family, and they were only too pleased to agree to come in to celebrate with us on the day. It was all hush-hush.

St. Patrick's Day, Darren's 21st birthday…there was a great surge of excitement all around. We had bottles stashed away in various places that Darren could not see and one of the Sisters, Sr. Marie, accidentally knocked over a bottle of champagne. She was so embarrassed that she crossed a busy main road and walked over to the local pub and bought a bottle of baby-Cham to replace it. This was unheard of, but this was the way that everyone was helping on the day. The orderly Joe also went over to the pub and carried back a pint of Guinness as a birthday present, without spilling a drop! He had asked for special permission from doctors and he was allowed to buy it as a special treat. So it was a great success. All his family and friends tiptoed into the waiting room which we had done up with some banners. When we gave the nod, the karaoke system began to play Tina Turner's "Simply the Best," song and we slowly pushed Darren's bed up to the waiting room. The party began. The look of shock on his face was priceless, and for that moment it didn't matter if the party was in the waiting room of a hospital, or the Gresham Hotel in Dublin! 21ST banners adorned the glass doors, and across the windows. We were all so happy, even the staff of the hospital helped out as much as they could. Darren got loads of beautiful presents from everyone, and the nurses presented him with a lovely book. Some of his scouting friends even turned up and helped with the music. To our surprise, our parish priest Fr. Hastings came in also, and neighbours and friends turned up, sixty-five in all. The sister in charge wished us well and left us to it. The singing and partying went on till 9.30pm. We had lovely food, a birthday cake, (and a little drink thrown in). We were nearly thrown out with the noise; well you're only twenty one once! I loved that day; it has bitter sweet memories for me. I am glad we did it, but still regret he was not out to celebrate in the normal way.

The next day he was taken to the operating theatre to have his line back in his neck, as it was pulled out on his birthday, with everyone hugging him.

Darren was still weak, and tried to walk some days, but found it very hard. He was relying on his T.P.N. (total parental nutrition) to keep him going.

The stomoligest was very kind. He came in most days to advise on how to manage the bag and maybe change it if it was leaking.

Amazingly Darren came home for a few months, as he needed this mentally also, and our sitting room was turned into his bedroom. We brought down his small bed from the bedroom and placed it in the corner. He had a bell at the side of his bed, so he could call us at any time of the night if he needed us. (Again, there were no mobile phones then!) The television was right facing him, so it continued to keep him amused. His friends came to visit. They laughed and joked together and told him all the gossip. It was great to have him home, sick and all as he was, and a great break for us as we did not have to be rushing out for visiting hours. It was at this time that his beautiful ring was robbed from the small table beside his bed in the sitting room. His Dad gave him a ring with a black stone in it to cheer him up. I had given it to his Dad when we were courting, so it was old! Darren placed it safely on the small table while he slept, and we had some of his friends in. They brought in some lads that we did not know too well, and when they were gone, so was the ring. We asked around discreetly, as he loved that ring, but he never got it back. He was a different person when he was home. It helped us all get through the following weeks, as we were waiting for the final operation. Mr. Howard told him that if he managed to come in by ambulance and secure a bed, (as beds were very scarce) then he would operate immediately. This we did, because he was extremely bad one morning with pain, so we called an ambulance. They brought him in to the hospital where they admitted him straight away. When the doctor did his rounds the next morning he was amazed to see him and said… "Well Darren you managed to get yourself a bed somehow, so now I will operate for you as soon as possible".

Chapter Sixteen

A few weeks later, after Darren's skin quality and overall medical condition improved, he went through the big operation to attach his bowel again. He was in a bad condition after it and it took months to recover, as his tummy would not close because it was open for so long. The skin would not repair itself anymore. He was left with just a light skin covering up the tummy area and he settled for that. But as usual, with the help of the good doctors and nurses, he bounced back.

We talked about it, and talked about it and counted down the weeks, and with many prayers and good nursing, (and Padre Pio) the day finally arrived and we went in to accompany him home. It was very emotional to help him pack his bags, to leave what was to become his home, and say goodbye to the doctors and nurses that had nursed him for eighteen long months, and had become his friends. Some of the nurses even shed a tear. He was institutionalised by now. This by far was the most traumatic time of his life, and he walked out of the hospital doors, to his Dad's waiting car.

I remember when we got there he said to me that he did not know if he was ready for this, he had no confidence. We understood this and persuaded him that everything would be ok, only then he got into the waiting car.

Such a long, complicated stay for such a young man. I can't believe we had finally reached this day, we were all so emotional.

Chapter Seventeen

A great function was organised by the local community, just before he got home and we kept it secret from Darren. This was very hard for me as I can't keep secrets. I nearly let it slip a few times, but somehow we got away with it, until his aunty Mary came in to visit that is. She innocently asked him what he might wear for his upcoming party. We all laughed as the secret was out now, so I had to tell him what was planned. It was very well organized and the very next day we headed off to the Noggin Inn pub in Sallynoggin. A couple of hundred people turned up to support the family. We had a brilliant band called Cool Breeze, and a very funny comedian called Sill Fox. We had a great laugh and I was so proud to have Darren with us. There were many spot prizes that were given out throughout the night. It was great to have all the family and friends together, and the nurses from the hospital came to meet us there. Even the headmaster and other teachers from Darren's school made an appearance to say hello. The place was packed!

Darren prepared a little speech and got up to say it. I noticed that through his little speech he blamed me for letting the secret of the party out of the bag. He did not want to get his aunty Mary into trouble. Such a cheer he got when he was finished. At that moment he could have been a famous pop-star. I wrote a poem, and I was very proud to read it out on the night. It went down very well, and the whole night was a success.

We have it recorded, and watch it on every anniversary of him getting home.

Darren's relationship with Lisa unfortunately ran its course, and they parted ways after a few months, but we will be forever grateful for her friendship, and wish her all the very best for the future. Her family were also very good to Darren, and all the presents they brought him in to the hospital, he really loved them. They had all helped him when he needed it most. After a few years, he met Edel. They were together for many years, and became engaged.

I was out shopping one day and just as I got to my driveway Darren rang me and asked me if I was in the house. I told him I was just there. He said he would ring me back when I got into the house. He did, and cried when he told me he was going to become a dad. We were all trilled for him and Edel. To everyone's delight, they became parents to Mia. After so much chemotherapy, Darren was told he would not be able to father children, so we were all over the moon when Mia was our third grandchild. We now have five grandchildren as our other son Johnny is father to Sean and Caitlin and recently a new baby girl Layla. My other son Anthony and his wife Michelle have a beautiful baby called Conor. They keep us all busy now.

Chapter Eighteen

After four years Darren and Edel went their separate ways, but they share minding Mia. They live quite near one another, which is handy now for babysitting.

Catherine, our eldest daughter moved to Jersey for a while. She deserved to make some life for herself after such a long time babysitting here for us. She remained there for many years and when she returned she took up work with a large communications company. She is in a long-term relationship with a lovely lad called Keith.

Johnny moved to Drogheda Co. Louth to live, and is a train-driver. He is engaged to a beautiful girl called Eimear, and they have just had their first baby girl called Layla.

Anthony married Michelle and moved to Delgany Co. Wicklow. He started his own business building and fitting kitchens and they are both now proud parents for the first time to Conor.

Fiona is a receptionist in a well known Dublin hairdressers, and is happily engaged to Patrick.

Richard is now a Garda in Dublin city and is in a long-term relationship with Leona. So all is well with them.

Darren's health remained very delicate, and it stood in the way of him moving forward in his management career. He had held down many positions of management in various shopping centres in the last few years and the R.D.S. in Dublin.

But despite his great enthusiasm for his work, his health continued to deteriorate, and he could not move on. He would be well for six months at a time, but then always had trouble with his health.

For the next few years, Darren was in and out of hospital with bowel trouble. This was caused by adhesions and bowel blockages, and no matter what he drank or ate, the pain could come on suddenly. It is also because his bowel is now very short as so much had to be removed. It was very distressing for him as the pain was so bad that he was afraid of his bowel bursting. Many times his sister or we would have to rush him into hospital to have emergency treatment for his pain. This usually consisted of being put onto a saline drip to try to clear the bowel blockage.

He also hated going into hospitals as now so many years had passed, he would have to explain the situation all over again, and sometimes he felt he was not being understood. At other times if he was admitted to a different Dublin hospital, the doctors did not know his history and they would not give him pain relief suspecting him of being a drug addict. This would cause such distress to Darren that we often went in to find him in tears. Many a time his Dad and I had to explain to the doctors that Darren had major surgery and that in fact he was not putting on these symptoms just to have medication. X-rays always would confirm that the problem was a blocked bowel, due to a twist occurring. We did come across our fair share of doubting Thomas's.

As he could not move on with his life, sometimes he would ask the doctors would they operate on him to take away the adhesions, and the blockage, but no one would take the risk of operating, not even Mr. Howard. He was such a complicated patient that doctors didn't want to operate on him again.

He was only getting three months before it would happen again, and each time was worse than the last. He would go through the usual waiting around A&E sometimes on a trolley for hours, vomiting! Eventually he would get a bed and he would be kept in, anything from three days to three months.

So his life was much disrupted, and we were desperate for an answer. We suggested everything from changing his diet, smaller meals, going to specialists, especially in America, and alternative medicine. But none of these things happened.

Darren crawled his way through the years not knowing what to do, and then faith took over. He had such a bad attack of pain, and was admitted to hospital again. On one particular night, he was so bad that the doctors were so afraid that his bowel would burst, they watched him all night. Before he came home, Mr. Howard agreed to operate. He said that he was happy enough with the skin quality, and it was now time to go ahead with the surgery.

It had been fourteen years since the last operation.

So on the 3rd of June, 2008, Darren once more had a large operation to have some bowel removed, the section that was twisted, and the adhesions were also removed. The operation went on for hours, and was a success. Although he was in a lot of pain, he was relieved it was all over. He didn't even have to go into I.C.U. this time.

We met one of the doctors immediately after the operation; I shook his hand, and thanked him for giving Darren back his life.

Chapter Nineteen

We brought Darren home on Friday 27th June, 2008 and he had community nurses coming to change the bandages every day until he healed a little. As I write this exactly two years later, he is still unwell and in a lot of pain every day. The gauze the doctor put in to his tummy to keep adhesions away has adhered to his bowel and causing problems. He cannot visit us often, as he has to be near a toilet all of the time. If he does take a chance to come out, he cannot eat. I have never heard of this happening before, but he can't be the first. He is constantly going septic, and it leaks out, to his great embarrassment. He has returned as an out-patient into the hospital and he is under the care of the pain-team. They have him on an enormous amount of pain-killers to help him manage the pain, but he will hopefully be able to get off them once he gets over the next operation to try to remove the gauze, and to eventually close up his tummy. He is looking at an open tummy for a long time, years! He has had to attend a different doctor in a different Dublin hospital for on-going problems and is waiting on this large operation there. He was sent there for a second opinion, and they are going to help him. I trust the doctors there, and I wish it would come soon before he gets any worse. The doctors are trying to get him to a stage where his skin quality is good enough to undergo such an operation. It is not without its risks and we are all aware of this. I would also like to thank the other doctors in the last hospital for all their help, but we have to see him get completely better soon. Nineteen years he is sick on and off for now, He can't take much more of sickness. He deserves a better life now, after all that he has gone through.

Chapter Twenty

There is good news to tell you all, he met a lovely girl who is now his Fiancée. Ekaterina is a children's teacher from Bulgaria, and working now here in Ireland. They became engaged two years ago and they are very happy. Most weekends Darren takes his daughter Mia for the weekend. Both he and Ekaterina are looking forward to a great healthy future together. He is due good health and happiness soon, after going through this terrible ordeal. He was only nineteen when he got sick first, nineteen years later he is still sick...

While there have been huge advances in surgical care in recent years, things still do occasionally go wrong. No operation is without risk, but patient safety should come first. Basic standards should be followed to ensure that each and every patient has a running chance of a good recovery after their operation.

Are doctors more trained to be on the lookout for the occasional mistakes? Are their teams willing to speak up when they suspect that all is not right with their patients? Have we moved on in hospital care since we went through all this? I sincerely hope so.

The aforementioned hospital is one of the major academic teaching hospitals, committed to patient focused care.

It is run by a prominent religious group.

Their mission statement is...

"We strive for excellence in meeting the holistic needs of our patients in a caring and healing environment in which the essential contribution of each member of staff is valued, the values of human dignity, compassion, justice, quality and advocacy, rooted in the mission and philosophy of the religious sisters, guide us in our work. We will within the foregoing context, make every effort to maintain excellence in clinical care, teaching and research."

Your rights as a patient in Ireland...based on European Charter of Patients Rights.

- Right to preventive measures.
- Right of access.
- Right to be informed.
- Right to free choice.
- Right to privacy and confidentiality.
- Right to respect of patients time.
- Right to the observance of quality standards.
- Right to safety.
- Right to innovation.
- Right to avoid unnecessary suffering and pain.
- Right to personalised treatment.
- Right to complain.
- Right to compensation.

I can count at least five of these that did not happen in Darren's case.

I asked Darren what he remembered about being in hospital at that time...

"I had every trust in the doctors. I believed what they told me when they said that I would be out with two small plasters on my tummy, after the laparoscopy. What annoys me is that they didn't even need to go in to do the operation after all! It was all so unnecessary.

I remember the pain and torture, I remember it all. Living in the hospital, not been able to get out of the bed and waiting on the painkillers.

My skin was been eaten away with the acid that came from the wounds. I will need hospital treatment for years to come.

My memory of coming home for Christmas day will never leave me.

I remember getting ready and the nurses and the porter Joe helping me to get dressed. Then I will never forget the ambulance men coming up to the ward and taking me down in a wheelchair.

The excitement of coming up the road was brilliant! I asked the ambulance driver to put on the sirens for me. It was a surprise to see all the neighbours and family standing outside waiting to greet me.

Then before long, after a few hours, I had to go back into the hospital.

The ambulance men came into the house to help me get organised and I hated leaving the house again.

When it came to coming home for good, I felt weak and skinny, but happy. I knew that there was a party organised, so I had to buy some new clothes for that. I wanted to be home but I was afraid I was not strong enough.

How am I now? Don't ask. After another couple of years I am still no better off. On one occasion I went into hospital with extreme pain. I had another operation to remove adhesions. It was then decided to insert gauze into my wound to try to avoid so much adhesions growing back. The idea was for the gauze to disintegrate after a while. Well this has not happened. When I was again hospitalised for having an infection in my tummy, the doctor could not remove the gauze, as it had adhered to my bowel. How unlucky can a person get? I don't think the doctors know what to do next with me to get me sorted. I have been left in this condition, and have an ongoing infection in the wound. I have been on antibiotics numerous times and I am attending the pain clinic to help me manage since I was discharged. I have written numerous letters to people I thought might be able to help me, but to no avail. Some politicians have answered, others haven't. Sometimes I find it very hard to acknowledge that this is my life at the moment and I have panic attacks. When will it ever finish?

I am back waiting for the rest of my life to begin with my Fiancée and daughter Mia, and family. But it will come...it will come."

PATIENT NUMBER 360993

As I write this Darren is waiting on his date to go back in for major surgery, any day now... wish him well.

The End (or is it)

Kay Morrison

Darren posing in his Scouts outfit.
He was only seventeen here, and very healthy.

PATIENT NUMBER 360993

*Darren and myself in the hospital waiting room.
This was his first visit to the waiting room, after ten
minutes he asked to be taken back to his room.*

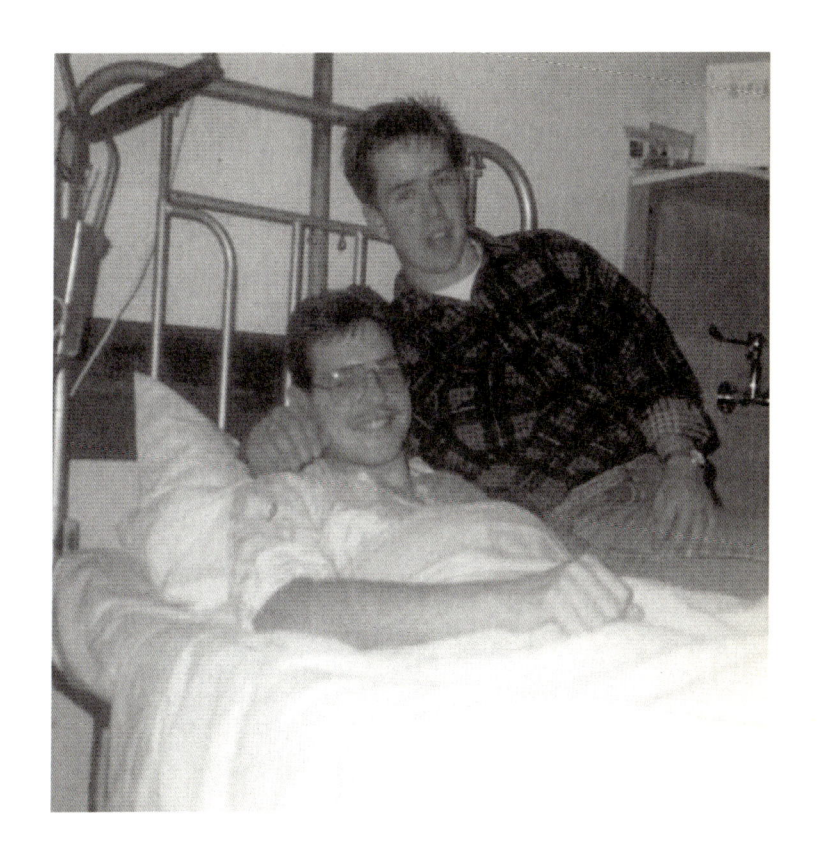

Darren with friend Thomas.
Darren loved to have visitors in to have a gossip.

PATIENT NUMBER 360993

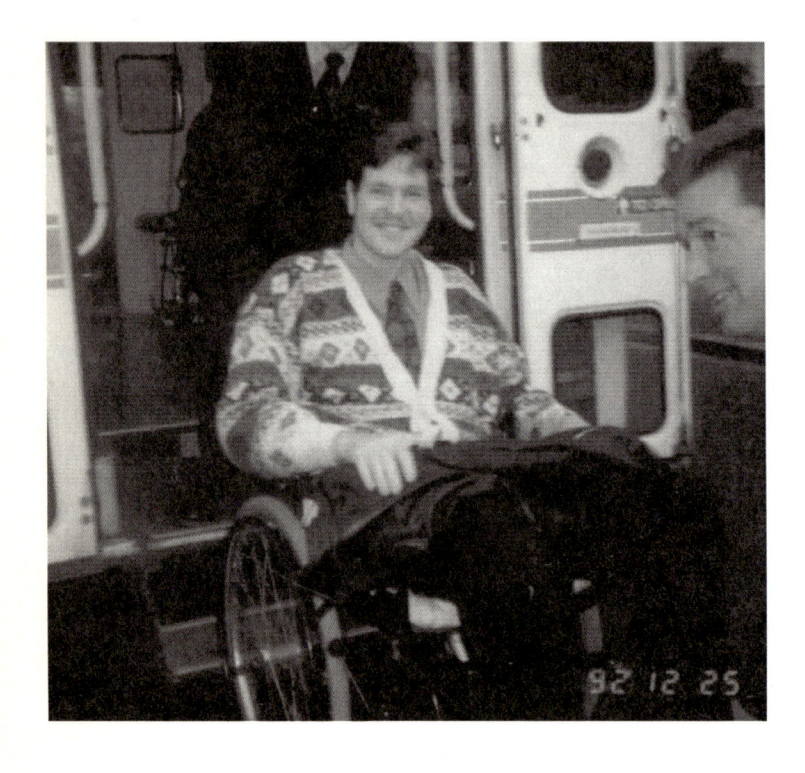

*Darren arriving home on Christmas day.
The smile says it all.*

All the neighbours and family gather to welcome him home for Christmas. Such an unusual day.

PATIENT NUMBER 360993

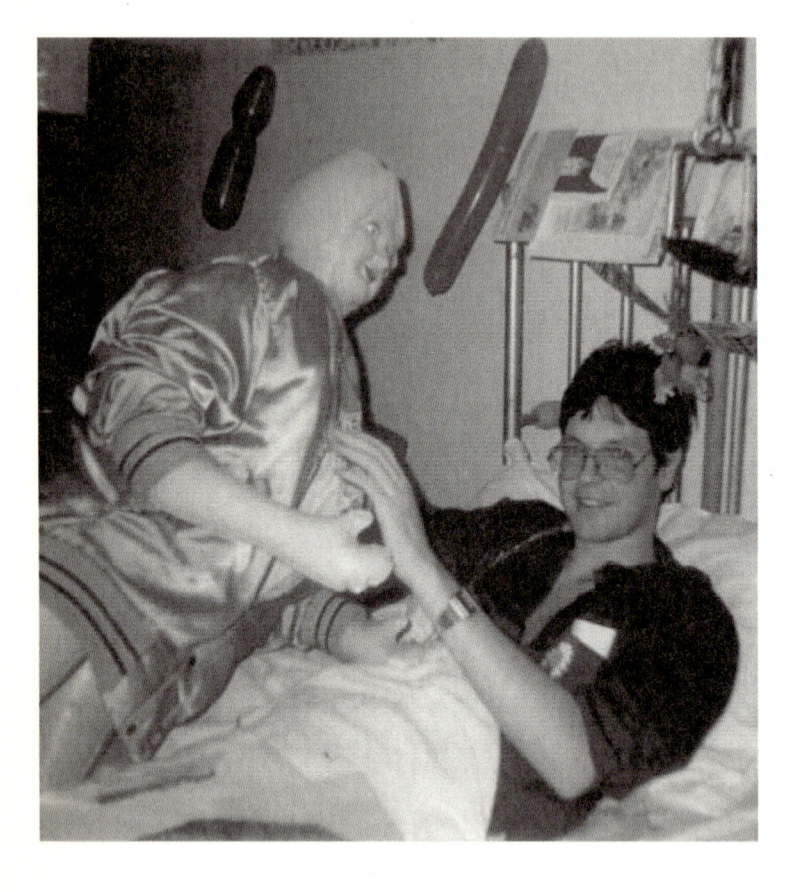

*Darren on his 21st birthday.
My sister Rosaleen brought over this doll from Scotland,
and we had to hide it behind the curtain in case it upset
the nuns*

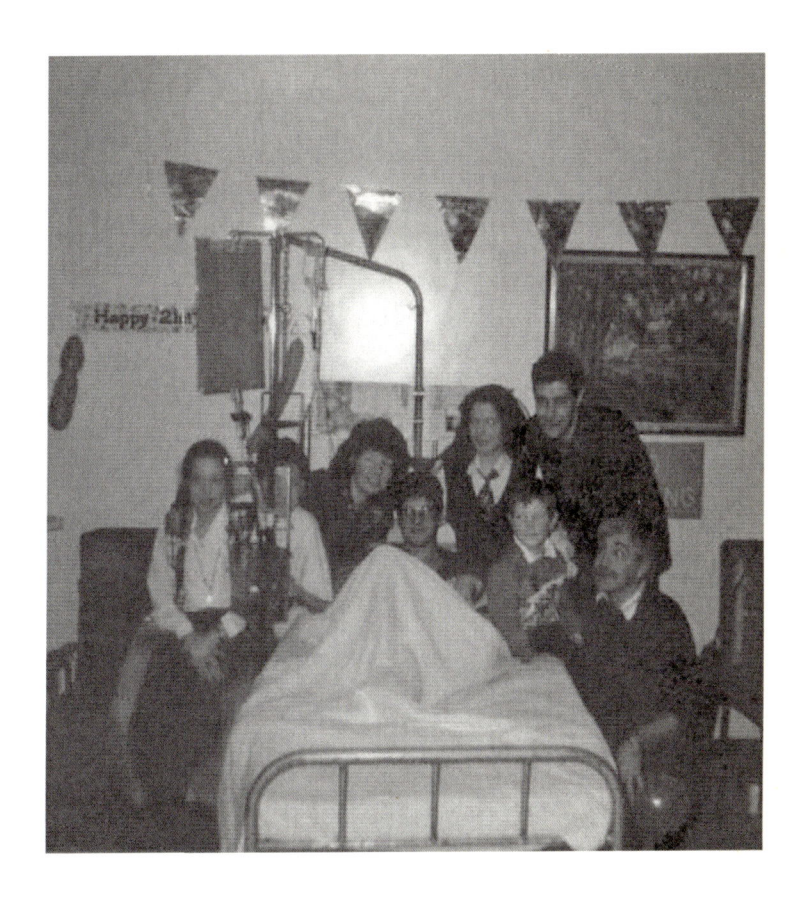

*The family look so young back then.
This was when the family gathered for Darren's 21st*

PATIENT NUMBER 360993

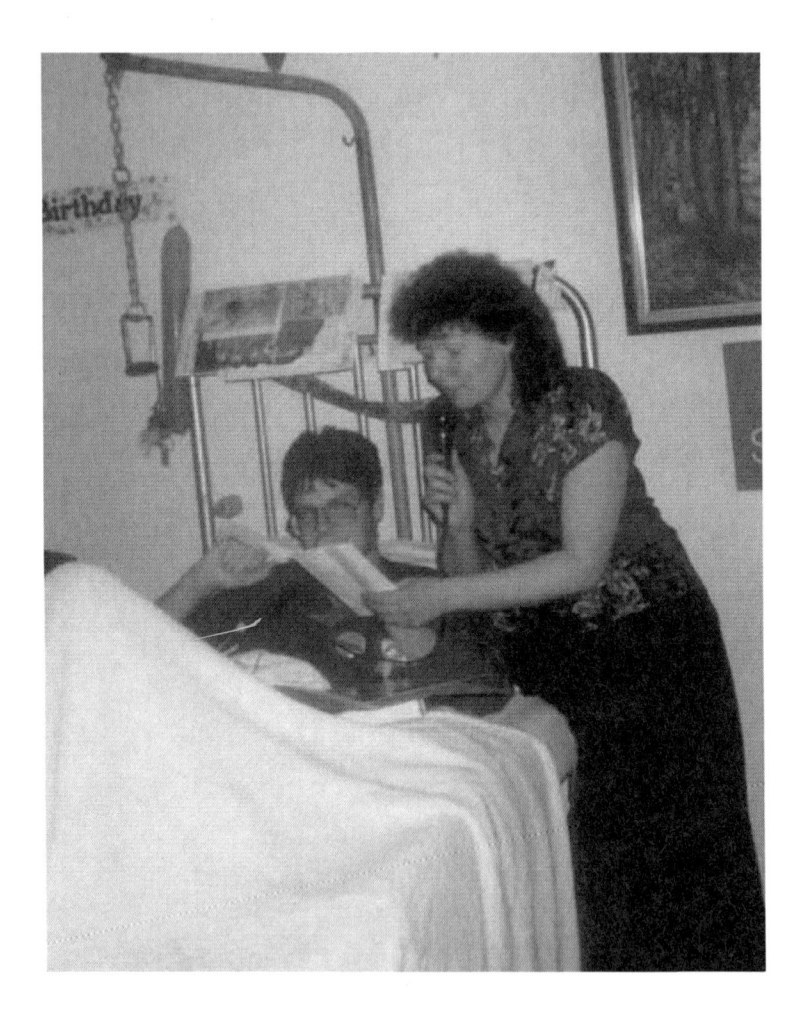

*I sang a song on his birthday.
We all took a turn, and sang our hearts out.*

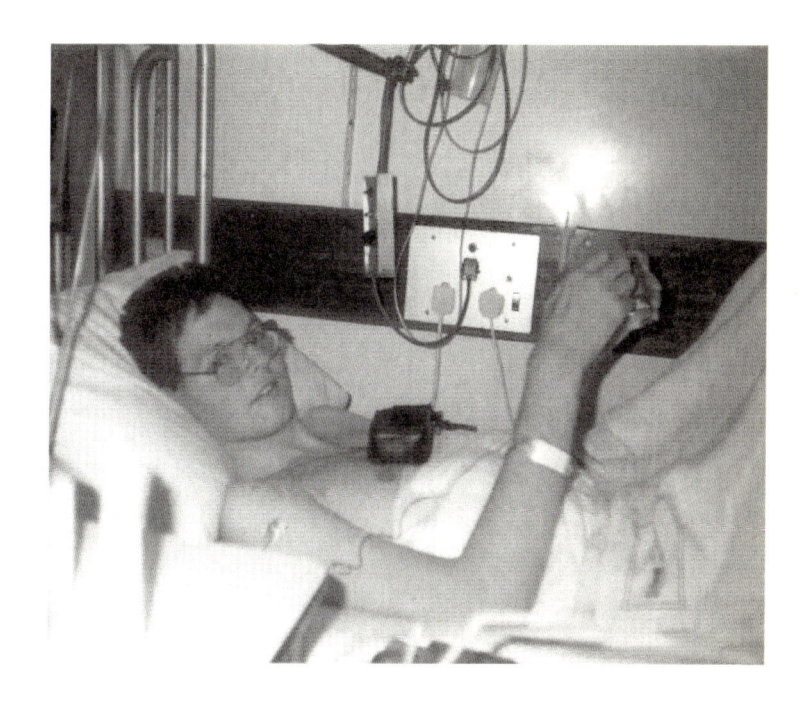

Darren in his own little ward. At this time he could not even get out of this bed for months.

PATIENT NUMBER 360993

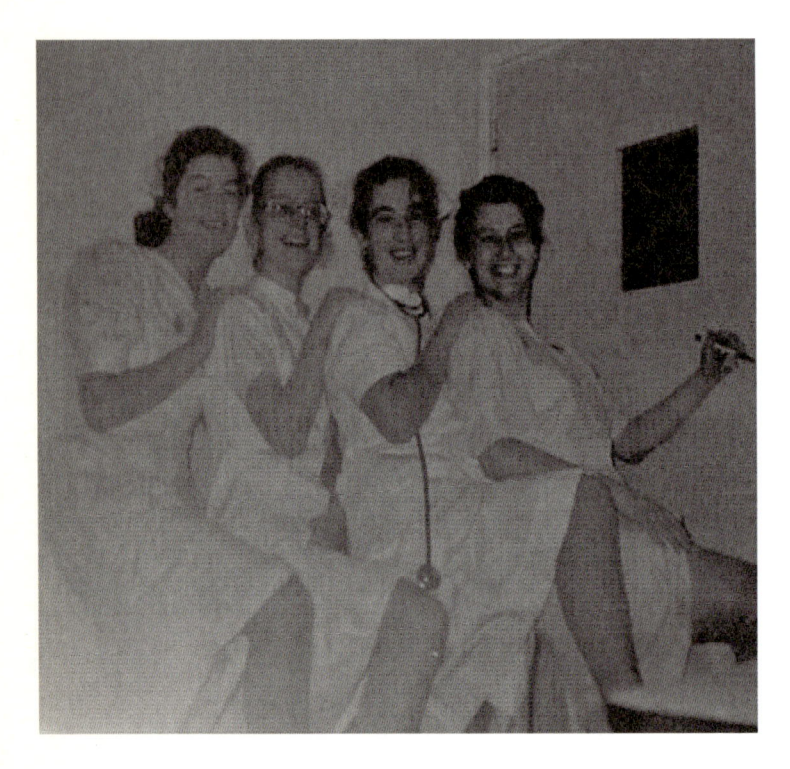

*Some of the nurses dancing for Darren
to keep his spirits high.*

Darren and myself on the way in to his special celebrations in the Sallynoggin Inn. We were all so excited, and had a wonderful night.

PATIENT NUMBER 360993

Darren today, awaiting what is hopefully, the operation which will finally give him back his life...